Samie — 266-1560

Jen

Jeannine

Jeannine — 996-1571
house

PA
Info
864 - 5672
864 - 5460

www.wadsworth.com

wadsworth.com is the World Wide Web site for
Wadsworth and is your direct source to dozens
of online resources.

At *wadsworth.com* you can find out about
supplements, demonstration software, and
student resources. You can also send e-mail to
many of our authors and preview new publications
and exciting new technologies.

wadsworth.com
Changing the way the world learns®

Wadsworth Developmental English

New for 2000

Writing

Rogers/Rogers, *Patterns and Themes: A Basic English Reader*, 4th Ed.
Tyner, *College Writing Basics: A Student-Writing Approach*, 5th Ed.
McDonald/Salomone, *The Writer's Response: A Reading-Based Approach to College Writing*, 2nd Ed.
McDonald/Salomone, *In Brief: A Handbook for Writers*

Reading

Maker/Lenier, *College Reading with the Active Critical Thinking Method, Book 1*, 5th Ed.
Maker/Lenier, *College Reading with the Active Critical Thinking Method, Book 2*, 6th Ed.
Sotiriou/Phillips, *Steps to Reading Proficiency*, 5th Ed.

Study Skills

Van Blerkom, *College Study Skills: Becoming a Strategic Learner*, 3rd Ed.

Other Developmental English Titles

Writing

Richard-Amato, *World Views: Multicultural Literature for Critical Writers, Readers, and Thinkers* (1998)
Salomone/McDonald, *Inside Writing: A Writer's Workbook, Form A*, 4th Ed. (1999)
Wingersky/Boerner/Holguin-Balogh, *Writing Paragraphs and Essays: Integrating Reading, Writing, and Grammar Skills*, 3rd Ed. (1999)

Reading

Atkinson/Longman, *Reading Enhancement and Development*, 6th Ed. (1999)
Maker/Lenier, *Academic Reading with Active Critical Thinking* (1996)

Study Skills

Longman/Atkinson, *College Learning and Study Skills*, 5th Ed. (1999)
Longman/Atkinson, *Study Methods and Reading Techniques*, 2nd Ed. (1999)
Sotiriou, *Integrating College Study Skills: Reasoning in Reading, Listening, and Writing*, 5th Ed. (1999)
Smith/Knudsvig/Walter, *Critical Thinking: Building the Basics* (1998)

TEXTS*AND* CONTEXTS

A Contemporary Approach to College Writing

Fourth Edition

William S. Robinson
Emeritus, *San Francisco State University*

Stephanie Tucker
California State University, Sacramento

Wadsworth
Thomson Learning™

Australia • Canada • Denmark • Japan • Mexico • New Zealand
Philippines • Puerto Rico • Singapore • South Africa • Spain
United Kingdom • United States

Executive Manager: *Elana Dolberg*
Print Buyer: *Barbara Britton*
Permissions Editor: *Susan Walters*
Production: *Hal Lockwood/Penmarin Books*
Designer: *Wendy Calmenson*

Cover Designer: *Laurie Anderson*
Cover Image: © *Richard Estes, Courtesy Marlborough Gallery, New York*
Compositor: *Thompson Type*
Printer: *R. R. Donnelley & Sons, Crawfordsville*

Printed in the United States of America

1 2 3 4 5 6 7 03 02 01 00 99

Library of Congress Cataloging-in-PublicationData
Robinson, William S., 1932–
    Texts and contexts : a contemporary approach to college writing / William S. Robinson, Stephanie Tucker.— 4th ed.
        p. cm.
    Includes indexes.
    ISBN 0-534-50773-5
    1. English language — Rhetoric. 2. English language — Grammar. 3. Report writing. I. Tucker, Stephanie, 1945– . II. Title.
PE1408.R6375   1999
808'.042 — dc21   99-34177

Instructor's Edition: 0-534-50775-1

For more information, contact:

Wadsworth/Thomson Learning
10 Davis Drive
Belmont, CA 94002-3098
USA
www.wadsworth.com

International Headquarters
Thomson Learning
290 Harbor Drive, 2nd Floor
Stamford, CT 06902-7477
USA

UK/Europe/Middle East
Thomson Learning
Berkshire House
168-173 High Holborn
London WC1V 7AA
United Kingdom

Asia
Thomson Learning
60 Albert Street #15-01
Albert Complex
Singapore 189969

Canada
Nelson/Thomson Learning
1120 Birchmount Road
Scarborough, Ontario M1K 5G4
Canada

This book is printed on acid-free recycled paper

This book is dedicated to the memory of
Susan Skov and Steve Stedman.
Their students never had better teachers.

One learns to write by writing and revising, not by consciously learning and rhetorically applying the "rules."

Robert J. Connors

Contents

*P*art I   *Writing from the Top Down*   1

Practice in developing the ability to read critically and to
summarize; learning the fundamentals of the academic
writing process through writing a short report; shaping texts
and sentences.

CHAPTER 1   THE WRITING PROCESS   3

*P*art II   Discovering and Writing   79

Cases for reading and writing: pre-reading and post-reading;
pre-writing and drafting; sentence combining and proofreading.

CHAPTER 5   ARGUING   246

CHAPTER 7   WRITING THE IN-CLASS ESSAY   447

*P*art III   *Proofreading Skills Workbook*   451

Self-teaching assignments for common usage problems.

*T*o the Student,

or, What You've Gotten Yourself Into
and How to Get Out of It

Here you are, after twelve years of school, and you're in still *another* English class, and you're probably thinking, "Now what?"

Meanwhile, your new English teacher is going to look at your first paper, which you are probably going to put a lot of work into and which you'll probably think is pretty good, and he or she is going to think, "How could anyone who's gone to school for twelve years write like this?"

And to make matters worse, the first time you and your fellow students hand in an essay test or a paper for some other college class, *that* teacher is going to groan, "Why don't they teach them to write anymore?"

On the one hand, the students are saying, "What's wrong with my writing anyway? Its always been okay before." And on the other hand, the teachers are saying, "This stuff is terrible. They can't even write a sentence."

What do we have here, a failure of communication?

I don't know whether it's going to make you feel any better about this or not, but college teachers have been complaining about their students' writing since people were dipping quill pens into little bottles of ink. And colleges have been running special writing classes for their weaker writers since long before you (or I) were born.

There are probably numerous reasons why college students don't write as well as their teachers think they ought to, but the main point is that for the most part they don't, and there are a few things you ought to know about this.

One is that the teachers are right; most students don't write as well as they should be able to.

Another is that if you think poor writing won't hold you back, you may be right, but there is a good chance that you're wrong. You can cast this proposition in the form of a bet, if you want. You can bet against needing to write fairly well; you can say, "Learning English is a pain, and I probably won't need it anyway, so why bother?" In this case, if you turn out to be wrong, you've lost the bet and suffered major financial and career disadvantages. Your poor writing has held you back from promotion or, in some cases, even employment in the first place.

Or you can bet the other way; you can say, "Learning English is a pain, but I might need it, so I better do it." In this case, if you turn out to be wrong (you didn't need to learn to write well after all), you haven't lost anything. But if you turn out to be right, you've gained a lot. So which bet makes more sense?

One of the mildly amusing things about all this from an English teacher's point of view is that in precisely the fields where the majority of students think writing is unimportant — business and engineering — the people who do the hiring think it's extremely important.

Anyway, regardless of how you bet, you still have to pass this course, so you might as well know what you're in for and why. This book is designed to help you improve your writing in certain very specific ways, for certain very specific reasons, and here's what they are.

First, the most important thing about writing is to be able to get your ideas across. Obviously. But that isn't always so easy. Someone once said, "Writing is God's way of showing you how sloppy your thinking is." So the main part of this book is a series of writing assignments like the ones you'll have to do in college, assignments in which you gather information either from personal observation or from readings, decide what you think the information means or shows, and then organize an essay to explain the issue and your ideas on it. You'll be working on summarizing, analyzing, classifying, comparing, and arguing, and you'll be working on organizing your ideas into coherent papers that will get them across. It is, literally, easier said than done.

Second, you'll be working on developing your sentences. A famous study of the writing of fourth graders, eighth graders, twelfth graders, and published writers showed a number of interesting differences among them. One difference was that as the writers got older and more experienced, their sentences got longer. The fourth graders wrote sentences averaging 13.5 words long, the eighth graders 15.9 words, the twelfth graders 16.9 words, and the published writers 24.7 words. (You might count the words in the sentences in a page of your writing and see where you come out.)

This doesn't mean that a long sentence is automatically better than a short one or that you should never write short sentences. It does mean that more capable writers are able to say more in each sentence and have more different ways of doing so. In other words, better writers have more tools.

Besides that, writing that averages seventeen words a sentence is so childish and monotonous that it would drive you, as a reader, crazy in fifteen minutes. You do want mainly to communicate, but you also want someone else to be able to read it.

So a major part of this book consists of what are called "sentence-combining" exercises, which are designed not just to enable you to get more into your sentences, as professional writers do, but also to begin using certain kinds of structures that most inexperienced writers tend to use very infrequently. If you apply what you learn in these exercises to your own writing, you will start sounding on the page like an intelligent human being.

Finally, and most uninterestingly, if you are still making mistakes in matters that you should have learned by the seventh grade — stuff like using apostrophes correctly — this book provides the usual explanations and exercises. For God's sake, learn it.

No book or workbook, no explanations or exercises, can make anyone into a good, or even capable, writer. You can no more learn how to write by reading a book than you can learn how to ride a bicycle, water-ski, or fly a jet fighter by reading a book. Learning *how to do* anything requires someone there to help you, to show you the right techniques and correct you when you do something wrong. That's the teacher's job. It also requires a learner who wants to learn, who is willing to learn both from the teacher and from his or her own mistakes, someone who will try to make active use of the lessons given. That's your job. This is your big chance.

WSR

Preface: To the Instructor

TOP-DOWN AND BOTTOM-UP

What do we do when we write? We think about what we want to say, formulate some sort of plan or goal, and get at it. In the process, we employ what we know about English in general and written English in particular. Seeing flawed and inexpert written texts, writing teachers used to think that the writer's main, or only, problem was error, and that the solution to that problem was to teach the writer grammar and the correction of errors. Of course, many writing teachers still advocate this approach.

But researchers in composition, linguistics, and psycholinguistics have found that this approach — which is now called the "bottom-up" approach — does not correspond with, to rephrase the question above, what we do when we write and so does not address the most basic difficulties writers have or the *sources* of their errors.

At least three sources of the writing problems that students encounter have been identified. One is the knowledge source — not knowing certain rules (and thus producing errors). A corollary of this is not using certain syntactic structures with the frequency competent writers use them (and thus producing choppy, monotonous, undeveloped sentences). A second is the process source — the writer's not understanding how capable writers work and therefore trying to write in unproductive ways, usually trying to produce perfect first drafts. Much has been written about these two sources, but somewhat less has been written about the third source, what we might call the text source.

Under one circumstance every basic writer faces, the text itself may be the source of numerous writing problems — everything from disorganized, undeveloped essays to errors of usage. That circumstance is *when the writer doesn't understand the characteristics of the text he or she is being asked to write.*

Students who have been put through drills in sentence structure, usage, and paragraph organization will still be completely at sea when asked to write an essay if they have no idea what an essay looks like — what its structural and substantive features are. Students who learn to write personal essays with competence characteristically fail at every level, from text to word, when required to write a piece of literary analysis. How can they not? They don't know what those texts look like.

The traditional solution to this problem has been the infamous five-paragraph essay, but the five-paragraph essay is not an example of academic, professional, or any other kind of writing, nor even a stepping stone to them, but merely a formula for getting words on paper.

Because doing exercises that do not involve communication is stultifying, because learning rules in a vacuum is fruitless, and because the text itself is a major source of problems for the inexperienced writer, it has become an axiom of current composition theory — as found, for instance, in Theresa Enos' *A Sourcebook for Basic Writing Teachers* — that we should tackle the job of teaching inexperienced writers in the same way writers write — from the top down — working on building meaning as a primary goal rather than attempting to extirpate errors first.

Yet most composition texts for basic writers still work from the contrary idea — that you can't write an essay until you can write a paragraph and that you can't write a paragraph until you can write certain esteemed kinds of sentences and that you can't even write those sentences until you have learned a lot of grammar. Thus, we find a bottom-up approach to a top-down activity.

An assumption of this book is, then, that if inexperienced writers are to learn to write essays, they must begin writing essays as soon as possible — that is, immediately — and that the part of the writing process most central to their learning is the one involving shaping the whole text. That is not to say that they won't need help at the lower levels; they will. And this text provides that help. It is to say that the traditional order of priorities has been reversed here.

GETTING PERSONAL

A second assumption behind this book is that students in developmental writing courses are still college students. That means that they are being assigned college-level readings and college-level writing tasks right away, depending to a limited extent on their majors and other curriculum requirements. What, then, are they to do in these other classes if their English curriculum defers until some later date their preparation for this work? Poorly prepared students need immediate help in doing college-level reading and writing.

A growing number of teachers has come to realize that we give these students the most effective help if we assign them not the traditional personal-experience essay, a form derived from the belletristic tradition, but essays more nearly of the kind they will be assigned in their other courses. There, characteristically, they must read and then write about their readings. They may have to summarize, analyze, synthesize, compare or contrast, figure out what they think and argue for it, discuss implications. They will be asked to make discoveries in fields alien to them and think about what those discoveries mean. In short, they will be asked to join the educational enterprise as the academic world defines it (not write five-paragraph essays).

And so the assignments in this book are based on readings or other data from which the student writers are asked to extract meanings and implications as the basis for their essays.

That does not mean that students must not draw on their own experience. It is surely a crucial part of their educations that students look at their own lives in the light of what they are learning, and so most assignments begin by asking them to think about questions related to the assignment that bear on their own experience. Additionally, some assignments require students to use what they know and can observe as an important part of their essays. The assignments vary considerably in this respect. But all emphasize making valid inferences about both the readings and the students' experiences.

WRITING TO WRITE OR WRITING TO LEARN

Another salient characteristic of the writing assignments is that they involve writing to learn rather than merely writing for writing's sake. Too many textbooks suggest, for instance, "classification" assignments in which the writer categorizes students into types (always three) or describes three different kinds of friends — in one classic case, "best friends," "good friends," and "hi and bye friends." Never is there an indication of why one would want to do such a thing nor what one would learn from doing it, and so the result is invariably vacuous and formulaic, the counterfeit of writing.

In the assignments in this text, students use common thinking strategies — classifying, comparing, arguing, discussing — for genuine purposes.

- They may classify a typical list of contemporary jobs in order to find out what kinds of skills, training, and education the job market today and tomorrow will be asking for, or they may set up their own research project to investigate ethnic or gender representation in Saturday morning children's television.

- They may compare American and Asian educational methods in order to learn the strengths and weaknesses of different approaches to education and thus to look at their own experiences in school, or they may compare the treatment in school and at home of boys and girls in the light of genetic and learned gender differences.

- They may examine the arguments for and against handgun control or the U.S. English movement in order to decide for themselves on an informed basis how they stand.

There is always a reason for the writing assignment and something to be learned by doing it.

CHALLENGE AND CONFIDENCE

It is a truism that the initial work in basic writing courses should, among other things, promote the confidence of student writers. No one performs well when he or she feels doomed to failure. The easy way to promote such confidence is to assign work that the student already knows how to do. Unhappily, such assignments do not promote learning.

Assignments must push students toward what Lev Vygotsky calls their "zone of proximal development" — that is, the next stage at which they can succeed *with help*. In short, from the very beginning, a skills course should work to edge the students' skill level ever higher. Consequently, this text includes enough assignments of every kind — both essay and sentence — that students can solidify in their new skill levels before they advance.

Some classes may need to spend more time in solidifying skills than others and so may not move as far through the book. In one of the courses we teach, the students take two full semesters to work through Chapter 5, while in another, many sections get into Chapter 6 in one semester. With the right pacing, all students begin to develop a strong sense that they can do college-level work.

ERROR'S ENDLESS TRAIN

Linguists have known for many decades that native speakers of English have mastered pretty much the entire grammar of English by the time they are four years old. This grammar is, of course, the grammar of speech rather than that of writing, but while the two differ in ways that may seem more or less obtrusive, depending on the spoken dialect, these grammars are, for all practical purposes — such as communication — virtually identical. If they weren't, we wouldn't be able to understand one another.

As we noted earlier, inexperienced writers face the problem that because the cognitive demands of written communication are so great, they may have difficulty using the grammar they know and so produce ungrammatical structures. A second problem is that they may use structures grammatical in speech but not in writing. And finally, and much more frequently and obtrusively, they usually demonstrate degrees of unfamiliarity with written usages, the kinds of things covered in handbooks and workbooks (and covered in Part III of this book). These elements, however, should not be confused with grammar.

In writing there are "errors" of omission as well as errors of commission, the kind of "error" represented by choppy, childish syntax. As Kellogg Hunt noted many years ago, while inexperienced writers use the same syntactic structures used by experienced writers, they don't use them as frequently. Even a fourth grader will turn up with an occasional appositive phrase, but the frequency of appositives in published writing will be scores of times greater.

Sentence combining, though no panacea, is helpful in dealing with many of the difficulties outlined above, and research strongly suggests that it is particularly effective with developmental writers. A consistent program of sentence combining, one in which the students do exercises one or more times a week, helps develop fluency and consequently a greater ability to produce grammatical structures. If properly designed, it can also promote the use of structures — such as concessive clauses, appositives, and verbal phrases — that inexperienced writers rarely use, structures that not only add texture to writing but also tend to promote more mature thinking.

Usage errors are another matter, and that is what the workbook section is for, though again it is important for the teacher to distinguish between usage errors that crop up as production problems and those that are truly knowledge problems. For knowledge errors, explanations and exercises are essential. For process errors, only practice and help in proofreading will do. (For a complete discussion of the different kinds and sources of error, see my article "Towards a Theory of Error" in the September 1998 *Teaching English in the Two-Year College,* reprinted in the Instructor's Manual.)

WRITING PROCESS, TEACHING PROCESS

As a result of the work of Nancy Sommers and others, we now understand that "the writing process" is not a linear, step-by-step affair, beginning, say, with invention activities, proceeding to an outline, moving on through various drafts, and winding up with proofreading, each step discrete and individual. We know that writers actually work in a much messier and more recursive fashion, one that involves these activities but tends to conflate them.

While this knowledge is very important to us as writing teachers, it is not necessarily very helpful to us as *basic* writing teachers. Learning specialists have also shown us that when we learn a new activity we go through (among others) three basic stages:

1. Ignorance of how to perform the activity
2. Ability to perform it only by closely following rules or directions
3. Ability to perform it without reference to rules or directions

Moreover, it is impossible to go directly from stage 1 to stage 3. Inexperienced writers, writers who may think, for example, that the way writers write is to sit down and produce polished, finished articles and stories, must have guidance, "rules" even, to help them achieve workable composing processes. Both Chapter 1 and the writing assignments in Chapters 3 through 6 attempt to give that guidance without being excessively prescriptive and linear. Still, carefully taking classes through recognizable steps in the process helps students to begin finding themselves as writers.

Examples of Student Writing

There are a number of examples of student writing in the text. They are used to demonstrate key points and as readings. You will find these examples in

- Chapter 2 (Student Writers at Work)
- Chapter 3 "We've Come a Long Way, but Magazines Stayed Behind"
- Chapter 4 "School Here in the United States and There in Vietnam"

In addition, the revised Instructor's Manual includes more examples of student writing, should you wish to use them in the course.

New to This Edition

- Twelve new readings on such topics as hot jobs for graduates, free speech on campus, single parenting, gun control, and child care.
- Updated and revised sentence-combining exercises throughout.

Teaching Aids

Print Supplements

- **Instructor's Manual** (0-534-50774-3). This edition has been revised to provide additional help, particularly to new users. It includes more examples of student writing, background and information on the elements of the text and how to use them, a sample course outline, a journal article on the approach of this text, chapter-by-chapter strategies for teaching the writing assignments, and teaching tips for using the Workbook.

- *Newbury House Dictionary* (0-8384-5613-8). Make this developmental-level dictionary available to your students at a reduced cost by bundling it with this textbook. Contact your sales representative for information about this option.

Electronic and Online Supplements

- **Web Site.** Visit Wadsworth's Developmental English web site at *http://www.devenglish.wadsworth.com.*

- **The Wadsworth Developmental English Internet-at-a-Glance Trifold** (0-534-54744-3). This handy guide shows your students where to find online reading and writing resources. Package this trifold card with any Wadsworth Developmental English textbook for a small cost. Contact your local Wadsworth representative for more information.

- **InfoTrac® College Edition.** A fully searchable, online database with access to full-text articles from more than six hundred periodicals provides a great resource for additional readings and/or research. Now available free if purchased with this textbook, InfoTrac® College Edition offers authoritative sources, updated daily and going back as far as four years. You and your students can receive unlimited online use for one academic term. (Please contact your ITP representative for policy, pricing, and availability; international and school distribution is restricted.)

- **Custom Publishing.** You can combine your choice of chapters from specific Wadsworth titles with your own materials in a custom-bound book. To place your order, call the ITP Custom Order Center at 1-800-355-9983.

- **Videos.** Wadsworth has many videos available to qualifying adopters on such topics as essay writing, improving your grades, note-taking practice, diversity, and many more. Contact your local Wadsworth representative for more information.

- **AT&T World Net.** Get your students on the Internet with AT&T— one of the fastest-growing Internet access service providers.

ACKNOWLEDGMENTS

The materials in this book are the result of a number of years of development and revision, trial and error and retrial, and we would like to express our obligations and thanks to the many instructors at San Francisco

State University and California State University, Sacramento, who have used them and made suggestions for improvements. We are also in debt to Shelley Circle for the hours she spent in gathering publishers' and writers' permissions and helping us with library research and to Randall Roorda, whose comments on the penultimate manuscript were of the greatest value.

First Edition

We would like to thank the following people for their help in reviewing the manuscript; we are grateful for the teaching wisdom they brought to the task and for the resulting suggestions and criticisms, which have improved this text immeasurably: Barbara Baxter, State Technical Institute at Memphis; Judith Boschult, Phoenix College; Barbara Carpenter, Marist College; Linda Daigle, Houston Community College; Laura Knight, Mercer County Community College; John C. Lovas, De Anza College; Milla McConnell-Tuite, College of San Mateo; Randall Popken, Tarleton University; Claudia Questo, Green River Community College; and Penny O. Smith, Gannon University.

We also want to thank Angela Gantner, our former editor at Wadsworth, for her faith in this project, her determination that we would do the job right whether we wanted to or not, and her unfailing good nature through even the most trying of times.

Second Edition

For help with the second edition thanks are owing to Pam Altman, whose generosity with her time and energy have been exceptional and gratefully received, and to Juanita Alunan, Doreen Deicke, Michael Martin, and Lisa Metge, all of San Francisco State, and to Marc Kemp of Fullerton College and Bill Sweigart of Indiana University, Southeast. I wish this edition were as good as they would have made it.

Third Edition

And for contributions to the third edition, I would like to add my thanks to Elizabeth Sommers, Karen Wong, and Susan Zimmerman of San Francisco State and Jim Bowsher of College of Marin. Thanks also to reviewers for this third edition: Donna Alden, Dona Ana Community College; Sandra Blakeman, Hood College; Natalie S. Daley, Linn-Benton Community College; Cindy Hicks, Chabot College; Pamela McDonough, Palomar College; and Robert T. Mundhenk, Northampton Community College.

Fourth Edition

Thanks are very much in order to Cindy Hicks of Chabot College and Pam Altman of San Francisco State for invaluable help with the fourth edition of this book.

Reviewers for the Fourth Edition

Nancy M. Anter, Wayne State University

Nora Bacon, University of Nebraska at Omaha

Elizabeth Jones, Fontbonne College

Laura Knight, Mercer County Community College

Michael Lomax, Hartnell College

Janet Madden, El Camino College

Ken McLaurin, Central Piedmont Community College

William Sweigart, Indiana University, Southeast

PART *I*

Writing from the Top Down

Writing is a lot like inflating a blimp
with a bicycle pump. Anybody can do
it. All it takes is time.

Kurt Vonnegut, Jr.

CHAPTER *1*

The Writing Process

In college, most of the writing you do will be based on other writing—on books and articles you dig up in the library. In this class, you will be doing the same thing except that you won't have to find the materials you write about; they are provided for you. In both cases, your writing process, like that of scholars, businesspeople, and professional writers, will start not with writing but with reading. And how well you manage to write will start with how well you read.

One can make two mistakes in reading done for writing. The first is just to read the stuff, whatever it is, assuming that you will remember it all. You won't. Nobody can. The second is to try to remember everything. You won't do that either. Some students buy highlighters and go through their textbooks highlighting everything, page after page, figuring that now they will remember it all. But when everything is highlighted, nothing is highlighted. The only difference is that the page is yellow instead of white.

READING ACTIVELY AND EFFICIENTLY

The first step in the writing process is reading actively. To read actively, you need to find the main points in what you read and work out a way of recording them so that you will be able to find them easily later on.

How do we know what the main points in a written text are? We first need to realize that all expository writing—the kind that explains something or argues a position—has a special shape. You can even draw it; it looks something like the chart on the preceding page. The dark areas represent general statements, ones that serve to introduce the reader to what's coming next. The first paragraph or so is, of course, the introduction, telling the reader what the whole essay or article will be about. The following paragraphs (however many there are) usually begin with their own general statements, a sentence or two called the topic sentence, which tells the reader what to expect in the paragraph.

Why do writers use topic sentences? Read the following sentence and ask yourself if you know what it's supposed to mean.

She was really annoyed, but she decided she had to go.

Obviously, you don't know who "she" is or why she was annoyed, or where she was supposed to go. Now read the same sentence with another one preceding it:

Joanne received an invitation to her ex-boyfriend's wedding. She was really annoyed, but she decided she had to go.

Now we can understand the second sentence (though we would have to read further to learn why she decided she had to go). Linguists call this issue "text coherence"—that is, what makes pieces of writing understandable. The same text coherence issue that works between sentences also works in paragraphs. Read the following paragraph:

The spectators enjoy the sun or the evening, chat, drink beer or soda, cheer or boo as the occasion demands, and hope for a victory by the home team. The analysts keep score, watch each pitch intently, note the strengths and weaknesses of the players, and follow managerial strategy with microscopic attention.

You may or may not have been able to figure out what this paragraph is supposed to be about. The problem is that it isn't coherent. Making a reader guess about a paragraph's meaning is not what writers want to do, because their readers will get irritated at having to do all that guessing and stop reading. (Or, in college, they may read it and give it a D or F.) Readers don't want to have to figure out each paragraph. That's why we use topic sentences; they make paragraphs more coherent, easier to read. Here's the incoherent paragraph again, but this time with a topic sentence:

At every baseball game, there are basically two kinds of fan—the spectators and the analysts. The spectators enjoy the sun or the evening, chat, drink beer or soda, cheer or boo as the occasion demands, and hope for a victory by the home team. The analysts keep score, watch each pitch intently, note the strengths and weaknesses of the players, and follow managerial strategy with microscopic attention.

This is how most informational paragraphs work; they usually begin with a general statement telling us what's coming up and then get into the specifics of their subject.

Here is another example. Which sentences contain the general point of the paragraph, which the specifics?

We [students] were forever being organized into activities that, I suspect, looked good on paper and in school board reports. New programs took over and disappeared as approaches to child education changed. One year we would go without marks, on the theory that marks were a "poor motivating factor," "an unnatural pressure." . . . Another year every activity became a competition, with posters tacked up on the walls showing who was ahead that week, our failures and our glories bared to all the class. Our days were filled with electrical gimmicks, film strips and movies and overhead projectors and tapes and supplementary TV shows, and in junior high, when we went audio-visual, a power failure would have been reason enough to close down the school.

Joyce Maynard, *Looking Back: A Chronicle of
Growing Up Old in the Sixties*

In this case, the first two sentences are the general introductory ones, and the rest are specific. The point of most paragraphs lies in a combination of their general and specific statements. Joyce Maynard's general sentences (the first two) introduce us to the idea that child education in the 60s didn't follow any set principles, and her specific sentences then give us illustrations of that idea, showing us that education was governed by gimmicks. If we summarized this paragraph for someone, we would include its main point, without going into its details. (If we covered all the details, we'd just be recopying the paragraph, not summarizing it.) We might write our summary this way:

Education in the 60s was ruled by gimmicks that looked good on paper rather than real principles.

As the two paragraphs above indicate, one clue as to which points are most important lies in the way in which most paragraphs are organized; their general sentences usually come first and their specifics follow them. Sometimes it will almost be possible to make an outline of a text just by noting the first two or three sentences of each of its paragraphs. It is important to remember, however, that not every paragraph works this way. The main exception is the paragraph in which all the sentences are about specifics; in these cases, the generalization covering them may be in a previous paragraph or the specifics may be so important that each one should be noted.

EXERCISE

Following are three paragraphs. Underline or highlight the general statements (the introductory sentences), write an *S* in front of the specific statements (the sentences giving details) in each of them, and write a one- or two-sentence summary of what each paragraph means.

Reagan's role in the 1988 election was of **incalculable** value to Bush. For one thing, Bush was basking in the glow of Reagan's successes, taking credit for being part of the team that was seen by many as having restored America's morale, rebuilt its defenses, tamed inflation, and brought down interest rates. Reagan's failures and embarrassments seemed to fade in people's memories as the year went on, and as he became a **nostalgic** figure about to leave the scene. The other way that Reagan helped was in giving his all-out support to Bush. The Reagan White House cooperated with the Bush campaign to an **unprecedented** extent—in having the President sign or veto bills as deemed helpful to Bush, in making appointments, in putting off unpleasant business until after the election.

Elizabeth Drew, "Letter from Washington,"
The New Yorker

Summary: _____

_____

_____

Of course, population growth is not occurring uniformly over the face of the Earth. Indeed, countries are divided rather neatly into two groups: those with rapid growth rates, and those with relatively slow growth rates. The first group, making up about two-thirds of the

---

incalculable: of great value;   nostalgic: fondly remembered;
unprecedented: not previously experienced

world population, coincides closely with what are known as the "un-developed countries" (UDCs). The UDCs are not industrialized, tend to have inefficient agriculture, very small gross national products, high illiteracy rates and related problems. That's what UDCs are technically, but a short definition of undeveloped is "starving." Most Latin American, African, and Asian countries fall into this category. The second group consists, in essence, of the "developed countries" (DCs). DCs are modern, industrial nations, such as the United States, Canada, most European countries, Israel, Russia, Japan, and Australia. Most people in these countries are adequately nourished.

Paul R. Erlich, The Population Bomb

Summary: _____

_____

_____

Comic books had been criticized in print since 1940 or so; because most of the readers were children, some people worried that comic books—crude and violent as many of them were—might be damaging young minds. The crime and horror comic books were found especially alarming, and a storm of **indignation** finally struck the industry with full force in 1954. Comic books were dumped on bonfires; comic books were denounced in Congress; comic books were solemnly condemned by psychiatrists as the root of a host of social evils. (And, more important for business, distributors started refusing to accept some comic books from the publishers.) As the movie producers had done twenty years earlier, the comic-book publishers responded to charges of immorality by drawing up an extremely strict code and entrusting its enforcement to a panel recruited from outside the industry. Only one major publisher—Dell, whose comic books starred such licensed characters as Donald Duck and the Lone Ranger and had attracted little criticism—could afford to **shun** the new Comics Code.

Michael Barrier and Martin Williams,
Introduction to A Smithsonian Book of
Comic-Book Comics

---

indignation: anger caused by an injustice;   shun: avoid, keep away from

Summary: _____

_____

_____

Following is a passage from a sociology textbook. Although not an essay in itself, it is organized like one except without the introduction and conclusion. Read the passage, underlining or highlighting the general, introductory statements of each paragraph:

What age is viewed as old depends, in part, on the age of the viewer. 1
A teenager may feel old in relation to a brother still in grammar school, but young in relation to a sister who already has a career and children. Forty may seem over the hill until we have reached that age. And a ninety-year-old may regard a retired person of seventy as a mere youngster.

More objectively, what age is old depends on the average life 2
expectancy in a particular society. This, in turn, is related to the society's overall standard of living and its technological ability to control disease and other threats to human life. Throughout most of human history, people's lives were quite short by current American standards. Teenagers married and had children, those in their twenties were middle-aged, and people became old by about thirty. Reaching the age of forty was rare in most societies until the late Middle Ages, when the rising standard of living and technological advances began to provide the means to control **infectious** diseases that were common killers of people of all ages.

Although elderly Americans experience less physical disability than 3
the cultural stereotype suggests, physical decline is indeed an important part of old age and can cause considerable emotional stress. Human beings at all stages of life are familiar with the problems caused by illness and physical injury. Pain, loss of activity, dependence on others, and reminders of our mortality can be sources of frustration, self-doubt, and depression. Since American culture so highly values youth, physical vitality, and good looks, changes in physical capabilities and physical appearance can threaten the self-esteem of older people. Unlike the young, however, the elderly must face the fact that their physical decline has no cure and is a prelude to ultimate death.

_____

infectious: transmittable

Psychologist Erik Erikson has described old age as a stage of life   4
in which individuals experience the tension of **"integrity** versus despair." However much they may still be learning and achieving, the
elderly must face the fact that their lives are nearing an end. Thus
old age involves reflection about one's past, which brings a variable
degree of satisfaction and regret. Erikson claims that people who are
able to maintain high self-esteem in the face of physical and social
decline, accepting their mistakes as well as their successes, are likely
to experience old age as a time of personal integrity. For those who
find little worth in their lives, however, old age may be a time of despair—a dead end that lacks positive meaning.

John J. Macionis, "Aging and the Elderly,"
Sociology

Besides improving your reading comprehension, active reading can improve
your writing by revealing the role of structure, as these questions illustrate:

1. Look back at the diagram at the beginning of this chapter showing
    how essays and paragraphs are organized. How does your underlining
    or highlighting compare with the shaded areas of the paragraphs in the
    diagram?
2. Go over the first two or three paragraphs again, this time reading them
    without reading your underlined or highlighted sentences. How does
    the passage read now?
3. What does this show you about how you should try to write your own
    paragraphs?

While most paragraphs in most informative writing (such as textbooks) are
organized like the ones above, not every single one necessarily is. Though writers do carefully follow the principle of starting with general, introductory statements and following up with specifics, they don't always do so in such clear
and highly organized ways.

Let's look now at a section of a text in which things aren't organized so
neatly paragraph by paragraph. Which are the general and which the specific
statements in this text? Again, write a short summary of what the *whole text*
means.

Why do I think network TV does a better job of informing than [the
newspapers]? Well, let's get the **partisan** bit over with. Television

---

integrity: commitment to personal values;
partisan: supports a particular idea

lives on advertising to an even greater extent than newspapers, and since advertising is big business, advertising is by nature Republican. Yet nowhere in network newscasts or network commentaries on current events have I encountered the intense partisanship, the often **rabid** bias that colors the editorial pages of the majority of newspapers in this country. Douglass Cater, in his book *The Fourth Branch of Government,* confines himself to only one **pungent** footnote on this subject. "I have deliberately avoided," he writes, "getting into the predominantly one-party nature of newspaper ownership. It is a fact of life." This particular fact of life is a shameful one: that newspapers whose duty it is to inform the American public give them only one side of the issues that affect them profoundly—the Republican side. This is shameful not only for Democrats—they have survived it before and will survive it again— but for the maturity of our people. Some of the same papers which loudly **extol** the virtues of free enterprise and a free press are consistently failing to print the facts on which a people can form a balanced and independent opinion. That balanced and independent opinion is our only real security as a nation.

Now, very often, television coverage of news is superficial and inadequate. Very often the picture takes precedence over the point. But by and large the news reports and commentaries on CBS and NBC and ABC make every effort to present viewers with more than one aspect of an issue, either by letting opposing spokesmen have their say, or by outlining the positions held by both major parties on the subject involved.

Television also provides a wide range of opinion by setting up four or five experts and letting them knock each other down. What has the local press of this nature? Is it discharging its duty to diversity by printing snippets of opinion from unqualified readers? Is this exploring an issue?

Marya Mannes, *But Will It Sell?*

Summary: _____

_____

_____

————————

rabid: fanatical, biased;   pungent: sharp, biting;   extol: give high praise

In addition to paragraph organization, the organization of whole texts also provides clues you can use in deciding which points to write down for easy reference. The introduction of an essay or article will tell you what it's going to be about, and that, of course, is the most important point of all. The conclusion of an essay or chapter often highlights for the reader the material the writer feels is most important. And sometimes texts will contain section headings to make it easy for the reader to see when a new point is coming up.

The active reader, then, sorts out the main general points from the text and writes them down *in his or her own words*. It is most important to use your own words rather than copying the author's because trying to put the ideas into your own words forces you to think about them closely and thus helps you remember them. Finally, when you make your notes, be sure to put page references after each idea you have jotted down so that when you later begin to use the information, you will be able to find again the specifics or quotations you may want to use.

WRITING SUMMARIES

A summary is a concise restatement, in one's own words, of another, longer document, usually an article or a report. Summaries are often used in business and academic settings in which a committee or a small group of teachers or students needs to grasp a great deal of material very quickly. In such cases, the group will often assign two or three articles or reports to each of its members to read and summarize for the group as a whole, so every person won't have to read every single document. Needless to say, in such cases, the summaries must be accurate as well as brief.

Summaries are also handy study tools for students, particularly those facing essay tests. Summarizing the chapters in a textbook or articles assigned to be read can help in reviewing the material and is a great help in remembering the material. Moreover, once you have written down the information, writing it again under the pressure of time, as during an essay test, becomes much much easier.

A summary written for a committee or similar group should be as carefully composed as an essay and have all of an essay's usual characteristics, including paragraphs with topic sentences. A working summary that you write for yourself need not be so formal; it may even be all one paragraph if that suits you.

A good working summary is written in your own words, though you may want to borrow key phrases from the original. It *must* have the following characteristics:

- Above all, it must maintain and communicate the meaning of the original.
- It must *not* contain your opinions or views on the original.

- It must stick strictly to what the original writer had to say.
- It must contain all the main points of the original.
- Usually it will not contain the supporting points, unless one or more of them is of unusual importance.

You can see that to write a good summary, you need to exercise a great deal of judgment about what is important and what isn't.

A good working summary should answer these questions:

1.   What is the subject of the original? What problem or situation is the writer addressing? (You might want to set this off as a separate paragraph, like an introduction, to make it stand out.)

2.   What are the main points of the original? The summary may or may not stick to the same order as the original. Normally summaries will cover the most important points first, although articles and reports often do not do that. If the original involves discussion of some pro/con issue or compares two things, the summary will usually give all the pro points together and all the con points together or keep the various points of the comparison together, even though the original might not be organized that way. (If the original covers many main points, you might again want to set them in separate paragraphs for clarity's sake.)

3.   What conclusions does the original reach?

STEPS IN WRITING A SUMMARY

How do you go about writing a good working summary? If you follow the steps below, you will have an excellent chance of producing a useful and accurate summary.

1.   Read through the entire original to get an understanding of the whole piece. On a piece of scratch paper, write in your own words the *point* of the piece, which you will usually find in the introduction, and its conclusion.

2.   Reread and underline or highlight the important ideas. Carefully check the beginnings of paragraphs for topic sentences that announce new points. Normally, you will not want to highlight supporting facts, but some may be so striking or otherwise important that you will want to include them in your summary.

3.   Now write the introductory statement of your summary, explaining what the original is about. Try to confine yourself to one sentence—two at the most.

4.   Decide on the order in which you want to present the main points of the original; you will probably need to do some scribbling on scratch

paper to do this. Review the materials you have highlighted to make sure you cover everything.

5.   Write the body of your summary, using your own words and making sure to cover all the key points.

6.   Write your last part, in which you explain what the original author's conclusions were. Be sure to keep your own opinions out of this part.

7.   Proofread for spelling, typographical errors, and the conventions of usage. In particular, compare the spelling of titles, authors, and other names and key terms with that in the original document.

AN EXPERIENCED WRITER WRITES A SUMMARY

Following is a short essay about one element in the history of the English language. It has been marked up by a person preparing to write a summary of it. While everyone will mark up a text somewhat differently, this kind of work will have some features in common regardless of who does it. For one thing, the words indicating the subject and main points are sure to be noted. Examine the essay to see how the writer marked it, what he noted, and what he didn't note. Following the essay is the summary written from the notes. Compare the two to see how the notes led to the summary.

Point: Because of Wm. the Conq., English (now heavily influenced by — originally Germanic language French)

HOW ENGLISH BECAME FRENCH

There is a question you won't find in the game "Trivial Pursuit" that will stump your audience every time: "Name the one person who had the greatest effect on the English language." You will get answers like "Shakespeare," "Samuel Johnson," and "Webster," but none of those men had any effect at all compared to a man who didn't even speak English—William the Conqueror.   1

subject — greatest effect on English

before William   Prior to 1066, in the land we now call Great Britain lived peoples belonging to two major language groups. In the west-central region   2
lived the Welsh, who spoke a Celtic language, and in the north lived the Scots, whose language, though not the same as Welsh, was also Celtic. The rest of the country was inhabited by the dominant Saxons, actually a mixture of Angles, Saxons, and other Germanic and Nordic peoples, who spoke what we now call Anglo-Saxon (or Old English), a Germanic language. If this state of affairs had lasted, English (which comes from *Engle,* the Angles) today would be close to German.

when it changed

But this state of affairs didn't last because a Norman Duke, William, living in the part of France called Normandy, decided to extend his domain over England. In 1066 the Normans under Duke William met the Saxons under King Harold in battle at a place called Hastings. *effects* There the French-speaking Normans defeated the Saxons and began their rule over England, establishing not only their political dominance but their linguistic dominance as well. [3]

For about a century, French became the official language of England while Old English became the language of peasants and outcasts. *① examples* As a result our current vocabulary of politics and the law comes from French rather than German. Such words as *nation, state, realm, capital, senate, president, legal, court, appeal*—even *politics* and *law*—as well as many others, come from French. On the other hand, words like *field, road, plow, bread, milk, water,* and *steal* come from Old English. *effects* [4]

② In some cases, modern English even shows a distinction between upper-class French and lower-class Anglo-Saxon in its vocabulary. *examples* Which is higher-class, *car* (from French) or *wagon* (from German)? What about *people* (French) and *folk* (German)? Or *chair* (French) and *stool* (German)? We even have different words for some foods, *③* meat in particular, depending on whether it's still out in the fields or *examples* at home ready to be cooked. The words *cow, sheep,* and *lamb* are, not surprisingly, all German, reflecting the fact that the Saxon peasants were doing the farming. But the words *beef, mutton,* and *veal* are French, perhaps indicating that the Norman nobility were doing most of the eating. [5]

When Americans visit Europe for the first time, they usually find Germany more "foreign" than France because the German they see on signs, posters, and advertisements seems much more different from English than French does. Few realize that our language is actually Germanic in its origins and that the French influences are all the result of one man's ambition. [6]

Summary

Because of a Norman duke, William the Conqueror, English, which is actually a Germanic language, is now heavily influenced by French.

The dominant people in England were the Saxons, who spoke Anglo-Saxon or Old English. When they were defeated in 1066 by the Normans, French became the official language of England. We can see three big results of that. One is that today many of our words in politics and law are from French rather than German. A second is that we even have upper-class words from French and lower-class words from German. Finally, we use French words for meat on the table but German words for the animal sources of the meat.

No other person ever had such a major effect on English as William the Conqueror.

EXERCISES

Mark up the following three essays and write summaries of them as indicated by your instructor.

Pre-reading

Some articles, particularly ones in the sciences and social sciences, and many textbooks will show you how they are organized or what their main points are through subtitles in the articles. Before you start reading Jane Brody's article on fatigue, look over the article to see what its subtitles are. Even before you begin writing your summary, you can see what the main points of Brody's article are. Next look to see whether one of the sections of the article is longer than the others. If it is, look at the topic sentences of its paragraphs to see whether this section contains a major point or example important enough so that it should be part of your summary.

FATIGUE
Jane Brody

Fatigue is one of the most common complaints brought to doctors, 1
friends, and relatives. You'd think in this era of labor-saving devices
and convenient transportation that few people would have reason
to be so tired. But probably more people complain of fatigue today
than in the days when hay was baled by hand and laundry scrubbed
on a washboard. Witness these typical complaints:

"It doesn't seem to matter how long I sleep—I'm more tired 2
when I wake up than when I went to bed."

"Some of my friends come home from work and jog for several 3
miles or swim laps. I don't know how they do it. I'm completely exhausted at the end of a day at the office."

"I thought I was weary because of the holidays, but now that 4
they're over, I'm even worse. I can barely get through this week, and
on the weekend I don't even have the strength to get dressed. I wonder if I'm **anemic** or something."

---

anemic: weak, listless

"I don't know what's wrong with me lately, but I've been so col- 5 lapsed that I haven't made a proper meal for the family in weeks. We've been living on TV dinners and packaged mixes. I was finally forced to do a laundry because the kids ran out of underwear."

The causes of modern-day fatigue are diverse and only rarely re- 6 lated to excessive physical exertion. The relatively few people who do heavy labor all day long almost never complain about being tired, perhaps because they expect to be. Today, physicians report, tiredness is more likely a consequence of underexertion than of wearing yourself down with overactivity. In fact, increased physical activity is often prescribed as a cure for sagging energy.

Kinds of Fatigue

There are three main categories of fatigue. These are physical fatigue, 7 **pathological** fatigue, and psychological fatigue.

Physical. This is a well-known result of overworking your muscles 8 to the point where metabolic waste products—carbon dioxide and lactic acid—accumulate in your blood and sap your strength. Your muscles can't continue to work efficiently in a bath of these chemicals. Physical fatigue is usually a pleasant tiredness, such as that which you might experience after playing a hard set of tennis, chopping wood, or climbing a mountain. The cure is simple and fast. You rest, giving your body a chance to get rid of accumulated wastes and restore muscle fuel.

Pathological. Here fatigue is a warning sign or consequence of 9 some underlying physical disorder, perhaps the common cold or flu or something more serious like diabetes or cancer. Usually other symptoms besides fatigue are present that suggest the true cause.

Even after an illness has passed, you're likely to feel dragged out 10 for a week or more. Take your fatigue as a signal to go slow while your body has a chance to recover fully even if all you had was a cold. Pushing yourself to resume full activity too soon could precipitate a relapse and almost certainly will prolong your period of fatigue.

Even though illness is not a frequent cause of prolonged fatigue, 11 it's very important that it not be overlooked. Therefore, anyone who feels drained of energy for weeks on end should have a thorough physical checkup. But even if nothing shows up as a result of the various medical tests, that doesn't mean there's nothing wrong with you.

---

pathological: caused by disease

Unfortunately too often a medical work-up ends with a **battery**   12
of negative results, the patient is dismissed, and the true cause of serious fatigue goes undetected. As Dr. John Bulette, a psychiatrist at
the Medical College of Pennsylvania Hospital in Philadelphia, tells it,
this is what happened to a Pennsylvania woman who had lost nearly
fifty pounds and was "almost dead—so tired she could hardly lift her
head up." The doctors who first examined the woman were sure she
had cancer. But no matter how hard they looked, they could find no
sign of malignancy or of any other disease that could account for her
wasting away. Finally, she was brought to the college hospital, where
doctors noted that she was severely depressed.

They questioned her about her life and discovered that her trou-   13
bles had begun two years earlier, after her husband died. Once
treated for depression, the woman quickly perked up, gained ten
pounds in just a few weeks, then returned home to continue her re-
covery with the aid of psychotherapy.

Psychological. Emotional problems and conflicts, especially depres-   14
sion and anxiety, are by far the most common causes of prolonged fatigue. Fatigue may represent a defense mechanism that prevents you
from having to face the true cause of your depression, such as the fact
that you hate your job. It is also your body's safety valve for expressing
repressed emotional conflicts, such as feeling trapped in an ungratify-
ing role or an unhappy marriage. When such feelings are not expressed openly, they often come out as physical symptoms, with
fatigue as one of the most common **manifestations.** "Many people
who are extremely fatigued don't even know they're depressed," Dr.
Bulette says. "They're so busy distracting themselves or just worrying
about being tired that they don't recognize their depression."

One of these situations is so common it's been given a name—   15
tired housewife syndrome. The victims are commonly young mothers who day in and day out face the predictable tedium of caring for
a home and small children, fixing meals, dealing with repairmen,
and generally having no one interesting to talk to and nothing en-
joyable to look forward to at the end of their boring and unreward-
ing day. The tired housewife may be inwardly resentful, envious of
her husband's job, and guilty about her feelings. But rather than face
them head-on, she becomes extremely fatigued.

---

battery: a large number, a series;   manifestations: signs

Today, with nearly half the mothers of young children working 16
outside the home, the tired housewife syndrome has taken a new
twist, that of conflicting roles and responsibilities and guilt over leaving the children, often with an overlay of genuine physical exhaus-
tion from trying to be all things to all people.

Emotionally **induced** fatigue may be compounded by sleep dis- 17
turbance that results from the underlying psychological conflict. A
person may develop insomnia or may sleep the **requisite** number of
hours but fitfully, tossing and turning all night, having disturbing
dreams, and awakening, as one woman put it, feeling as if she "had
been run over by a truck."

Understanding the underlying emotional problem is the **crucial** 18
first step toward curing psychological fatigue and by itself often results in considerable lessening of the tiredness. Professional psychological help or career or marriage counseling may be needed.

Pre-reading

As you have learned, topic sentences may be one sentence or they may
be more than one, though not usually more than two. It is also true that
what makes a sentence a topic sentence may be no more than one key word
in that sentence. Before reading all of the following essay, read only the first
three paragraphs—these are the introduction—and then underline or highlight or jot down in the margin the kinds of violence McGrath says he is
going to cover.

After you have done that, go through the essay looking only at the first
sentence of each paragraph. In that sentence find the word (or words) that
tell the reader what the paragraph will be about. Write down these words in
order, paragraph by paragraph, along with the number of each paragraph.
For example, in paragraph 4, the topic word in the first sentence is "robbery," one of the forms of violence McGrath notes in his introduction. So
for the first entry in your outline you should write

robbery (4)

When you have written down these words and their paragraph numbers, you will have an outline of McGrath's essay, and this can serve as the
basis for your summary.

---

induced: caused; requisite: needed, required;
crucial: of supreme importance

THE MYTH OF VIOLENCE IN THE OLD WEST
Roger D. McGrath

It is commonly assumed that violence is part of our frontier heritage. 1
But the historical record shows that frontier violence was very different from violence today. Robbery and burglary, two of our most
common crimes, were of no great significance in the frontier towns
of the Old West, and rape was seemingly nonexistent.

Bodie, one of the principal towns on the trans-Sierra frontier, il- 2
lustrates the point. Nestled high in the mountains of eastern California, Bodie, which boomed in the late 1870s and early 1880s, ranked
among the most **notorious** frontier towns of the Old West. It was, as
one prospector put it, the last of the old-time mining camps.

Like the trans-Sierra frontier in general, Bodie was indisputably 3
violent and lawless, yet most people were not affected. Fistfights and
gunfights among willing **combatants**—gamblers, miners, and the
like—were regular events, and stagecoach holdups were not unusual.
But the old, the young, the weak, and the female—so often the victims of crime today—were generally not harmed.

Robbery was more often aimed at stagecoaches than at individ- 4
uals. Highwaymen usually took only the express box and left the passengers alone. There were eleven stagecoach robberies in Bodie
between 1878 and 1882, and in only two instances were passengers
robbed. (In one instance, the highwaymen later apologized for their
conduct.)

There were only ten robberies and three attempted robberies of 5
individuals in Bodie during its boom years, and in nearly every case
the circumstances were the same: the victim had spent the evening
in a gambling den, saloon, or brothel; he had revealed that he had
on his person a significant sum of money; and he was staggering
home drunk when the attack occurred.

Bodie's total of twenty-one robberies—eleven of stages and ten 6
of individuals—over a five-year period converts to a rate of eighty-
four robberies per 100,000 inhabitants per year. On this scale—the
same scale used by the FBI to index crime—New York City's robbery
rate in 1980 was 1,140, Miami's was 995, and Los Angeles's was 628.
The rate for the United States as a whole was 243. Thus Bodie's robbery rate was significantly below the national average in 1980.

---

notorious: widely and unfavorably known;   combatants: fighters

Between 1878 and 1882, there were only thirty-two burglaries— 7
seventeen of homes and fifteen of businesses—in Bodie. At least a
half-dozen burglaries were **thwarted** by the presence of armed citizens. The newspapers regularly advocated shooting burglars on
sight, and several burglars were, in fact, shot at.

Using the FBI scale, Bodie's burglary rate for those five years was 8
128. Miami's rate in 1980 was 3,282, New York's was 2,661, and Los
Angeles's was 2,602. The rate of the United States as a whole was
1,668, thirteen times that of Bodie.

Bodie's law enforcement institutions were certainly not responsi- 9
ble for these low rates. Rarely were robbers or burglars arrested, and
even less often were they convicted. Moreover, many law enforcement officers operated on both sides of the law. Perhaps the greatest
deterrent to crime in Bodie was the fact that so many people were
armed. Armed guards prevented bank robberies and holdups of
stagecoaches carrying shipments of **bullion**, and armed homeowners and merchants discouraged burglary.

It was the armed citizens themselves who were the most po- 10
tent—though not the only—deterrent to **larcenous** crime. Another
was the threat of **vigilantism.** Highwaymen, for example, understood that while they could take the express box from a stagecoach
without arousing the citizens, they risked inciting the entire popu-
lace to action if they robbed the passengers.

There is considerable evidence that women in Bodie were rarely 11
the victims of crime. Between 1878 and 1882 only one woman, a
prostitute, was robbed, and there were no reported cases of rape.
(There is no evidence that rapes occurred but were not reported.)

Finally, juvenile crime, which accounts for a significant portion 12
of the violent crime in the United States today, was limited in Bodie
to pranks and malicious mischief.

If robbery, burglary, crimes against women, and juvenile crime 13
were relatively rare on the trans-Sierra frontier, homicide was not:
thirty-one Bodieites were shot, stabbed, or beaten to death during
the boom years, for a homicide rate of 116. No U.S. city today comes
close to this rate. In 1980, Miami led the nation with a homicide rate
of 32.7; Las Vegas was a distant second at 23.4. A half-dozen cities

---

thwarted: prevented;   deterrent: prevention;
bullion: pure gold or silver;   larcenous: having to do with theft;
vigilantism: people taking the law into their own hands

had rates of zero. The rate for the United States as a whole in that year was a mere 10.2.

Several factors contributed to Bodie's high homicide rate. A majority of the town's residents were young, adventurous, single males who adhered to a code of conduct that frequently required them to fight even if, or perhaps especially if, it could mean death. Courage was admired above all else. Alcohol also played a major role in **fostering** the settlement of disputes by violence. 14

If the men's code of conduct and their consumption of alcohol made fighting inevitable, their **sidearms** often made it fatal. While the carrying of guns probably reduced the incidence of robbery and burglary, it undoubtedly increased the number of homicides. 15

For the most part, the citizens of Bodie were not troubled by the great number of killings; nor were they troubled that only one man was ever convicted of murder. They accepted the killings and the lack of convictions because most of those killed had been willing combatants. 16

Thus the violence and lawlessness of the trans-Sierra frontier bear little relation to the violence and lawlessness that **pervade** American society today. If Bodie is at all representative of frontier towns, there is little justification for blaming contemporary American violence on our frontier heritage. 17

Pre-reading

The following essay will be more difficult to summarize than the preceding ones because the signals that Heilbroner gives at the beginnings of his paragraphs are quite subtle. But if you skim the first few lines of each paragraph, you will begin to see that the essay has distinct sections. Notice that the title of the essay is a warning to us about a problem. So it will make sense to think of this essay as setting forth a problem (that would be one section), showing us how the problem comes about (that would be another), and offering us possible solutions to the problem (that would be a third).

DON'T LET STEREOTYPES WARP YOUR JUDGMENT
Robert L. Heilbroner

Is a girl called Gloria apt to be better-looking than one called Bertha? 1
Are criminals more likely to be dark than blond? Can you tell a good

---

fostering: encouraging;   sidearms: small weapons carried at the side;
pervade: spread through

deal about someone's personality from hearing his voice briefly over the phone? Can a person's nationality be pretty accurately guessed from his photograph? Does the fact that someone wears glasses imply that he is intelligent?

The answer to all these questions is obviously, "No."   2

Yet, from all the evidence at hand, most of us believe these   3
things. Ask any college boy if he'd rather take his chances with a Gloria or a Bertha, or ask a college girl if she'd rather blind-date a Richard or a Cuthbert. In fact, you don't have to ask: college students in questionnaires have revealed that names **conjure up** the same images in their minds as they do in yours—and for as little reason.

Look into the favorite suspects of persons who report "suspicious   4
characters" and you will find a large percentage of them to be "swarthy" or "dark and foreign-looking"—despite the testimony of criminologists that criminals do not tend to be dark, foreign or "wild-eyed." **Delve** into the main asset of a telephone stock swindler and you will find it to be a marvelously confidence-inspiring telephone "personality." And whereas we all think we know what an Italian or a Swede looks like, it is the sad fact that when a group of Nebraska students sought to match faces and nationalities of 15 European countries, they were scored wrong in 93 percent of their identifications. Finally, for all the fact that horn-rimmed glasses have now become the standard television sign of an "intellectual," optometrists know that the main thing that distinguishes people with glasses is just bad eyes.

Stereotypes are a kind of gossip about the world, a gossip that   5
makes us prejudge people before we ever lay eyes on them. Hence it is not surprising that stereotypes have something to do with the dark world of prejudice. Explore most prejudices (note that the word means prejudgment) and you will find a cruel stereotype at the core of each one.

For it is the extraordinary fact that once we have typecast the   6
world, we tend to see people in terms of our standardized pictures. In another demonstration of the power of stereotypes to affect our vision, a number of Columbia and Barnard students were shown 30 photographs of pretty but unidentified girls, and asked to rate each in terms of "general liking," "intelligence," "beauty" and so on. Two months later, the same group were shown the same photographs,

---

conjure up: call up as though by magic;   delve: dig

this time with fictitious Irish, Italian, Jewish and "American" names attached to the pictures. Right away the ratings changed. Faces which were now seen as representing a national group went down in looks and still farther down in likability, while the "American" girls suddenly looked decidedly prettier and nicer.

Why is it that we stereotype the world in such irrational and   7
harmful fashion? In part, we begin to type-cast people in our child-hood years. Early in life, as every parent whose child has watched a TV Western knows, we learn to spot the Good Guys from the Bad Guys. Some years ago, a social psychologist showed very clearly how powerful these stereotypes of childhood vision are. He secretly asked the most popular youngsters in an elementary school to make errors in their morning gym exercises. Afterwards, he asked the class if any-one had noticed any mistakes during gym period. Oh, yes, said the children. But it was the unpopular members of the class—the "bad guys"—they remembered as being out of step.

We not only grow up with standardized pictures forming inside   8
of us, but as grown-ups we are constantly having them thrust upon us. Some of them, like the half-joking, half-serious stereotypes of mothers-in-law, or country yokels, or psychiatrists, are dinned into us by the stock jokes we hear and repeat. In fact, without such stereo-types, there would be a lot fewer jokes. Still other stereotypes are **perpetuated** by the advertisements we read, the movies we see, the books we read.

And finally, we tend to stereotype because it helps us make sense   9
out of a highly confusing world, a world which William James once described as "one great, blooming, buzzing confusion." It is a curi-ous fact that if we don't know what we're looking at, we are often quite literally unable to see what we're looking at. People who re-cover their sight after a lifetime of blindness actually cannot at first tell a triangle from a square. A visitor to a factory sees only noisy chaos where the superintendent sees a perfectly **synchronized** flow of work. As Walter Lippmann has said, "For the most part we do not first see, and then define; we define first, and then we see."

Stereotypes are one way in which we "define" the world in order   10
to see it. They classify the infinite variety of human beings into a con-venient handful of "types" towards whom we learn to act in stereo-

---

perpetuated: made to last longer;   synchronized: operated together typed fashion. Life would be a wearing process if we had to start from scratch with each and every human contact. Stereotypes economize on our mental effort by covering up the blooming, buzzing confusion with big recognizable cutouts. They save us the "trouble" of finding out what the world is like—they give it its accustomed look.

　　Thus the trouble is that stereotypes make us mentally lazy. As S. 　11 I. Hayakawa, the authority on **semantics**, has written: "The danger of stereotypes lies not in their existence, but in the fact that they become for all people some of the time, and for some people all the time, substitutes for observation." Worse yet, stereotypes get in the way of our judgment, even when we do observe the world. Someone who has formed rigid preconceptions of all Latins as "excitable," or all teenagers as "wild," doesn't alter his point of view when he meets a calm and deliberate **Genoese**, or a serious-minded high school student. He brushes them aside as "exceptions that proved the rule." And, of course, if he meets someone true to type, he stands triumphantly **vindicated**. "They're all like that," he proclaims, having encountered an excited Latin, an ill-behaved adolescent.

　　Hence, quite aside from the injustice which stereotypes do to 　12 others, they impoverish ourselves. A person who lumps the world into simple categories, who type-casts all labor leaders as "racketeers," all businessmen as "reactionaries," all Harvard men as "snobs," and all Frenchmen as "sexy," is in danger of becoming a stereotype himself. He loses his capacity to be himself—which is to say, to see the world in his own absolutely unique, **inimitable** and independent fashion.

　　Instead, he votes for the man who fits his standardized picture 　13 of what a candidate "should" look like or sound like, buys the goods that someone in his "situation" in life "should" own, lives the life that others define for him. The mark of the stereotype person is that he never surprises us, that we do indeed have him "typed." And no one fits this strait-jacket so perfectly as someone whose opinions about other people are fixed and inflexible.

　　Nor do we suddenly drop our standardized pictures for a blind- 　14 ing vision of the Truth. Sharp swings of ideas about people often just

---

semantics: the study of the meaning of language;　Genoese: a person from Genoa, Italy;　vindicated: shown to be correct; inimitable: unable to be imitated substitute one stereotype for another. The true process of change is a slow one that adds bits and pieces of reality to the pictures in our heads, until gradually they take on some of the blurriness of life itself. Little by little, we learn not that Jews and Negroes and Catholics and Puerto Ricans are "just like everybody else"—for that, too, is a stereotype—but that each and every one of them is unique, special, different and individual. Often we do not even know that we have let a stereotype lapse until we hear someone saying, "all so-and-so's are like such-and-such," and we hear ourselves saying, "Well—maybe."

Can we speed the process along? Of course we can.   15

First, we can become aware of the standardized pictures in our   16 heads, in other people's heads, in the world around us.

Second, we can become suspicious of all judgments that we   17 allow exceptions to "prove." There is no more chastening thought than that in the vast intellectual adventure of science, it takes but one tiny exception to topple a whole **edifice** of ideas.

Third, we can learn to be **chary** of generalizations about people.   18 As F. Scott Fitzgerald once wrote: "Begin with an individual, and before you know it you have created a type; begin with a type, and you find you have created—nothing."

Most of the time, when we type-cast the world, we are not in   19 fact generalizing about people at all. We are only revealing the embarrassing facts about the pictures that hang in the gallery of stereotypes in our own heads.

ANALYZING AND EVALUATING YOUR INFORMATION

When most people think about writers, if they ever do, they probably imagine someone sitting at a typewriter and writing. If writers aren't people who write, who are they? Actually, people who write usually spend a lot more time getting ready to write than they do writing. The writing process starts long before the actual writing does.

Many people think that writers know something others don't know, have some secret about writing that makes them good writers. They do. In fact, they have two secrets. We're going to save one secret to tell you later,

---

edifice: structure;   chary: careful, wary

but here's the first secret: *The more carefully you think about what you are going to write, the easier it will be to write it. And conversely, the less you think and prepare ahead of time, the harder the writing will be.*

In reading preparatory to writing summaries, you have already engaged in reading actively. But when you read in preparation for writing your own essay, rather than merely summarizing someone else's, you need to take active reading one small step further. Sometimes in doing your reading—but more often when you reread—you will find yourself getting ideas about what you've read, seeing connections or contradictions, often finding material relevant to your own experience. When you are making your notes, be sure to write down the ideas or questions that come to you, perhaps putting them in the margin or in parentheses so that you don't confuse them with your notes. These materials, the results of your own thinking, will help you enormously in the next crucial step, analyzing what you have been reading.

For the most part, your analysis of each item of information should cover three points:

1. What is the *relevance* of this item to what you're going to be writing about? For instance, if you were doing a paper on rates of Chinese immigration to the United States in the nineteenth century, you might come across some fascinating material on social life in west coast Chinese communities. However, you would realize that this material had no bearing on immigration rates, and so you would discard it (or save it for another paper).

2. Closely related to relevance is *importance*—that is, given that a particular item is relevant, how important is it? Writers will often put asterisks or stars alongside materials they think are especially important.

3. Finally, what is the *relationship* of each item to other items? If some items support each other, you will want to know that before you start writing. If an item contradicts or proves wrong another item, you will again need to know that. The important point here is that you won't know what your information means until you get it organized. *This is not the same as organizing your essay.* That comes later.

ORGANIZING AND FINDING YOUR POINT

In some of your college writing, including some of the assignments for this course, you will be asked to explain something, to show what a group of data means. In other assignments, you will have to argue a position, to make up your mind which side seems to you to have the stronger points on a particular issue and argue for that side.

In both cases, you have to decide what your point is before you can start. If you have analyzed and organized your information, you will have little trouble deciding on your point.

The single biggest mistake a writer can make is to decide on his or her point without having gone carefully over the available information. It is unfortunately true that most people form opinions on important matters without carefully investigating them first. If challenged, they then say, "Well, I'm entitled to my opinion." That's true. They are. But the opinion is probably worthless if they haven't analyzed and organized their information.

Even so, it is important for a writer to draw on the knowledge he or she does possess as a way of *beginning* to think about a topic. Although you may not realize it, you bring an enormous amount of knowledge and information into this course, the result of your age, experience, and education. Although you may not be an expert in every topic assigned (who is?), you probably know something about each one and therefore have an opinion about it. One way to find out what you already know about a topic is to ask yourself general questions before you start examining the available information—not as a way of arriving at definitive answers, but as a way of beginning to think about a topic. We call this *pre-reading.*

WRITING A REPORT

Following are two short essays on the same subject, a problem in male-female relationships that often has serious effects: how men and women verbally communicate with each other.

Imagine that you are serving as a consultant to a marriage guidance class. The instructor of the class gives you the following task:

Writing Assignment

Write a report indicating which of the two following essays you think newly married couples attending the marriage guidance class should read. Your report should consist of three parts: a short introduction about the general problem of male-female communication, summaries of each of the two essays, and a concluding recommendation about which one you think should be required reading. The recommendation section should compare the strengths and weaknesses of the two essays to show *why* you recommend one over the other.

Before you read the two essays, spend a few moments on *pre-reading*—that is, thinking in a fairly organized way about the subject you are going to tackle.

Pre-reading

Ask yourself the following questions (or ones like them):

- Have you ever noticed, on a date for example, that you and the opposite sex don't always want to talk about exactly the same things—that sometimes you have to listen to your partner talk about something that doesn't really interest you at all?

- Who spends more time on the phone—your women friends (or sister) or your men friends (or brother)?

- What do women use the phone for primarily? How about men?

- If you have a sibling of the opposite sex, have you noticed that he or she talks with his or her friends about different things than you like to talk about with your friends?

- On social occasions, have you noticed that married couples often split up, with the women getting in one group and the men in another?

- Do your mother and father tend to want to talk about different topics? Do they have different conversational styles? Does one tend to talk more than the other?

After you've given this subject some thought from your own experience, you're ready to read what others think about it. Keep an open mind as you read; you may learn something new.

Reading

Read the following essays, underlining or highlighting and making notes on their main points and anything else you think is particularly important. (If a piece of information is something that *you* didn't know before and are glad you learned, that's a sign that it's important.) As you did in writing your previous summaries, first skim these two essays, looking for their introductions and indications of what their main sections are, what main points they cover. Notice, however, that the first essay, by Joyce Maynard, is organized in a completely different way from the essays you've previously worked on and from the second essay, by Sherman and Haas. Maynard's is a very informal essay written for a newspaper column and so she doesn't use a conventional introduction but instead drifts into her main subject. Sherman and Haas write the kind of standard introduction your teachers in college will expect you to write.

HIS TALK, HER TALK
Joyce Maynard

It can be risky these days to suggest that there are any **innate** differ-   1
ences between men and women, other than those of anatomy. Out
the window go the old notions about man and aggression, woman
and submission (don't even say the word), man and intellect, woman
and instinct. If I observe that my infant son prefers pushing a block
along the floor while making car noises to cradling a doll in his arms
and singing lullabies (and he does)—well, I can only conclude that,
despite all our earnest attempts at nonsexist childrearing, he has already suffered environmental contamination. Some of it, no doubt
unwittingly, came from my husband and me, **reared** in the days
when nobody **winced** if you recited that old **saw** about what little
girls and little boys are made of.

    I do not believe, of course, that men are smarter, steadier, more   2
high-minded than women. But one or two notions are harder to
shake—such as the idea that there is such a thing as "men's talk" or
"women's talk." And that it's a natural instinct to seek out, on occasion, the company of one's own sex, exclude members of the other
sex and not feel guilty about it.

    Oh, but we do. At a party I attended the other night, for instance,   3
it suddenly became apparent that all the women were in one room
and all the men were in the other. Immediately we redistributed ourselves, which was a shame. No one had suggested we segregate. The
talk in the kitchen was simply, all the women felt, more interesting.

    I think I know my husband very well, but I have no idea what   4
goes on when he and his male friends get together. Neither can he
picture what can keep a woman friend and me occupied for three
hours over a single pot of coffee.

    The other day, after a long day of work, my husband Steve and   5
his friend Dave stopped at a bar for a few beers. When he got home,
I asked what they had talked about. "Oh, the usual." Like what? "Fire-
wood. Central America. Trucks. The Celtics. Religion. You know."

    No, not really. I had only recently met with my friend Ann and   6
her friend Sally at a coffee shop nearby, and what we talked about
was the workshop Sally would be holding that weekend concerning

---

innate: possessed at birth;   reared: brought up, raised;   winced: flinched;
saw: saying

women's attitudes toward their bodies, Ann's 11-year-old daughter's upcoming slumber party, how hard it is to buy jeans, and the recent dissolution of a friend's five-year marriage. Asked to **capsulize** our afternoon's discussion, in a form similar to my husband's outline of his night out, I would say we talked about life, love, happiness and heartbreak. Larry Bird's name never came up.

I don't want to reinforce old stereotypes of bubble-headed   7 women (Lucy and Ethel), clinking their coffee cups over talk of clothes and diets while the men remove themselves to lean on mantels, puff on cigars and **muse** about world politics, machines and philosophy. A group of women talking, it seems to me, is likely to concern itself with matters just as pressing as those broached by my husband and friends. It might be said, in fact, that we're really talking about the same eternal conflicts. Our styles are just different.

When Steve tells a story, the point is, as a rule, the ending, and   8 getting there by the most direct route. It may be a good story, told with beautiful precision, but he tells it the way he eats a banana: in three efficient chews, while I cut mine up and savor it. He can (although this is rare) spend 20 minutes on the telephone with one of his brothers, tantalizing me with occasional exclamations of amazement or shock, and then after hanging up, reduce the whole conversation for me to a one-sentence summary. I, on the other hand, may take three quarters of an hour describing some figure from my past while he waits—with thinly veiled impatience—for the point to emerge. Did this fellow just get elected to the House of Representatives? Did he die and leave me his fortune?

In fairness to Steve, I must say that, for him, not talking about   9 something doesn't necessarily mean not dealing with it. And he does listen to what I have to say. He likes a good story, too. It's just that, given a choice, he'd rather hear about quantum mechanics or the history of the Ford Mustang. Better yet, he'd rather play ball.

MAN TO MAN, WOMAN TO WOMAN
Mark A. Sherman and Adelaide Haas

When it comes to conversation, husbands and wives often have   1 problems that close friends of the same sex don't have. First, they

---

capsulize: summarize;   muse: think about

may not have much to talk about, and second, when they do talk, misunderstandings often develop that lead to major fights. Our research concludes that these problems are particularly resistant to solution. Not only do men and women like to talk about different topics, spoken language serves different functions for the sexes.

Our findings are based on responses to a nationally distributed 2 questionnaire, in-depth interviews and observation of same-sex conversations. We found much variation within each gender and no verbal absolutes to differentiate the sexes. But whether we look at topics of conversation or at the role language plays for each gender, we see enough difference to explain why men and women are, to use Lillian Rubin's book title, "intimate strangers."

One hundred sixty-six women and 110 men, ranging in age 3 from 17 to 80, returned a questionnaire asking how often they discussed each of 22 topics with friends of the same sex. For some topics there is little difference—work, movies and television are, in that order, frequent topics of conversation for both sexes. On the other hand female friends report more talk than do men about relationship problems, family, health and reproductive concerns, weight, food and clothing. Men's talk is more likely than women's to be about music, current events and sports. Women's topics tend to be closer to the self and more emotional than men's (in another questionnaire item, 60 percent of the women but only 27 percent of the men said that their same-sex conversations were often on emotional topics). A common topic, and one generally reserved for one's own sex, is the other sex and sexuality. Interestingly, women talk about other women much more than men talk about other men (excluding sports heroes and public figures). This includes "cattiness," a feature of conversation that many women wished to see eliminated. "Keep the gossip but get rid of the cattiness" is how one put it.

Of course, there are men who are eager to talk about family mat- 4 ters and women who love to talk about sports, but for a typical couple, there will be areas of personal importance that the other partner is simply not interested in and, in fact, may **deride**. "Trivial" is a term used often by both sexes to describe topics of obvious significance to the other.

But the difference in topics is not so damaging to intimate male- 5 female relationships as are the differences in the style and function of conversation. For men, talks with friends are enjoyed primarily for

---

deride: make fun of;

their freedom, playfulness and **camaraderie**. When we asked men what they liked best about their all-male talk, the most frequent answer had to do with its ease. "You don't have to watch what you say" is how one young man put it. Some men commented on enjoying the fast pace of all-male conversation, and several specifically mentioned humor. A number of men said that they liked the practical aspects of these talks. As one wrote, "We teach each other practical ways to solve everyday problems: New cars, tax handling, etc."

A different picture emerged when we asked women what they 6 liked best about talking with other women. While many mentioned ease and camaraderie, the feature mentioned most often was empathy or understanding, which involves careful listening as well as talking. "To know that you're not alone." "The feeling of sharing and being understood without a sexual connotation." "Sensitivity to emotions that men feel are unimportant." In questionnaire responses and interviews, women spoke of their same-sex conversations not as something they merely liked, but truly needed.

Women's greater need for same-sex conversation was shown by 7 responses to other questions. When we asked how important such conversations were, 63 percent of the women, but only 43 percent of the men, called them important or necessary. Women are also far likelier than men to call up a friend just to talk. Nearly half the women in our sample said they made such calls at least once a week, whereas less than one man in five said he did. In fact, 40 percent of the men said they never called another man just to talk (versus 14 percent of the women). Men use the phone a great deal for business, and in the context of a business call they may have friendly conversation. But a call just to "check in" is a rare event.

Consider then the marriage of a man who has had most of his 8 conversations with other men, to a woman who has had most of hers with other women, probably the typical situation. He is used to fast-paced conversations that typically stay on the surface with respect to emotions, that often enable him to get practical tips or offer them to others and that are usually **pragmatic** or fun. She is used to conversations that, while practical and fun too, are also a major source of emotional support, self-understanding and the understanding of others. Becoming intimate with a man, the woman may finally start expressing her concerns to him as she might a close friend. But she may find, to her dismay, that his responses are all wrong. Instead of

camaraderie: friendship; pragmatic: practical, useful

making her feel better, he makes her feel worse. The problem is that he tends to be direct and practical, whereas what she wants more than anything else is an **empathetic** listener. Used to years of such responses from close friends, a woman is likely to be surprised and angered by her husband's immediate "Here's what ya do . . ." Adding to her anger may be her belief, as expressed by many women in our survey, that men don't credit her with good sense and intelligence, and that perhaps that is why he is advising her. The fact is, he does the same with male friends.

Men can be good listeners, of course, and women can give direct advice. But just as women read books and take courses on how to be assertive, men take courses on how to become better listeners. Indeed, whether it was Shakespeare—"Give every man thine ear but few thy voice"—or Dale Carnegie—"Be a good listener"—men have impressed on each other the value of good listening. The advice, however, must often fall on deaf ears. Women continue to be seen as better listeners. 9

Many books and articles have been written on how language discriminates against women, and there is no doubt that it does. Attempts have been made to change this—in the last couple of years, for example, we have heard men say "he or she" instead of the generic "he" in all-male conversation—but as long as boys play with boys, and girls with girls the sexes will use language in different ways and for different purposes. Whether it is for the feeling of freedom that comes from not having to watch what you say, or the feeling of relief and joy that comes from another human being truly understanding you, we will continue to seek out those of our own sex to talk to. There is no reason each must adopt the other's style. What is necessary is to recognize and respect it. 10

Post-reading

Your assignment here is to prepare the following in order to write a first, or *idea,* draft of the report.

- Notes on the two articles, legibly written, with comments of your own about the importance of the points noted
- A rough outline of the report with the main points written under each section

---

empathetic: understanding

Remember that you are *both* summarizing the articles *and* writing a recommendation and that your recommendation should cover both the strong and the weak points of each of the two essays.

THE IDEA DRAFT

A lot of people think that when writers actually begin to write, the words flow out of them the way they will appear in the book or newspaper or magazine article that eventually gets published. That is far, far from being the case. In fact, it almost never happens that way. On the next page, for instance, is a page from a piece of writing by one of the authors of this book.

This is the place where we get to tell you the second secret professional writers have. Here it is:

- *Nobody gets it right the first time. Everybody* has to rewrite. Kurt Vonnegut, Jr., a well-known and successful American novelist, said this about himself and his fellow writers: "Our power is patience. We have discovered that writing allows even a stupid person to seem halfway intelligent, if only that person will write the same thought over and over again, improving it just a little bit each time. It is a lot like inflating a blimp with a bicycle pump. Anybody can do it. All it takes is time."

There are two pieces of good news here, and one other bit of news that you may find surprising. The good news is

1. you have an edge; because you aren't stupid (or you wouldn't be in college), you have a head start on the writing process, and
2. hard as it is, writing is a lot easier than filling a blimp with a bicycle pump.

The (perhaps) surprising news is what Vonnegut is saying about rewriting. Notice that he doesn't talk about rewriting as going back to look for spelling mistakes or other kinds of errors; he talks about rewriting as improving the *ideas.*

Your first draft is not one in which you try to get everything right, try to get all the words spelled correctly, all the apostrophes in the right places, all the sentences correct. Not at all. If you try to do all that stuff, you won't be able to concentrate on your ideas. The human mind can only do so much work at one time. Ever try to drive in heavy traffic and hold a serious or intense conversation at the same time? Or talk on the phone when someone in the room is talking to you? That's what you ask your mind to do if you try to get your ideas down *and* get all the mechanics correct too.

Life, as we all know, is fu~~y~~ll of unan~~w~~sera~~v~~ble questions. In the area
of food, I can easily understand how someone discovered ~~how to get~~ the *the way*
skin off the garlic clove. He, or ①more likely, she got fed up one day
trying to peel the stupid stuff off~~, and just~~ whacked the clove with her
fist in a fit of temper, and lo! off it came. But how did mayonnaise
ever get invented? *Dida* ~~What made the~~ woman from Mayonne say to herself,
"Let's see. If I put an egg yoke, some mustard, and some vinegar in a
bowl, whip them up, then add oil slowly until the whole thing ~~forms a~~ *though,*
thick emulsion, that ought to taste pretty good"? *I know, why American*
chemical companies decided to make phoney mayonnaise.
~~In the same way,~~ I have trouble understanding why the ~~very first people~~
to live where ~~Sacramento now is~~ thought it would be a ~~good idea to~~
~~settle there.~~ It's ~~very hard~~ for me to ~~imagine~~ the following going
through someone's mind: "Okay, ~~here's~~ a place where it's over a 100 ~~all~~
~~the time~~ during the ~~summer,~~ where it rains ~~like hell~~ and floods during
the winter, ~~and~~ where various vicious ⓐattack pollen ~~thrive~~ in b~~v~~etween
so the ~~few~~ people who can breathe are always coughing or sneezing their
heads off. ~~I think I'll live here."~~ This seems like a good place to
~~live."~~

one ⏀
like
everyone
else?

But my
speculations
lately
have been
occasioned
not by
food or
chemicals,
but by

~~But the questions bothering me lately have been occasioned by~~
~~But this is just background to my real subject, which is~~ (the 90 mile①s
of Interstate 80 between San Francisco and Sacramento, ~~90 miles of~~
~~heavy, often stop-and-go traffic—90 miles of traffic congestion—~~90
miles of heavy traffic and crappy scenery. ~~(And speaking of~~
~~unanswerable questions, how does one explain Vacaville? At least~~
~~Sacramento has rivers.)~~ In my view of the thing, I-80 falls ~~into three~~
~~parts:~~ going east, these are the part from San Francisco to the
Carquinez ~~Bridge,~~ a 25 minutes drive if you ~~do it~~ at midnight but an
hour or more under ~~all~~ other conditions; the section from Vallejo to
Vacaville, a transition zone ~~that gets~~ you ready for the horrors still
ahead; and finally, ~~when~~ you cross one ~~last ridge~~ line, the last 30
miles, a dead ~~flat,~~ dead straight shot to our glorious ~~state~~ capital,
farmland ~~on~~ which little or nothing ~~seems to grow~~ seething under ~~a~~ clear
sky ~~turned~~ slate blue with heat and haze.

                does answer a
Interstate 80 ~~answers one~~ question ~~many people have, particularly~~
visitors from other states~~:~~ *have* namely, (~~W~~hy can't ~~your~~ *the Calif* Highway Patrol use
radar~~)~~ The answer is that our state legislators want to ~~be able to~~
speed as fast as they can from Sacramento to San Francisco, and they
don't want to get caught doing it. But even though I-80 an~~s~~①wers th①is
question, it raises a number of others.
A big one has to do with the drivers, you see.
While most drivers on I-80 out in the wilds beyond Vallejo are content
to poke along at a sedate and conservative 65 to 70 miles per hour,
there are a few, the mad dogs, who regard this as an impediment to the
natural order of things~~,~~ ~~infringement~~ on their rights. These ~~folks~~ *people*
barrel through the traffic, or try to, at ~~speeds~~ in the 90's, changing
lanes without signalling (they probably don't have ti~~i~~me to, actually),
viciously tailgating anyone in their way. Then there are the unconⓒious
tailgaters~~,~~ ~~Maybe they don't have adequate~~ depth perception~~,~~ ~~In any~~ *Whatever,*
~~case,~~ *maybe people with inadequate*
                                    maybe just morons.

Your first draft is your *idea draft*. That's when you just get your ideas on paper. In the idea draft you try to say *what* you want to say (not *how* you want to say it) and get things in the order you want them. It's a draft that's a total mess. It looks horrible. But in many ways, the worse it looks, the better it is, because lots of changes and written-in stuff and crossed-out stuff all means that you are getting your ideas—the most important part of the paper—in shape.

Although the first draft is an idea draft, it's also the time to try to get the ideas in the order you want them, and part of that process is grouping them in paragraphs. You will learn more about paragraphs later, but you've already learned a lot. If you remember the diagram of an essay at the beginning of this chapter and all the paragraph examples you've seen, you will remember that paragraphs tend to be written in one way: with an introductory sentence or two telling what the paragraph will be about and then specific sentences that give the details.

In getting ready to write your first draft, group your ideas as you think you will write them in paragraphs. Organize the groups in the order you think you will want them. Write introductory (topic) sentences that seem to you to cover each of the groups. You might change your mind about the groupings or the order or what you have written as topic sentences later. That's not a problem. But you do have to start somewhere, and this is the place.

Idea Draft Assignment

Using your notes, write an idea draft of your report. Remember: This draft is *only* for getting your ideas on paper and in the order you want them. Many people like to double-space this draft so that when it becomes a mess, they can still read it. Others feel that single spacing makes it easier for them to see the whole thing. If you write your draft by hand, you may want to leave yourself wide margins for making changes.

LATER DRAFTS

Many college professors and many businesspeople have to write for professional audiences, people in their own fields. Papers explaining new ideas or giving critiques of old ones, discussing new theories or discoveries, reporting on matters assigned by the firm, and so on are the bread and butter of professional life. When a professional person works on a paper or report, he or she will almost always try to write a pretty good draft—usually the second or third draft—and then show it to a trusted colleague, someone he or she knows will offer constructive criticism. All professional people realize that no matter how good their ideas are, other people will always find weaknesses in them that can be corrected or see ways their ideas could be expressed better. People who write for professional reasons never write alone. When they have got things about as good as they think they can get them, and often well before, they always try to get extra help from others.

After you have completed the idea draft, the one that's a total mess, you should rewrite it, again concentrating mostly on its content rather than on mechanics, and get a friend to read it. But here you need a friend who will really read it critically, looking for problems of logic or other weaknesses in the content and giving specific suggestions.

After this part of the process, when the content is as good as you can get it, you are usually prepared to start working on the mechanics of the paper, cleaning it up for "publication," even though in college, publication may mean just handing it in to a teacher.

The very last step, after you have produced the final neat version, is to proofread it carefully, word by word and line by line. Proofreading is a difficult skill; few people enjoy it. But even the most carefully typed text will contain surprising numbers of errors, and so proofreading is an absolute necessity. An otherwise intelligent, well-written essay full of spelling errors or other mistakes a reader would consider stupid creates so bad an impression that most readers simply won't bother reading the whole piece. And in the professional world, that's a killer.

FINAL DRAFT ASSIGNMENT

Turn the first draft of your report into a final draft. First, write the first draft out in good form and then get together with at least one other student in the class to go over each other's drafts, making suggestions about content and organization.

Concentrate on the ideas and their order in this draft. If something in the other student's report doesn't make sense, sounds confusing, or doesn't seem to belong where it is (or in the report at all), speak up. Even if you can't *label* what the problem is, trust your instincts. By the same token, *listen* to what the reader of your report says about your ideas and organization. Pay attention to his or her questions. Remember: *A report is written to be read by other people, and if they have questions or don't understand it, the report fails at its job.*

If time permits, you may be able to do this in class, but if not, get together at the student center or library to share drafts. Remember: *There is not necessarily one right way to organize your material or one right conclusion to come to.* You and your colleague may find that you differ in various ways, but as long as you back up your general points with good specific ones, you may both produce excellent papers.

After you have discussed your report with another student or students, revise it, taking into consideration the constructive criticism you have received. When you've written this draft, you're ready to look at sentence-level or mechanical issues. Read your draft aloud, listening for any places that seem "wrong," even if you're not sure what's "wrong" with it. If this happens, ask yourself: "What do I want to say here?" Answer yourself aloud and quickly write down what you've said. If you can't answer that question, you need to do more thinking about it in order to be able to say or write what you mean. You may have to write one or two additional drafts before you are satisfied with your essay. (Remember Kurt Vonnegut's point about blowing up a blimp with a bicycle pump.)

Now write a final draft—one ready for "publication." Finally, proofread your report as carefully as you can. If you have done everything this assignment has called for, you have worked hard on this report. Therefore, make sure that, by being as professional looking as possible, your final draft reflects the care and effort you have expended. You may want to exchange your report with another student's—even right before you submit it—and each of you proof the other's, marking the following *with a pencil:* typos, words you think are misspelled, or possible punctuation errors.

USING QUOTATIONS

Quoting the words of an author you are referring to is a very good and very convenient way of helping to back up a point you are making. Here is part of a paragraph written by a student on a writing assignment that comes later in this book. Notice how she has incorporated quotations into her paragraph:

> Working long hours under stressful conditions, especially in fast-food restaurants, appears to promote some forms of delinquent behavior. Lou DeRosa, a 29 year old manager of a McDonald's, said, "This is a survival job. A lot of people can't handle it." In addition to low wages and a hot, high-speed work environment, some employees complain of poor treatment by managers. Through Mark Kershaw's own experience as a manager he agrees that "there are some managers who treat them like slaves."

You can incorporate quotations into your report on men's and women's talk too, and you will certainly want to do it both in later assignments and in papers you write for your other courses. Fortunately, it is both easy and effective.

Punctuating Quotations

As in the paragraph above, when you want to introduce a quotation with words like "she said" or "he wrote," you put a comma after your introductory phrase and capitalize the first word in your quotation:

Lou DeRosa said, "This is a survival job."

If you want to incorporate the quoted words right into your own sentence, you use the word *that* instead of the comma, and you don't capitalize the first quoted word:

Mark Kershaw agrees that "there are some managers who treat them like slaves."

Punctuating Titles of Works

The general rule is that we underline (in print, as in this book, underlining is turned into italicizing) the titles of long works and put quotation marks around the titles of short works. So the names of books, movies, magazines, newspapers, and record albums get underlined:

The Great Gatsby

Citizen Kane

Cosmopolitan

The Atlanta Constitution

But we put quotation marks around the titles of essays or articles, short stories, songs, and so on.

Introducing Quotations

Let us suppose we are going to quote from an article by Leon Cheung and Marlene Johnson. The article is entitled "Three Issues in AIDS Research," and it appeared in *Current Social Issues,* a magazine. In our first reference to this article, we would give the names of the authors, the complete title of the article, and the name of the magazine. Here are three ways of doing this:

In their article, "Three Issues in AIDS Research" in *Current Social Issues,* Leon Cheung and Marlene Johnson write, "Now that we have . . ."

In "Three Issues in AIDS Research" in *Current Social Issues,* Leon Cheung and Marlene Johnson write, "Now that we have . . ."

According to Leon Cheung and Marlene Johnson in "Three Issues in AIDS Research" (*Current Social Issues*), "Now that we have . . ."

Note that these three sentences are based on two simple patterns. The first two follow this pattern:

In + title, + authors *write,* + quotation

The third uses a different pattern:

According to + authors & title, + quotation

In later references, we would simply use the last names of the two authors with no further mention of the title of the article or the name of the journal:

Cheung and Johnson write, "The evidence shows . . ."
According to Cheung and Johnson, "The evidence shows . . ."

EXERCISE
_____

Following are exercises in using quotations. Here are the quotations you will use:

A. Although the breakup of the Soviet Union marked the end of the Cold War, in Eastern Europe Communism has been replaced by new ethnic strife.
    Mario Cuellar, *The More Things Change*

B. It is difficult to defend free speech when groups exploit it, as is done in some popular music, to foment racial and sexual prejudices.
    Sarah Murray, "The Aesthetics of Injustice," in *Current Social Issues*

1. Referring back to the sections "Punctuating Quotations," "Punctuating Titles of Works," and "Introducing Quotations," write four sentences using quotation A. Each time, you should introduce the quotation in a different way. In your first sentence, assume that you are quoting this author for the first time. In the next three sentences, assume that you have already quoted him before.

2. Referring back to the sections "Punctuating Quotations," "Punctuating Titles of Works," and "Introducing Quotations," write four sentences using quotation B. Each time, you should introduce the quotation in a different way. In your first sentence, assume that you are quoting this author for the first time. In the next three sentences, assume that you have already quoted her before.

PARAPHRASING

One of the meanings of the prefix *para-* is "alongside" or "near." We use it with this meaning in terms like "paralegal," a legal worker who is not actually a lawyer, one who works with or alongside lawyers, and "paramilitary," armed forces that are not actually members of armies. A *paraphrase,* then, is a phrasing or wording of an original meaning that is not quite the same as the original wording. It is the same thing in different words. Usually a paraphrase is a shorter, more condensed version of a much longer original. Writers often paraphrase other writers in order to get their meaning on paper without having to quote all of the original. You will often find this to be a useful tool when you are writing about an article you've read in this book, but you don't want to spend a page or most of it just copying the original words. Paraphrasing is frequently very close to summarizing.

There are three important steps to paraphrasing.

First, make sure you've really understood the original passage; a paraphrase has to be an accurate account of the original.

Second, write your paraphrase using your own words; you can, of course, use key terms from the original, and you may often find it helpful even to quote short phrases because you can't think of a better way to write them, but a good paraphrase is someone else's idea expressed in your words.

Third, compare your completed paraphrase with the original to make sure you haven't changed the meaning.

A good method for writing a paraphrase is to read the original passage, jotting down the key points, the ones you know you'll want to include in your paraphrase. (That's point 1 above.) The best thing to do is to write these points in short phrases rather than complete sentences. Make them reminders of what's in the original rather than copies of what's there. When you've done that, put the original aside and, just using your notes, write out your paraphrase. (That's point 2.) Then compare your version with the original to make sure what you've written is accurate. (That's point 3.)

Here is a paragraph from the essay "Man to Man, Woman to Woman," which appears earlier in this chapter:

A different picture emerged when we asked women what they liked best about talking with other women. While many mentioned ease and camaraderie, the feature mentioned most often was empathy or understanding, which involves careful listening as well as talking. "To know that you're not alone." "The feeling of sharing and being understood without a sexual connotation." "Sensitivity to emotions that men feel are unimportant." In questionnaire responses and interviews, women spoke of their same-sex conversations not as something they merely liked, but truly needed.

Here is one possible paraphrase of this paragraph:

The women who were surveyed tended to use same-sex talk for different reasons than men. They especially liked it for "empathy or understanding" and for sharing their feelings. Unlike men, they didn't just like this kind of talk but felt they needed it.

IMPORTANT! Remember that when you paraphrase another writer's ideas, you must *always* give the original writer credit. Not doing so is just as bad as copying the original writer's words without giving credit. It's called plagiarism, and most colleges will expel students caught doing it.

A Problem

Sometimes students start a sentence with a prepositional phrase, particularly one beginning with *in,* and then get stuck for how to continue. Introductory prepositional phrases are very handy for referring the reader to a document you previously mentioned, as in these cases:

In this article
In this book
In the essay I previously mentioned

In such cases, remember that the word after the *in* (*article, book, essay*) cannot be the subject of the sentence. In other words, the following sentence is incorrect:

In this article stated that Ethiopia is once again facing a famine.

Students sometimes try to solve this problem by putting the word *it* in as the subject, but this is again incorrect. *Do not use the word* it *as the subject when* it *refers to a noun immediately preceding it.* In other words, the following sentence is incorrect:

In this article, it stated that Ethiopia is once again facing a famine.

How do you handle such a situation? If you know the name of the author, use that as the subject:

In this article, Fernandez stated that Ethiopia is once again facing a famine.

If you don't know the author, then don't start the sentence with the *in* phrase. (If you've already started it, go back and scratch it out.) Use the word *article* itself as the subject:

This article stated that Ethiopia is once again facing a famine.

EXERCISE

Correct the following sentences:

1. In an article from a Seattle newspaper stated that a study revealed that of gun-shot deaths in a white, urban county in Washington State, 53 percent took place in the home.

2. Over the sixteen-year survey of Cuyahoga County's accidental firearm fatalities, it showed that during four consecutive years, the number of deaths tripled the average rate of the first ten years.

3. In a pamphlet called "It Could Happen to You" by the National Rifle Association, it stated that "firearms in the hands of law-abiding citizens can and do produce a chilling effect on criminal behavior."

4. In another study of gun-shot deaths in a white, urban county in Washington revealed that over half of the killings took place in the homes where guns were kept.

5. Recently from a study of firearm fatalities in one Washington State county, it showed that 53 percent of homicides took place in gun-protected homes.

6. When looking at the pros and cons of owning a gun, it tells me that a gun is not the right answer for protection.

7. After reading the reasons for owning a gun and the results of having one, it changed my point of view.

8. In a survey done by two major women's magazines unveiled that a fast-growing number of women see firearms as a possible means of self-defense.

Sentence Combining

SHAPING SENTENCES

One of the problems with improving one's sentences is that understanding sentences means understanding at least some grammar, but at the same time studies have shown that very few people remember the grammar they study. And even more studies have shown that no one ever learned to write better by studying grammar. What to do?

One solution to the problem is called *sentence combining*. One of the signs of improved writing is longer, more varied, better shaped sentences. Studies have shown that the sentences of sixth graders are longer and more varied than those of fourth graders, those of eighth graders are longer and more varied than those of sixth graders, and so on. Professional writers write the longest and most varied sentences of all, and they go to a lot of trouble to shape them well.

Actually, there are good reasons why the sentences of less experienced writers tend to be shorter and more monotonous than those of more experienced writers. We can't get into all of these here, but we can tell you that knowing or not knowing grammar has nothing to do with it. And we can follow that up with two more reassuring points:

1. If you were born in this country or have lived here since you were very young, you probably know as much English grammar as any professional writer in America.

2. Professional writers don't use any grammatical structures when they write that fourth graders—or you—don't also use.

So how do their sentences become longer and more varied? There are two primary reasons. One reason is that they make their sentence length and construction follow their ideas. That's what we mean when we talk about *shaping* sentences. That in turn means they don't chop up a single idea into several little sentences. The other reason is that although they don't use any constructions you don't know about and use, they do use some of them far more often than you probably do.

Let's look at an example of these two principles in action. Earlier in this chapter you read some paragraphs and wrote short summaries of them. Here is part of one of those paragraphs, as an inexperienced writer might have written it:

> The Reagan White House cooperated with the Bush campaign to an unprecedented extent. It had the President sign or veto bills. These bills were judged helpful to Bush. It had him make appointments. It had him put off unpleasant business until after the election.

This passage doesn't read too badly—until you imagine trying to read ten or twelve pages of writing like it. You would drop dead from boredom. The thing is that while there are five sentences here, there aren't five ideas; there's only one idea, the idea that the White House helped the Bush campaign in a variety of ways. Here is what was actually written:

> The Reagan White House cooperated with the Bush campaign to an unprecedented extent—in having the President sign or veto bills as deemed helpful to Bush, in making appointments, in putting off unpleasant business until after the election.

The writer, Elizabeth Drew, used structures here called verbal phrases. (As you will shortly learn, *-ing* words—*having, making, putting off*—are verbals.)

Instead of new sentences, she used verbals to keep all the parts of her idea together, to shape her sentence. You use verbals yourself all the time, but in writing an idea like the example just given, you might not think of using them as Drew did. That's where sentence combining comes in.

Sentence combining concentrates on the structures that experienced writers are most likely to use a lot and inexperienced writers are most likely to use very little, and it gives you practice in using them. It gives you the feel of using those structures frequently, and it tries to get you to remember to do so.

To help you remember what you learn in your sentence-combining work, we will give you reminders of it with each one of your writing assignments. But don't worry about combining your sentences when you are working out your idea draft. That's a time for concentrating on the ideas, not the writing. When you have all your ideas in place and your first draft completed, *then* go over your sentences to see whether you can combine some of them—or even add further information—using the sentence-combining techniques you have learned. Shaping sentences—and this is true for professional writers as well as those of us with less experience—is mainly a *second draft* operation.

And finally, don't worry that your sentences will get too long. There is really no such thing as a too-long sentence. And don't worry about mistakes. That's the way we learn.

The first three lessons of sentence combining are designed primarily to familiarize you with how it works, to get you acquainted with what sentence combining is and how sentence shaping works. The first lesson, "Recognizing Verb Forms," will help you eliminate a verb problem that often crops up in student writing, and it will prepare you to do the next sentence-combining lesson. Lessons 2 and 3 will show you easy ways to make crucial parts of your sentences say more, and lessons 4 through 9 will give you practice with key structures found frequently in the work of experienced writers, structures all your college teachers will, without even thinking about it, expect to find in your written work. Lesson 10 gives explicit practice in a structure that you will find yourself using in all the previous lessons.

RECOGNIZING VERB FORMS FOR WRITING AND SENTENCE COMBINING

Have you ever been stumped about whether to write "we had swam in the pool" or "we had swum in the pool"? Or "she has run for president twice" or "she has ran for president twice"? This lesson will give you a brief overview of the basic verb forms in English to help you solve such problems in the future as well as to prepare you for work in sentence combining that you will shortly be doing.

In addition to having forms that make the present, past, future, and other tenses, all English verbs have three forms that do not make tenses; these three forms together are called *verbals* to distinguish them from the normal verbs. The three verbal forms are the *base* form, the *-ing* form, and the *-ed* or *have* form.

The base form of a verb is the one you find in the dictionary when you look up the verb. If you were to look up the verbs *walk, sing, think,* and *abolish,* those words would be the base forms of those verbs. If you were to look up a verb form that was not the base form—say, *is* or *has*—the dictionary would tell you that they were forms of the verbs *be* and *have.* So base forms are easy to spot. Base forms may also have the word *to* in front of them, as *to walk, to sing, to think, to abolish, to be,* and *to have.*

Every English verb has an *-ing* form also, and the *-ing* form always consists of the base form with *-ing* added. Thus, the verbs above all have the following forms: *walking, singing, thinking, abolishing, being,* and *having.* If the base form of the verb ends in *e,* as *give,* drop the *e* before adding the *-ing* (*giving*); if the base form of the verb ends in a single consonant (a letter other than *a, e, i, o,* or *u*), like the verb *get,* usually you should double the consonant (*getting*).

And finally, all verbs have a *have* form. We call this form the *have* form because it is the verb form that follows the word *have,* as in these cases:

I have *walked*

I have *sung*

I have *thought*

I have *abolished*

The *have* form of most verbs consists of the base form with *-ed* added, and in most cases the *have* form of the verb and its past-tense form are spelled in exactly the same way:

Base	**Past Tense**	***Have* Form**
walk	walked	walked
abolish	abolished	abolished
pause	paused	paused
open	opened	opened

But a great many of our verbs—the ones we use most frequently—have *have* forms that do not end in *-ed.* Again, however, their past-tense and *have* forms are identical:

Base	**Past Tense**	***Have* Form**
find	found	found
think	thought	thought
feel	felt	felt
have	had	had

Still another group has *have* forms that are spelled differently from the past-tense forms:

Base	**Past Tense**	*Have* **Form**
sing	sang	sung
drive	drove	driven
swim	swam	swum
be	was/were	been

Usually we can easily think of any verb's *have* form simply by asking ourselves what form of the verb we would use after *have*, but in cases of doubt, look up the verb in the dictionary. All dictionaries list verb forms in the same way. First they give the base form, then the past-tense form, then the *have* form, then the *-ing* form. If the past-tense and *have* forms are spelled the same way, the dictionary will list only the past-tense form.

EXERCISE

To ensure that you can spell the common *have* forms correctly and to enable you to do future exercises in this book, you will need to get a little practice in finding past-tense and *have* forms of verbs. Using your dictionary, find the past-tense and *have* forms of the following verbs:

advance	eat	ride
become	fly	see
blur	lead	sink
buy	mark	suppose
choose	pay	teach
deplore	play	use

Following is a short passage to be written in the past tense. Most of the verbs are given in parentheses in their base forms. Write out the passage completely on a sheet of paper, putting the verbs in their proper forms. The verbs following *was, had,* and *grew* should be put into their *have* forms:

Martin was a person who (dislike) Christmas. He knew that he was (suppose) to see it as a happy, festive time, but he (see) only the commercialization. As a child, he had (know) happy Christmases and he (use) to look forward to them, but as he (grow) up, he grew (disgust) by the pressures to buy and buy. He (learn) that the suicide rate always rose on Christmas, and he (see) this as a sign that it was an unhappy rather than a happy time. Every December 1, he (post) above his desk his Christmas motto, which he (steal) from a writer named Quentin Crisp: "I try at Christmas time to carry on as though nothing unpleasant were happening."

SHAPING SENTENCES WITH ADJECTIVES AND VERB FORMS

A *modifier* is a word or group of words that adds to the meaning of another word or group of words. You may once have learned that a noun is a word naming a person, place, or thing. That is true, but nouns have many other functions as well. In doing the exercises in this section, you will, by good fortune, not have to worry about identifying nouns; they will be identified for you. Soon you will have a good feel for what nouns are, if you don't already, but more importantly, you will have learned something about how writers write that you can use whether you know what a noun is or not.

In the following exercises, you will be given a sentence such as this one in which the nouns are underlined:

The car drove down the road.

After it will be one or more short sentences containing the underlined words along with other words telling something about them—modifiers, in other words. You will add these modifiers to the original sentence to make one longer sentence. Here are three examples:

1.   The car drove down the road.
     The car was old.

     Solution: The old car drove down the road.

2.   The car drove down the road.
     The road was bumpy.

     Solution: The car drove down the bumpy road.

3.   The monster arose from the swamp.
     The monster was huge.
     The monster was ugly.
     The swamp was smelly.

     Solution: The huge, ugly monster arose from the smelly swamp.

Several different kinds of words can modify nouns. In the preceding examples, all the modifiers—*old, bumpy, huge, ugly,* and *smelly*—are adjectives. In addition to adjectives, verb forms, in particular the *-ing* and *have* forms, can modify nouns. When one of these forms all by itself modifies a noun, we put it in front of the noun:

1. A <u>monster</u> arose from the swamp.

    A monster was <u>groaning</u>.

    Solution: A groaning monster arose from the swamp.

2. A <u>monster</u> arose from the swamp.

    A monster was <u>bored</u>.

    Solution: A bored monster arose from the swamp.

However, if the *-ing* or *have* form has other words attached behind it or begins a phrase, then we must put it behind the noun we want it to modify:

1. A <u>monster</u> arose from the swamp.

    A monster was <u>groaning loudly</u>.

    Solution: A monster groaning loudly arose from the swamp.

2. A <u>monster</u> arose from the swamp.

    A monster was <u>bored by the company of frogs</u>.

    Solution: A monster bored by the company of frogs arose from the swamp.

EXERCISE

Witchcraft 101

1. A <u>student</u> is strolling to class.
    The student is tall.
    The student is good-looking.

2. The student is walking with a <u>friend</u>.
    The friend is pretty.
    The friend is well dressed.

3. The two <u>students</u> seem to be relaxed and enjoying each other's company.
    The two students are walking along together.

4. The <u>student</u> is thinking about asking her for a date.
    The student is tall.
    The student is walking with his friend.
    His friend is attractive.

5. The attractive student thinks her friend is a dope.

   She is known for her high standards.

   The dope is hopeless.

   The dope is simple-minded.

6. The students walked into the classroom.

   The students were laughing.

   The students were happy.

   The classroom was bright.

   The classroom was sunny.

7. They were greeted by their witchcraft instructor.

   Their witchcraft instructor was ancient.

   Their witchcraft instructor was ugly.

   Their witchcraft instructor was staring at them from the front of the room.

8. Switching his tail, the instructor spoke in a voice.

   The instructor was frowning.

   His voice was deep.

   His voice was menacing.

9. On their midterm exams, almost half of them had changed their frogs into real-estate brokers instead of into princes or princesses.

   Their frogs were harmless.

   Their frogs were little.

   The real-estate brokers were aggressive.

   The princes were handsome.

   The princesses were beautiful.

   The princesses were charming.

10. While going over these midterms, the instructor was talked into buying a condominium.

    The midterms were wretched.

    The instructor was furious.

    The condominium was extremely expensive.

    The condominium was located at the edge of a swamp in Florida.

REVIEW

Since you probably are able to recognize nouns by this time and understand how to do this kind of exercise, the nouns in the review exercises are not underlined.

The Sounds of Music

1. Four music students hoped to find work.
   The music students were young.
   The music students were talented.
   The music students were graduating from college.
   The work was playing classical music.

2. They formed a group called the Family Rat Quartet, but no one wanted to hear quartets played by musicians.
   The quartets were famous.
   The musicians were unknown.
   The musicians were scruffy.
   The musicians were wearing faded jeans.

3. So they changed their appearance; now they had hair, suits, neckties, and shoes.
   The hair was short.
   The hair was neatly trimmed.
   The suits were dark blue.
   The neckties were red.
   The shoes were polished.

4. They looked like funeral directors.
   The funeral directors were unemployed.
   The funeral directors were soliciting new business.

5. They found that audiences would not pay to hear musicians.
   The audiences were middle aged.
   The audiences were attracted to string quartets.
   The musicians were young.
   The musicians were neatly dressed.
   The musicians were unknown.
   The musicians were wearing blue suits.

6. The concerts were those by string quartets.
   The concerts were well attended.
   The string quartets were established.
   The string quartets were made up of well-known players.

7. So the Family Rat changed its name to the Franz Joseph Haydn String Quartet and adopted hair, leotards, tennis shoes, and instruments.
   The hair was wild.
   The hair was Day-Glo orange.

The leotards were grass green.

The leotards were skin tight.

The tennis shoes were worn out.

The instruments were amplified.

8. They played music that killed insects, made dogs howl, and made bodies walk around.

The insects were flying and crawling.

The dogs were deaf.

The bodies were unburied.

The bodies were dead.

9. They gave concerts, made bundles of money, and, according to the critics, wrote music.

The concerts were jammed with admirers.

The music was grotesque.

The music was reflecting the death of Western civilization.

10. Between their concerts, during which their fans almost destroyed themselves, they gathered quietly in warehouses, got out their original instruments, and played the quartets.

The concerts were frantic.

The concerts were orgiastic.

Their fans were churning.

Their fans were writhing.

The warehouses were isolated.

The quartets were beautiful.

The quartets were intricate.

The quartets were written by the composers they loved.

SHAPING SENTENCES WITH PREPOSITIONAL PHRASES

Another noun modifier that we commonly use is the *prepositional phrase*. A prepositional phrase consists of a preposition followed by a noun (and any modifiers that noun may have). Prepositions are among the most common words in the language; you've seen and used them millions of times. They are little function words, like these: *in, on, up, down, across, from, to, of,* and *at.* Prepositional phrases serve a wide variety of purposes. Here is a sentence with all its prepositional phrases underlined:

Without a doubt, the horse in the lead at the end of the second turn will finish in front of the field.

Prepositional phrases often tell location:

on the water	up the street
in the water	down the street
across the river	inside the box
over the river	beside the box

Sometimes they indicate time:

    in a minute   at the moment

But they perform a variety of other functions as well:

of the dog	for a friend
about George	with her mother

In the following exercises, you will use prepositional phrases to modify—add meaning to—nouns, as in these examples. The prepositional phrases are underlined to help you spot them.

1. A bird is worth two.

    The bird is in the hand.

    The two are in the bush.

    Solution: A bird in the hand is worth two in the bush.

2. A stone gathers moss.

    The stone is in a swamp.

    The moss is on its surface.

    Solution: A stone in a swamp gathers moss on its surface.

3. A flight is a beautiful sight.

    The flight is of pelicans.

    The pelicans are over the water.

    The sight is in the late afternoon.

    Solution: A flight of pelicans over the water is a beautiful sight in the late afternoon.

In the last example, note that the second prepositional phrase—*over the water*—modifies a noun in the prepositional phrase preceding it. Prepositional phrases frequently work this way, coming in a series with each modifying the noun of the phrase before it:

    the people / with a canoe / on a lake / in Canada

However, long strings of prepositional phrases generally don't sound good and are usually considered bad style.

In the following exercises, the prepositional phrases are underlined to aid you in locating them.

EXERCISE

Buying a Bathing Suit

1. A sale attracted a crowd.

    The sale was at the local shopping center.

    The crowd was of bargain hunters.

2. A friend wanted to find a new swimsuit.

    The friend was of mine.

    The swimsuit was in the latest style.

3. The store was mobbed with people.

    The store was with the biggest sale.

    The people were of every age.

4. The bathing suit always looks better than the one, but we found a promising one.

    The bathing suit is on the rack.

    The one is on the body.

    The one was on the sale table.

5. People were standing in a long line.

    The people were with all kinds of clothes.

    The line was for the dressing rooms.

6. The person was a woman who didn't seem to have any clothes to try on.

    The person was in front of us.

    The woman was in her thirties.

    The clothes were in her hands.

7. Finally, we noticed a small piece, a swimsuit.

    The piece was of nylon.

    The nylon was in her hand.

    The swimsuit was of a truly astounding size.

8. It was a tiny garment.

    The garment was from a collection.

    The collection was by a Brazilian designer.

9. When we found the racks, we saw other tiny pieces.

   The racks were <u>of designer swimsuits</u>.

   The racks were <u>down another aisle</u>.

   The pieces were <u>of nylon</u>.

   The pieces were <u>in violent reds, bright blues, blazing yellows</u>.

10. The tiny pieces of nylon bore large cardboard tags; when we reached the parking lot, we agreed that since the swimsuits were about the size, it was appropriate that they bore the price.

    The tags were <u>with prices of astronomical size</u>.

    The parking lot was <u>outside the store</u>.

    The size was <u>of diamonds</u>.

    The price was <u>of diamonds</u>.

REVIEW

In the following exercises, you will practice using all the modifiers you have worked with so far.

Round-Trip

1. The student waited at a bus stop in the rain.

   The student was shivering.

   The student was suffering from a cold.

   The bus stop was on a wind-swept corner.

   The rain was pouring.

2. When the bus arrived, it was jammed with people.

   The bus was overcrowded.

   The people were depressed.

   The people were dripping water on each other.

3. At that moment, the student decided it was time to buy a car.

   The student was disgusted.

   The student was standing between two people.

   The two people were sneezing on her.

   The car was nice.

   The car was clean.

   The car was convenient.

   The car was for the commute.

   The commute was to school.

4. Several days later, she went to a dealer and selected a car.

   The dealer was reputable.

   The car was attractive.

   The car was used.

   The car was apparently in good condition.

5. The student loved her car, which kept her out of buses.

   Her car was new.

   Her car was used.

   The buses were crowded.

   The buses were full of people.

   The people were miserable.

   The people were suffering from colds.

6. The student gave her car a name, Fritz.

   The student was happy.

   The car was friendly.

7. One morning, Fritz the car showed some symptoms.

   The morning was gloomy.

   The morning was threatening.

   The symptoms were alarming.

   The symptoms were of trouble.

8. Fritz developed a disposition, so she took him to a garage.

   The disposition was surly.

   The disposition was uncooperative.

   The garage was recommended by a friend.

   The friend was trustworthy.

9. The mechanic said that Fritz was suffering from old age in many of his parts.

   The mechanic was sympathetic.

   The mechanic was at the garage.

   His parts were most essential.

10. In particular he pointed out Fritz's oil pump, his radiator, his cylinders, and others.

    His oil pump was ailing.

    His radiator was leaking.

    His cylinders were worn out.

    The others were of equal importance.

11. The student waited at a bus stop in the rain.
    The student was shivering.
    The student was remembering her car.
    Her car was cozy.
    Her car was warm.
    Her car was named Fritz.
    The bus stop was on a wind-swept corner.
    The rain was pouring.

CHAPTER *2*

The Shape of Texts

In Chapter 1, you began, through your work in analyzing essays and writing summaries, to see how texts are shaped. In this chapter, we will look closely at four key elements of texts: introductions, paragraphs, topic sentences, and conclusions.

INTRODUCTIONS AND THESIS STATEMENTS

Introductions are an essential part of life. How would we ever get to know one another if it weren't for introductions? How would we bring up an item of conversation or change the subject? It would be an odd class if, at the first meeting of the semester, the instructor walked in and just plunged into the material of the course without first introducing himself or herself and the subject to be studied. Unconsciously, you use or hear some form of introduction every day, probably many times a day.

Essay introductions, like other kinds of introductions, are nothing more than a way of telling the reader what's coming up. Along with the title, they help the reader find out whether this is a piece he or she is going to enjoy or be interested in or learn from.

The kinds of introductions we encounter in life tend to follow standard forms:

"John, I'd like you to meet Mary. Mary, this is John."

"You know that movie we saw last Friday? Well, . . ."

"Hello, class. My name is Professor Burpsmith, and I'd like to welcome you to English 565, a course in which we'll cover the American novel from Melville through Twain."

Essay introductions also follow formats, but you have a fair amount of leeway in how you handle the opening paragraph of your essays.

Basically, essay introductions take two different forms. One is the form used by most articles in popular magazines, the other the form used in academic work and in many articles in more intellectual magazines. The popular, or "Wowee!," introduction is often, for reasons that are ill understood, taught in high school and even some college English classes. This introduction is supposed to *grab* the reader in some way or other. Here is one by a well-known American writer:

Thirty-nine years old! A recluse! Bonafide! Doesn't go out, doesn't see the light of day, doesn't put his hide out in God's own unconditioned Chicago air for months on end; *years.* Right this minute, one supposes, he is somewhere there in the innards of those forty-eight rooms, under layers and layers of white wall-to-wall, crimson wall-to-wall, Count Basie—lounge leather, muffled, baffled, swaddled, shrouded, closed in, blacked out, shielded by curtains, drapes, wall-to-wall, blond wood, screens, cords, doors, buzzers, dials, Nubians—he's down in there, the living Hugh Hefner, 150 pounds, like the tender-tympany green heart of an artichoke.

What on earth is that all about? It's by a writer named Tom Wolfe, and it's the introduction to an essay ("King of the Status Dropouts") about Hugh Hefner, founder and publisher of *Playboy* magazine. Sometimes grabber introductions get a little far out. Here's another, more conservative one:

As it happens I am in Death Valley, in a room at the Enterprise Motel and Trailer Park, and it is July, and it is hot. In fact it is 119 degrees. I cannot seem to make the air conditioner work, but there is a small refrigerator, and I can wrap ice cubes in a towel and hold them against the small of my back. With the help of the ice cubes I have been trying to think, because *The American Scholar* asked me to, in some abstract way about "morality," a word I distrust more every day, but my mind veers inflexibly toward the particular.

Like Wolfe's introduction, this one by Joan Didion hints at its subject (the title of the essay is "On Morality"), but it certainly does not explain what the essay will be about. Rather, it tries to engage readers so that they will be intrigued to continue. That's fine, but grabber introductions are not in great demand in academic work or in the business world. The last thing you want to do is begin a paper for a history or sociology or business class with an introduction like Tom Wolfe's. In these contexts, your teachers expect you to get to the point with a minimum of fuss. Here is a fairly typical academic introduction:

When we talk about history, there is always the danger of oversimplifying. In reflecting upon recent times we often focus on their uniqueness and turbulence, ignoring what they have in common with previous eras. When we consider the more distant past, we tend to think of a more serene age; the sharp edges of controversy and uncertainty become blunted by the passage of time. Yet even in acknowledging these tendencies, I think we can also acknowledge that the past two decades of our profession's history have been extraordinary.

As is often, but not always, the case, the last sentence of this introduction states the point of the essay—to review the "extraordinary" events of the past twenty years of "our profession's history." There it is, no bones about it, no guessing what's going on. A sentence like this one in an introduction, one that states the point of the whole essay, is often called a *thesis sentence*. Strictly speaking, the thesis part of this thesis sentence is only the part underlined:

> Yet even in acknowledging these tendencies, I think we can also acknowledge that the past two decades of our profession's history have been extraordinary.

Just as the thesis sentence of an introduction might be less than a complete sentence, so it may sometimes be more than one sentence. There are no rules involved here; writers just do what makes the most sense in the circumstances.

Here are the introductions from the two essays on male and female talk that are reprinted in Chapter 1 of this book. One of the essays first appeared as a newspaper column, the other in *Psychology Today*. Reread them and answer the questions following them:

It can be risky these days to suggest that there are any innate differences between men and women, other than those of anatomy. Out the window go the old notions about man and aggression, woman and submission (don't even say the word), man and intellect, woman and instinct. If I observe that my infant son prefers pushing a block along the floor while making car noises to cradling a doll in his arms and singing lullabies (and he does)—well, I can only conclude that, despite all our earnest attempts at nonsexist child-rearing, he has already suffered environmental contamination. Some of it, no doubt unwittingly, came from my husband and me, reared in the days when nobody winced if you recited that old saw about what little girls and little boys are made of.

I do not believe, of course, that men are smarter, steadier, more high-minded than women. But one or two notions are harder to shake—such as the idea that there is such a thing as "men's talk" or "women's talk." And that it's a natural instinct to seek out, on occasion, the company of one's own sex, exclude members of the other sex and not feel guilty about it.

Joyce Maynard, "His Talk, Her Talk"

When it comes to conversation, husbands and wives often have problems that close friends of the same sex don't have. First, they may not have much to talk about, and second, when they do talk, misunderstandings often develop that lead to major fights. Our research concludes that these problems are particularly resistant to solution. Not only do men and women like to talk about different topics, spoken language serves different functions for the sexes.

Mark A. Sherman and Adelaide Haas,
"Man to Man, Woman to Woman"

- Which introduction seems to be aimed at a popular audience (that is, is more of a "grabber" introduction) and which seems to be aimed at a more academic audience?
- What seems to be the thesis sentence (or sentences) of the first introduction?
- What is the thesis sentence of the second introduction?
- Where in their introductions do these writers put their thesis sentences?

In popular writing, the writer wants to lure you into reading the piece. In academic writing, the writer wants to give you enough information so that you can decide whether you want to read the piece or not. In the school writing you do, your teachers will expect you to follow the academic model, even though they have no choice about whether to read your work. They will, however, evaluate your introduction for its accuracy in setting up the problem you are going to be dealing with or stating your intentions, and they will usually expect to see a thesis sentence or sentences—a very clear and direct indication of what your essay will be about.

In your next writing assignments, it will be best if you use the following form in your introductions:

- First, a sentence or two of background on why (theoretically) you are writing the essay; the introduction by Sherman and Haas is a good model here.
- Second, a simple statement of what you intend to do, what you have been assigned to do (your thesis sentence).

For instance, suppose you were assigned in a business class, or even in a real job, to survey computer programs concerning the organization of personnel files. Your task would be to find out what types of programs existed within the general category outlined by your teacher or boss and describe the characteristics of those in each category. Your introduction might read something like this:

> The number of programs available for use in helping organize personnel files is fairly limited, but they do fall into four recognizable types. In the following report, *I will describe these types and the chief characteristics of each.*

STUDENTS AT WORK: INTRODUCTIONS

In Chapter 3 is a writing assignment in which students read two essays about gender and ethnic representation in 1987 Saturday morning television programs and advertisements for children. Students are then asked to conduct their own study of *either* the programs *or* the advertisements today to see whether there seems to be a problem in one or more of the following areas:

> more or less equal representation of both boys and girls
>
> fair representation of the different ethnic groups in our society
>
> presence or absence of sexual stereotyping in the ways boys and girls are portrayed

Students are not asked to compare the 1987 studies with today's programing, though they may do so if they wish. Nor do students have to cover all three of the points above. Students are, however, expected to discuss the meaning of their findings. Following are four student introductions to essays on this topic. Read them and then consider the questions in the introduction checklist.

Commercials in general are detrimental to society. After viewing many commercials aimed at children, I saw many incidents of racism

and sexism. When our population views these commercials it reinforces the sexist and racist behaviors in each of us.

In the United States every Saturday morning, young children begin
watching their programs on television. Many people wonder if the
commercials will affect their children. Are the programs showing or
teaching good or bad values? In this essay, I will discuss the commercials in 1987 and in 1992. Then I will give my opinion about the
commercials.

There haven't been many improvements in television ads shown to
children today compared to 1987, although certain changes have
taken place. Certain stereotypes in gender and also in race still seem
to exist. Most of the commercials on Saturday mornings today are
still about sugary cereals, sweet drinks, fruit-flavored candies, toys,
etc. Besides all of the exploitative products that they're trying to sell
to children, language, attitudes, and values are also being sold.

The 1980s was a time when the commercials showed little or no ethnicity and only males were present in the commercials. Children's
commercials consisted of cereals loaded with sugar, drinks that
clogged your throat, fruity candies, and of course, who could forget
those wonderful blue-eyed, blond-haired dolls with a great figure.
Those were the days when boys played with rough, masculine toys,
and the girls played with dolls.

For each of the introductions above, answer the following questions.
Note that you probably won't always be able to give a simple yes or no answer to each question. Some of the introductions will be stronger in some
ways and weaker in others.

Introduction Checklist

1. Is it clear what the subject of the essay is—what it's about, why it's
    being written?
2. Is it clear what *specific* aspects of that subject this essay will dis-
    cuss? (To judge this point, see the paragraph preceding the intro-
    ductions, in which the different aspects of the assignment are
    explained.)
3. Does the introduction make clear that the essay will discuss both
    the nature of either the programs or the advertisements and what
    that means for children and for society?

4. Does the introduction contain a clear, specific thesis statement? (Note that the thesis statement doesn't have to give the writer's conclusions about the subject; those can come at the end of the essay.)

5. Is there anything in the introduction that seems irrelevant or pointless as far as the assignment is concerned?

6. What do you feel are the strong and weak points of these introductions? What did you like or dislike about each one? What did each teach you about what you'd like to do or not do in your own introductions?

Writing Your Introduction

Using the checklist above or one of your own making, decide on the points you want to put in your introduction *before* you start writing it.

Some writers prefer to wait until they have finished at least the idea draft of their essays before they write an introduction. They feel that it's better to know ahead of time what the introduction is going to introduce.

Others, however, use the introduction as a way of getting the essay going, of getting into it. If you like to write your introduction first, that's okay, but be sure that it doesn't limit you in what you want to say. Consider it a draft, subject to revision. You may even change your mind entirely about what you want to say as you write your essay, and if you do that, you'll want to go back and change your introduction. That's what happened in the case of Vanessa Thai, a student writing on the question of whether high school students should take part-time jobs. Here is the first version of her introduction:

Nowadays, teenagers are very anxious about having a job. As a student who worked during high school, I believed that the major reason why teenagers work is because they want to have more work experience and they can also make extra money for their own spending. However, working while in high school is quite stressful. It has both advantages and disadvantages, as I discovered from reading three articles, "Part-Time Work Ethic: Should Teens Go For It?" by Dennis McLellan, "McJobs," by Ben Wildavsky, and "Why Fast-Food Joints Don't Serve Up Good Jobs for Kids," by Amitai Etzioni. Nevertheless, I truly recommend that high school students should look for a part-time job because there's a profit that one could encounter from having a job. A part-time job might teach you lots of valuable things, yet it might give you some harm too.

After getting well into her essay, Vanessa changed her mind, and went back and crossed out everything from "Nevertheless" to the end of her introduction and replaced that part with these words:

After reading the three articles, I do not encourage high school students to look for a part-time job unless it's really necessary. The reason is that although a job might be valuable to a student's life, it might also be harmful to a student's life as well.

The end of this introduction could well be a lot more specific about good and bad points, particularly the bad ones since that's what Vanessa wanted to stress in her essay, but the main point is that she didn't let what she first wrote (and thought) force her to write something she ended up not believing. Moral: Start with your introduction if you want to, but don't let it lock you into a position you won't be happy with.

PARAGRAPHS: PROVING YOUR POINTS

Everybody knows what a paragraph looks like—it looks like any other group of sentences except that the first one is indented several spaces—but most people, even experienced writers, would be hard put to say what a paragraph is. For one thing, paragraphs come in radically different lengths. For instance, if you look at the first page of any newspaper, you will find that the paragraphs are extremely short, often only one sentence long. If you then look at any page of a college textbook, you will of course find that the paragraphs are much longer and that one-sentence paragraphs are rare. Paragraphs in popular magazines lean somewhat toward the newspaper kind while paragraphs in more intellectual magazines are like those in textbooks. Why is that?

Newspapers and popular magazines are designed to be read by everybody, even people who aren't such good readers and who may not be much interested in reading at all. So the editors of these periodicals keep the paragraphs short to create a maximum amount of white space in the columns of text. The extra white space makes the columns of print seem easier to read, more open. But books and magazines designed for good readers, people who read often, do not need to provide a lot of white space. Their readers aren't intimidated by long columns of print and will read them easily without the help of extra white space.

Newspaper paragraphs are, in a sense then, artificial paragraphs, or rather chunks of paragraphs, and to see what real paragraphs are, we need to look at the other kind, the kind you will run into in your college reading and be expected to write in your college writing. When we ask what a paragraph is, we are really asking the wrong question. A paragraph isn't what it is; a paragraph is what it does. Paragraphs are units of meaning within a book or an essay, and what they do is set up a point or a question (usually expressed in the *topic sentence* of the paragraph) and either explain it or prove it or illustrate it or discuss it or some combination of those things.

But it is not important to try to remember these things. What is important is to remember what you learned in writing summaries—that paragraphs go from general to specific. If your paragraphs consist of appropriate topic (or introductory) sentences backed up with specifics, you will be on the road to good paragraphs whether you know the four or fourteen types of paragraph development or not.

In academic and business writing, you basically *prove* or *show*. If you make a statement that requires proof, you must get specific to provide that proof. Look at this example:

> The reason the North won the American Civil War was that it was much stronger than the South. The North was a far more powerful part of the country than the South. The South just wasn't as strong as the North and so it was really impossible for the South to win.

Does this paragraph prove anything? Why not? Does it go from general to specific? Compare it with this one:

> The reason the North won the American Civil War was that it was much stronger than the South. The white population of the North was 22,340,000 while that of the South was only 5,600,000. The North had 105,000,000 acres of land under cultivation, mostly devoted to food, whereas the South had 57,000,000 acres, much of it devoted to cotton. The North had 22,000 miles of railroad to the South's 9,000 and 1,300,000 industrial workers to only 110,000 in the South.

The first paragraph, of course, is simply a succession of general sentences that all say the same thing. It proves nothing. The second one, however, gets into the specific, concrete reasons why the North was stronger than the South and, because of those specific reasons, presents a very strong case for its topic sentence.

Of course, not every paragraph you write is going to be full of specific facts like the one about the Civil War. Frequently, we argue for our ideas simply by giving our opinions, but again, the more specific (rather than general) and concrete (rather than vague) those opinions are, the more effective our argument will be. Again, compare the following two paragraphs:

> Watching a movie at home on videotape seems to me to be far more enjoyable than seeing one at a movie theater. When you're at home, you can just relax and be yourself. It's much less of a hassle than going out. I hate the nuisance of having to find the movie I want when I can just rent one and enjoy it in the comfort of my own living room.

> Watching a movie at home on videotape seems to me to be far more enjoyable than seeing one at a movie theater. Movie theaters are usually crowded at the times I can go, and there is always someone right behind me who

explains the whole movie to his friend. At the theater, I have to endure the sounds and smells of popcorn being chewed all around me, while at home I can eat and drink whatever I want, whenever I want, with no fear of bothering anyone else and no worry about anyone bothering me. Finally—and this is important to someone who has to watch his expenses—the price of renting a videotape is a third or less that of going to a movie.

The second paragraph doesn't *prove* that watching videotaped movies at home is better than going to a movie theater, but it makes a good case for that view because of the concrete, specific reasons offered.

EXERCISE

Write a paragraph modeled on the second example in which you argue one of the following points:

- Watching movies in movie theaters is preferable to watching them at home on videotape.
- Commuting to work or school on public transit is preferable to doing so by car.
- Commuting by car is preferable to public transit.
- Watching a sport (specify which sport) on television is preferable to being on the scene.
- Attending a sports event (specify which kind) is preferable to watching it on television.
- Living at home while going to college is preferable to living in a dormitory.
- Living in a dormitory is preferable to living at home.
- For a college student, living in one's own apartment is preferable to living at home or in a dorm.
- Living at home or in a dorm (specify which one) is preferable to living in one's own apartment.

TOPIC SENTENCES AND
THE ORGANIZATION PROCESS

Where do topic sentences come from? It would be nice if the stork or the tooth fairy or Santa Claus or someone would bring them, but we've learned from hard experience that they don't. By the same token, we've found that sitting down and scratching our heads and fretting and stewing and foaming at the mouth (all normal parts of the writing process) also won't bring them. Topic sentences come from the material you are working with. As you become more accustomed to doing academic writing, you will find that they usually come without your even thinking about them. But that won't happen right away. As you have seen in the paragraph examples you've already looked at, the topic sentence tells both you, the writer, and your reader what the paragraph is going to be about. Thus, it is easy to see that topic sentences come from your organization.

When you plan an essay, whether the plan is extremely detailed or just a kind of loose list, what you are doing is setting up the points you will cover and, usually, the order you will cover them in. Remember the planning process you went through in writing the report on men's and women's talk.

Let's say, as an example, that you have been assigned an essay in an American history class and that your subject is the relative strengths of the North and the South at the beginning of the Civil War. In your research you discover the facts about population, acreage under cultivation, railroads, and other points given in the paragraph you read earlier.

But then you discover that those facts are somewhat misleading. They make the North seem stronger than it really was. The Northern population figures, for instance, are inflated and unrealistic because they include the populations of "border states" like Missouri and Maryland, many of whose men fought for the South. They also include the populations of far western states, which contributed nothing to the North. The figures for Southern population are misleadingly low because they don't include the number of slaves in the South, and yet the slaves did valuable work that helped support the South's war effort. And so on.

Because of these complexities, you decide to organize your essay according to three main categories of strength and weakness:

Population
    white population
    black population

Economic strength
    industrial and agricultural strength
    railroad networks

Military strength
    weapons available
    leaders

This organization suggests that the completed essay might have an introduction and three body paragraphs, each with its topic sentence announcing the subject of the paragraph. But the great thing about organizations is that you never know whether they're going to work until you start writing. For example, further thought and perhaps writing might reveal that the paragraph on population should actually be two paragraphs because the population issue for both black and white populations is fairly complex, so that trying to cover both subjects in one paragraph would result in a paragraph that ran to more than a page. While there's nothing wrong with such a long paragraph, even experienced readers prefer to have them somewhat shorter.

Let's assume that you decide to give two paragraphs to population. Since the issue of white population is complicated for the North by the question of how you count the border states and whether you count the far western states at all, two questions the paragraph will have to discuss, a possible topic sentence for this paragraph might read something like this:

> The relative strength of the white populations of the North and South is complicated by which people one counts as belonging to the North.

The paragraph on black population would have to discuss not just the number of slaves in the South and the effect they had on the South's strength, but also the number of freed slaves who fought for the North. So its topic sentence might go like this:

> As complicated as counting the white population for the North is, trying to estimate the importance of the black population for the two sides is equally complex.

This topic sentence begins, as topic sentences often do, with a transition from the previous paragraph. But the important point is to see how the topic sentence develops from what you want to say in the paragraph. For instance, let's say that you wanted to make essentially the same points in this paragraph but wanted to stress that traditional history books make the mistake of over-estimating the *effective* population of the North and underestimating that of the South. The topic sentence for such a paragraph would reflect that point:

> Because traditional history books usually count whites who did not help the North and ignore blacks who did help the South, they overestimate the effective population of the North and underestimate that of the South.

It all depends on what you want to say.

Let's now assume that the material on economic strength is not so lengthy or complicated that it won't go easily into one paragraph. Since you know that the North had a huge advantage over the South in this area, your topic sentence might as well say it:

> In economic strength, the North had a huge advantage over the South.

Finally, you had thought that one paragraph might take care of the military strengths and weaknesses of the two sides, but further study revealed, again, a number of complications. Although the North began with an army and a navy, while the South had neither, the Southern states quickly seized

Union war materiel within their borders, and many more Southern men owned firearms than did their Northern brothers. This issue would take a whole paragraph, as would the issue of the leaders on both sides. Topic sentences would be required for each of these paragraphs.

The result of all this thinking might be an outline similar to this one:

white populations (North and South)

black populations (North and South)

economic strengths (North and South)

military strengths (North and South)

leaders available (North and South)

We see now that what had looked like a simple essay with an introduction, three paragraphs, and a conclusion turned out to be a somewhat more extensive one with an introduction, five central paragraphs, and a conclusion. And even this outline might turn out to be misleading, since some of these points, especially those about populations and military strengths, might require more than one paragraph.

We can see also how *the topic sentences of each paragraph are the result of our knowing what we wanted to write in those paragraphs.* They are the general statements expressing what the specifics of the paragraphs will tell the reader. Although the topic sentence comes first in the written paragraph, the paragraph idea has to come first before you can write the topic sentence.

Remember the steps of the thinking-writing-revising process and how topic sentences fit into it:

1. *Analyze* and *evaluate* your information.
2. *Organize* your material and *find your point.* (Here you begin grouping your material in ways that might lead to paragraphs.)
3. Write the *idea draft.* (As you write, you will find out whether your first ideas about grouping your materials will work. If they do, you are ready to write your topic sentences for each paragraph. If they don't, you can regroup your materials and then write.)
4. Write the *later drafts.* (Here you can review your paragraphs and your topic sentences, making any changes that seem necessary.)

STUDENTS AT WORK: PARAGRAPHS

When we are actually writing, it is often difficult to remember how paragraphs are shaped—that they normally start with a general sentence, the topic sentence, which introduces the ideas to be covered. Similarly, it is often hard to be sure what kind of evidence, and how much of it, one should include in a paragraph in order to make one's point adequately. Moreover, hard as these two essentials are, they are even more difficult to get right the first time—that is, as one writes one's idea draft.

In the first few papers in college English classes, teachers are used to seeing paragraphs that are faulty in either having no topic sentences or containing inadequate proof or evidence of the point being made. Here are two paragraphs from the middle of a paper about the content of Saturday morning children's television. Can you tell what points the writer is trying to make?

Dating back to God knows when, the blonde Barbie doll was introduced to a generation of young girls. The Barbie doll is a huge success, even in today's market, being sold to girls living out their fantasies through a doll who had it all. I can imagine that many of the girls, of all races, wished that they had blonde hair, lived in a Malibu beach home, drove a Porsche, and had a man like Ken. Barbie may have broken many dreams. Adding to the negative impact, an article last week had math teachers upset at the Barbie doll because Barbie has spoken. Now, 20 years later, Teen Talk Barbie, introduced in July by Mattel, Inc., is chattering away in the playrooms across the country, and this is what she has waited so long to say: "Math class is tough." This is the sort of thing that perpetuates the myth that girls find math harder than boys do.

One of the commercials about a new hockey game featured four white boys playing with one another. Even though professional hockey is dominated by white men, the typical minority may feel that this game may not be for him. On the other hand, many producers feature blacks playing basketball in their new hi-top basketball shoes trying to target young blacks, meanwhile it is very stereotypical to visualize that blacks always play basketball and care mostly of the shoes they wear. But we can't question the success of their methods.

Jerrold Gor, Student

Without topic sentences for these paragraphs, it is really impossible to tell what general point or points the writer was trying to make. His material is interesting, and much of his writing is very good, but what's his point? This is wonderful material for an idea draft, but it needs to be shaped to move from general to specific before it's ready for the finished paper. In a later paper, the same student did an excellent job of providing topic sentences and well-developed paragraphs. Notice here how the first sentence tells us exactly what point he wants to make:

The involvement of Asian parents may be the key in why the development of their children has escalated to such high plateaus. In the article "Japan's School System," by James Kilpatrick, Japanese parents play a major role in their children's learning process. The parents are expected to attend PTA meetings and to reinforce the school's training in "punctuality, neatness and respect for authority." I feel that the bond created between parents and their children motivates them because knowing that they have the love and support of their family gives the children incentive to do well and therefore succeed. Since American parents don't have such a close bond with their children, many students are unsure of their future and lack some incentive to learn because their parents care only about the final grades received and not how they got it. The first step in improving the American system is to have parental involvement in their children's education.

Jerrold Gor, Student

In working on the development of your paragraphs—what goes into them—the best procedure will usually be to follow these steps:

First, using your class notes, a review of the readings, and your notes on them if you have any, decide on the main points you want to make *in your essay* and list them in the order that looks best to you. This rough outline of the whole paper will make everything else much much easier to do.

Second, under the main points on your list or outline, jot down any subpoints you want to make (so you don't forget them later).

Third, using these materials write your idea draft; don't worry about spelling, punctuation, grammar, and the like—just get your ideas into writing.

Fourth, make sure your paragraphs have topic sentences that tell what each paragraph will be about. Then, go back over the readings and look to see whether you've forgotten any important points; look also for any good quotations you can use to support your ideas.

After this, you'll be pretty much ready to start on the final form of your rough draft; in some cases, you may find that what you've just done is your final rough draft.

Following are some pages from students who went through this process. You'll notice that in some cases, they didn't have much to add during their fourth step, while in other cases, they felt they had a lot to add.

In the first case, Peggie Van developed one paragraph into two. Here is
the paragraph in her idea draft:

> There are many advantages for a student to work while going to
> school. For the most part, students want to earn money. If they have
> money, they will have independence. They can spend the money
> they earned any way they want to. Besides having money to spend,
> students are able to save money either to buy a car, for leisure spend-
> ing, or to save for college use. Students can also gain work experi-
> ence while they work. Depending on the job they have, they are able
> to learn a variety of skills such as operating a cash register or food
> preparation machine, learn inventory controls, bookkeeping and ac-
> counting skills, teamwork, and deal with customers. They also learn
> responsibility, for example, being on time and going to work regu-
> larly, taking directions and finishing assigned tasks, and also be reli-
> able and presentable all the time.

Here is Peggie's revision of this part of her idea draft. After going back over
the readings involved in this assignment, she realized that she hadn't covered the subject adequately. She also realized that when she included the
important material she'd left out, she would have an unusually long paragraph, so one of her notes on her idea draft said, "Split into two paragraphs."

> There are advantages for a student to work while going to school.
> One of the advantages is that you can ~~gain~~ earn money. For the most
> part, students work to earn money for their own use. Earning their
> own money allows them the independence to spend as they please.
> They would not have to ask their parents for money or for permission
> to do something with the money. The money they earned are ~~either~~
> used for leisure ~~luxury~~ spending such as going out with friends or
> buying a car, or ~~for~~ saving up for college or future use. Some students
> may also contribute some of their money to help out the family. ~~Al-~~
> ~~though most students work to earn money for use of buying things~~
> ~~and not to save up for future use.~~ But as I said in the beginning,
> students usually work for money to buy personal things. It is very
> seldom that they chip in to help out the family.
>   ~~Another Gaining experience from working is another advantage~~
> ~~of working during highschool.~~
>   Besides earning money, a student can also gain work experience
> from working. Once a student works, he/she will learn to be responsi-

One student said that the money she earned goes to support myself, my car and clothes and just stuff I do like going out."

ble. By ~~saying~~ being responsible, the student must go to work regularly and be on time, taking directions and finishing assigned tasks, and also be reliable and presentable all the time. Depending on the job they have, the students are able to learn a variety of skills such as operating a cash register or food preparation machine, learning inventory controls, bookkeeping and accounting skills, teamwork, ~~and~~ dealing with customers *and* ~~They also learn~~ supervising skills. ~~These are~~ Although these are general skills, they will help the students to find other jobs in the future in one way or another. An example of this is a highschool graduate who worked at McDonald's after graduation and worked her way up to being a professor at Hamburger University, "the McDonald's manager-training center, famous for issuing each graduate of its one- and two-week intensive courses a degree in Hamburgerology with a minor in fries."

Another student, Janet La, used the margins of her idea draft to write notes to herself about examples from her own experience of the advantages of students working. Among her notes she wrote the following, to be inserted into her final version:

> "Students who work gain benefits from work. They get discounts and free things from the store and also special occasions off."
>
> "My friend who works in a public library gets days off on holidays and two months of free holidays."
>
> "And my other friend who works in a retail store gets a discount on everything she purchases at her job."

CONCLUSIONS

We have seen in hundreds of composition textbooks many heroic efforts to break down essay conclusions into different types for students to imitate. And we know that students do get anxious about the conclusions of their essays, worried that they might not end them "right," whatever "right" is. With this in mind, we were mildly tempted to entitle this section "The Bitter End."

Since there's no getting over the fact that essays do have conclusions, the best thing to do, we feel, is look at some of them. Let's review three essays from the first chapter of this book to see how their authors handled conclusions.

In the essay by Jane Brody, "Fatigue," the author tells us in her thesis sentences that "there are three main categories of fatigue"—physical, pathological, and psychological—and then describes each in turn. Here is her conclusion:

Understanding the underlying emotional problem is the crucial first step toward curing psychological fatigue and by itself often results in considerable lessening of the tiredness. Professional psychological help or career or marriage counseling may be needed.

Brody has simply finished her description of the third kind of fatigue, psychological fatigue, and stopped. She hasn't written a conclusion to the whole essay because there would be nothing to do except repeat what she said in her introduction, that there are three main kinds of fatigue. One might say that this kind of nonconclusion conclusion comes from the "When You're Finished, Stop" school, one we rather admire.

Here are the introductory and concluding paragraphs from Roger D. McGrath's essay, "The Myth of Violence in the Old West":

It is commonly assumed that violence is part of our frontier heritage. But the historical record shows that frontier violence was very different from violence today. Robbery and burglary, two of our most common crimes, were of no great significance in the frontier towns of the Old West, and rape was seemingly nonexistent.

McGrath's thesis sentence is: "But the historical record shows that frontier violence was very different from violence today." That is what he is going to prove in his essay.

Thus the violence and lawlessness of the trans-Sierra frontier bear little relation to the violence and lawlessness that pervade American society today. If Bodie is at all representative of frontier towns, there is little justification for blaming contemporary American violence on our frontier heritage.

Notice that McGrath has essentially just repeated the idea in his thesis sentence as the first sentence of his conclusion, adding to that a sentence relating to the underlying reason behind his study. Again, McGrath keeps his ending short and to the point.

Robert L. Heilbroner begins his essay, "Don't Let Stereotypes Warp Your Judgment," with a series of examples of common ways in which we tend to stereotype people and then comes to the point of his essay, his thesis sentences: "Stereotypes are a kind of gossip about the world, a gossip that makes us prejudge people before we ever lay eyes on them. Hence it is not surprising that stereotypes have something to do with the dark world of prejudice." Here is his conclusion:

Most of the time, when we type-cast the world, we are not in fact generalizing about people at all. We are only revealing the embarrassing facts about the pictures that hang in the gallery of stereotypes in our own heads.

Because Heilbroner is concerned about the way stereotypes lead to prejudices, he emphasizes that point in his conclusion, again, as does McGrath, tying it back in closely with his thesis sentences.

The writers of these three essays reveal several interesting similarities in their conclusions:

- They keep them as short as possible; after all, the essay has made their points and so there is no need to repeat them.
- Two of the three writers essentially repeat their main point, their thesis statements, and then stop.
- They don't use the phrase "in conclusion," and they don't repeat their thesis statements word for word.

You can conduct your own research on conclusions by looking back in Chapter 1 to see how Maynard in her essay and Sherman and Haas in theirs handle their conclusions. Essentially, most writers prefer to wrap up their essays with a minimum of fuss. We have generally found that most students manage to end their essays with no great difficulty, and our chief advice to you is not to worry about it. Most of the time, your material will tell you how to conclude.

PART II

Discovering and Writing

A writer is someone for whom writing is harder than it is for other people.

Thomas Mann

CHAPTER *3*

Learning by Sorting It Out

AN IMPORTANT THINKING TOOL: MAKING INFERENCES

Certainties and Probabilities

In most of our daily actions, we govern ourselves as though our lives were surrounded by certainties—that is, truths we can count on absolutely. To illustrate, let us take a morning in the life of Mary X. She sets her electric clock for 6:00 A.M., certain that its alarm will go off at that time. She is certain that she will be able to take a shower when she gets up and that the food she has bought will still be there for her to eat at breakfast time. She is certain that her car will start, and she is certain that when she arrives at work, her job will be waiting for her. Her only concern is that sometimes the traffic is so bad, because of accidents or stalls, that the time it normally takes her to get to work may not be sufficient. Usually, however, it is.

Mary is guiding her behavior according to what, without thinking about it, she considers five certainties and one probability (that the traffic will be normal instead of slow). But of course none of these "certainties" is really certain. Power failures do occur from time to time, so that her clock may not go off at 6:00. Even if she has a battery backup for her clock, the battery may fail. Water systems fail also, especially water heaters. Perhaps Mary left her food out on the counter and her dog or roommate ate it. This could be the morning that her car battery dies, and it could also be the morning her boss decides the firm doesn't need her anymore. In other words, Mary is really dealing with six probabilities and no certainties. It is *probably* true that the morning will go as she assumes it will, but there are no certainties about it.

Still, not all probabilities are equally probable. We have degrees of probability, including, at one end of the scale, what are called *high probabilities* and, at the other end, *low probabilities.*

As a probability gets really high or really low, it gets nearer and nearer to being a certainty. For instance, if a teacher gives you a schedule of six quizzes for a course, and the first five quizzes appear exactly as scheduled, the probability that quiz number six will appear as scheduled is very high. Or, looked at another way, the probability that the quiz will be canceled or rescheduled is very low. Either way, it is almost a certainty that the quiz will appear as advertised. If, on the other hand, the teacher gave quiz number two a week after it was scheduled and skipped quiz number three altogether, the probability that number six will appear on schedule has dropped, and the class would have the right to feel very uncertain about whether it would be given and, if so, whether it would be given on its scheduled date.

In most aspects of our lives, we decide, mostly unconsciously, on the probability of an event on the basis of past experience. For instance, we know that light bulbs burn out, but we also know that they don't do so very often. We know that when we flip the light switch, there is a high probability that the light will go on, but we also know that it isn't a certainty. So we are not surprised when the light goes on, but we are mildly surprised, though not astonished, when it doesn't.

EXERCISE

On the basis of what you know about the world, evaluate the relative probability of the following events in Mary's morning. Rate them on a four-point scale:

4 certainty
3 high probability
2 low probability
1 uncertainty

Her alarm will go off at 6:00 A.M.

The water system will be functioning.

The water heater will be working.

Her food will still be there.

Her car will start.

There will not be a traffic tie-up.

She will still have her job.

In doing this exercise, you probably had difficulty rating two of the items—*her car will start* and *she will still have her job*. From your experience, you probably know that whether or not cars start as expected usually depends on various factors—the age and upkeep of the car, the temperature— and since you weren't given any of that information about Mary's car, you didn't have enough to go on to make a good judgment. Similarly, whether a person's job will be there on a given morning depends on a lot of things, including the kind of job it is, how well one does it, the economic health of the company, the economy in general, and so on.

Because people like to feel secure in their lives, they unconsciously treat as certainties matters that are only probabilities, and they often ignore evidence that makes their probabilities less and less certain. For instance, drivers who know that speeding under most circumstances increases their chances of having an accident will still speed, treating it as a certainty that they won't have an accident. Sometimes one member of a married couple will ignore numerous signs that the other member is unhappy and continue to act as always, treating it as a certainty that the other member won't end the marriage. People in these and similar circumstances are often shocked when their "certainties" turn out not to be certain at all.

EXERCISE

Using the four-point scale again, rate the probability of the following events:

You will attend your next class.

You will get an A on the next exam you have.

You will have or be able to get enough money to go out this
    weekend.

You will one day get married.

If you get married within the next two years, you will never be involved in
    a divorce.

You will not be involved in an automobile accident this week.

You will never be involved in an automobile accident.

If you do not wear a seatbelt the next time you are in a car, you will still
    not be injured .

If you never wear a seatbelt when riding in a car, you still will not be
    injured.

Try to think of at least one occasion when one of your "certainties" turned out to be wrong.

Inferences and Guesses

There is a famous short story entitled "The Lady or the Tiger," at the end of which the main character winds up alone in a room with only two doors, one of which he must go through to get out. Behind one is a beautiful lady with an agreeable disposition; behind the other is a ferocious and hungry tiger. There are no clues of any kind as to which door leads to the lady, which to the tiger. The man in the story has to guess which door to open. A *guess* is a decision based on inadequate evidence. It's a shot in the dark.

Let's play around with the lady and the tiger for a minute. Suppose our man puts his ear next to door A and hears, faintly, a low, rumbling growl of the type most of us hear only at the zoo; suppose he then listens at door B and hears nothing. Everything else being equal, he is now in a position to make a decision based on some evidence—his knowledge that tigers growl whereas people don't, or at least not like that. He can now infer that door B is the one to open. An *inference* is a conclusion drawn from evidence.

Good Inferences and Bad Inferences

Inferences are often labeled as *legitimate* or *reasonable*, on the one hand, or *illegitimate* or *unreasonable*, on the other. A reasonable inference is one based on adequate evidence or at least a well-considered judgment of the evidence available. Suppose you are in a position to hire a person to fill a particular job. The person, Michael Z, appears at his interview looking well groomed and neatly dressed. He is pleasant and answers your questions well. His work experience includes the kind of work you are hiring for, and he demonstrates an excellent command of that work. You infer from these matters that he would make a good employee, and that is a reasonable inference. If he turns out to be a poor employee, frequently late, often absent, always unproductive, you had no way of knowing that that would turn out to be the case. Your inference was still reasonable, a legitimate one, because it was logical given the evidence available.

Suppose, in another case, Henry R applies for a job. He is well groomed, well dressed, and pleasant, and he answers the questions intelligently, but he has never done this kind of work before. He is also a member of an ethnic group different from that of the interviewer. At the end, the interviewer decides not to offer Henry R the job, and this is the reasoning: "The last time we hired a member of this ethnic group without job experience we had a problem with her; she just couldn't learn the work fast enough and never did really get the hang of it. We finally had to let her go. These people just seem to be dumb." This is an example of an illegitimate and unreasonable inference, as prejudice often is. From one instance, the interviewer has categorized all members of an ethnic group as lacking in intelligence.

In this case, two big mistakes are present. The first is to overgeneralize from too little evidence. The inference about Henry R was based on only a single example, and there is no reason to believe that one example, in a situation like this, is representative of the group. The second is to assume that all members of a group containing millions of people share a particular characteristic. It is a certainty of the same kind as our knowing that the sun will rise in the east tomorrow morning that any extremely large group of people, regardless of ethnicity, will be very diverse in all human characteristics. In this case, Henry R may or may not be bright enough to learn the job, but the inference that denied it to him was an unreasonable and illegitimate one.

EXERCISE

In the following four short cases, a certain amount of evidence is presented along with a possible conclusion. Evaluate each situation to decide whether the conclusion represents a reasonable and legitimate inference or an unreasonable and illegitimate one.

1. X rides the bus to school every Monday, Wednesday, and Friday morning at about 7:30, and almost every morning he notices another student who is always studying, reading one textbook or another. Most of the rest of the "regulars" study their work only occasionally, presumably when they've got an exam coming up. X concludes, "Boy, this must be a good student. She works all the time."

2. On the first day of his math class, X's teacher, whom X knows nothing about, comes into class smiling, a young attractive man. He reads the class roll, acknowledging each student individually, introduces the subject very entertainingly, making several genuinely funny jokes along the way, and then announces that he will give out a list of the books required and an outline of the semester's work and course requirements at the next class. With twenty-five minutes left, he dismisses the class. X is impressed. "This looks like a good teacher," he says to himself.

3. Z has been saving her money to buy a car and is now ready to do so. She consults her brother, a car buff, who tells her about a model that has been named "Car of the Year" by an auto magazine. In the library, she checks the back issues of a consumer magazine that tests cars and finds the "Car-of-the-Year" model has had only an average frequency of repair record in the past. The company that makes it has recently had a below-average record for quality control. In a section on shopping for a new car, the magazine advises that car dealers give better prices on less popular cars than on highly popular ones. The "Car-of-the-Year" model gets excellent gas mileage, has the features she wants, and is within her price range. Z likes the way it looks. She decides not to buy it.

4. While trying to decide on a car, Z considers another model being advertised
    by a company that promises it makes quality the very first consideration in
    building its cars. The motto of this company's ad campaign is: "Quality is
    our middle name." However, a friend of Z bought one of this company's
    cars and had a lot of trouble with it. The local dealer tried to fix it seven
    times but was unable to do so. The company refused to replace the car, and
    Z's friend finally got her money back only when she went to a lawyer spe-
    cializing in such cases. Z decides, "This company's ads are just designed to
    cover up poor quality control."

Making inferences is one of the tools we use to group or classify things. For
example, Professor Drywit places John Woo and Nancy Williams in the same
freshman English class because she infers that, as the result of attending the
same honors English class in high school, the students have acquired equivalent skills in English. By so doing, the professor has "classified" the two
students on the basis of inference. Does the professor's classification seem
to you to be based on a strong inference or a weak one? Why?

CLASSIFYING TO DISCOVER

The writing assignments in this section are based on *classification*. Classification is a system for organizing things or ideas into groups according to
their similarities, to make them more manageable or understandable. You
encounter classification systems every day. When you go into a store, you
know that the goods are going to be classified in particular ways so that
you can find what you want without having to search throughout the store.
In a record store, the albums will be grouped according to kind of music—
all the rock in one place, all the country and western in another, all the classical in a third; in a supermarket, the foods and other goods are grouped
according to type, the pickles in one place, the paper goods in another. At
school, courses are grouped into departments set up according to subject
matter. City zoning laws govern where businesses can be located and what
kinds of housing can be built in what areas. These laws organize or classify
the city for us. This useful tool is, naturally, extremely common in academic
and business work for helping us to understand large bodies of data.

Scholars and businesspeople use the tool of classification to discover
underlying patterns and meanings that might not be apparent otherwise.
For instance, imagine that you work for an advertising agency with an account for "Hard Rock Hairspray for Hunks," and your job is to determine in
which magazines your client ought to advertise. To do so, you would want
to examine carefully the kinds of items advertised in several magazines in
order to draw conclusions about the audiences of those magazines. A few
magazines might jump to mind as fairly obvious candidates—*GQ* and *Playboy*, for example. But what about, say, *Modern Drummer*? If you think about

the bands you've seen, you would probably agree that most of them have male drummers, and so you might infer that *Modern Drummer* magazine might be a good place to advertise Hard Rock Hairspray. If you examined the magazine, you would find that while it doesn't carry as many male grooming ads as *Playboy* or *GQ*, its audience is composed for the most part of young men. From that determination, it would be reasonable to infer that *Modern Drummer's* audience might well be interested in your client's product. Of course, your next question might be, "Yes, but does the absence of male grooming ads mean that rock musicians don't use hairspray?" That would be another possible inference.

In the early 1970s, a sociologist, William C. Martin, decided to look at the colorful world of professional wrestling in Houston, Texas. Attending some matches and studying the literature of the sport, he noticed that it was possible to classify the wrestlers—at first sight an incredible collection of colorful and outlandish characters—into several different types. First, he noticed that most of them fell into two large categories—heroes and villains. Looking more closely, he saw that even among the heroes and villains there were other smaller categories. In outline form, here is how he classified them:

Villains
    Foreign Menaces
        Nazis
        Japanese
        Russians
    Titled Snobs and Intellectuals
    Big Mean Sonofabitches
Heroes
    Clean-Cut Young Men
    Blacks and Browns
    Native Americans
Masked Men

Notice that Martin arranged both his heroes and his villains in three main classes, though he could have had four classes by making separate classes for Titled Snobs and Intellectuals, among the villains, and Blacks and Browns, among the heroes. Notice also that he found three subclasses under his Foreign Menace class. Sometimes, in classifying, one finds items that are hard to fit into one's system. This was a problem Martin ran into with his third group of wrestlers, Masked Men. The trouble with the Masked Men was that they crossed both main categories, appearing sometimes as villains, sometimes as heroes.

When one looks at Martin's classification of wrestlers, one can see that classification sometimes produces surprising results. Martin found that black and brown wrestlers were almost always cast as heroes, that Native Americans were never villains, and that Japanese usually were. An interesting and important limitation of classification is that while it reveals patterns, it doesn't necessarily reveal the *reasons* for the patterns. Further analysis and inference are almost always necessary if we are to understand what lies behind the patterns revealed by classification.

In this case, Martin found out that Japanese appeared among the villains because the audiences remembered Japan as being our enemy during World War II and because few Japanese-Americans attended wrestling matches in Houston. On the other hand, many blacks and Hispanics as well as whites attended, and so promoters, unwilling to risk racial strife in the audiences, generally cast black and brown wrestlers as heroes. American folklore pictures Native Americans as upright, dignified, and honorable, and we admire traditional Native American clothing and arts. Those facts, along with, perhaps, some guilt about the way our government has treated Native Americans, combine to make the Native American an ideal hero.

Frequently we can classify a set of data—that is, a set of individual pieces of information—in various different ways, depending on what we want to learn or how we want to look at the data. In classifying, we look for similarities between items in our data set. For instance, suppose we were going to classify the following sports: swimming, baseball, football, boxing, and water polo. We might decide to divide them into sports in which a ball is involved and those that do not use a ball, in which case we would get these categories:

Sports that use balls
    baseball
    football
    water polo

Sports that do not use balls
    swimming
    boxing

Or we could divide them into sports played in the water and those played on land:

Sports played in water
    water polo
    swimming

Sports played on land
    baseball
    football
    boxing

Or we could categorize them according to ones involving teams and ones played individually:

Team sports
    baseball
    football
    water polo
Individual sports
    swimming
    boxing

By looking at these sports lists, what immediate and general inference can
you make about a way that team and individual sports differ? Does your inference *always* hold true? With what sports not listed above does it lose its
legitimacy? Here is a larger list of sports. See how many different ways they
can be categorized:

baseball	hockey
football	table tennis
water polo	tennis
swimming	soccer
boxing	wrestling
track	gymnastics
golf	volleyball
racquetball	diving
fishing	basketball

In the following assignments, you will be asked to classify information
to discover what it means and to make reasonable inferences from your classifications.

*A*ssignments and Readings

ANALYZING TELEVISION FOR CHILDREN

In every city and town in the United States, every Saturday morning,
young children settle down in front of their parents' television sets to begin
watching programs—and advertisements—developed just for them.

The enormous audience of children held spellbound by stories and sales
pitches beamed into their homes has left parents, educators, child psychologists, and others worried about the effects of this programing. Studies have
been done from time to time looking at the amount and kinds of advertising directed at children on Saturday mornings, at the nature of the programs
designed for them and the values those programs seem to teach, and at

whether all segments of our society are represented on children's TV—girls as well as boys, black, Hispanic, and Asian children as well as white.

In the first of the following essays, a writer in the *New York Times* argues that children's television is doing poorly in all of these important areas; the second article reports the results of a study of gender and ethnic bias in commercials aimed at children.

Reading Assignment

Pre-reading

Before reading the following essays, think about your own experience as a child with Saturday morning television. On a piece of paper, jot down what you remember in these three categories:

- Commercials: What were they for? As you recall, were they designed to exploit children or not? Why?
- Gender representation: Do you remember the characters of children's programs as being primarily male or female?
- Ethnic representation: Do you remember the characters of children's programs as being primarily white, or not?

WHAT ARE TV ADS SELLING TO CHILDREN?
John J. O'Connor

About 20 years ago, the new Action for Children's Television, started 1 by mothers in the Boston area, prompted a national crusade when it attacked commercials in children's programing as being **exploitative** and a disservice to society. For the past couple of weeks, I have been dipping into the children's schedule and watching endlessly repeated sales pitches for sugary cereals, sweet drinks, fruit-flavored candies and blond, blue-eyed dolls with "fabulous hair" and "the hottest clothes."

Things haven't changed much in the television business of chil- 2 dren's merchandising, and some aspects of the scene are even more appalling.

Considering the feminist gains of the past couple of decades, for 3 instance, it is little less than astonishing to discover the **rampant** sexist stereotypes in the bulk of commercials. Boys still get to play sports

---

exploitative: using selfishly or unethically;   rampant: widespread

and be charmingly rowdy; girls play with dolls that look like "Char-
lie's Angels" rejects and that can be bought with such added-cost extras as nail polish, makeup, perfume and, of course, cool blond hair.

The message: little girls must be prepared for a life of buying 4
clothes and cosmetics and all those other wonderful things that will
make them irresistibly **alluring** objects. Life, it seems, is a look.

The role of television in the development of youngsters is, of 5
course, crucial and inevitably subject to public hand-wringing every
decade or so. The time has probably arrived for another national debate. Headlines once again are telling unsettling stories about troubled and seemingly **disaffected** teen-agers, the more notable of
recent instances involving black and Hispanic youths in gritty urban
New York, and whites in manicured suburban New Jersey.

Not surprisingly, a good many people waste no time in pounc- 6
ing on television as the culprit. Being trotted out once again are the
familiar statistics about the tens of thousands of hours of programing and the millions of commercials the average student has con-
sumed by the end of high school.

Certainly, the commercials specifically aimed at young audiences 7
are, at the very least, suspect. They don't only sell products—sugar-
saturated and grease-clogged junk food—that arrogantly ignore
today's nutritional campaigns. They sell language. ("Ain't life deli-
cious," says the candy spot.) More to the point, they sell attitudes
and values. Equally as disturbing as the sexism on so many commercials is the racism, even if unintentional, although Madison Avenue
puts so much research into its products that nothing is likely to be
unintentional.

Consider the parade of blue-eyed dolls—Beach Blast Barbie, 8
Hula-Hoop Maxie, Cool Times Barbie and the rest of the somewhat
tarty gang. Just about every commercial makes a point of mentioning the doll's hair, which is invariably blond and silky. "She's got the
best hair," brags one commercial. Is there a message here for the
black and Hispanic children with dark curled hair? It could hardly be
plainer; they do not have the best hair. They are clearly inferior. They
live in a society in which they can never be considered the best. And
then public leaders scratch their heads over the very pronounced
phenomenon of **alienation** among certain groups.

---

alluring: attractive;   disaffected: antisocial;   alienation: being an outsider

Considerably more subtle, there is the role given to "minority" 9
children in well over 90% of the commercials. In fact, in the New
York City area, black and Hispanic children are in the majority, but
they nevertheless will have a hard time finding their reflections in
the commercials surrounding the Saturday morning cartoons.

Black children are just about always placed in supporting roles. If 10
a basketball game is used to promote the virtues of a soft drink or cereal, the single black youth will barely get into the picture frame. The
leader of the pack is invariably a white boy, preferably blond. The
name of the game remains **tokenism.** One of the few commercials to
give a starring role to a black youth is for a cereal and, in that case, all
the players are black. Segregation lives, and in the oddest places.

It is distressing enough that Madison Avenue's constant message 11
of "buy, buy, buy" is being delivered to homes that in many instances may not be able to afford the products in question. But it is
downright infuriating when large sections of the audience being **tantalized** are left with the message that they are not important enough
to merit equal visibility. The disservice to society noted back in 1968
is still very much with us.

FEMALES AND MINORITIES IN TV ADS
IN 1987 SATURDAY CHILDREN'S PROGRAMS
Daniel Riffe, Helene Goldson, Kelly Saxton, and Yang-Chou Yu

This study updates research—some a decade old—on females and mi- 1
norities in children's television advertisements, examining how often
minorities and females are present, and in what proportions, settings
and kinds of white-minority interaction they are presented. . . .

Method

Our goal was to generalize about how minorities and females are 2
represented in the overall "world" of children's Saturday morning
television commercials, regardless of which network's program a
child might select. . . .

Two non-consecutive (Feb. 7 and Feb. 28, 1987) Saturdays were 3
selected for this study, in order to increase representation of *different*
spots *and* total numbers of spots. . . .

---

tokenism: representing a minority group by using only one or two
individuals;   tantalized: teased or tormented

All national commercials on both Saturday mornings (7–11 A.M.,   4
CST) on ABC, CBS and NBC were recorded. We coded each commercial, including repeats, that appeared, assuming greater impact
for repeated messages. . . .

Product and setting were recorded for each ad, while *individual*   5
character **variables** included: race, age, gender, speaking role and
interaction with minority characters. Three coders collected the data
after revision of coding instructions, group training sessions and
three reliability checks. . . .

Findings and Discussion

ABC presented 147 commercials, CBS 139, and NBC 133. "Snack   6
food" was the most frequently advertised (29%) product category,
followed by "cereal" (25%), "toys" (tied at 15%), "miscellaneous
other products" (tied at 15%), "fast food" (8%), "public service an-
nouncements" (5%) and "soft drinks" (3%). . . .

As predicted, the 419 commercials were populated primarily by   7
males. Three times as many (29%) used only human male characters
as used only females (9%). Nearly a fourth used only animated characters.

When animated-only spots are excluded, nearly 38% of the 323   8
human-only commercials used only males while just over 11% had
only females. Overall, females were represented in 62% of ads. Previous comparable estimates of total female representation were 51%
in 1971 and 60% in 1973, suggesting that female representation
may have increased over the last 15 years. . . .

Our [next] prediction (no commercials with only minority char-   9
acters present) was also confirmed. Two-thirds of humans-only ads
were white-only. None were minority-only; white characters were
present in 100% of commercials. However, nearly a third had at least
one non-white character present. This may indicate increased non-
white representation. In 1974, minorities were in a fifth of Saturday
morning commercials.

But non-white "presence" is diminished even further when the   10
focus changes from percentage of commercials with "at least one"
minority, to proportion of characters who are minority. Whites . . .
totaled nearly 60% of all animated and non-animated characters,

---

variables: things likely to change

non-whites totaled 8.2% (5.9% were black) and animated non-human characters made up 32% of all characters.

When analysis is limited to "real" human characters, 86.5% were   11
white and 13.5% were non-white. Census data in 1985 placed the non-white percentage of the U.S. population at 15%. . . .

Gender and race were significantly related, . . . with a higher   12
percentage of males among minority characters. Overall, white males were the most prevalent race/gender "combination," accounting for a majority (52%) of all 1,429 real human characters, with white females 34.5% of characters, minority males 9.2% of characters, and minority females 4.3% of characters. Census projections, however, show 1985's white *females* a plurality (43.5%) with white males 41.5%, non-white males 7.2%, and non-white females 7.9%.

Conclusions

In 1968 the Kerner Commission warned that, "If what the white   13
American reads in newspapers or sees on television conditions his expectations of what is ordinary and normal in the larger society, he will neither understand nor accept the black American." With slight **emendation**, that warning could still apply, and it could apply to the television depiction of females and minorities other than blacks.

In the 1970s, scholars spurred by minority and feminist concern   14
demonstrated that racial minorities and females were underrepresented on television and, if present, were used as background in large groups, as token representatives, or to fill roles secondary to those of white males. Similar criticism was directed at television advertising aimed at children.

Minorities and females, in short, were shown less often than their   15
numbers in society would lead one to anticipate, *and* less often in roles of authority or competence than logic would demand.

How have females and racial minorities fared since that 1970s   16
flurry of research? Our 1987 data *suggest* that female and non-white *presence* (i.e., the presence of at least one) in children's commercials has increased.

But despite those increases, the world of children's television ad-   17
vertising remains predominantly male and white. In its whiteness, that television world mirrors the real world, according to census esti-

---

emendation: correction

mates (86.5% white characters on television and 85% white in the U.S. population). But by presenting a world with only 39% females, children's television commercials seriously distort the real world population, where a majority—51%—is female.

Further, a form of tokenism may remain: non-white presence (33% of commercials have *at least one* minority character) exceeds non-white proportion (15%) of characters in the population of television characters. And, for the most part, non-whites have non-speaking roles, and tend to be shown interacting among themselves and not with whites. 18

Minority characters were less likely than whites to be shown in home settings and adult minority males were seldom shown. Absence of adult male role models in many black children's lives has long concerned those who study urban families. Absence of such models in children's "prime time"—Saturday morning—commercials is chilling. . . . 19

Post-reading

John J. O'Connor has written his *impressions* of some of the effects of children's television, impressions obtained, as he says, by "dipping into the children's schedule." In other words, he did not carefully or systematically study the advertising on Saturday mornings or the presence of women and minorities in children's programing. Impressions may be interesting and worthwhile, but they are still impressions.

The article by Riffe, Goldson, Saxton, and Yu represents a very careful study, rather than impressions, but it is a study only of advertising, not of the programs aimed at children on Saturday mornings. Nevertheless, it does seem to confirm many of O'Connor's impressions.

Compare the main points of O'Connor's essay and the article by Riffe *et al.* with your own pre-reading notes about your memories of Saturday morning TV. Were your impressions like or unlike those of O'Connor? Did they tend to confirm or not to confirm the conclusions of the study?

There are a few other matters to consider here too, before you go any further. One is whether minorities and women *should* be represented in television in proportion to their numbers in the population as a whole. Because women represent 51 percent of the total US population, it is pretty clear that they should receive half of the roles in television, but what about minorities? Should they get only about 15 percent of the roles just because they represent only about 15 percent of the population? What does a black, Hispanic, or Asian child learn by watching programs in which virtually all of the main characters are white?

The Kerner Commission's question is also an interesting one. What is the effect on white children's attitudes toward minority groups if they hardly ever see them on television?

O'Connor raises two related questions. He asks whether seeing one's own ethnic group or gender poorly represented on television would produce a sense of being inferior and of not really belonging to the larger society. And he also questions the values taught to young girls about what womanhood should be—whether they should come to feel that the most important thing about being a woman is to be an attractive sex object, desirable to men.

All of these issues are worth serious exploration.

Essay Assignment

Write an essay in which you examine Saturday morning television programing aimed at children.

For more discussions of this issue and suggestions about organizing your essay, log on to http://devenglish.wadsworth.com.

Pre-writing

There are many different ways to apply classification techniques to children's television. For instance, if you wanted to examine the shows, rather than commercials, for treatment of minorities, you might decide, on the basis of watching a few programs, that characters tend to fall into four groups: leading characters, important characters, minor characters, and background figures. You could then count ethnic representation in each category.

Together with your teacher and your fellow students, you will need to decide what you are going to study and how you are going to proceed. Working together, your class will have to answer the following questions:

- What do we want to learn about television's treatment of gender and/or ethnicity on Saturday mornings? (Consider the questions raised by O'Connor's article and the study by Riffe *et al.*; look again at the questions in the post-reading section.)

- What system of classification will we use? (This will be determined largely by what you decide you want to find out.)

- Will each of us do our own individual study, or will we work together in pairs or small groups? Will the entire class cooperate in the same project, or will we do both, producing a series of individual papers that, when put together, offer a larger view of the issues we work on?

- Will all or some of us study the offerings of one or more of the three major networks, or will we study a local channel to see how it treats the issue we decide to study?
- Will all or some of us try to replicate—that is, redo in order to verify—the study of advertising, or will we examine the programs themselves?
- How many hours of broadcasting will we try to cover?
- Will we be able to videotape the programs or commercials we want to study? (If one person can make a videotape, two people or a small group can more easily work together on the analysis.)

When you have completed your study, you will be prepared to decide what your discoveries mean. Once again, the two articles and the questions listed in the post-reading section above may help you with this, but you will also want to examine your own reaction to what you have learned. How *you* feel about your findings is an important consideration and should be part of your essay.

Writing

In your introduction, describe briefly what you have chosen to investigate.

In the body of your essay, you should first describe the method you used—that is, the aspects of children's television you chose to look at and how you proceeded. This is the part of your paper also where you report your findings. You may find that the article by Riffe *et al.* is a helpful model.

Conclude by discussing what your discoveries mean. You may also, although this is not necessary, make recommendations for changes in Saturday morning television.

Be sure to review the Writer's Checklist on pages 154–155.

ANALYZING THE JOB MARKET

Many, if not most, college students either hold jobs while they go to college or have had jobs while in high school or both. They are aware of the positive and negative benefits of work and usually plan, or at least hope, to find careers that will be a lot more rewarding, both personally and financially, than their part-time jobs. It comes as a surprise to most people to learn that the great majority of job holders got into their careers more or less by accident, that most people are doing work they didn't anticipate doing or prepare for when they were in college. This condition is likely to accelerate in the future, since the kinds of jobs available to Americans are changing at a very rapid rate, and most people are not even aware of the kinds of jobs that will be most in demand in the future.

To help you think about your own career in the world of work and give you some perspective on the rapidly changing nature of the job market, here are three readings: an article by a noted economist outlining the new categories of jobs a global market is producing in the United States, a listing by *U.S. News & World Report*, written in 1995, of 20 hot job tracks, and a list of several dozen representative present-day jobs listed in the classified section of a large metropolitan newspaper.

Reading Assignment

Pre-reading

Before you begin your reading, take out two pieces of paper and label them *Worksheet A* and *Worksheet B*. Write on them the answers to the questions below; it is important to do this carefully, since these worksheets will be important in your writing assignment.

Worksheet A

List *all* of the work characteristics in the columns below that you enjoy or think you would enjoy:

working with my hands	working independently
working with machines	working in groups
working at a desk	serving others
working with numbers	helping others
reading	working at home
writing	working in an office
drafting	working with animals
fixing things	helping animals
making things	owning own business
solving problems	working with food
meeting deadlines	working with computers
working under pressure	working outdoors
working with children	working indoors
working with senior citizens	traveling
meeting new people	working in a store

List any other job characteristics you like or might like that aren't listed above:

Write a summary of the kinds of work activities you like:

Worksheet B

Work experience you've had

Jobs:

Training required or received:

Skills acquired (list any of the following that are appropriate and add any others not on the list):

being on time	following directions
teamwork	dealing with people
training others	taking responsibility
supervising others	using your own initiative

Write a summary of your work experience. Indicate how you think it has prepared you for school and how it has helped you prepare for your future career. What have you learned from this experience that tells you what you might or might not want to do in the future?

Reading

Reminder: Highlight or underline the thesis statement and the topic sentences of each paragraph, and note the more important points in the margins. In short, *read actively.*

U.S. INCOME INEQUALITY KEEPS ON RISING
Robert B. Reich

Between 1978 and 1987, the poorest fifth of American families be- 1
came eight percent poorer, and the richest fifth became 13 percent

richer. That leaves the poorest fifth with less than five percent of the nation's income, and the richest fifth with more than 40 percent. This widening gap can't be blamed on the growth in single-parent lower-income families, which in fact slowed markedly after the late 1970s. Nor is it due mainly to the stingy social policy of the Reagan years. Granted, Food Stamp benefits have dropped in real terms by about 13 percent since 1981, and many states have failed to raise benefits for the poor and unemployed to keep up with inflation. But this doesn't come close to accounting for the growing inequality. Rather, the trend is connected to a profound change in the American economy as it merges with the global economy. And because the merging is far from complete, this trend will not stop of its own accord anytime soon.

It is significant that the growth of inequality shows up most strik- 2
ingly among Americans who have jobs. Through most of the **post-war era,** the wages of Americans at different income levels rose at about the same pace. Although different workers occupied different steps on the escalator, everyone moved up together. In those days poverty was the condition of *jobless* Americans, and the major economic challenge was to create enough jobs for everyone. Once people were safely on the work force escalator, their problems were assumed to be over. Thus "full employment" became a liberal rallying cry, while conservatives fretted over the inflationary tendencies of a full-employment economy.

In recent years working Americans have been traveling on two 3
escalators—one going up, the other going down. In 1987 the average hourly earnings of nonsupervisory workers, adjusted for inflation, were lower than in any year since 1966. Middle-level managers fared much better, although their median real earnings were only slightly above the levels of the 1970s. Executives, however, did spectacularly well. In 1988 alone, **CEOs** of the hundred largest publicly held industrial corporations received raises averaging almost 12 percent. The **remunerations** of lesser executives rose almost as much, and executives of smaller companies followed close behind.

Between 1978 and 1987, as the real earnings of unskilled work- 4
ers were declining, the real incomes of workers in the securities industry (investment bankers, arbitrageurs, and brokers) rose 21

---

postwar era: period since World War II;   CEOs: Chief Executive Officers; remunerations: salaries

percent. Few investment bankers pocket anything near the $50 mil-
lion lavished yearly upon the partners of Kohlberg, Kravis, Roberts &
Company, or the $550 million commandeered last year by Michael
Milken, but it is not unusual for a run-of-the-mill investment banker
to bring home comfortably over a million dollars. Partners in America's largest corporate law firms are comparatively deprived, enjoying average yearly earnings of only $400,000 to $1.2 million.

Meanwhile, the number of impoverished *working* Americans 5
climbed by nearly two million, or 23 percent, between 1978 and
1987. The number who worked full time and year round but were
poor climbed faster, by 43 percent. Nearly 60 percent of the 20 million people who now fall below the Census Bureau's poverty line are
from families with at least one member in full-time or part-time work.

The American economy, in short, is creating a wider range of 6
earnings than at any other time in the postwar era. The most basic
reason, put simply, is that America itself is ceasing to exist as a system of production and exchange separate from the rest of the world.
One can no more meaningfully speak of an "American economy"
than of a "Delaware economy." We are becoming but a region—
albeit still a relatively wealthy region—of a global economy, whose
technologies, savings, and investments move effortlessly across borders, making it harder for individual nations to control their economic destinies.

By now Washington officials well understand that the nation's 7
fiscal and monetary policies cannot be set without taking account of
the savings that will slosh in or slosh out of the nation in consequence. Less understood is the speed and ease with which new technologies now spread across the globe, from computers in, say, San
Jose, to satellite, and then back down to computers in Taiwan.
(America's efforts to stop the Japanese from copying our commercial
designs and the Soviets from copying our military designs are about
equally doomed.) And we have yet to come to terms with the rise of
the global corporation, whose managers, shareholders, and employees span the world. Our debates over the future of American jobs
still focus on topics like the competitiveness of the American automobile industry or the future of American manufacturing. But these
categories are increasingly irrelevant. They assume the existence of a

---

albeit: although

separate American economy in which all the jobs associated with a particular industry, or even more generally with a particular sector, are bound together, facing a common fate.

New technologies of worldwide communication and transporta- 8 tion have redrawn the playing field. American industries no longer compete against Japanese or European industries. Rather, a company with headquarters in the United States, production facilities in Taiwan, and a marketing force spread across many nations competes with another, similarly **ecumenical** company. So when General Motors, say, is doing well, that probably is good news for a lot of executives in Detroit, and for GM shareholders across the globe, but it isn't necessarily good news for a lot of assembly-line workers in Detroit, because there may, in fact, be very few GM assembly-line workers in Detroit, or anywhere else in America. The welfare of assembly-line workers in Detroit may depend, instead, on the health of corporations based in Japan or Canada.

More to the point: even if those Canadian and Japanese corpora- 9 tions are doing well, these workers may be in trouble. For they are increasingly part of an international labor market, encompassing Asia, Africa, Western Europe—and perhaps, before long, Eastern Europe. Corporations can with relative ease relocate their production centers, and alter their international lines of communication and transportation accordingly, to take advantage of low wages. So American workers find themselves settling for low wages in order to hold on to their jobs. More and more, your "competitiveness" as a worker depends not on the fortunes of any American corporation, or of any American industry, but on what function you serve within the global economy. GM executives are becoming more "competitive" even as GM production workers become less so, because the functions that GM executives perform are more highly valued in the world market than the functions that GM production workers perform.

In order to see in greater detail what is happening to American 10 jobs, it helps to view the work Americans do in terms of **functional categories** that reflect the real competitive positions of workers in the global economy. Essentially, three broad categories are emerging. Call them symbolic-analytic services, routine production services, and routine personal services.

---

ecumenical: worldwide;   functional categories: categories indicating the nature of work performed

1. *Symbolic-analytic services* are based on the manipulation of in- 11
formation: data, words, and oral and visual symbols. Symbolic analysis comprises some (but by no means all) of the work undertaken by
people who call themselves lawyers, investment bankers, commercial bankers, management consultants, research scientists, academics, public-relations executives, real estate developers, and even a
few creative accountants. Also: advertising and marketing specialists,
art directors, design engineers, architects, writers and editors, musicians, and television and film producers. Some of the manipulations
performed by symbolic analysts reveal ways of more efficiently
deploying resources or shifting financial assets, or of otherwise saving time and energy. Other manipulations grab money from people
who are too slow or naive to protect themselves by manipulation in
response. Still others serve to entertain the recipients.

Most symbolic analysts work alone or in small teams. If they 12
work with others, they often have partners rather than bosses or supervisors, and their yearly income is variable, depending on how
much value they add to the business. Their work environments tend
to be quiet and tastefully decorated, often within tall steel-and-glass
buildings. They rarely come in direct contact with the ultimate beneficiaries of their work. When they are not analyzing, designing, or
strategizing, they are in meetings or on the telephone—giving advice or making deals. Many of them spend **inordinate** time in jet
planes and hotels. They are articulate and well groomed. The vast
majority are white males.

Symbolic analysis now accounts for more than 40 percent of 13
America's gross national product, and almost 20 percent of our jobs.
Within what we still term our "manufacturing sector," symbolic-
analytic jobs have been increasing at a rate almost three times that
of total manufacturing employment in the United States, as routine
manufacturing jobs have drifted overseas or been mastered by
machines.

The services performed by America's symbolic analysts are in 14
high demand around the world, regardless of whether the symbolic
analysts provide them in person or transmit them via satellite and
fiber-optic cable. The Japanese are buying up the insights and inven-
tions of America's scientists and engineers (who are only too happy

---

deploying: using;   inordinate: too much

to sell them at a fat profit). The Europeans, meanwhile, are hiring our management consultants, business strategists, and investment bankers. Developing nations are hiring our civil and design engineers; and almost everyone is buying the output of our pop musicians, television stars, and film producers.

It is the same with the global corporation. The central offices of 15 these sprawling entities, headquartered in America, are filled with symbolic analysts who manipulate information and then export their insights via the corporation's far-flung enterprise. IBM doesn't export machines from the United States; it makes machines all over the globe, and services them on the spot. IBM world headquarters, in Armonk, New York, just exports strategic planning and related management services.

Thus has the standard of living of America's symbolic analysts 16 risen. They increasingly find themselves part of a global labor market, not a national one. And because the United States has a highly developed economy, and an excellent university system, they find that the services they have to offer are quite scarce in the context of the whole world. So elementary laws of supply and demand ensure that their salaries are quite high.

These salaries are likely to go even higher in the years ahead, as 17 the world market for symbolic analysis continues to grow. Foreigners are trying to learn these skills and techniques, to be sure, but they still have a long way to go. No other country does a better job of preparing its most fortunate citizens for symbolic analysis than does the United States. None has surpassed America in providing experience and training, often with entire regions specializing in one or another kind of symbolic analysis (New York and Chicago for finance, Los Angeles for music and film, the San Francisco Bay area and greater Boston for science and engineering). In this we can take pride. But for the second major category of American workers—the providers of routine production services—the laws of supply and demand don't **bode** well.

2. *Routine production services* involve tasks that are repeated over 18 and over, as one step in a sequence of steps for producing a finished product. Although we tend to associate these jobs with manufacturing, they are becoming common in storage and retrieval of informa-

---

bode: be an omen of

tion. Banking, insurance, wholesaling, retailing, health care—all employ hordes of people who spend their days processing data, often putting information into computers or taking it out.

Most providers of routine production services work with many 19 other people who do similar work within large, centralized facilities. They are overseen by supervisors, who in turn are monitored by more senior supervisors. They are usually paid an hourly wage. Their jobs are monotonous. Most of these people do not have a college education; they need only be able to take directions and, occasionally, undertake simple computations. Those who deal with metal are mostly white males; those who deal with fabrics or information tend to be female and/or minorities.

Decades ago, jobs like these were relatively well paid. Henry Ford 20 gave his early production workers five dollars a day, a remarkable sum for the time, in the (correct) belief that they and their neighbors would be among the major buyers of Fords. But in recent years America's providers of routine-production services have found themselves in direct competition with millions of foreign workers, most of whom are eager to work for a fraction of the pay of American workers. Through the miracle of satellite transmission, even routine data-processing can now be undertaken in relatively poor nations, thousands of miles away from the skyscrapers where the data are finally used. This fact has given management-level symbolic analysts ever greater bargaining leverage. If routine producers living in America don't agree to reduce their wages, then the work will go abroad.

And it has. In 1950 routine production services constituted 21 about 30 percent of our national product and well over half of American jobs. Today such services represent about 20 percent of national product and one-fourth of jobs. And the scattering of foreign-owned factories placed here to circumvent American protectionism isn't going to reverse the trend. So the standard of living of America's routine production workers will likely keep declining. The dynamics behind the wage concessions, plant closings, and union-busting that have become commonplace are not likely to change.

3. *Routine personal services* also entail simple, repetitive work, 22 but, unlike routine production services, they are provided in person. Their immediate objects are specific customers rather than streams of metal, fabric, or data. Included in this employment category are restaurant and hotel workers, barbers and beauticians, retail sales personnel, cabdrivers, household cleaners, day-care workers, hospi-

tal attendants and orderlies, truck drivers, and—among the fastest-
growing of all—custodians and security guards.

Like production workers, providers of personal services are usu-   23
ally paid by the hour, are carefully supervised, and rarely have more
than a high school education. But unlike people in the other two categories of work, these people are in direct contact with the ultimate
beneficiaries of what they do. And the companies they work for
are often small. In fact, some routine personal-service workers turn
entrepreneurial. (Most new businesses and new jobs in America
come from this sector—now constituting about 20 percent of GNP
and 30 percent of jobs.) Women and minorities make up the bulk of
routine personal-service workers.

Apart from the small number who strike out on their own, these   24
workers are paid poorly. They are sheltered from the direct effects of
global competition, but not the indirect effects. They often compete
with illegal aliens willing to work for low wages, or with former or
would-be production workers who can't find well-paying production
jobs, or with labor-saving machinery (automated tellers, self-service
gas pumps, computerized cashiers) dreamed up by symbolic analysts
in America and manufactured in Asia. And because they tend to be
unskilled and dispersed among small businesses, personal-service
workers rarely have a union or a powerful lobby group to stand up
for their interests. When the economy turns sour, they are among the
first to feel the effects. These workers will continue to have jobs in the
years ahead and may experience some small increase in real wages.
They will have **demographics** on their side as the American work
force shrinks. But for all the foregoing reasons, the gap between their
earnings and those of the symbolic analysts will continue to grow.

These three functional categories—symbolic analysis, routine   25
production, and routine personal service—cover at least three out of
four American jobs. The rest of the nation's work force consists
mainly of government employees (including public school teachers),
employees in regulated industries (like utility workers), and govern-
ment-financed workers (engineers working on defense weapons systems), many of whom are sheltered from global competition. One
further clarification: some traditional job categories overlap with sev-

---

entrepreneurial: like a person who founds a business;
demographics: characteristics of the population

eral functional categories. People called "secretaries," for example, include those who actually spend their time doing symbolic-analytic work closely allied to what their bosses do; those who do routine data entry or retrieval of a sort that will eventually be automated or done overseas; and those who provide routine personal services.

The important point is that workers in these three functional cat- 26 egories are coming to have a different competitive position in the world economy. Symbolic analysts hold a commanding position in an increasingly global labor market. Routine production workers hold a relatively weak position in an increasingly global labor market. Personal-service workers still find themselves in a national labor market, but for various reasons they suffer the indirect effects of competition from workers abroad. . . .

Unlike America's old . . . economy, . . . the global economy im- 27 poses no particular limit upon the number of Americans who can sell symbolic-analytic services. In principle, all of America's routine production workers could become symbolic analysts and let their old jobs drift overseas. . . .

The number of such technologically empowered jobs, of course, 28 is limited by the ability of workers to learn on the job. That means a far greater number of Americans will need good health care (including prenatal and postnatal) and also a good grounding in mathematics, basic science, and reading and communicating. So once again, comfortably integrating the American work force into the new world economy turns out to rest heavily on education. . . .

20 HOT JOB TRACKS
U.S. News & World Report, October 30, 1995

Accounting

International Accountant

As fast as the economies in Eastern Europe, Latin America, and China have opened up, U.S. companies have rushed in to capitalize: exporting, buying firms, building plants, planning joint ventures. The North American Free Trade Agreement provided $20 billion in new trade with Mexico alone in 1994. To make the deals happen, companies need accountants who know international financial-reporting standards, merger-and-acquisition protocol, and foreign business customs. The number of international accountants at the accounting firm Deloitte & Touche has increased more than fourfold in the past five years and is expected to double again in the next five.

Hot Tracks Salaries (Average)
ENTRY LEVEL: $28,000–$32,250; MANAGER: $43,000–$62,500; PARTNER: $55,000–$84,500.

Training
An accounting or business degree and another language. Overseas experience helps.

Runner-up Hot Track
Forensic accountant. Companies and law firms hire them to check financial reports for signs of fraud or evidence of criminal conduct.

What Accounting Jobs Pay

Accounting Clerk	$19,500–$24,500
Internal Auditor	*$24,000–$30,000
Assistant Credit Manager	$24,500–$42,000
Senior Budget and Cost Analyst	$38,000–$46,500
Manager, Public Accounting Firm	$42,000–$62,500
Corporate Tax Manager[†]	$67,000–$105,000

Note: Average salaries for 1995. *Entry level. [†]At companies with more than $250 million in volume

Architecture

Design/Build Specialist
Traditionally, an architect handles the design and a contractor is hired to execute it—and both, plus the owner, frequently end up mad. Now many architectural firms are offering clients designer and builder as a package deal. Instead of becoming an observer when the blueprints are complete, the design/build architect works closely with the contractor to execute the design and make modifications where necessary. About 28 percent of new nonresidential buildings are now put up through the design/build process, up from about 10 percent in 1989. By 2005, that share could reach nearly 50 percent.

Hot Track Salaries (Average)
ENTRY LEVEL: $30,300; MIDLEVEL: $44,900; TOP: $61,500 and up.

Training

A bachelor's degree in architecture and passage of the architect registration examination. People with coursework in construction-related fields and business have an edge.

Runner-up Hot Track

High-tech home office specialist. These pros ensure that the home offices of telecommuters and entrepreneurs are designed to handle the equipment to get the job done.

What Architecture Jobs Pay

Drafter	$24,600
Landscape Architect	$35,600
Architect	
3–6 Years' Experience	$30,300
6–8 Years' Experience	$34,400
8–10 Years' Experience	$39,000
Manager in a Firm	$44,900
Principal/Partner	$61,500

Consulting

Human Resources Pro

The army of re-engineers charged with routing corporate fat has often taken an early whack at the human resources department. Experts say the "outsourcing" of HR duties to independent contractors now represents about a quarter of the $20 billion yearly consulting revenue in the United States; that $5 billion is expected to grow about 10 percent in the next two to three years. Human resources specialists might be hired to install an automated system so employees can monitor their retirement plans, say, or to recruit a top executive. Or they could get extended duty: Benefits specialists might be retained to evaluate health plans, handle enrollment, and field employee questions.

Hot Track Salaries (Median)

ENTRY LEVEL: $40,200; MIDLEVEL: $43,700; TOP: $62,000.

Training

A bachelor's degree in business, math, or accounting; an M.B.A. or master's in labor relations is a plus.

Runner-up Hot Track

Management consultant. The explosion of global trade has created a need for advisers with language skills and knowledge of emerging Eastern European and Asian markets.

What Consulting Jobs Pay

Consultant (Entry)	$46,900
Strategic Planner (Entry)	$50,000
Management Consultant	$67,000
Strategic-Planning Consultant	$78,700
Senior Consultant	$92,100
Senior Strategic Planner	$118,400

Note: Median earnings, including bonus, for 1994

Education

Specialist in English as a Second Language

Half the student population of Fairfax County, Va., has a native language other than English; some 100 languages are spoken in the school system. All told, the population of U.S. students who are designated as "limited English proficient" has jumped 22 percent in just two years. Teachers of English as a Second Language (ESL) take students in small groups for a period each day to instruct them in basic English or team-teach in the classroom to help students understand the work. They rarely use the students' languages to get their message across, unlike bilingual programs. Bilingual education has created a raging controversy over whether teaching kids in their native tongues does them a disservice in the long run.

Hot Track Salaries (Average)

ENTRY LEVEL: $21,900; MIDLEVEL: $25,200; TOP: $40,500.

Training

A degree in education with emphasis on foreign language is typically required; however, fluency in another language is not mandatory. Some states also require ESL certification, which may mean two years of study in multicultural education and linguistics.

Runner-up Hot Track

Special-education teacher. Estimates show schools are short 30,000 or so special-ed teachers, who work with learning-disabled and emotionally disturbed kids in small-group settings.

What Education Jobs Pay

Beginning Teacher	$ 24,400
Teacher (16 Years' Experience)	$ 37,300
Principal	$ 68,000
Superintendent	$ 90,000
Associate Professor	$ 47,000
Professor	$ 63,500
Dean (Undergraduate)	$ 57,740
University President	$103,301

Engineering

Software Engineer

It shouldn't come as a revelation that software is hot—or that the engineers who feed the hunger have become a precious commodity. Sales in the United States have been up 27 percent yearly, on average, since 1982; last year's $35.6 billion in revenue from packaged software is expected to more than double by the year 2000. As rapidly as computers and networks become more sophisticated, so do consumer expectations; thus, programming must constantly be upgraded to do a better, quicker, or fancier job. Carnegie Mellon University reports that recruitment of its software engineering students is up this year by more than 20 percent.

Hot Track Salaries (Median)

ENTRY LEVEL: $30,000; MIDLEVEL: $45,000; SENIOR: $60,000.

Training

A computer science degree is the most common preparation, but some schools offer computer engineering programs. Programming experience is helpful.

Runner-up Hot Track

Environmental engineer. . . . Engineers who guide [waste site cleanup programs] will be in great demand for years to come.

What Engineering Jobs Pay

Industrial	$39,200–$138,800
Aerospace	$40,200–$104,000
Environmental	$40,200–$108,000
Agricultural	$41,500–$101,400

Electrical	$42,000–$103,000
Chemical	$48,500–$130,500
Petroleum	$51,600–$165,200

Entertainment

Computer Animator

Anyone who has experienced the roaring dinosaurs of *Jurassic Park* or Jim Carrey's facial contortions in *The Mask* will understand why computer animation is a sizzling medium. Filmmakers, television show creators, video game producers, and advertisers are rushing to add dazzling computer effects; Industrial Light & Magic in San Rafael, Calif., one of the top computer effects shops, has seen its computer graphics staff grow from two in 1985 to more than 295 today. Much of the demand will be at smaller firms focused on television and video game animation, which are springing up rapidly as equipment prices plummet. (One complete top-of-the-line package of animation hardware and software has gone from as much as $100,000 in price three years ago to less than $20,000.)

Hot Track Salaries (Average)

ENTRY LEVEL: $27,000–$40,000; MIDLEVEL: $40,000–$80,000; TOP: $80,000 and up.

Training

A two- or four-year degree from a computer animation or graphics program. Two years of experience is desirable at top firms.

Runner-up Hot Track

Entertainment lawyer. Changing technology has made copyright and trade issues devilishly complex. Entertainment companies need lawyers with the know-how to protect their products.

What Entertainment Jobs Pay

Dancer/Choreographer	$24,200
Art Director	$33,800
Staff Video Editor	$45,430
Chief Video Engineer	$47,300
Staff Director (Commercials)	$57,250
Vice President (Entertainment Company)	$86,100

Note: Average salaries for 1994; dancer/choreographer salary is for 1992–93

Environment

Computer Mapper

When a city-planning agency is debating the best location for a new waste dump, or a manufacturer the site of a new plant, the decision makers are apt to first commission a computer-created geographic map of current sites; many are hiring folks who do the job in-house. Geographic information systems software allows a visual understanding of a project's impact on surrounding areas; GIS specialists are the technical pros who create the maps and help analyze the results. Last year, sales of GIS software reached $760 million worldwide, up 15 percent over 1993; sales are expected to keep growing by 12 percent a year through 1999.

Hot Track Salaries (Average)

ENTRY LEVEL: $26,000–$35,000; MIDLEVEL: $45,000–$50,000; TOP: $75,000 and up.

Training

A bachelor's or master's degree in geography or computer science is preferred. Familiarity with the software is helpful.

Runner-up Hot Track

Environmental technician. Manufacturers used to hire techs with master's degrees to collect water, soil, and air samples; they now realize those with two-year degrees can do the job at a fraction of the former cost.

What Environmental Jobs Pay

Waste Site Facility Foreman	$32,000–$42,000
Chemist	$25,000–$35,000
Environmental Auditor	$33,000–$48,000
Air Quality Specialist	$40,000–$55,000
Risk Assessment Specialist	$40,000–$50,000
Project Manager	$45,000–$55,000

Note: Average salaries for 1995; five years' experience

Finance

Investment Manager

Lending money isn't such a hot way to make money anymore: Banks have seen their profit margins from loans eaten away by a third in the past four years because of competition and a glut of capital. Managing money, however, offers real potential. Hungry for fee-generating business, financial institutions have rapidly expanded their mutual fund and pension fund operations—and they need pros to manage the investments. All told, banks now hold some 13.5 percent of the industry's $2.6 trillion in assets. J. P. Morgan Investment Management, for example, hired more than 100 professionals this year and expects to add even more than that in '96.

Hot Track Salaries (Average)

ANALYST: $40,000–$55,000; PORTFOLIO MANAGER: $110,000–$160,000; CHIEF INVESTMENT OFFICER: $175,000–$325,000.

Training

A B.S. degree in economics or business; an M.B.A. is a plus.

Runner-up Hot Track

Derivatives consultant. Companies using these complex instruments need help assessing the risks and monitoring the investments.

What Finance Jobs Pay

Foreign-Exchange Clerk	$ 28,000–$40,000
Vice President (Consumer Lending)	$ 60,000–$95,000
Settlements Manager (Brokerage)	$ 75,000–$95,000
Vice President (International Bank)	$ 85,000–$165,000
Senior Derivatives Trader	$ 95,000–$135,000
Manager of Trading (Brokerage)	$125,000–$175,000

Note: Average salaries for 1995

Health Care

Information Specialist

Any hospital, clinic, health maintenance organization, or medical practice that wants to work cheaper and faster—all health care providers, in other words—either has scrapped or soon will scrap paper medical records in favor of digital data. Advantages: Electronic data can be updated and retrieved quickly, specialists can tap into a patient's records and consult on a case long distance; and research can be conducted more easily. According to one estimate, the need for staffers conversant with medical information and computer databases is expected to outstrip supply by 54 percent by the year 2000.

Hot Track Salaries (Average)

ENTRY LEVEL: $27,500; MIDLEVEL: $47,500; TOP: $82,500.

Training

A two- or four-year health information management degree is required, as is passage of a national certification exam.

Runner-up Hot Track

Physical therapist. According to the American Hospital Association, there's a 15 percent vacancy rate—at least—in the field.

What Health Care Jobs Pay

Medical Technician	$19,000–$20,000
Medical Technologist	$23,000–$24,000
Dietitian	$27,924
Staff Nurse, RN	$35,464
Speech Therapist	$36,036
Pharmacist	$49,608
Physician Assistant	$50,000–$55,000
Nurse Practitioner, RN	$50,000–$55,000

Note: Median salaries for 1994

Hospitality

Food Service Manager

A study by the National Restaurant Association found that when a woman works outside the home, she and her family are more apt to dine out or order in than to have a home-cooked supper. Little wonder the food service industry now takes about 44 cents of every dollar spent on food. The Bureau of Labor Statistics predicts that by 2005, jobs in food service management will jump by 44 percent; besides restaurants, hotels, hospitals, and contract food service companies will be recruiting. Food service managers purchase food and supplies, hire, plan menus, and oversee operations.

Hot Track Salaries (Median)

ENTRY LEVEL: $30,000; MIDLEVEL: $37,000; TOP: $48,000.

Training

More than 60 percent of restaurant owners and managers began as dishwashers, servers, and cooks, so experience is important. A degree in hotel or restaurant management may mean faster advancement.

Runner-up Hot Track

Hotel general manager. The travel industry is booming—by year's end, there will be 40 percent more hotel jobs than there were in 1992. Managers oversee all hotel employees, operations, and sales marketing.

What Hospitality Jobs Pay

Flight Attendant (Entry)	$13,700
Travel Agent (3–5 Years' Experience)	$19,500
General Manager (Fast-Food Restaurant)	$27,000
Executive Chef	$37,000
Hotel General Manager	$56,000
Hotel Chief Financial Officer	$95,000

Note: Median salaries for 1994–95

Human Services

Residential Counselor

Group homes for the developmentally disabled have grown in number by 29 percent in the past two years, as governments continue to close mental institutions. For troubled or drug-abusing teens and former prisoners, too, residential services have become a favored way to deliver therapy and ease the transition to a normal life. Counselors supervise residents in housekeeping tasks, provide emotional support and counseling, and lead recreational activities. They also analyze each client's needs by reviewing records, talking with families, and conferring with medical personnel.

Hot Track Salaries (Average)

ENTRY LEVEL: $15,000–$23,000; MIDLEVEL: $18,000–$27,000; TOP: $25,000–$35,000.

Training

A degree in human services, with coursework in crisis intervention, drug and alcohol counseling, and mental health. Many two-year colleges offer degrees in human services.

Runner-up Hot Track

Life skills instructor. Developmentally disabled clients learn from these pros to handle tasks such as cooking, using public transportation, and mixing with people.

What Human Services Jobs Pay

Life Skills Instructor	$15,000–$23,000
Home Health/Hospice Aid	$15,000–$23,000
Case Manager	$19,000–$27,000
Residential Manager	$19,000–$27,000
Group Home Director	$30,000–$45,000
Social Science Administrator	$40,000–$50,000

Note: Average salaries for 1994–95

Information Services

Web Master

The cyberpros who design and maintain a company's World Wide Web site on the Internet are a new species; headhunters say the job title is only about a year old. A home page is becoming *de rigueur* as a way to create awareness of a company and advertise its products; Yahoo!, the largest guide to Web sites, reports the list is growing by 10 to 15 percent monthly. Responsibilities include the graphics and editorial content of the home page, the public relations and marketing message, and overseeing technical decisions—the choice of software and hardware, for example.

Hot Track Salaries (Average)

ENTRY LEVEL: $50,000; MIDLEVEL: $75,000; Senior: $100,000 and up.

Training

A Web master might have a background in computer science, marketing, or English. What's key: online experience, knowledge of computer technology, and writing skills.

Runner-up Hot Track

Online-service developer. Corporations in virtually every industry are developing moneymaking online ventures—BellSouth's electronic phone directories, for example.

What Information Jobs Pay

Programmer	$26,000–$37,500
Systems Analyst	$36,000–$55,000
PC Network Specialist	$45,000–$61,000
Systems Manager	$46,000–$76,000

Database Analyst (Large Firm)	$46,000–$58,000
Database Manager (Large Firm)	$63,500–$79,000
Software Product Manager	$62,500–$90,000

Note: Median salaries for 1995

Law

Employment Lawyer

In 1994, the Equal Employment Opportunity Commission received 14,420 complaints regarding sexual harassment, up from 5,623 a mere five years earlier. Since 1992, when the EEOC began enforcing the Americans with Disabilities Act, some 50,000 claims of discrimination against disabled workers have been counted. The evolution of workplace law, plus the greater willingness of workers to come forward, means more jobs for lawyers on both sides of the courtroom. The choice, high-paying jobs tend to be at large firms, which usually consult with and defend corporate clients. One New York legal recruiter, Ann Israel & Associates, has seen the number of requests for employment lawyers jump 200 percent in the past year alone.

Hot Track Salaries (Average)

PARALEGAL: $43,262; ASSOCIATE: $63,001–$77,131; PARTNER: $173,774–$191,300.

Training

Besides a J.D., firms want their hires to have an interest in litigation and employment issues.

Runner-up Hot Track

Corporate securities lawyer. Mergers are in vogue; these lawyers are needed to verify financial statements and draw up the forms required to get sales approved by the SEC and others.

What Legal Jobs Pay

Paralegal (Business Law)	$ 43,414
FBI Attorney/Adviser, GS-14	$ 64,000
Associate (Real Estate)	$ 81,560
Trial Court Judge	$ 85,699
U.S. Bankruptcy Court Judge	$122,912
U.S. Supreme Court Justice (Associate)	$164,100

| Partner in Firm (Litigation) | $189,462 |
| Partner (Tax) | $207,700 |

Note: Average salaries for 1995

Media

Online Content Developer

Electronic newspapers now number around 500, up from virtually zero a few years ago; media watchers expect that number to triple or quadruple in the next two years. Magazines and newsletters, too, are creating online editions—and new slots for pros who can infuse text with visual and audio life. Online content developers produce stories, commission others to write for the publication, and repackage previously published material (all articles on O. J. Simpson, say, might be made accessible). They also might host chat sessions with readers and update news throughout the day. Further, they might help the company produce other electronic products, such as CD-ROMs.

Hot Track Salaries (Average)

ENTRY LEVEL: $25,000–$35,000; MIDLEVEL: $50,000; TOP: $80,000.

Training

A bachelor's degree is communications or journalism; experience in publishing, graphic design, or multimedia programming is also helpful.

Runner-up Hot Track

Online marketer. All those new online publications require sales pros to sell ads and subscriptions.

What Media Jobs Pay

Magazine Ad Sales Manager	$44,300
Magazine Senior Editor	$44,500
Magazine Editor-in-Chief	$67,100
Newspaper Reporter (Entry)	$19,700
Newspaper Editor	$67,600
Radio News Announcer	$27,900
Radio Program Director	$53,900
TV News Director	$60,000

Note: Median salaries for 1995 (for magazines, averages; for newspaper reporter, average for 1994)

Medicine

Internist in Infectious Diseases

Specialists in infectious diseases don't face quite the level of crisis that Dustin Hoffman did in *Outbreak*. But the medical profession is very worried that the rise of antibiotic-resistant "superbugs" could mean a serious increase looms in dangerous—even deadly—diseases. Since 1989, the incidence of drug-resistant infection in hospitals has increased a whopping 34-fold. Last month, the Centers for Disease Control and Prevention strongly warned doctors to use germ-fighting drugs more sparingly. The spread of hepatitis, gonorrhea, tuberculosis, and HIV is contributing to demand for the doctors who treat—and when possible, prevent—contagious diseases.

Hot Track Salaries (Average)

ENTRY LEVEL: $117,048; MIDLEVEL: $145,300; TOP: $214,637.

Training

College, medical school, a residency in pediatrics or internal medicine, and a period of specialization in infectious diseases.

Runner-up Hot Track

Geriatrician. The explanation is in the numbers: It won't be that long until the baby boomers are senior citizens.

What Medical Jobs Pay

Family Practitioner	$122,000
Pediatrician	$126,401
Psychiatrist	$132,929
Internist	$133,581
General Surgeon	$200,211
Pathologist	$208,694
Ob-Gyn	$210,703
Anesthesiologist	$244,600
Radiologist	$264,446
Orthopedic Surgeon	$292,000

Note: Median salaries for 1994 for doctors in group practice

Sales

Wireless Salesperson

The Federal Communications Commission raked in more than $7 billion earlier this year when it auctioned off 99 licenses for broadband

---

geriatrician: specialist in aging

personal communications services (PCS). The new services will push state-of-the-art wireless technology—mobile cordless phones, for example—and challenge cellular firms; the number of wireless providers per market should rise from two to as many as eight. Salespeople will be needed to market not only the new phones but mobile fax machines and pagers, too. The best-paid sales jobs tend to be with manufacturers who sell to retailers and other companies.

Hot Track Salaries (Average)
ENTRY LEVEL: $41,000; MIDLEVEL: $50,000–$60,000; TOP: $70,000.

Training
A degree in engineering or a strong sales background is helpful, but many companies will train staffers in the new technologies.

Runner-up Hot Track
Computer equipment salesperson. Pros are needed who can sell rapidly changing technology—from computer monitors to fax machines to virtual-office products.

What Sales Jobs Pay

Entry-Level Sales Rep	$27,600
Senior Sales Rep	$47,000
Major Account Rep	$49,300
District Sales Manager	$54,800
National Account Rep	$57,600
Regional Sales Manager	$58,600
National Account Manager	$62,800
Top Sales Executive	$81,000

Note: Average salaries for 1995 for average performers, including bonuses

Science Research

Genetic Researcher

The scientists who are mapping human chromosomes are well along toward their goal: Nearly half of the body's 80,000 genes have been located so far. Every new discovery spells possibility for the pharmaceutical industry, which has used the information to seek new treatments for diseases like diabetes, schizophrenia, and cancer. Some $15 billion will be spent on drug development this year, nearly double 1990's investment; much of that will fund genetic research at university laboratories and in-house. There should be plenty of work for such researchers well beyond 2002—when the mapping is likely to be complete.

Hot Track Salaries (Average)

ENTRY LEVEL: $47,000; MIDLEVEL: $60,000; TOP: $80,000.

Training

A B.S. in biology or chemistry; increasingly, a Ph.D. in molecular or human genetics is needed. Postdoctorate work in genetics can also be important.

Runner-up Hot Track

Computer-trained biologist. Computers often supply answers faster than test tubes do. Scientists who know how to ask a computer to process and analyze data are needed.

What Research Jobs Pay

Biologist (B.S.)	$29,000
with Ph.D.	$53,100
Medical Scientist	$36,296
Physicist (B.S.)	$37,566
with Ph.D.	$54,750
Geologist (B.S.)	$54,100
with Ph.D.	$70,600
Chemist (B.S.)	$29,625
with Ph.D.	$60,000

Note: Median salaries for 1994

Social Work

Geriatric Case Manager

Two trends account for the emergence of this new professional: the distances that often separate the elderly from their children and the swelling ranks of the "oldest old." The number of people age 85 and up—now 3.5 million—will more than double by 2025, the year the whole baby boom bulge will pass 65. Case managers assess the physical and mental health of elderly clients and make sure they get care; advise on living arrangements; point to sources of financial and legal aid; and counsel the families. Many case managers are entrepreneurs; larger firms are also becoming common. Nursing homes have slots, too.

Hot Track Salaries (Average)

ENTRY LEVEL: $30,000; MIDLEVEL: $36,000; TOP: $45,000.

Training

A master's degree in social work, with a certificate in gerontology or experience with the elderly.

Runner-up Hot Track

Employee assistance counselor. Some 90 percent of *Fortune* 500 companies have employee assistance programs in place to provide counseling to workers with emotional, job-related, or substance abuse problems.

What Social Work Jobs Pay

Public Welfare Caseworker	$30,000
Court Social Worker	$32,000
School Social Worker	$32,500
HMO Social Worker	$36,000
Member-Private Practice	$40,000
Employee Assistance Counselor	$43,000
Solo Private Practitioner	$50,000

Note: Average salaries for 1993 (latest available)

Sports Management

Corporate Sales Representative

It costs $3,500 to be top sponsor of the Hoopla Aurora Youth Basketball Tournament in Colorado; $200,000 buys the honors for college football's Peach Bowl. At all levels of play, sporting events, teams, and the arenas they compete in are aggressively selling sponsorships as a way to make money: Companies in North America will spend a stunning $3.05 billion as sponsors this year, up 44 percent since 1992. The sales force cuts the deals, which generally give a company logo rights . . . , TV advertising during an event, and free tickets.

Hot Track Salaries (Average)

ENTRY LEVEL: $18,000; MIDLEVEL: $60,000; TOP: $80,000 and up.

Training

A business degree with an emphasis in marketing is helpful but not necessary. A background in sales or media plus knowledge of the sports industry should open doors.

Runner-up Hot Track

Sports marketer. These pros battle for spectators by devising the right PR and advertising message. The number of sports-marketing firms has grown from 110 in 1980 to about 800 today.

What Sports Management Jobs Pay

Public Relations Staffer (Entry)	$ 19,000
Assistant Athletic Director (College)	$ 45,710
General Manager (Minor League)	$ 60,280
Ticket Sales Director	$ 75,000
Chief Financial Officer (Pro Team)	$ 90,000
Executive Vice President (Arena)	$191,670

Note: Average salaries for 1993–94 (latest available)

Telecommunications

Computer Security Expert

The rapid move by corporate America to computer networks, plus the explosive surge in Internet traffic, has created real opportunity for high-tech snoops and cyberthieves. The annual loss to U.S. businesses is estimated at $6.5 billion to $9 billion and is expected to swell by 25 percent in 1996. Result: Companies want computer security pros to design and monitor protections for computer-stored trade secrets, employee data, etc. They might install software that mandates password changes every so often, say, or develop an encryption technique that converts all sensitive information into code.

Hot Track Salaries (Average)

ENTRY LEVEL: $30,000–$40,000; MIDLEVEL: $65,000–$78,000; TOP: $90,000 and up.

Training

A degree in computer science, engineering, or telecommunications, plus an understanding of networking and communication systems, is required. To reach the top, security experience is key.

Runner-up Hot Track

Wireless specialist. Desire for ever smaller, more sophisticated cellular phones and pagers drives demand for these designers and technicians.

What Telecommunications Jobs Pay

Sales Rep (Entry Level)	$22,000
Junior Technician	$25,500
Midlevel Technician	$29,400
Entry-Level Engineer	$40,600
Sales/Marketing Executive	$53,100
Top-Level Engineer	$59,100
Online Content Project Manager	$80,000

Note: Average salaries for 1995

PRESENT-DAY JOBS

Accountant. For firm handling grants. Degree required, plus minimum one year exp. in midsize office. Prefer exp. in working with grants and analytical ability. Benefits.

Admin Asst/Acctng Clerk for sm const firm; phone, typing, w/p, purchasing, 10key touch, data input. Must possess exc English skills.

Advertising Sales. Prestigious bridal publication. Exp pref but will train. Entry level. Ideal for recent college grad or housewife returning to work.

Air Cargo Agent. Experience req. working with international airlines.

Baker. Asst Baker and Baker's Apprentice. Exper. necessary. Call for interview.

Barmaids/Waitress. F/M No exp. nec. 21 & over. F/T & P/T. Must have outgoing personality, good appearance.

Bartender. Some exp. necessary. Personable, flexible, various shifts avail. Apply in person.

Bicycle Mechanic/Sales/Asst. Mgr. 2 yrs. min. shop exp., exc. interpersonal skills.

Busboy needed. P/T. No exper. nec.

Cashier, adult bookstore. P/T eves. Over 21. Cash register expr. helpful.

Cataloguer/Reader. Position in news bureau cataloguing & reading newspapers. Must be interested in news. F/T. Benefits. Will train. Perm.

Chauffeurs. P/T or F/T. Airport shuttle.

Clerk. Med size fin. dist. law firm seeks highly organized case clerk. Send resume.

Cocktailpersons. Cats Nightclub.

Cook. P/T saute/broiler, nights.

Dancers, F/M. No experience nec. Top pay, excel. working cond. 18 & older. Apply in person. Alhambra Club.

Dental Tech. Hi qual. dental lab looking for motivated D.T. Exper. reqd. Models, wax-up, metal finishing. Grt oppty to learn porcelain, dicor and dentocolor.

Drafter/Graphic Artist w/AutoCAD exper. Oppty to work w/latest in CAD and rendering software. We are moving into full 3-D rendering and solid modelling and need a CAD artist w/combo technical and artistic ability. Prefer degree in architecture or graphics, w/exp. in drafting/technical illustration and graphics. NOT an entry level position. Send resume.

Draftsperson. Landscape design/build co. has immed opening for qualified individual. Strong drafting skills, knowledge of landscape graphics pref'd. Able to execute drawings with speed, clarity and accuracy. Fax resume.

Driver. Bakery wholesaler seeks Delivery/Bakery Prep person. F/T. Clean DMV. 21+ years. English a must. Will train. Bnfts. Apply in person.

Engineer. Will train selected individual for this entry level position with sprinkler contractor. BSME required. Send resume and salary.

Exec Secty/Admin Asst to president of growing mfg co. Exc. skills essential: typing 80+, shorthand 90+, MS Word, compose own correspondence, able to work independently, top phone skills. Min. 7 yrs exper. Ref. All app. will be screened and tested. Good benefits and exc. salary. Send resume.

Financial Planner. Full service financial planning firm seeks experienced Financial Planner or Broker for association.

Floor Refinishers, vinyl laying or carpet cleaning. Experience necessary. Salary negotiable. Driver's license a plus.

Floral Designer wanted. Min. 5 yrs exp.

Glazier/Auto Glass. Min. 2 yrs exp. Top pay.

Hotel Desk Clerks and Maids. Will train.

Housekeeper for a rest home. Exp'd, live-in. Engl. spkg.

Insurance Sales. We train on a P/T basis for a F/T agent's pos. Comm.

Janitorial/Maintenance. Must have janitorial exper., own tools & transport.

Legal Secretary (entry level) for small law firm. Requires MS Word and grammar skills, neat appearance, pleasant phone voice, transcribing ability.

Management Trainee. Degree pref. Unique oppty in travel/trans. Computer & acct. exper. helpful. Position reports to President/VP. Gd advancement pot. for right indiv. Send resume.

Management Trainee. Publicly traded nat'l corp. seeks ambitious, self-motivated individual for entry-level position. A short training period provides instruction in all phases of operations and leads directly to management. Exc. co. benefits. College degree.

Marketing. Entry level pos. for college grad. Duties incl. telemarketing. Gd commun. skills a must. Resume.

Mechanic, diesel, own tools. 2 yrs commercial exper. req.

Messenger. Large fin. dist. firm seeks msngr. for a variety of duties.

Nuclear Med. Tech. Immed. opening avail. for registered or registree eligible Nuclear Medicine Tech. Excel. career oppty and benefits, pay commens. with exper.

Occupational therapist.

Plumber. Journeyman, min. 5 yrs exper.

Promotional Models. Females. For shows locally.

Program Analyst. Cash/invest. mgt. system.

Programming. Above avg. salary and creative benefits.

Receptionist. To enroll students for driving school. No exper. necessary.

Retail salesperson, FT/PT. Volume mens & boys clothing. Good job & benefits.

Roofers wanted. Exp. req. No hot work.

Sales. Cosmetics. Drugstore exp. pref. P/T.

Sales. Engineering: specialty aerospace fasteners.

Teacher. Special Education P/T for small therapeutic pre-school/work as part of team of treatment specialists. MUST be eligible for Special Education Credential.

Teacher, F/T. Science/math. 7th/8th grade. Exc. district.

Telephone sales, sell show tix for estab. public safety sponsor.

Waitress. M/F, Brkfst lunch.

Warehouse work. Min. wage.

Post-reading

At the top of a sheet of paper, write the words *Worksheet C.*

In the first article, Reich argues that jobs fall into three categories. Identify these categories, make sure you understand what each of them means, and, working with a classmate, match the jobs in "20 Hot Track Jobs" with Reich's categories and write this information on Worksheet C. This will give you a good start on understanding precisely what kinds of jobs hold most promise. Again working with a classmate, classify the newspaper jobs according to Reich's three categories, and add this information to Worksheet C. For each job you list, note the kind of education or training it requires. You will now have a good idea of what kind of promise many currently available jobs hold for the future.

Essay Assignment

Write a report that will inform one of your classmates about his or her present and future employment prospects. To do so, use the information you found in the two articles and the newspaper listings. Illustrate the job trends you found with examples from the readings. Finally, use your findings to show your classmate how his or her job preferences match with job prospects for the future and make recommendations about how he or she might prepare for a career.

For more discussion of this issue and suggestions about organizing your essay, log on to http://devenglish.wadsworth.com.

Pre-writing

In order to learn how job trends for the future match the experiences and hopes of one of your classmates, you will need to interview him or her.

Use the following worksheet as a guide and ask any additional questions that seem to you important.

Worksheet D

What kind of jobs has he/she had? How did he/she like each of them?

What were the hours?	What about vacation time?
Were these desirable?	Was this satisfactory?

How long did he/she work at each of these jobs?

What were the prospects for promotion and/or pay raises?

Description of the work done (get specifics; for example, have the person describe in detail the first four hours of a typical day)

What aspects of the work did he/she like best?

What aspects did he/she like least?

Does he/she have any specific or general career aspirations now?

If so, how did he/she decide on them?

Writing

The introduction should explain what the report will be about, in this case to inform your classmate about his or her prospects for the future.

The essay's body paragraphs should develop your main points—what you learned about work prospects in the future and the kinds of jobs available now, including the relationship between education and good work prospects. Be sure not to write just in general terms but to give specifics and examples. Additionally, don't feel that each of your points necessarily deserves its own paragraph. More important points may require you to write two or more paragraphs in order to develop them fully.

Your conclusion will probably contain your final recommendations to your classmate about how to achieve his or her goals.

Note: When you are writing, remember that a job is not the same as the person doing the job. In other words, a busboy, a cashier, a sales manager, and a teacher *are not jobs*. Jobs are busing dishes, working as a cashier or sales manager, and teaching. Be sure not to confuse the two. Review the Writer's Checklist on pages 154–155.

LEARNING WHAT OUR MAGAZINES TELL ABOUT US

In studying human societies, anthropologists have learned that we invent the worlds we live in and then believe that these made-up worlds of ours are "natural" and "real." Not only that, but we think our own made-up views of the way human beings behave represent the truth for everyone. This habit can produce two bad results. One is that when we encounter a world different from ours, one made up by a different society, we usually consider it wrong— perhaps even barbarian or primitive or evil.

For example, during World War II, the Japanese armed forces treated prisoners of war with contempt and brutality as a matter of course, outraging their Western enemies, who believed prisoners should be treated humanely. Thus, Western societies viewed the Japanese as barbaric and even subhuman. In Western societies, surrendering to an enemy when one's cause is hopeless is considered not dishonorable but only sensible. But the Japanese just as firmly believed that surrender was cowardly and that the only honorable end for a defeated soldier was death. Most Japanese soldiers simply could not imagine living on after surrendering. As a result, the Japanese saw Allied prisoners of war as cowardly, contemptible, and subhuman.

There can be another bad result of holding that one's own view of the world is the only one possible. If this view turns out to be destructive, it may be difficult or even impossible to change it. For instance, in some cultures certain food sources that we accept as normal are considered holy and untouchable, and people will literally starve to death rather than eat them. While many people in the United States think that Hindus are foolish for not wanting to eat cows, what would you think of having dog for dinner? In many lands, dog meat is a natural part of the diet. In our own culture, we value certain social behaviors so highly—thinking them only natural—that we find it virtually impossible to change them even though they are poisoning our environment.

In the first of the following articles, Mary Kay Blakely discusses the kind of world women's magazines have "made up" for their readers. In this world women are told they must always look beautiful and never gain weight or grow old. In the second article, Susan Dudash has examined the articles in these magazines and come to the conclusion that they do not represent the reality of women's lives today.

Reading Assignment

Pre-reading

Before you begin your reading, think about the women's magazines you have read or glanced at (*Cosmopolitan, Seventeen, Redbook, Vogue*). You may want to go to a nearby book or magazine store and skim the table of contents of several traditional women's magazines; students who have copies of these magazines may wish to bring them to class for discussion purposes.

What are the kinds of articles in these magazines? What kinds of topics are their readers interested in? What things do their readers *value*—that is, what is important to them? When you categorize these articles, do you notice any patterns? If you do, what do these patterns suggest about the world these magazines present to their readers, a world their readers clearly think valuable since they continue to buy the magazines?

Remember to take notes as you examine and discuss this topic. And remember to read the following article *actively*, underlining or highlighting the thesis and topic sentences and making notes in the margins when you happen upon some interesting point or observation.

HELP OR HINDRANCE?: WOMEN'S MAGAZINES OFFER READERS LITTLE BUT FEAR, FAILURE

Mary Kay Blakely

Journalist Maggie Scarf stumbled upon the following finding during 1
her 10-year study of women and depression: "For every male diagnosed as suffering from depression, the head count was anywhere from two to six times as many females." The late Professor Marcia Guttentag, director of the Harvard Project on Women and Mental Health, confirmed the fact, calling depression "epidemic" among women. The strongest clue Guttentag's team of psychologists had unearthed about the reason so many women are depressed had come from a 1974 analysis of articles in women's and men's magazines.

The content of men's magazines "tended to concern adventure, 2
the overcoming of obstacles; the preoccupations were with mastery and triumph," Scarf reports in her subsequent book, *Unfinished Business: Pressure Points in the Lives of Women* (Doubleday, 1980). In magazines written for women, however, "the clear preoccupation was with the problem of loss—loss of attractiveness, loss of effectiveness." The message women's magazines sent to 65 million readers was this: Whatever it is that makes you happy, you are about to lose it.

Twelve years after Guttentag's exhaustive study at Harvard, I 3
conducted an informal, unscientific survey of my own. I spent $16.58 for 10 recent issues of the 10 largest magazines about women to study the reflection of women as it came back to me through 2,793 magazine pages. (The top 10 women's magazines are *Family Circle, Women's Day, McCall's, Ladies' Home Journal, Redbook, Cosmopolitan, Glamour, Mademoiselle, Woman's World,* and *Vogue.*)

Judging from the headlines on the covers, the foremost concern 4
of women today is not to grow wiser but to grow smaller. The Average Reader, magazines assume, is on a perpetual diet. There were "Exercise and Diet Tips for Your Over-Fat Zones" and "The Four Hot Diets—What's Good, What's Not." The preoccupation with fat appeared as headlines on 60 percent of the covers, as articles in nine out of 10, and as advertisements in all of them.

Could this obsession with thinness contribute to women's **per-** 5
vasive depression? A recent study of bulimia, a disorder in which victims force themselves to vomit after eating, would indicate that it does. Alarming reports of bulimia among college-age women have been circulating for some time, and now there are symptoms of the illness among 30-year-old executives.

The obsession with thinness was never labeled clearly as "van- 6
ity"; it masqueraded as "health." Celebrities such as Jane Fonda, Cher, Raquel Welch and Stephanie Powers were offered as "health experts" to advise readers on how to maintain a 25-year-old physique well past 40. The clear message was that whatever growing and changing a woman must do psychologically to prevent depression, she had better accomplish it in a body that never grew or changed past 25. A youth/confidence equation appeared in several hundred pages of ads promising to fend off wrinkles with "anti-aging complexes," "age-zone protectors," "cellular-replacement therapy" and "line preventers." Again, unwrinkled skin was described as "healthy" skin.

Articles creating anxiety about "what's wrong with you" pre- 7
ceded ads supplying the remedies. One feature called "Quick Lifts for the Morning Uglies," a peculiar form of depression suffered by young readers, mentioned seven tips for "improving your outlook." Five of them involved the purchase of a bath gel, a blemish cover, a blusher, a scarf, a perfume. Because a woman, if she lives to old age, will become wrinkled, will shift in weight, there will always be the need for more treatment. The Average Reader is not encouraged to look forward to her old self as a woman of achievement, but as a waste. "How you look" was synonymous with "who you are," and for older women that means "invisible."

Not only does the Average Reader have to achieve her growing 8
and changing without bulges and wrinkles, but the current **purge** of

---

pervasive: complete, total;   purge: removal

serious issues means that she must proceed without information. As Elizabeth Sloan, the editor in chief of *McCall's*, recently told the press, the magazine's past issues had been "too text-oriented. We're going to have pictures of girls spinning, kicking, swirling. We're going to be much younger." She promised an end to "essays on serious issues, society issues. They just didn't belong." The decision not to shock the Average Reader, however, can **inadvertently** contribute to another kind of depression women suffer: the prolonged, debilitating feeling of powerlessness.

Surveys indicated the Average Reader liked how-to features, es- 9 pecially how-tos that would solve a problem by next weekend. The quick-fix approach permeated the pages of the recent issues: "How to Stop the One You Love from Drinking," "Loving Ways to Talk Out Anything—So Your Marriage Wins," and "How Not to Look and Feel Tired." There is hardly a problem in America the Average Reader can't somehow solve with health or beauty techniques. The beauty tricks recommended made the sad-looking woman in the "before" photo look decidedly more cheerful, but can a cold, a quarrel, and a hangover really be cured by applying mascara? "The articles speak to us as if women are extremely simple-minded," says science writer K. C. Cole, a panel member for a recent symposium on the trivialization of women in magazines at the New School for Social Research in Manhattan. "Problems are cast in terms of before and after, do's and don't's, yes and no. There are rarely shades of gray. It's the language a mother uses with a child, not the language of women dealing with extremely complicated issues."

As the late physicist Frank Oppenheimer once explained to his 10 students, "We don't live in the real world. We live in a world we made up." The world made up for women through 2,793 pages of the magazines I selected was this: 40-year-old bodies can look like 25 if women would only try hard enough; if "anti-aging" formulas fail to keep wrinkles off women's skin, surgery is available; and marriages can be saved in three easy steps. If women feel depressed about any of this, they probably need more blusher.

The "Unfinished Business" Scarf wrote about six years ago is still 11 vastly undone. Instead of encouraging women to grow beyond childish myths and adapt to the changes of life, women's magazines have readers running in place, exhausted. The anxieties and depression

inadvertently: accidentally

instilled by these magazines have risen so high that executive women are submitting to surgery. This is the world we have "made up" for women, and it is a perilous place to exist.

WE'VE COME A LONG WAY, BUT MAGAZINES STAYED BEHIND
Susan Dudash, Student

When she wrote this essay, Susan Dudash was a French major at Penn State University. The essay (in a slightly different form) appeared in 1989 in The Daily Collegian, *the Penn State student newspaper.*

When well-known newscaster Christine Craft lost her job several   1
years ago, many people assumed that she simply was not performing her job effectively. Instead, according to my sociology professor,
Dr. Mari Molseed, Craft was fired because her employers found her
to be "Too old and unattractive. . . . [Also, she] didn't show enough
deference towards men." In an age where a woman sits on the
Supreme Court and women may vote, this certainly seems ridiculous. However, this example shows the media's important role in
maintaining the **status quo** as well as in informing the public. The
information that we receive from our media can be especially misleading when they purport to be conveying a different image about
women.

One media form, working women's magazines, generally pre-   2
sents an image of women as incompetent; its traditional view mars
the chance for the status quo perceptions of women to change.
Magazines such as *Cosmopolitan, Working Woman, Mademoiselle,
Glamour*—even *Ms.*—claim to be up to date, yet still portray women
as incompetent in regard to appearance, work and knowledge.

The magazines portray women as appearance oriented, which   3
isn't in itself a problem, but the extent to which this image is presented may be. Articles and advertisements deal with clothes, hair,
make-up—not business success or how to play the stock market. In
three consecutive issues of *Glamour* I found a grand total of four articles that dealt specifically with women's occupations. "Should You
Quit Your Job If You're Not Getting Respect?" turned out to be a survey, simply stating the dissatisfaction of women with their superiors,

---

deference: respect;   status quo: existing situation

though the author *did* demonstrate that women shouldn't have to put up with disrespect or degradation. Another of these, "Is That Just-Right Job Really All Wrong?" was a disappointing and **patronizing** list of do's and don'ts. This particular article gives good hints on what to watch out for in choosing a new occupation, but by the same token, these bits of advice should be common sense. The article tells the reader to beware of jobs whose employees say the company is a bad place to work, or to watch out for companies with high turnover, little financial security and "nonexistent or vague" job descriptions. The third article, "Managing Your Money in the 90's: Which Old Rules Still Apply? Which Don't?", gave some useful information for those not up to date on expectations for the economy in the 1990's. This is to their credit. However, most women in the business field have probably had an elementary economics course, which makes some of the article's suggestions seem obvious. For example, of course it is better to buy a new car on credit when interest rates are lower **in lieu of** paying cash or even renting. In sum, even though these articles do deal with the job market, their advice tends to be either common sense or persuades the reader to change occupations.

This may be more apparent with our next example. The final article deals with "computeritis," a disease the article suggests is primarily caused by the repetitive motion of typing on a keyboard without enough little "breaks." Here, the article fails to follow up on the second cause of this disease: namely, thoracic outlet syndrome, a **hereditary** and easily treatable disorder. Here, the emphasis is on the work as a main cause of numb or tingly hands, not on the other causes. The article suggests that the "inflicted" worker take more breaks, hence work less. 4

In addition to these articles, I've found only one out of approximately fifty articles had anything to say about the woman and her job. In these same three issues, I also noted a total of three articles on the *work wardrobe*. This is not to say that there weren't countless articles on fashion, methods of seduction, and sex-related issues. These articles, along with those concerning make-up, or parties, constitute the remainder of the approximately fifty articles per issue. 5

The articles and advertisements in magazines for working women show perfect and unattainable images of women. Most of 6

---

patronizing: talking down to, condescending;   in lieu of: instead of;
hereditary: acquired by birth

us don't realize the models themselves don't look this good; trick photography, silk screening, and expert make-up application present the image desired by these magazines.

These images lead women to believe their success lies not in   7 their knowledge, but in their appearance. For example, a Nivea Skin Cream advertisement proclaims, "Is Your Face Paying the Price of Success?" A Forever Krystle cologne ad states, "CREATE YOUR OWN DYNASTY"; the accompanying photo shows a woman, arms wrapped around her man as he's dressing for work, a hard day at the office. A Pantene shampoo ad tells you to "Risk everything except your hair." Showing the **paramount** importance of the perfect appearance, a woman's face dominates the ad—a face devoid of any possible fault of complexion or hair. After skillfully applied make-up, and photo retouching, the woman is nearly perfect. Another ad for cologne, this time from Coty, tells us that we can "Make A Statement Without Saying A Word," and the beautiful flawless woman in the ad reinforces the fact; **diligence** or competence aren't required here.

According to these magazines, success depends on women's ap-   8 pearance, and their accomplishments are secondary. Women may work, state these magazines; however, the importance of their occupations is overshadowed by numerous articles dealing with non-occupational topics and ads. Out of about fifty features in a typical issue of *Cosmopolitan,* I found four articles that were occupation-oriented; one of these even dealt with purchasing real estate. *Cosmo* scored better than most magazines of its type in this category. In place of sound advice for the working woman, this issue chose to emphasize such things as "Living with a Difficult Man," "Women Who Attract Men (And Women Who Don't)," "How Much Sex Is *Enough?*" "Beauty Bar: What a Great Smile You've Got!" The list goes on and on, and these are only the articles dealing with men. The food and decorating section boasts a feature on "Bad Girl Beds," while other sections emphasize health, the importance of staying soft, smooth, young and physically fit. The Beauty and Health Report in October's issue of *Glamour* tells its women readers to "Exercise your breasts." In November's issue, *Glamour* urges women to "Stop obsessing

---

paramount: highest, greatest;   diligence: constant effort

about your thighs, hair, breasts." I'm not making this up. These magazines are sending out conflicting signals, in addition to placing their emphasis on image and appearance.

You can take the analysis further by looking at the advertise- 9 ments yourself. In a particular issue of *Cosmopolitan* (November, 1989) at least 45 ads dealt with skincare, haircare, and make-up; 35 ads dealt with cologne; and 19 sold clothing. Also prevalent were cigarette and alcohol advertisements. Nothing occupationally oriented whatsoever was to be found. True, in some ads women were wearing work clothes; but it just so happens that none of the ads mention the workplace. The underlying message is the improvement of a woman's appearance—her skin and hair must look young, healthy; her scent must be attractive, if not seductive.

Advertisements abound demonstrating this point—women are 10 imperfect, but need to be perfect to succeed. Advertisements such as for Episage Ultra (THE CELLULITE SOLUTION), or Clairol haircolor (Whether you want to be noticed a little or a lot, the Clairol Highlighting Collection is who you really are), are prime examples. Countless ads for make-up—L'Oreal, Clinique, Estee Lauder, CoverGirl, Max Factor, Almay—all show models with flawless skin and hair, telling us that they use a particular brand of make-up and look so refined. Women just aren't good enough as they are.

The magazines imply that working women must accept double 11 duty—as employees in the workplace and in the traditional roles as mother and housewife. Nona Glazer, an authority in the field of women's studies and a writer for *Women's Studies International Quarterly,* put it this way: from ". . . cooking ahead . . . supervising children's homework and spending quality time with them . . . relaxing with one's husband, studying to improve oneself for the job," women are expected to retain their traditional homemaker roles in addition to their new jobs.

Advice and articles in women's magazines therefore range from 12 advice for quick one-pot meals to the proper dress-for-success attire. After work, women have to deal with decisions about whether 15-second make-up applications are better than the 12-hour process. A Coors ad states, "Our Women's Work Is Never Done." The tone of some magazines suggests that success comes with sexuality.

Even when these magazines deal specifically with the idea that 13 women work a "double" shift, they usually only address the situation and expect the reader to accept it. Not surprisingly, studies conducted within the last decade show that women are becoming more discontented with their situations in general. Women are expected to perform a double-duty job, yet the magazines often consider them so incompetent. How are they to perform these duties at all? These magazines consistently show an attitude of patronization. Typical articles give advice such as: "How to Enjoy the Superbowl— Whether You Like It or Not" or "Meeting His Mother: A Survival Guide," or "Create a New You—the Plastic Surgery Primer."

The available working women's magazines fail to give women   14 enough suggestions for future success, other than that related to a man. The available magazines take the general attitude that women are incompetent in respect to their appearance and work. Looking at women in this way negates their importance in society. And the effects of the ideals behind these magazines are all the more powerful because of their subtlety.

If these modern working women's magazines are sending out   15 conflicting messages, you can only wonder what the rest of the media are doing. Are women's stereotypes really changing? If so, then why are women in occupations traditionally held by men switching out of these jobs only a few years after entrance? Why are women's *firsts* emphasized (first woman to run for vice president, first woman astronaut)? Even in an issue of *Ms.* only 15% of the articles dealt specifically with women and work; about half of these addressed the problems or obstacles that women are facing on the job. Are things really changing?

It is not merely enough to be aware of this misleading percep-   16 tion of women held by the magazines; we must demonstrate the need for more concrete changes to give women the place in society that, according to these magazines, is already theirs.

Post-reading

Blakely has classified certain articles in women's magazines; go back over her article and write down her classifications. Under each one write what it suggests about the world we have made up for women. Then write out *your* summary of what that world's main characteristics are, what its values are. Make a few notes for yourself about whether you think these characteristics and values are good or bad and why. Refer to the notes you've already taken.

Essay Assignment

Write an essay in which you examine three of the top magazines listed in Blakely's article, classify the *leading articles only* according to their content, and explain what these classifications suggest about the world these magazines project to their readers. You may use Blakely's classification if you wish, or you can make and use your own.

For more discussion of this issue and suggestions about organizing your essay, log on to http://devenglish.wadsworth.com.

Pre-writing

After you have chosen the three magazines and classified the leading articles, choose two or three of the categories that best represent the world *you* think these magazines suggest. Using your pre-reading, reading, and post-reading notes, write out a brief description of that world. What are its characteristics? What are the values it projects? Then choose several *specific* articles that best exemplify that world.

At this point jot down a brief outline, ordering the categories that represent the world.

Writing

In your introduction, describe briefly the situation you are investigating. Review the section on introductions in Chapter 2 for help with this task.

In the body of your essay, describe the categories you have found, giving specific examples to illuminate the categories—to make them clear to the reader.

Conclude by discussing the values these magazines project and whether they are ones with which you agree or disagree. Review the section on conclusions for help with this task. Be sure to review the Writer's Checklist on pages 154–155.

Here are three alternate assignments:

1. Write an essay following the steps outlined above, but instead of looking at three different magazines, choose one magazine from the top ten and examine its three most recent issues.
2. Write an essay following the steps outlined above, but instead of examining one or more of the top ten magazines, study one or

more of the less traditional women's magazines such as *Lear's, Working Woman,* or *Playgirl.* (Be sure you get a representative sample, at least three issues of one magazine or one copy of three magazines.)

3. Guttentag's study indicated that men's magazines "tended to concern adventure, the overcoming of obstacles; the preoccupations were with mastery and triumph." Examine three issues of a popular, general-interest magazine for men (that is, don't choose one aimed at a specific group like hunters and fishermen). Following the steps outlined above, write an essay in which you classify the leading articles according to their content and come to your own conclusion about the messages men receive from these articles. What world do these magazines "make up"? (Compared with women's magazines, most magazines for men have very small circulations, and no other magazine for men is close to the top three— *Playboy, Penthouse,* and *Esquire*—in numbers sold.)

*A*ssignments

HOW DO ADVERTISERS
TRY TO MANIPULATE US?

Americans may be the most advertisement-bombarded people on earth. Daily we are exposed to advertisements from television and radio, in newspapers and magazines, on signs we see as we go about our business, and even in our mailboxes. Often we think we see how advertisers are trying to sell us something, but what's really going on? Jib Fowles, a professor at the University of Houston, has studied and written about advertisements, and here he outlines fifteen basic emotions that advertisers try to appeal to.

Reading Assignment

Pre-reading

Before you read this article, think about a couple of advertisements you remember having seen recently, ones that struck you for one reason or another. You may not be interested in the product advertised, and you may not even remember what it was. But you remembered the ad, so it must have appealed to something in you. Jot down a list of any such ads you can recall, and when you finish the article, see whether you can figure out which of the fifteen emotional appeals Professor Fowles describes were the ones in your ads.

ADVERTISING'S FIFTEEN BASIC APPEALS

Jib Fowles

Emotional Appeals

The nature of effective advertisements was recognized full well by   1
the **late** media philosopher Marshall McLuhan. In his *Understanding Media*, the first sentence of the section on advertising reads, "The continuous pressure is to create ads more and more in the image of audience motives and desires."

By giving form to people's deep-lying desires, and picturing   2
states of being that individuals privately yearn for, advertisers have the best chance of **arresting** attention and affecting communication. And that is the immediate goal of advertising: to tug at our psychological shirt sleeves and slow us down long enough for a word or two about whatever is being sold. . . .

An advertisement communicates by making use of a specially   3
selected image (of a **supine** female, say, or a curly-headed child, or a celebrity) which is designed to stimulate "**subrational** impulses and desires" even when they are at ebb, even if they are unacknowledged by their possessor. Some few ads have their emotional appeal in the text, but for the greater number by far the appeal is contained in the artwork. This makes sense, since visual communication better suits more primal levels of the brain. If the viewer of an advertisement actually has the **importuned** motive, and if the appeal is sufficiently well-fashioned to call it up, then the person can be hooked. The product in the ad may then appear to take on the **semblance** of gratification for the summoned motive. Many ads seem to be saying, "If you have this need, then this product will help satisfy it." It is a primitive equation, but not an ineffective one for selling.

Thus, most advertisements appearing in national media can be   4
understood as having two orders of content. The first is the appeal to deep-running drives in the minds of consumers. The second is information regarding the good or service being sold: its name, its manufacturer, its picture, its packaging, its objective attributes, its functions. For example, the reader of a brassiere advertisement sees a partially undraped but blandly **unperturbed** woman standing in an otherwise

---

late: now dead;   arresting: getting;   supine: lying on one's back;
subrational: not consciously aware;   importuned: being addressed;
semblance: appearance;   unperturbed: undisturbed

commonplace public setting, and may experience certain sensations; the reader also sees the name "Maidenform," a particular brassiere style, and, in tiny print, words about the material, colors, price. . . .

People involved in the advertising industry do not necessarily 5 talk in the terms being used here. They are stationed at the sending end of this communications channel, and may think they are up to any number of things—Unique Selling Propositions, explosive copywriting, the optimal use of demographics or psychographics, ideal media buys, high recall ratings, or whatever. But when attention shifts to the receiving end of the channel, and focuses on the instant of reception, then commentary becomes much more elemental: an advertising message contains something primary and primitive, an emotional appeal, that in effect is the thin end of the wedge, trying to find its way into a mind. Should this occur, the product information comes along behind.

When enough advertisements are examined in this light, it be- 6 comes clear that the emotional appeals fall into several distinguishable categories, and that every ad is a variation on one of a limited number of basic appeals. While there may be several ways of classifying these appeals, one particular list of fifteen has proven to be especially valuable.

Advertisements can appeal to: 7

1. The need for sex
2. The need for affiliation
3. The need to nurture
4. The need for guidance
5. The need to aggress
6. The need to achieve
7. The need to dominate
8. The need for prominence
9. The need for attention
10. The need for autonomy
11. The need to escape
12. The need to feel safe
13. The need for **aesthetic** sensations
14. The need to satisfy curiosity
15. Physiological needs: food, drink, sleep, etc. . . .

---

aesthetic: artistic

Fifteen Appeals

1. Need for sex. Let's start with sex, because this is the appeal   8
which seems to pop up first whenever the topic of advertising is
raised. Whole books have been written about this one alone, to find
a large audience of mildly **titillated** readers. Lately, . . . concern with
sex in ads has redoubled.

The fascinating thing is not how much sex there is in advertis-   9
ing, but how little. Contrary to impressions, **unambiguous** sex is rare
in these messages. Some of this surprising observation may be a matter of definition: the Jordache ads with the lithe, blouse-less female
astride a similarly clad male is clearly an appeal to the audience's sexual drives, but the same cannot be said about Brooke Shields in the
Calvin Klein commercials. Directed at young women and their credit-
card-carrying mothers, the image of Miss Shields instead invokes the
need to be looked at. Buy Calvins and you'll be the center of much
attention, just as Brooke is, the ads imply; they do not primarily **inveigle** their target audience's need for sexual intercourse.

In the content analysis reported in *Mass Advertising as Social Fore-*   10
cast, only two percent of ads were found to **pander** to this motive.
Even *Playboy* ads shy away from sexual appeals: a recent issue contained eighty-three full-page ads, and just four of them (or less than
five percent) could be said to have sex on their minds.

The reason this appeal is so little used is that it is too blaring and   11
tends to obliterate the product information. Nudity in advertising
has the effect of reducing brand recall. The people who do remember the product may do so because they have been made indignant
by the ad; this is not the response most advertisers seek.

To the extent that sexual imagery is used, it conventionally   12
works better on men than women; typically a female figure is offered up to the male reader. A Black Velvet liquor advertisement displays an attractive woman wearing a tight black outfit, **recumbent**
under the legend, "Feel the Velvet." The figure does not have to be
horizontal, however, for the appeal to be present, as National Airlines revealed in its "Fly me" campaign. Indeed, there does not even
have to be a female in the ad: "Flick my Bic" was sufficient to con-
vey the idea to many.

---

titillated: excited;   unambiguous: clear, plain;   inveigle: use;
pander: appeal to;   recumbent: reclining

As a rule, though, advertisers have found sex to be a tricky ap- 13
peal, to be used sparingly. Less controversial and equally fetching
are the appeals to our need for affectionate human contact.

2. *Need for affiliation.* . . . The need to associate with others is 14
widely invoked in advertising and is probably the most prevalent appeal. All sorts of goods and services are sold by linking them to our
unfulfilled desires to be in good company.

According to Henry Murray, the need for affiliation consists of 15
desires "to draw near and enjoyably cooperate or reciprocate with
another; to please and win affection of another; to adhere and remain loyal to a friend." The manifestations of this motive can be seg-
mented into several different types of affiliation, beginning with
romance.

Courtship may be swifter nowadays, but the desire for pair 16
bonding is far from satiated. Ads reaching for this need commonly
depict a youngish male and female **engrossed** in each other. The
head of the male is usually higher than the female's, even at this late
date; she may be sitting or leaning while he is standing. They are not
touching in the Smirnoff vodka ads, but obviously there is an inti-
macy, sometimes **frolicsome**, between them. The couple does touch
for Martell Cognac when "The moment was Martell." For Wind Song
perfume they have touched, and "Your Wind Song stays on his
mind."

Depending on the audience, the pair does not absolutely have 17
to be young—just together. He gives her a DeBeers diamond, and
there is a tear in her laugh lines. She takes Geritol and preserves herself for him. And numbers of consumers, wanting affection too, follow suit.

Warm family feelings are fanned in ads when another genera- 18
tion is added to the pair. Hallmark Cards brings grandparents into
the picture, and Johnson and Johnson Baby Powder has Dad, Mom,
and baby, all fresh from the bath, encircled in arms and emblazoned
with "Share the Feeling." A talc has been fused to familial love.

Friendship is yet another form of affiliation pursued by advertis- 19
ers. Two women confide and drink Maxwell House coffee together;
two men walk through the woods smoking Salem cigarettes. Miller
Beer promises that afternoon "Miller Time" will be staffed with three

---

engrossed: involved;   frolicsome: playful

or four good buddies. Drink Dr. Pepper, as Mickey Rooney is coaxed to do, and join in with all the other Peppers. Coca-Cola does not even need to portray the friendliness; it has reduced this appeal to "a Coke and a smile." . . .

As well as presenting positive images, advertisers can play to the need for affiliation in negative ways, by invoking the fear of rejection. If we don't use Scope, we'll have the "Ugh! Morning Breath" that causes the male and female models to avert their faces. Unless we apply Ultra-Brite or Close-Up to our teeth, it's goodbye romance. Our family will be cursed with "House-a-tosis" if we don't take care. Without Dr. Scholl's anti-perspirant foot spray, the bowling team will keel over. There go all the guests when the supply of Dorito's nacho cheese chips is exhausted. Still more rejection if our shirts have ring-around-the-collar, if our car needs to be Midasized. But make a few purchases, and we are back in the bosom of human contact. 20

As self-directed as Americans pretend to be, in the last analysis we remain social animals, hungering for the positive, endorsing feelings that only those around us can supply. Advertisers respond, urging us to "Reach out and touch someone," in the hopes our monthly bills will rise. 21

3. *Need to nurture.* Akin to affiliative needs is the need to take care of small, defenseless creatures—children and pets, largely. **Reciprocity** is of less consequence here, though; it is the giving that counts. Murray uses synonyms like "to feed, help, support, console, protect, comfort, nurse, heal." A strong need it is, woven deep in our genetic fabric, for if it did not exist we could not successfully raise up our replacements. When advertisers put forth the image of something **diminutive** and furry, something that elicits the word "cute" or "precious," then they are trying to trigger this motive. We listen to the childish voice singing the Oscar Mayer wiener song, and our next hot-dog purchase is prescribed. Aren't those darling kittens something, and how did this Meow Mix get into our shopping cart? 22

This pitch is often directed at women, as Mother Nature's chief nurturers. "Make me some Kraft macaroni and cheese, please," says the **elfin** preschooler just in from the snowstorm, and mothers' hearts go out, and Kraft's sales go up. "We're cold, wet, and hungry," whine the husband and kids, and the little woman gets the 23

---

reciprocity: mutual exchange;   diminutive: very small;   elfin: like an elf

Manwiches ready. A facsimile of this need can be hit without children or pets; the husband is ill and sleepless in the television commercial, and the wife grudgingly fetches the NyQuil.

But it is not women alone who can be touched by this appeal. The father nurses his son Eddie through adolescence while the John Deere lawn tractor survives the years. Another father counts pennies with his young son as the subject of New York Life Insurance comes up. And all over America are businessmen who don't know why they dial Qantas Airlines when they have to take a trans-Pacific trip; the koala bear knows.   24

4. *Need for guidance.* The opposite of the need to nurture is the need to be nurtured: to be protected, shielded, guided. We may be **loath** to admit it, but the child lingers on inside every adult—and a good thing it does, or we would not be instructable in our advancing years. Who wants a nation of nothing but flinty personalities?   25

Parent-like figures can successfully call up this need. . . .   26

A celebrity is not a necessity in making a pitch to the need for guidance, since a fantasy figure can serve just as well. People accede to the Green Giant, or Betty Crocker, or Mr. Goodwrench. Some advertisers can get by with no figure at all: "When E. F. Hutton talks, people listen."   27

Often it is tradition or custom that advertisers point to and consumers take guidance from. Bits and pieces of American history are used to sell whiskeys like Old Crow, Southern Comfort, Jack Daniels. We conform to traditional male/female roles and age-old social norms when we purchase Barclay cigarettes, which informs us "The pleasure is back."   28

The product itself, if it has been around for a long time, can constitute a tradition. All those old labels in the ad for Morton salt convince us that we should continue to buy it. Kool-Aid says, "You loved it as a kid. You trust it as a mother," hoping to get yet more consumers to go along. . . .   29

So far the needs and the ways they can be invoked which have been looked at are largely warm and affiliative; they stand in contrast to the next set of needs, which are much more **egoistic** and assertive.   30

5. *Need to aggress.* The pressures of the real world create strong retaliatory feelings in every functioning human being. Since these   31

---

loath: reluctant;   egoistic: self-centered

impulses can come forth as bursts of anger and violence, their display is normally tabooed. Existing as harbored energy, aggressive
drives present a large, tempting target for advertisers. It is not a target to be aimed at thoughtlessly, though, for few manufacturers
want their products associated with destructive motives. There is always the danger that, as in the case of sex, if the appeal is too blatant, public opinion will turn against what is being sold. . . .

. . . When Exxon said, "There's a Tiger in your tank," the implau- 32
sibility of it concealed the **invocation** of aggressive feelings.

Depicted arguments are a common way for advertisers to tap 33
the audience's needs to aggress. Don Rickles and Linda Carter trade
gibes, and consumers take sides as the name of Seven-Up is stitched
on minds. The Parkay tub has a difference of opinion with the user;
who can forget it, or who (or what) got the last word in?

6. *Need to achieve.* This is the drive that energizes people, caus- 34
ing them to strive in their lives and careers. According to Murray, the
need for achievement is signalled by the desires "to accomplish
something difficult. To overcome obstacles and attain a high standard. To excel one's self. To rival and surpass others." A prominent
American trait, it is one that advertisers like to hook on to because it
identifies their product with winning and success. . . .

Sports heroes are the most convenient means to snare con- 35
sumers' needs to achieve, but they are not the only one. Role models
can be established, ones which invite **emulation**, as with the profiles
put forth by Dewar's scotch. Successful, **tweedy** individuals relate
they have "graduated to the flavor of Myer's rum." Or the advertiser
can establish a prize: two neighbors play one-on-one basketball for a
Michelob beer in a television commercial, while in a print ad a bottle
of Johnnie Walker Black Label has been gilded like a trophy.

Any product that advertises itself in superlatives—the best, the 36
first, the finest—is trying to make contact with our needs to succeed.
For many consumers, sales and bargains belong in this category of
appeals, too; the person who manages to buy something at fifty percent off is seizing an opportunity and coming out ahead of others.

7. *Need to dominate.* This fundamental need is the craving to be 37
powerful—perhaps **omnipotent**. . . . We drink Budweiser because it
is the King of Beers, and here come the powerful Clydesdales to

---

invocation: calling forth;   emulation: imitation;   tweedy: dressed in tweed
jacket or suit;   omnipotent: all-powerful

prove it. A taste of Wolfschmidt vodka and "The spirit of the **Czar** lives on."

The need to dominate and control one's environment is often 38 thought of as being masculine, but as close students of human nature, advertisers know it is not so **circumscribed**. Women's aspirations for control are suggested in the campaign theme, "I like my men in English Leather, or nothing at all." The females in the Chanel No. 19 ads are "outspoken" and wrestle their men around.

Male and female, what we long for is clout; what we get in its 39 place is Mastercard.

8. *Need for prominence.* Here comes the need to be admired and 40 respected, to enjoy prestige and high social status. These times, it appears, are not so **egalitarian** after all. Many ads picture the **trappings** of high position; the Oldsmobile stands before a **manorial** doorway, the Volvo is parked beside a **steeplechase**. A book-lined study is the setting for Dewar's 12, and Lenox China is displayed in a dining room chock full of antiques.

Beefeater gin represents itself as "The Crown Jewel of England" 41 and uses no illustrations of jewels or things British, for the words are sufficient indicators of distinction. Buy that gin and you will rise up the prestige hierarchy, or achieve the same effect on yourself with Seagram's 7 Crown, which **unambiguously** describes itself as "classy."

Being respected does not have to **entail** the usual **accou-** 42 **trements** of wealth: "Do you know who I am?" the commercials ask, and we learn that the prominent person is not so prominent without his American Express card.

9. *Need for attention.* The previous need involved being *looked* 43 *up to*, while this is the need to be *looked at*. The desire to exhibit ourselves in such a way as to make others look at us is a primitive, insuppressible instinct. The clothing and cosmetic industries exist just to serve this need, and this is the way they pitch their wares. Some of this effort is aimed at males, as the ads for Hathaway shirts and Jockey underclothes. But the greater bulk of such appeals is targeted singlemindedly at women.

Czar: former king of Russia;   circumscribed: limited;
egalitarian: politically or socially equal;   trappings: physical objects;
manorial: like a manor or estate;
steeplechase: kind of horse race favored by the wealthy;
unambiguously: clearly;   entail: require;   accoutrements: physical objects

To come back to Brooke Shields: this is where she fits into Amer- 44
ican marketing. If I buy Calvin Klein jeans, consumers infer, I'll be the
object of fascination. The desire for exhibition has been most strik-
ingly played to in a print campaign of many years' duration, that of
Maidenform lingerie. The woman exposes herself, and sales surge.
"Gentlemen prefer Hanes" the ads **dissemble**, and women who
want eyes upon them know what they should do. Peggy Fleming
flutters her legs for L'eggs, encouraging females who want to be the
star in their own lives to purchase this product.

The same appeal works for cosmetics and lotions. For years, the 45
little girl with the exposed backside sold gobs of Coppertone, but
now the company has picked up the pace a little: as a female, you
are supposed to "Flash 'em a Coppertone tan." Food can be sold the
same way, especially to the diet-conscious; Angie Dickinson poses
for California avocadoes and says, "Would this body lie to you?" Our
eyes are too fixed on her for us to think to ask if she got that way by
eating mounds of guacamole.

10. *Need for **autonomy**.* There are several ways to sell credit card 46
services, as has been noted: Mastercard appeals to the need to dominate, and American Express to the need for prominence. When Visa
claims, "You can have it the way you want it," yet another primary
motive is being beckoned forward—the need to endorse the self.
The focus here is upon the independence and integrity of the individual; this need is the antithesis of the need for guidance and is unlike any of the social needs. "If running with the herd isn't your style,
try ours," says Rotan-Mosle, and many Americans feel they have finally found the right brokerage firm.

The photo is of a red-coated Mountie on his horse, posed on a 47
snow-covered ledge; the copy reads, "Windsor—one Canadian
stands alone." This epitome of the solitary and proud individual may
work best with male customers, as may Winston's man in the red
cap. But one-figure advertisements also strike the strong need for
autonomy among American women. As Shelly Hack strides for Char-
lie perfume, females respond to her obvious pride and flair; she is
her own person. The Virginia Slims' tale is of people who have come
a long way from **subservience** to independence. . . .

---

dissemble: pretend;   autonomy: independence;
subservience: being subordinate

11. *Need to escape.* An appeal to the need for autonomy often 48
co-occurs with one for the need to escape, since the desire to duck
out of our social obligations, to seek rest or adventure, frequently
takes the form of one-person flight. The dashing image of a pilot, in
fact, is a standard way of quickening this need to get away from it all.

Freedom is the pitch here, the freedom that every individual 49
yearns for whenever life becomes too oppressive. Many advertisers
like appealing to the need for escape because the sensation of pleasure often accompanies escape, and what nicer **emotional nimbus**
could there be for a product? "You deserve a break today," says Mc-
Donalds, and Stouffer's frozen foods chime in, "Set yourself free." . . .

12. *Need to feel safe.* Nobody in their right mind wants to be in- 50
timidated, menaced, battered, poisoned. We naturally want to do
whatever it takes to stave off threats to our well-being, and to our
families'. It is the instinct for self-preservation that makes us respon-
sive to the ad of the St. Bernard with the keg of Chivas Regal. We
pay attention to the stern talk of Karl Malden and the plight of the
vacationing couples who have lost all their funds in the American Express travelers cheques commercials. We want the **omnipresent** stag
from Hartford Insurance to watch over us too. In the interest of keeping failure and calamity from our lives, we like to see the durability of
products demonstrated. Can we ever forget that Timex takes a lick-
ing and keeps on ticking? When the American Tourister suitcase
bounces all over the highway and the egg inside doesn't break, the
need to feel safe has been adroitly plucked.

We take precautions to diminish future threats. We buy Volkswa- 51
gen Rabbits for the extraordinary mileage, and MONY insurance
policies to avoid the tragedies depicted in their black-and-white ads
of widows and orphans.

We are careful about our health. We consume Mazola margarine 52
because it has "corn goodness" backed by the natural food traditions of the American Indians. In the medicine cabinet is Alka-Seltzer,
the "home remedy"; having it, we are snug in our little cottage.

We want to be safe and secure; buy these products, advertisers 53
are saying, and you'll be safer than you are without them.

13. *Need for aesthetic sensations.* There is an undeniable aesthetic 54
component to virtually every ad run in the national media: the pho-

---

emotional nimbus: feeling;   omnipresent: being everywhere

tography or filming or drawing is near-perfect, the type style is well chosen, the layout could scarcely be improved upon. Advertisers know there is little chance of good communication occurring if an ad is not visually pleasing. Consumers may not be aware of the extent of their own sensitivity to artwork, but it is undeniably large.

Sometimes the aesthetic element is expanded and made into an 55 ad's primary appeal. Charles Jordan shoes may or may not appear in the accompanying avant-garde photographs; Kohler plumbing fixtures catch attention through the high style of their desert settings. Beneath the slightly out of focus photograph, languid and sensuous in tone, General Electric feels called upon to explain, "This is an ad for the hair dryer."

This appeal is not limited to female consumers: J and B scotch 56 says "It whispers" and shows a **bucolic** scene of lake and castle.

14. *Need to satisfy curiosity.* It may seem odd to list a need for in- 57 formation among basic motives, but this need can be as primal and compelling as any of the others. Human beings are curious by nature, interested in the world around them, and intrigued by tidbits of knowledge and new developments. Trivia, percentages, observations counter to conventional wisdom—these items all help sell products. Any advertisement in a question-and-answer format is strumming this need. . . .

15. *Physiological needs.* To the extent that sex is solely a biologi- 58 cal need, we are now coming around full circle, back towards the start of the list. In this final category are clustered appeals to sleeping, eating, drinking. The art of photographing food and drink is so advanced, sometimes these temptations are wonderously caught in the camera's lens: the crab meat in the Red Lobster restaurant ads can start us salivating, the Quarterpounder can almost be smelled, the liquor in the glass glows invitingly. **Imbibe**, these ads scream. . . .

Analyzing Advertisements

When analyzing ads yourself for their emotional appeals, it takes a 59 bit of practice to learn to ignore the product information (as well as one's own experience and feelings about the product). But that skill comes soon enough, as does the ability to quickly sort out from all the non-product aspects of an ad the chief element which is the most

---

bucolic: in the country;   imbibe: drink

striking, the most likely to snag attention first and penetrate brains furthest. The key to the appeal, this element usually presents itself centrally and forwardly to the reader or viewer.

Another clue: the viewing angle which the audience has on the   60 ad's subjects is informative. If the subjects are photographed or filmed from below and thus are looking down at you much as the Green Giant does, then the need to be guided is a good candidate for the ad's emotional appeal. If, on the other hand, the subjects are shot from above and appear **deferential**, as is often the case with children or female models, then other needs are being appealed to.

To figure out an ad's emotional appeal, it is wise to know (or   61 have a good hunch about) who the targeted consumers are; this can often be inferred from the magazine or television show it appears in. This piece of information is a great help in determining the appeal and in deciding between two different interpretations. For example, if an ad features a partially undressed female, this would typically signal one appeal for readers of *Penthouse* (need for sex) and another for readers of *Cosmopolitan* (need for attention).

It would be convenient if every ad made just one appeal, were   62 aimed at just one need. Unfortunately, things are often not that simple. A cigarette ad with a couple at the edge of a polo field is trying to hit both the need for affiliation and the need for prominence; depending on the attitude of the male, dominance could also be an ingredient in this. An ad for Chimere perfume incorporates two photos: in the top one the lady is being commanding at a business luncheon (need to dominate), but in the lower one she is being **bussed** (need for affiliation). Better ads, however, seem to avoid being too diffused; in a study of post–World War II advertising . . . , appeals grew more focused as the decades passed. As a rule of thumb, about sixty percent of ads make one paramount appeal; roughly twenty percent have two conspicuous appeals; the last twenty percent have three or more. Rather than looking for the greatest number of appeals, decoding ads is most productive when the loudest one or two appeals are discerned, since those are the appeals with the best chance of grabbing people's attention.

Finally, analyzing ads does not have to be a solo activity and prob-   63 ably should not be. The greater number of people there are involved, the better chance there is of transcending individual biases and dis- . covering the essential emotional lure built into an advertisement. . . .

---

deferential: respectful;   bussed: kissed

Essay Assignment

Write an essay in which you examine a selection of advertisements from a magazine you read, whether one you read frequently or infrequently. Examine ten full-page advertisements,
preferably ones in color. Working with a classmate, try to figure
out which of Fowles' fifteen appeals is working in each ad.
Come to a conclusion about how advertisers see the readers of
the magazine.

    For more discussion of this issue and suggestions about orga-
nizing your essay, log on to http://devenglish.wadsworth.com.

Pre-writing

    Working with a classmate, choose a magazine both of you enjoy read-
ing. Decide together which ads you will examine. It doesn't matter which
ones you choose, but it will be best if they seem on the surface to be more
or less representative of the ones in the magazine. Then reviewing the descriptions of the fifteen appeals, see which ones seem best to describe each
of your ads. You can do this together with your partner, or you can each do
it separately and then get together to see how well you agree. In case of dis-
agreements, go back over the descriptions of the appeals to check more carefully which seem best to apply. Remember that some ads do contain more
than one appeal.

    As you analyze the ads, make notes for each one about not only which
appeal or appeals it seems to contain but *why* you think so. Your reasons
will be extremely important for your paper.

    When you have found the pattern of appeals in the magazine you've
studied, you are ready to make an inference about how the advertisers see
the readers—who they think they are, what emotions they think are dominant in them. And then you are ready to make a further inference about
how the advertisers have stereotyped the readers. You should then ask yourself what you think this means. After all, you are the one being stereotyped
in a particular way.

Writing

    In your introduction, briefly describe your study and why you are making
it. Review the section on introductions in Chapter 2 for help with this task.

    In the body of your essay, describe the categories of appeals that you
found, giving specific examples to make clear to the reader why those are
the correct appeals. Note how Fowles has done this in his essay.

Conclude by explaining the inferences you have made about how the advertisers see the readers of the magazine you studied and what that seems to mean to you. Review the section on conclusions for help with this task. Be sure to review the Writer's Checklist below.

THE WRITER'S CHECKLIST

The Idea Draft

1. Does your idea draft *respond fully* to the assignment?
2. Are your ideas *organized* in the way you want?
3. Does your *introduction* explain what the essay will be about and what its purpose is?
4. Do you have a *thesis* that states your point or indicates the issue the essay will address?
5. Do the *body paragraphs* each have a *topic sentence*? Do they develop the main points by giving *specifics and examples* to support those points?
6. Does your *conclusion* either summarize the main points or make a recommendation?
7. Have you *collaborated* with at least one trusted friend or fellow student who has read your draft *critically*, looking for lapses in logic or other weaknesses in content?

Sentence Combining

As part of your revision process, think consciously of using coordinators and subordinators if you have done sentence-combining work with them at this point. Be especially alert for places where *but, because* (or *for*), and *while* might clarify your meaning for your readers.

In his article on children's television programs, John J. O'Connor finds numerous occasions to use coordinators and subordinators. Here are three of them:

> **Equally as disturbing as the sexism on so many commercials is the racism, <u>even if</u> unintentional, <u>although</u> Madison Avenue puts so much research into its products that nothing is likely to be unintentional.**

> **In fact, in the New York City area, black and Hispanic children are in the majority, <u>but</u> they nevertheless will have a hard time finding their reflections in the commercials surrounding the Saturday morning cartoons.**

Remember that you can use the FANBOYS to introduce sentences, as in the following passage from the first paragraph of Robert Reich's essay, "U.S. Income Inequality Keeps on Rising":

> **This widening gap can't be blamed on the growth in single-parent lower-income families, which in fact slowed markedly after the late 1970s. Nor is it due mainly to the stingy social policy of the Reagan years. Granted, Food Stamp benefits have dropped in real terms by about 13 percent since 1981, and many states have failed to raise benefits for the poor and unemployed to keep up with inflation. But this doesn't come close to accounting for the growing inequality. Rather, the trend is connected to a profound change in the American economy as it merges with the global economy. And because the merging is far from complete, this trend will not stop of its own accord anytime soon.**

Why do you think Reich began three of his sentences with coordinators rather than joining them with the preceding sentences? Do you agree with his decisions?

Later Drafts

1. Taking into account the constructive criticism you have received, have you *revised* accordingly—that is, reorganized, if that was a problem, or given additional support, if that was?

2. Have you read your essay *aloud*, listening closely to what it *actually says* (not just what you think it says)?

3. Have you *revised your sentences* if they seemed unclear or awkward as you read them aloud?

4. Have you checked for those *mechanical difficulties* that you know you sometimes have? Have you used the dictionary to check words that you think may be *misspelled*?

Final Draft

If you have followed this assignment step by step, you have worked exceedingly hard on this essay. Therefore, make sure your final draft reflects your care and effort by being as professional looking as possible.

1. Type it neatly, using the format your instructor has assigned.

2. Proofread slowly and carefully, word by word, line by line. (One last time, ask a trusted friend to proofread it *after* you have, or exchange your essay with another student and proof each other's.)

*S*entence Combining

JOINING IDEAS TO SHOW BASIC LOGICAL RELATIONSHIPS

Coordinating Conjunctions

The most common way we have of joining sentences is to use words called *coordinators*, or coordinating conjunctions, and the ones we use most frequently are *and, but,* and *so.*

John took typing lessons, and he never regretted it.
Mary took flying lessons, but she couldn't afford to fly often.
I needed to relax, so I put away my work.

The coordinators not only join the two sentences but also show the logical relationship between the ideas in them. *And* indicates the addition of two similar ideas; *but* tells us that there is some kind of logical opposition between them; *so* indicates that the first one is the reason for the second one. In addition to these three words, we use four others in the same way—to join sentences while showing the logical relationship between the ideas in them: *or, for, yet, nor.*

It is easy to remember these seven words if you remember the word FANBOYS. FANBOYS is an acronym, a word formed from the first letters of other words. The word *FANBOYS* is made up of the first letter of the seven coordinators:

For   And   Nor   But   Or   Yet   So

There are two reasons for remembering the FANBOYS words, the coordinators. The first is that, as in the sentence examples just given, when we use one of these words to join two complete sentences, we normally put a comma *between* the two sentences and *in front* of the coordinator. We do not do this with other connective words.

A second reason for remembering FANBOYS is that unlike other joining words, which you will learn about in the next lesson, the coordinators can introduce sentences, serving as transition words. In other words, every one of the example sentences above could have been written as two complete, separate sentences with the coordinator capitalized, as in these examples:

John took typing lessons. And he never regretted it.
I needed to relax. So I put away my work.
There was nothing for us to fear. For we were safe from any possible harm.
She did not want to marry him. Nor was he interested in marrying her.

The reason for punctuating coordinators this way is to give greater emphasis than otherwise to the idea in the second sentence. If the idea does not deserve such emphasis, the sentences should be joined rather than separated. Finally, two of the coordinators can function a little differently than the others. These two, *so* and *yet*, can be used together with the coordinator *and* to make a two-word coordinator— *and so* and *and yet*:

> I needed to relax, and so I put away my work.
> There was no reason for a war to take place, and yet they went to war
> with each other.

As you can see, the meaning does not change depending on whether one uses *so* and *yet* by themselves or with *and*. The tone becomes a little more conversational with the *and*, but that is the only difference.

Here is a summary of the logical relationships expressed by the coordinators:

- *For*—expresses a result-cause relationship:

   She flew as much as she could [result], for she loved flying [cause].

- *And*—expresses the idea of adding something like what one has just written:

   His job brought in several thousand dollars a month [one source of his money], and he got another large sum from an inheritance [a second source].

- *Nor*—Expresses a relationship like *and*, one of addition, except that *nor* relates negative statements to each other. Notice that when a sentence begins with *nor*, we must reverse the normal subject-verb positions:

   John did not like horror movies, nor did Mary like violent adventures.

- *But*—expresses opposition between two ideas:

   She got the job she wanted, but she discovered that she hated it.

- *Or*—indicates alternatives:

   She will have to find a new job, or she will continue to be unhappy.

- *Yet*—functions as does *but*, expressing opposition between ideas:

   She got the job she wanted, yet she discovered that she hated it.

- *So*—while *for* shows us *result-cause* relationships, *so* shows *cause-result* relationships:

   She loved flying [cause], so she flew as much as she could [result].

EXERCISE

Combine the following pairs of sentences using one of the coordinators. The first ten pairs are followed by an indication of the logical relationship you should express, as in these examples:

John ate too many plums. He got pretty sick. [cause-result]

Solution: John ate too many plums, and so he got pretty sick.

John ate too many plums. He got pretty sick. [result-cause]

Solution: John got pretty sick, for he ate too many plums.

The Swimming Lessons

1. John decided to take swimming lessons. He had always had a morbid fear of drowning. [result-cause]
2. He enrolled in a swimming camp on Lake Gotcha. Mary decided to enroll in it too. [addition]
3. John was in training to become a cactus inspector in the Mojave Desert. He had no real need to learn to swim. [cause-result]
4. He realized that he was doing something pointless. He felt compelled to do it anyway. [opposition]
5. Mary already knew how to swim. She thought it would be fun watching John try not to drown. [opposition]
6. The camp owners promised to teach John to swim. They would give him his money back. [alternatives]
7. Secretly, John did not believe he could learn how to swim. Mary did not think it was possible either. [addition of negatives]
8. For one week, John sank like a stone whenever he entered the water. Mary nearly drowned laughing at his antics. [addition]
9. His beautiful young instructor was about to dump him. He suddenly started swimming like an alligator. [cause-result]
10. Now that he can swim, he has decided to become a sailor. He will always have a fond spot in his heart for cactus. [opposition]

EXERCISE

What are the relationships between the ideas in the following pairs of sentences, result-cause [for] or opposition [but, yet]?

Our basketball team had an undefeated season.
Our football team lost most of its games.

Our football team lost most of its games.
The coach was really an English teacher.

The basketball team had a terrific record.
They did not get a national ranking.

What are the relationships between the ideas in the following pairs of sentences, cause-result [so] or opposition [but, yet]?

Our football coach was really an English teacher.
He knew very little about football.

He was a pretty bad coach.
The players liked him personally.

The basketball players were exciting and talented.
The students enjoyed watching them play.

What are the relationships between the ideas in the following pairs of sentences, alternatives [or] or cause-result [so]?

Our school realized it had to hire a real football coach.
We would never win any games.

We could have a team that played good football.
We could have a team that wrote great essays.

The school decided it wanted a good football team.
It started looking for a real coach.

What are the relationships between the ideas in the following pairs of sentences, cause-result [so] or result-cause [for]?

The school asked the coaches of its neighboring schools to recommend a new coach.
It thought they might know of some good prospects.

They all recommended that the English teacher be kept as coach.
They liked beating our team.

Finally the school hired a football coach.
Our old coach went back to just teaching English.

EXERCISE

The following exercise is like *The Swimming Lessons* except that you are not given the relationship between the sentences. Choose the coordinator you think most appropriate to join the sentences and be prepared to defend your choice by telling what the relationship between the sentences is.

Mervyn's Major

1. Mervyn Rutabaga had his heart set on being a physics major. He was hopeless at math.
2. He took extra classes. He got a tutor.
3. He could not pass the classes. The tutor couldn't seem to help him.
4. He worked incredibly hard. Everyone in the math department was willing to help him.
5. He realized he was going to have to improve. He was going to have to give up his ambition to become a great physicist.

6. In addition to his math problems, he was the despair of his physics teacher. His experiments never worked.

7. The other students could produce vacuums when they had to. Nature abhorred Mervyn's vacuums.

8. Mervyn's experiments were always unique. They inevitably proved that some basic law of nature no longer existed.

9. Mervyn finally realized that he did not have it in him to become a great physicist. He changed his major to English.

10. He believes that he can write the Great American Novel. At least he thinks he might learn to spell better.

Subordinating Conjunctions

Although coordinators enable us to express a fairly wide range of logical relationships, another group of words provides us with an even greater resource of this kind. These words are called subordinators. There are a great many subordinators, and there is no point in trying to remember all of them. Some of the most common are *because, if, since, although, while,* and *unless.*

Subordinators function in a somewhat different way from coordinators, the FANBOYS words. While coordinators go between sentences to join them, subordinators do not. Instead, subordinators *attach* to sentences, and when a subordinator attaches to a sentence, it turns a sentence into a *dependent clause*—that is, a group of words that is no longer a sentence. You will remember that coordinators can introduce complete sentences. Subordinators cannot do that; they can introduce only *former sentences*, sentences that have become dependent clauses. Go over the following examples carefully:

Coordinators

She entered law school.	[sentence]
And she entered law school.	[sentence]
For she entered law school.	[sentence]
Or she entered law school.	[sentence]
But she entered law school.	[sentence]

Subordinators

She entered law school.	[sentence]
Because she entered law school.	[not a sentence]
If she entered law school.	[not a sentence]
Although she entered law school.	[not a sentence]
While she entered law school.	[not a sentence]

The dependent clauses created by subordinators may come either at the beginning or at the end of the sentence they are attached to. Look at these examples, and notice how the dependent clauses are punctuated:

Because he was hungry, he ate the apple.
He ate the apple because he was hungry.
Although he ate the apple, he was hungry.
He was hungry although he ate the apple.
If he got hungry, he could eat the apple.
He could eat the apple if he got hungry.

Here is an easy question: When do we set dependent clauses off with commas and when do we not?

Subordinators show some logical relationships that coordinators also show, but they show some that coordinators do not show. Like the coordinators *but* and *yet*, some subordinators can show opposition:

We lost the game, but we were happy.
Although we lost the game, we were happy.
While we lost the game, we were happy.

Others can show effect-cause as *for* does:

She dumped John, for he wore cheap aftershave.
She dumped John because he wore cheap aftershave.
She dumped John since he wore cheap aftershave.

Subordinators cannot show addition, like *and*, or alternatives, like *or*, but they can show time and condition, which no coordinator can do:

Time
<u>When</u> you get there, I'll be gone.
<u>After</u> you've gone, I'll be sorry.
Don't leave the house <u>until</u> she tells you to.
You may go <u>as soon as</u> you are ready.

Condition
<u>Unless</u> we hurry, we are going to be late.
You can succeed at learning French <u>if</u> you really want to.

Here is a summary of the logical relationships expressed by the most commonly used subordinating conjunctions:

Opposition/concession: although, though, even though, whereas, while
Effect-cause: because, since, as
Condition: if, unless
Time: after, before, until, when, as soon as, while, since

You may have noticed that two words, *while* and *since*, appear under more than one heading. Because these two words can express more than one logical relationship, it is important to use them carefully so that your readers will not be confused about your meaning.

EXERCISE

Combine the following pairs of sentences by using subordinators. The sentence to be made into a dependent clause is underlined, and the logical relationship you should express is indicated, as in these examples (be sure to pay attention to the punctuation of dependent clauses in this exercise):

She had a baby. She took time off from work. [cause]
Solution: Because she had a baby, she took time off from work.

He was laid off from his job. He was a hard worker. [opposition]
Solution: He was laid off from his job although he was a hard worker.

Melanie's Masterpiece

1. No one can understand it. Melanie Birdseed considers herself a talented artist. [opposition]
2. Anyone is unfortunate enough to visit her apartment. She immediately shows them her last twelve paintings. [time]
3. It is absolutely impossible to avoid this fate. You can convince her that your ancient and beloved grandmother is dying and needs your immediate attendance at her side. [condition]
4. Melanie's paintings are so awful. They have never been exhibited outside of her living room. [cause]
5. She showed me her latest masterpiece. I couldn't figure out what it was. [time]
6. I stared at it. My eyes started to cross. [time]
7. I was trying my best to see something there. What it really looked like to me was a pile of tangled coat hangers. [opposition]
8. I finally guessed a wheat field. I knew she would never paint a pile of coat hangers. [cause]
9. I had actually put a foot through her canvas. Her reaction couldn't have been worse. [condition]
10. It was obvious I knew nothing about art, she said. At least she thought I would recognize coat hangers when I saw them. [opposition]

EXERCISE

What are the relationships between the ideas in the following pairs of sentences, result-cause [because] or opposition [although, etc.]?

Carmen decided she would go to law school.
Her parents felt that the legal profession would guarantee her a good income.

She majored in political science.
Several people told her that would be good preparation for studying law.

She spent three years studying governments and politics.
She would have preferred studying biology.

What are the relationships between the ideas in the following pairs of sentences, opposition [although, etc.] or condition [if, unless]?

Carmen did a minor in biology.
She would have liked to do a major in it.

She had reluctantly agreed to be a lawyer.
She tried to convince her parents that biologists could make a good living too.

She would become a prosecuting attorney.
She felt she had to pursue a legal career.

What are the relationships between the ideas in the following pairs of sentences, time [when, after] or effect-cause [because]?

She became a prosecuting attorney.
She could put a lot of people in jail.

She could punish the wicked.
They deserved to be punished.

She learned the law.
She could jail parents who made their children follow careers they didn't want to follow.

EXERCISE

The following exercise is like *Melanie's Masterpiece*, except that you are given no information about how to join the sentences. Choose the subordinator you think most appropriate to join the sentences, and be prepared to defend your choice by stating what the relationship between the sentences is.

The Chocolate Addicts

1. Almost everyone loves chocolate. John and Mary were virtually addicted to it.

2. They could not have at least one piece of chocolate every day. They started to twitch.

3. They were able to eat an entire candy bar. Their eyes gleamed with new life.

4. Their dispositions became sunny, and their coats got glossy. They were able to acquire a chocolate truffle.

5. John preferred chocolate with nuts. Mary was a purist who preferred chocolate with chocolate.

6. Mary liked a cup of chocolate in the morning and a piece of chocolate at noon. John preferred a cup of chocolate at noon and a piece of chocolate in the evening.

7. They did not get their chocolate fix when they wanted it. They got sulky and hard to be around.

8. One day John was ordered to stop eating so much chocolate. It was rotting his teeth.

9. At about the same time, Mary was told to lay off the chocolate. It was affecting her complexion.

10. They attempted to commit suicide by leaping into a vat of chocolate at the candy factory. They were saved by an alert guard and are now in a Hershey's Half-Way House.

REVIEW: COORDINATORS AND SUBORDINATORS

In the following exercises, you are asked to combine sentences using only coordinators and subordinators. You will have to do the following things in order to do these exercises:

- Decide what the logical relationship between the sentences is. (Be prepared to defend your choice; do not just leap at the first meaning that springs to mind.)

- Decide what words express that relationship. If the relationship can be expressed with either a coordinator or a subordinator, decide which you will use.

At first, you will be working only with pairs of sentences, but as you go along, you will find some triplets. As a general stylistic principle, remember that it is *usually* (not always) better *not* to join more than two sentences with coordinators. Joining three or more sentences with coordinators usu ally produces a sentence that sounds stringy and clumsy to most readers. For example:

John bought a cat.
Mary bought a dog.
They both really wanted a kangaroo.

The relationship between the first two sentences is one of addition, so putting an *and* there makes sense:

John bought a cat, and Mary bought a dog.

The relationship between those two sentences and the third one is op-position (what they bought is not what they wanted), and so one could use the coordinators *but* or *yet* or the subordinators *although, though, whereas,* or *while*. In speech, we would probably automatically use *but:*

John bought a cat, and Mary bought a dog, but they both really wanted a kangaroo.

That would sound all right in talk, but in writing it has a stringy effect. Using a subordinator instead of *but* would help a great deal:

Although John bought a cat, and Mary bought a dog, they both really wanted a kangaroo.

Or:

John bought a cat, and Mary bought a dog though they both really wanted a kangaroo.

Combine the following sentence pairs or triplets using coordinators and subordinators. If you think that some of the completed combinations could or should be joined with each other (for instance, sentence one with sentence two), make that connection also. As an aid to doing this exercise, here is a table of the meanings of the coordinators and the most common subordinators:

Meaning	Coordinators	Subordinators
addition	and, nor	——
alternatives	or	——
cause-effect	so, and so	——
effect-cause	for	because, since, as
opposition	but, yet, and yet	although, though, even though, while, whereas
condition	——	if, unless
time	——	after, before, until, when, as soon as, while, since

Jim the Consumer

1. Jim, who had been unemployed, got a job.
   He could barely afford to buy lunch.

2. He finally got a very well-paying job.
   He thought he was Diamond Jim.

3. His friend Robert advised him not to spend his money as fast as he earned it.
   He paid no attention.

4. He did not seek Robert's advice.
   He did not welcome it.

5. He did not know anything about either music or electronics.
   He bought a set of expensive stereo equipment.

6. He played it at full volume one evening.
   The mice all left the building.
   His downstairs neighbor thought the Russians had attacked.

7. His landlord ordered the stereo out of the building.
   It had damaged the foundation and cracked the plaster.

8. Jim had to get rid of it in thirty days.
   The landlord would move him into the street.

9. The landlord could not be reasoned with.
   Jim moved to a new place rather than get rid of his sounds.
   The mice moved back in.

10. Next Jim bought a lot of new clothes.
    His mother had chosen most of his old clothes.
    He didn't have the same taste in shirts as his mother.

11. Robert saw Jim in one of his new outfits.
    He closed his eyes.
    The glare off the sportcoat nearly blinded him.

12. Jim had to bury that sportcoat, Robert said.
    He would not be seen on the street with him.
    He would not even visit him at home.

13. Jim finally realized that his purchases were ruining his life.
    He began to rethink how he was living.

14. He did not do something about his spending.
    He was going to lose his best friend.

15. He hated to stop spending money extravagantly.

    He decided to save his money.

    He could become a college student and live happily ever after.

Transition Words

English has another group of words, besides coordinators and subordinators, that are used to show relationships between ideas. These *transition words* do *not* join sentences; they merely show the logical relationship between them. The most common of these words are:

however	moreover
therefore	then
thus	also

Understandably, some students believe that these words actually join sentences and punctuate them as though they were coordinators or subordinators:

John leapt to his feet in alarm, however Mary remained calm.

This sentence is incorrectly punctuated. Since these transition words do not function like coordinators and subordinators—do not actually join sentences—the comma above is wrong; instead, there should be a period or a semicolon, as in the sentence you are now reading.

John leapt to his feet in alarm; however, Mary remained calm.
John leapt to his feet in alarm. However, Mary remained calm.

Unlike coordinators and subordinators, transition words are movable; you can put them at the beginning of the sentence or after the subject or at the end. They are words you can plug into a sentence, not words you join sentences with. You can see the difference between transition words and the real joining words in these two sentences:

John leapt to his feet in alarm; Mary, however, remained calm.
John leapt to his feet in alarm; Mary remained calm, however.

A final note about transition words. Despite what many textbooks and some teachers say, writers rarely use specific transition words or phrases to make transitions from one idea to another. If you've been taught to use "tran sitions" or transition words, you can easily check to see whether what you've been taught is true or not. Go to the bookstore to where the freshman English books are sold and pick up a collection of essays, any collection. Then open it and start looking for the transition words and phrases you've been taught about. Look in particular for the so-called transition words— *therefore, however, thus, moreover,* and so on. See if you can find even one per page. See if you can find one every five pages or every ten pages. You will probably find occasional sentences and even paragraphs beginning with the words *and* or *but,* but you will not find the transition words used much.

Transitions in real writing are more a result of good organization than anything else. If your planning has been good and your essay is well organized, transitions will, for the most part, take care of themselves. That is, your paper will read well. If it doesn't, if a reader (or your teacher) finds new points coming unexpectedly, you have an organization problem, not a transition problem.

Don't sprinkle your papers with *thus* and *therefore* and *however.* It's a sign of amateurishness. Use the coordinators and subordinators instead—and work on your organization.

REVIEW

In the following exercises, you will practice using materials from all your sentence-combining lessons so far. To assist you with coordinators or subordinators, places where they should be used to connect complete sentences are marked, as in this example:

[subord] The defense attorney argued for his client's innocence.
The defense attorney was tall.
He was wearing expensive clothes.
The Assistant District Attorney presented a case.
She was wearing an ordinary brown skirt and jacket.
The case was more effective.
[coord] The defendant was convicted.

Solution: *Although* the tall defense attorney wearing expensive clothes argued for his client's innocence, the Assistant District Attorney wearing an ordinary brown skirt and jacket presented a more effective case, *and so* the defendant was convicted.

Look Up and Say "Cheese"

1. Flying and photography are technologies.
   The technologies are two.
   The technologies are relatively new.
   The technologies are in the history of human experience.
   [coord] They are still developing.

2. The photographs were taken in 1858 by a Frenchman.
   The photographs were first.

The photographs were primitive.

The photographs were from the sky.

The Frenchman was named Felix Tournachon.

[subord] He photographed Paris from a gas balloon.

3. During the American Civil War, the Union army occasionally used balloons.

    [subord] It wished to spot Confederate troop dispositions.

    [coord] Photography did not yet have applications.

    The applications were military.

4. [subord] Aerial photography was developed in World War I.

    Aerial photography was for military purposes.

    It found its uses.

    Its uses were most numerous.

    Its uses were sophisticated.

    Its uses were in World War II.

5. [subord] Aerial photography was absolutely essential.

    It was used for spotting enemy troop movements.

    It was used for locating targets for bombers.

    Both the armies used it extensively.

    The armies were Allied.

    The armies were Axis.

6. Bombing raids were devastating.

    The raids were on military targets.

    [coord] Every nation made efforts to fool the aerial photographers.

    Every nation was warring.

    The efforts were strenuous.

7. Both sides used camouflage and other forms of deception.

    The forms of deception included building fake airfields.

    They included building fake camps.

    They were building fake supply dumps.

8. Today, cameras are equally useful.

    The cameras are ultra-sensitive.

    The cameras are in airplanes.

    The airplanes are flying at more than 80,000 feet.

    The cameras are in satellites.

    The satellites are orbiting the earth at 100 to 22,300 miles up.

    [coord] They enable each side to monitor the other's military activities.

9. Pictures from weather satellites enable us to see storms.
   The storms are developing far out at sea.
   [coord] Aerial photographs can help in flood control.
   They can help by locating snow packs.
   The snow packs are unusually dense.
   The snow packs are in mountains.

10. [subord] We have made aerial photography a tool.
    The tool is for space exploration.
    One day we will see photographs.
    They will be of other worlds.
    They will amaze us even more than those.
    Those have been produced so far.

The Little Record That Can

1. A revolution has taken place.
   The revolution is in the recording and playback of music.
   [coord] This revolution has been felt.
   It has been felt in shops and stores.
   The shops sell records.
   The stores sell stereos.

2. The product of the revolution is the compact disc.
   The product is the most obvious one.

3. Compact discs are called compact.
   [subord] They truly are much smaller than other records.

4. [subord] It is only 300 millimeters in diameter.
   It is 1.5 to 2.3 millimeters thick.
   A long-playing record (LP) was still fairly large.

5. [subord] It is only 120 millimeters in diameter.
   It is 1.2 millimeters thick.
   The compact disc is much smaller.

6. Compact discs (or CDs) have advantages.
   The advantages are numerous.
   The advantages are over the LP.
   They have advantages because of the way they are made.
   They have advantages because of the way they are played.

7. They are made of a sheet of plastic.

   The sheet is thin.

   The plastic is transparent.

   The plastic is coated with aluminum.

   The plastic is coated with protective lacquer.

   [coord] They are almost impervious to damage.

   The damage is the kind that would harm an LP.

8. LPs, of course, had to be cleaned.

   The cleaning had to be careful.

   The cleaning had to be before each playing.

   [coord] They would become scratchy.

   [coord] CDs require no such preparation before use.

9. Even LPs wore out.

   The LPs were clean.

   The LPs became noisy quite rapidly.

   [coord] They were played by a stylus.

   The stylus was diamond tipped.

   The stylus scraped their plastic grooves.

   The stylus wore out their plastic grooves.

10. There is nothing to wear out a CD.

    [subord] It is played by a laser beam.

    [coord] Nothing ever touches its surface.

11. The advantage of CDs is that all cueing is done electronically.

    The advantage is final.

    The advantage is great.

    The cueing is of the disc.

    [coord] The CD player will find the selections for you.

    The selections are desired.

CHAPTER 4

Learning by Comparing

COMPARING AND CONTRASTING TO DISCOVER

In this section, the writing assignments require you to notice the similarities and differences between things. Compare and contrast assignments simply reflect on paper an organizational strategy our minds use all the time. To make sense out of the disorderly and, frequently, confusing world around us, we compare (note similarities) and contrast (note differences), draw conclusions, and make decisions or recommendations accordingly.

> "I think I'll spend my day off on the beach; I've had enough sky diving for a while."
>
> "Take Professor James's astronomy class; Professor Stone's is impossible."
>
> "I hate horror movies. I'd rather see a good adventure."

Whether they realized it or not, these speakers made decisions or recommendations after examining two similar options (two outings, two classes, two kinds of movies) and after taking into account how these options differ.

Scholars and businesspeople compare and contrast constantly, and not only as a means of making a decision. Close examination of the similarities and differences between two or more items often leads to discovery. Take, for example, the student who is trying to decide between going to a state university and going to a private university.

Here is Olivia, a young woman with her A.A. degree from Centropolis City College, who has been working as a teller for River Valley Bank for six years. She has decided that she likes the world of finance, the work itself, and the people she works with, but she is getting a bit bored with her job as a teller. To move up the banking industry's corporate ladder, however, she needs to have her Bachelor of Arts degree, preferably with a major in finance and banking or business. So it's back to school.

The city of Centropolis has two universities—Universal University and Addams State—each of which offers a B.A. degree with a major in finance and banking. Located four blocks from River Valley Bank, Universal is a private university whose faculty consists of people who work within the disciplines they teach. A bank officer, for example, may teach a course in estate planning. Because this university is geared toward students who already have full-time jobs, it offers classes in the evening and does so all year round. A student enrolls in one course a month, two evenings a week; at the end of the month, she begins another course.

Olivia is quick to understand the benefits of this plan. She can keep her job at River Valley Bank and not take any time off from work to attend class. Additionally, she can concentrate on one course at a time and take courses during the summer. If she goes to Universal full time, Olivia can complete her B.A. degree in fifteen months. It will, however, cost her $7,500—not including textbooks.

Five miles away is Addams State, a public university whose faculty consists mainly of scholars and researchers who teach full time. Its student body consists primarily of full-time students, so it offers most of its undergraduate courses during the day. Unlike Universal's students, State's students enroll in five courses a semester, two semesters a year. The B.A. degree in banking and finance takes four semesters to complete and will cost Olivia $400 a semester—excluding textbooks, but including parking fees. (Universal has free parking.) Although Olivia can plan her schedule so that she takes courses only on Mondays and Wednesdays, or Tuesdays and Thursdays, she would still have to juggle her hours at work and make up the hours lost by doing fairly dull bookkeeping tasks two evenings a week at River Valley Bank.

In making an important decision like this one, Olivia would be wise to make a chart like the following one to help sort out her options and examine the similarities and differences (and the pros and cons) of each.

Issue	Universal U.	Addams State U.
Location	Centropolis (downtown)	Centropolis (edge of town)
Degree	B.A.	B.A.

(continued)

Issue	Universal U.	Addams State U.
Major	Banking and Finance	Banking and Finance
Minor	None	Business
Cost	$500 per month	$100 per month
Length of Program	15 months	16 months
Student Body	People employed full time	Full-time students
Faculty	Full-time professionals who teach part time	Full-time teachers and scholars
Number of Courses	One a month	Five a semester

ORGANIZING ESSAYS BASED ON COMPARISON AND CONTRAST

How do writers organize compare/contrast essays? That depends a lot on their material and what their point is. In "The Myth of Violence in the Old West," in Chapter 1, you will remember that McGrath compares the kinds of violence characteristic of frontier towns in the nineteenth century with the kinds characteristic of our cities today. Because most readers know what kinds of violence and crime we have today but not most common on the frontier, he concentrates on the latter, referring to the former only occasionally to make his point—that the two are totally different.

In most compare/contrast pieces, you will probably have to concentrate equally on both things to be compared or contrasted. In these cases, two standard organizations are usually recommended. In one, the writer first examines all the important characteristics of thing A or phenomenon A and then does the same for thing B or phenomenon B in this organization:

Introduction

Section on A
    Characteristic 1
    Characteristic 2
    Characteristic 3
    Characteristic 4

Section on B
    Characteristic 1
    Characteristic 2
    Characteristic 3
    Characteristic 4

Conclusion

Teachers sometimes advise that the characteristics be taken up in the same order in both sections, but rarely are organizations quite that mechanical.

More often, writers will discuss them in what they feel are their order of importance, which may be different for the two things under discussion.

Another approach is to tackle similar and different characteristics point by point. This organization would look like this:

Introduction
Characteristic 1 of A and B
Characteristic 2 of A and B
Characteristic 3 of A and B
Characteristic 4 of A and B
Conclusion

A variation of this organization might lay out first the similar characteristics and then the different ones (or the other way around). Such an organization might look like this if there were more important differences than there were similarities:

Introduction
Similar characteristics of A and B
    Characteristic 1
    Characteristic 2
Different characteristics of A and B
    Characteristic 3
    Characteristic 4
    Characteristic 5
Conclusion

The most important points in working out an organization are to make sure that it fits your material and that your reader will be able to follow it. When you work on the following assignments, be sure to discuss possible organizations, along with their strengths and weaknesses, in class.

*A*ssignments and Readings

CHANGING TASTES IN TELEVISION: 1970 AND TODAY

As you know, society's tastes, like those of individuals, change over time. Fashions in clothing come and go, and so do fashions in entertainment. One of the many subjects studied by sociologists is just such changes in society's tastes. In addition to that, societies face different problems at different times. To take two extreme examples, the United States in the 1930s was in the midst of a terrible economic depression in which the majority of its population was unemployed, while in the 1940s, we faced a completely different kind of problem, the Second World War.

In this writing assignment, you have the opportunity to make your own comparative sociological study of American television in two eras, 1970 and today. Your study can concentrate on either of two characteristics of television then and now. You can either

study the changes in American tastes in television programing then and now,

or

compare the way television in 1970 and television today have responded to the major social problems facing the country.

In the following reading assignment is a complete listing of the prime-time (8:00 to 11:00 P.M.) offerings of ABC, CBS, and NBC for the first week of March 1970. Depending on which study you intend to make, you can do one of two things.

1.   You can compare these with today's television offerings by the major networks in order to see how American tastes in television have changed and remained the same over two decades. In this case, you will want to ask yourself what these changing tastes seem to indicate about American values then and now. How do we seem to feel about war? About violence? About traditional family values? About sexuality? About minorities? Have our entertainment interests changed for the better or the worse?

2.   You can compare 1970 television's treatment of the major social problems in 1970 with today's television treatment of today's problems. In the Reading section below, you will find a short list of the problems facing Americans in 1970. To do this kind of study, you will need to make a list of the 1970 problems and then, with your friends or classmates, make a list of the major problems facing American society today—for instance, the problems of homelessness, teen violence, and the AIDS epidemic, just to name a few. To what extent did television in 1970 seem to reflect the problems of the day, and to what extent does television today seem to reflect our problems? Has TV changed for the better or the worse in this respect?

Reading Assignment

Pre-reading

To make this study, the first thing you will have to do is classify the programs according to type so that you can see what types were offered in 1970 and are offered now. The best place to start your classification is not with the 1970 programs but with those you are most familiar with, the ones broadcast now.

Step one in discovering the types of programs can be either of two activities: (1) going through a week's TV prime-time listings of the major networks, establishing categories for the programs as you go, or (2) working out possible categories ahead of time and then going through the listings and putting the programs into the prearranged categories.

The first way has the advantage of enabling you to actually see what's there before trying to set up categories. It has the disadvantage of being work that no more than two or possibly three people can do together.

The second way has the advantage of enabling your whole class to work together to come up with the categories. But its disadvantage is that when you actually study the programs, you may find some that don't fit into your prearranged categories. In this case, you will have to be prepared to invent new categories as you go along.

In addition to establishing the types of programs shown today, you will need to figure out how popular each type is. There are two ways of discovering this, and you will need to use both of them. One is simply to count how many programs of each type are offered during the week. The second is to count how much time each type is given during the week. For example, your study might reveal that the major networks offer twenty comedy shows a week and only ten police dramas. That would seem to indicate that comedies are twice as popular as police dramas. But further study might reveal that all the comedies are half-hour shows and all the police dramas are sixty-minute shows; the two types receive exactly the same amount of time—ten hours—during prime time each week, and so, we can assume, they are equally popular.

The task of identifying the program types will be more difficult in the case of the programs from 1970 because, in many instances, all you will have to go on will be the titles, and from them you will have to try to figure out what the program consisted of. In some cases, the program listing will help you by identifying particular programs by type, and in others the brief descriptions will be helpful. Here is one hint, though: In 1970, as now, comedies were almost always half-hour shows, while most dramas were an hour long. Remember too that we categorize movies according to their different types—dramas, suspense, westerns, science fiction, and so on—and some other general kinds of television programs—in particular dramas—may perhaps be divided into smaller categories also. For instance, at different moments in television history, different kinds of dramas have been very popular—police dramas, westerns, medical dramas, and spy stories, for example.

Reading

In 1970, the United States was in the midst of three major social upheavals. For about fifteen years, the civil rights movement, centered in the

South, had been fighting to achieve equal social and political rights for African-American citizens. This fight was continuing in 1970. Since 1964, students on hundreds of American college campuses had been in more or less active rebellion against their universities for a whole variety of reasons, some of them having to do with the civil rights movement, some of them with rules governing student conduct, some of them with American involvement in Vietnam. In 1970, the United States was fighting the Vietnam War, and many in this country were demonstrating against our involvement in that war. In May 1970, just two months after the television listings below, American troops invaded Cambodia, a country neighboring Vietnam, and in huge demonstrations and strikes on many college campuses, students protested the invasion.

In 1970, the United States was a country deeply involved in radical social change and in a war, and it was very much divided on both of these issues. Do you find any of this turmoil reflected in the television offerings or not? Are there a large number of programs that seem to feature violent themes? Does television seem to be trying to escape into comedies and into the past?

Remember to read actively, making notes in the margins or on a separate sheet of paper.

NETWORK PRIME-TIME PROGRAMING

Sunday, March 1

7:30	NBC	"Walt Disney: Menace on the Mountain." A 14-year-old boy is faced with the responsibility of caring for his mother and family while his father is off at war.
	CBS	"To Rome with Love"
8:00	CBS	"Ed Sullivan Show" (variety)
	ABC	"The FBI": Erskine gambles with his life to effect the release of a kidnap victim.
8:30	NBC	"Bill Cosby Show"
9:00	NBC	"Bonanza": Hoss, an overzealous fan of a visiting actress, becomes a suspect when the lady's leading man is fatally shot.
	CBS	"Glen Campbell Goodtime Hour" (variety)
	ABC	Movie: *Sons of Katie Elder*. A western adventure about the efforts of four brothers to clear their family name. (1965)
10:00	NBC	"The Bold Ones": Doctors Craig, Stuart, and Hunter search for a rapid cure for a seriously stricken US Presidential aide.

> CBS "Mission Impossible": Phelps assumes a risky pose as a drug addict with information to sell so he can get behind the Iron Curtain and try to stop an unknown plotter from attacking an unknown victim.

Monday, March 2

7:30 CBS "Gunsmoke": An outlaw and his gang capture Dodge City and hold Kitty, Doc, Festus, and Newly hostage.

ABC "It Takes a Thief": Mundy's plan to steal a painting for the SIA pits him against his old nemesis, con woman Charlene.

8:00 NBC "Rowan and Martin's Laugh-In"

8:30 CBS "Here's Lucy"

ABC Movie: *Heroes of Telemark*. Drama of Norwegian saboteurs who make a desperate attack against a Nazi-held factory that produces heavy water for a German atomic bomb. (1965)

9:00 CBS "Mayberry, RFD"

NBC Movie: *Ambush Bay*. The story of a nine-man Marine commando group that prepared the way for the American invasion of the Philippines in 1944. (1966)

10:00 CBS "Carol Burnett Show"

Tuesday, March 3

7:30 NBC "I Dream of Jeannie"

CBS "Lancer": After a religious band saves Scott from death on the desert, he provides them with supplies for their journey west.

ABC "The Mod Squad": Pete announces he plans to quit his police undercover work.

8:00 NBC "Debbie Reynolds Show" (variety)

8:30 NBC "Julia"

CBS "Red Skelton"

ABC Movie: *Mister Jerico*. Two con men, one with **scruples** and one with none, are involved in the theft of the famous Gemini diamond. (Made for TV)

9:00 NBC "First Tuesday" (news)

---

scruples: moral principles

10:00   CBS   "60 Minutes" (news)
        ABC   "Marcus Welby, M.D."

Wednesday, March 4

6:00   ABC   Movie: *North by Northwest.* A Hitchcock thriller about
              a Madison Avenue executive who is mistaken for a
              CIA man. (1959) (Part II)
7:30   NBC   "The Virginian": A young gunslinger accuses Clay
              Grainger of doing away with his father and threatens
              violence.
        CBS   "Hee Haw"
        ABC   "Nanny and the Professor"
8:00   ABC   "The Courtship of Eddie's Father"
8:30   CBS   "The Beverly Hillbillies"
        ABC   "Room 222"
9:00   NBC   "Kraft Music Hall" (variety)
        CBS   "Medical Center": Shelby Grant plays a tour director
              who falls in love with Dr. Joe Gannon while he is on
              vacation in Mexico.
        ABC   "Johnny Cash Show"
10:00   NBC   "Then Came Bronson": Bronson's motorcycle trip
              through the mountains of the Big Sur country
              becomes a fight for survival against time and the
              elements.
        CBS   "Hawaii Five-O": McGarrett has 12 hours to find a
              test tube filled with deadly Q strain, which science
              genius Alexander Kline has **secreted**. (Part II)
        ABC   "The Englebert Humperdinck Show"

Thursday, March 5

7:30   NBC   "Daniel Boone": Daniel poses as a notorious river pi-
              rate in a scheme to capture a confidence man.
        CBS   "Family Affair"
        ABC   "Pat Paulsen's Half a Comedy Hour"
8:00   CBS   "Jim Nabors Show"
        ABC   "That Girl"
8:30   NBC   "Ironside": The detective fights to save an organiza-
              tion dedicated to rehabilitation of ex-convicts when
              a member is accused of a jewel theft.

----

secreted: hidden

	ABC	"Bewitched"
9:00	CBS	Movie: *The African Queen*. An adventure story of a prim old maid missionary who enlists the aid of a tough riverboatman for a daring and dangerous venture. (1951)
	ABC	"This Is Tom Jones" (variety)
9:30	NBC	"Dragnet 1970"
10:00	NBC	"Dean Martin Show"
	ABC	"Paris 7000": Brennan helps to restore the confidence of a former actor whose disfigured face has forced him into seclusion.

Friday, March 6

7:30	CBS	*The Trail of the Feathered Serpent*. Documentary of archeological explorer Gene Savoy during his 2,000-mile voyage on a raft.
	ABC	"Flying Nun"
8:00	CBS	"Tim Conway Show"
	ABC	"The Brady Bunch"
8:30	NBC	"Name of the Game": Despite the fact that she loves him, a magazine writer tries to prove that a building tycoon is bribing city officials.
	CBS	"Hogan's Heroes"
	ABC	"The Ghost and Mrs. Muir"
9:00	CBS	Movie: *The Sandpiper*. A vibrant and compelling love story set against a background of some of the world's most beautiful scenery. (1965)
	ABC	"Here Come the Brides"
10:00	NBC	"Bracken's World": Grant cannot get an author to change the ending of a script even though the movie is nearly completed.
	ABC	"Love American Style"

Saturday, March 7

7:30	NBC	"Andy Williams Show" (variety)
	CBS	"Jackie Gleason Show: The Honeymooners"
	ABC	"Let's Make a Deal" (game)
8:00	ABC	"Newlywed Game"
8:30	NBC	"Adam 12"
	CBS	"My Three Sons"
	ABC	"Lawrence Welk Show" (variety)

9:00	NBC	Movie: *The War Lord*. The story of an eleventh-century Norman knight who establishes rule of a primitive Druid village on the shores of the North Sea. (1966)
	CBS	*Johnny Cash at San Quentin*. Documentary of the singer's concert visit to the California prison.
9:30	ABC	"Jimmy Durante Presents the Lennon Sisters Hour" (variety)
10:00	CBS	"Mannix": Investigating a crime that involves a television commentator, Mannix realizes nobody wants him on the case, including the chief suspect and her twin sister.
10:30	ABC	"One Man Show: Jerry Lester"

Post-reading

When you have completed your classification of the programs from 1970 and from today and worked out the number of programs in each type and the amount of time given to them, you will *almost* be ready to write an essay on the similarities and differences between American tastes in television in 1970 and today. Almost but not quite. There remains one more question for you to consider as you look at your tabulations: What do your findings mean?

Suppose you find that in 1970 a large number of programs seemed to feature violent themes. Or suppose that you find an extraordinary number of comedies. You would then want to look at your figures for today's programs to see how they compare and to see what the numbers seem to indicate about us in 1970, us now, or us consistently as a society.

When you have figured out what you want to say, what your comparisons have shown you, what you have learned, you are prepared to write an essay.

Essay Assignment

Write an essay in which you compare 1970 television programing with today's and explain the changes in American tastes in television programing then and now, or compare the way television in 1970 and television today have responded to the major social problems facing the country.

For more discussion of this issue and suggestions about organizing your essay, log on to http://devenglish.wadsworth.com.

Pre-writing

This assignment could very well result in a book-length study, so one of your tasks—and a very important one—is to focus your essay. You won't be able to discuss everything you've discovered about tastes in TV entertainment, nor will you use every TV show as support for your points. What you must do is decide which changes or similarities are the most significant and which TV shows are the best examples of those changes and similarities.

Once you have decided on your main points, jot down a brief outline ordering those points and noting which TV shows you are planning to use to support them. At this time, write a working thesis to help you focus and direct your idea draft.

Writing

In your introduction, briefly explain your study and the reasons for it—what you hoped to learn about television programing in 1970 and today. Your thesis should point to what your comparative study has revealed to you about either the changing tastes of American audiences or the different degrees of social responsibility of major network television.

In the body of the essay, show first what your findings reveal and then explain what you think they mean. Review the opening section of this chapter for suggestions about organizing the essay. Be sure to review the Writer's Checklist on pages 231–233.

COMPARING AMERICAN FAMILIES IN THE PAST AND PRESENT

The concept of hierarchy is an important one in human experience. A hierarchy among things is a graded order. For instance, if you classified all your possessions according to their value to you, with those most valuable at one end of your classification scheme and those least valuable at the other end, and all the others ranked between them, you would have created a hierarchy of your possessions. Human societies often involve hierarchies too, because we consider some people to be more important than others.

Of course, in a society in which the concept of equality is particularly important, we don't like to think of hierarchies among people, although every bureaucratic organization, whether military, governmental, academic, or business, is organized hierarchically. But equality is in many ways a modern concept, and before the eighteenth century, hierarchies were considered to be the natural state of things in all aspects of human life. In those times, most people believed that the entire universe was organized as a hierarchy, with God at the very top, the angels next, mankind in the middle, evil spirits below mankind, and the devil at the bottom. On earth, mankind was at the top followed by the animals (with the lion as most important), then birds (led by the eagle), then fish (led by the whale). Even minerals were organized hierarchically, with gold, naturally, at the top.

It followed, then, that among human beings there would also be a hierarchy, and there was. The king came first, followed by the various orders of nobles, then merchants, and so on. People who deeply believe that all things must be ordered in hierarchies will naturally organize their own affairs in the same way—even when it comes to family structure.

In colonial New England, for example, the man was at the top of the familial hierarchy, his wife and children ordered below him. Over the past three hundred years, the concept of hierarchies within families, along with the roles, responsibilities, and expectations of family members in this country, appears to have changed dramatically. Or has it?

Reading Assignment

Pre-reading

Psychologists and sociologists who study families find that most families are structured rigidly with certain family members habitually assuming certain roles, doing certain kinds of tasks, interacting in predictable ways, and having clear expectations of each other. All of these characteristics suggest an individual family's values in the same way that the hierarchical organization of colonial New England families illustrates their values.

Before you read about families in seventeenth-century New England, think about your own family. What roles do certain members of your family assume—your parents, your siblings (brothers and sisters)? Who usually does the cooking? Who gets served (or serves himself or herself) first? Who is expected to repair the roof, do the housework, discipline the children, bring home the paycheck, pay the bills, and so on? What do the individual roles and expectations suggest about your family's values?

It might be helpful to make a chart to classify the kinds of tasks and responsibilities the various members of your family have. You would want to list those of the individual adults, teenagers, and children. This will help you see how your family is organized and, perhaps, what values underlie that organization.

Reading

The following passages written by and about seventeenth-century New Englanders and twentieth-century Americans discuss the roles, expectations, and values of family members in these two different times.

THE SOCIAL ORDER IN COLONIAL NEW ENGLAND

The essence of the [Puritan] social order lay in the superiority of hus- 1
band over wife, parents over children, and master over servants in
the family, ministers and elders over congregation in the church,
rulers over subjects in the state. A child might possess superior talents and ability to his father, but within the family his father remained superior. A church member might be the richest man in the
community, but his pastor held authority over him in the church. In
each relationship God had ordained that one party be superior, the
other inferior. . . . As man ruled over the creatures and as God ruled
over man, so parents ruled over children and kings over subjects. . . .
Servants were exhorted to regard their masters as gods and to serve
them as though they were serving God. Wives were instructed that
woman was made ultimately for God but immediately for man. . . .
All social relations must be maintained with a respect to the order of
things, in full recognition of the fact that man ought to make God
his immediate end.

Edmund S. Morgan, *The Puritan Family: Religion*
and Domestic Relations in Seventeenth-Century
New England

The Role of Men and Women in Colonial New England

Since marriage was an **ordinance** of God and its duties commands 1
of God, the Puritan courts enforced these duties not simply at the
request of the injured party but on their own . . . initiative. . . .
Husbands and wives were forbidden to strike each other, and the
courts enforced the provision on numerous occasions. But they did
not stop there. Henry Flood was required to give bond for good
behavior because he had abused his wife by "ill words calling her
whore and cursing of her." The wife of Christopher Collins was
presented for railing at her husband and calling him "**Gurley** gut-
ted divill. . . ."

The duty of a husband to support his wife was . . . [also] enforced 2
by judicial action. English common law provided that when a woman
married, her property passed to her husband and that he must fur-
nish her support. These provisions suited Puritan **conceptions**, and
New England courts enforced them. . . . James Harris was fined ten

---

ordinance: law;   gurley: surly, ill-humored;   conceptions: ideas shillings and required to give bond for good behavior . . . because of "disorderly carriage in his family neglecting and refusing to provide for them and for quarrelling with his wife. . . ."

In order to prevent adultery, the most grievous cause of divorce, 3 the New England governments did not rely solely upon the dread of capital punishment. To comply with the laws of God, Massachusetts, Connecticut, and New Haven made adultery a capital offense, but they seem to have carried out that punishment only three times. For the most part they sentenced offenders to fines, whippings, brandings, the wearing of a letter "A," and symbolical executions in the form of standing on the gallows with a rope about the neck. . . .

In seventeenth-century New England no respectable person 4 questioned that woman's place was in the home. By the laws of Massachusetts . . . a married woman could hold no property of her own. When she became wife, she gave up everything to her husband and devoted herself exclusively to managing his household. Henceforth her duty was to "keep at home, educating of her children, keeping and improving what is got by the industry of the man." She was "to see that nothing is wasted, or **prodigally** spent; that all have what is suitable in due season." What the husband provided she distributed and transformed to supply the everyday necessities of the family. She turned flour into bread and wool into cloth and stretched the pennies to purchase what she could not make. Sometimes she even took care of the family finances. . . .

Whatever financial or managerial ability she might possess, the 5 colonial dame remained subject to her husband's authority. Her place was "to guid[e] the house and not guid[e] the Husband." . . . She was expected to depend entirely upon his judgment. Though she clearly possessed the mental powers required for balancing family budgets, she supposedly lacked strength for more serious intellectual exercise. She never attended college, whatever intellectual prowess she might display in any secondary school. The accepted estimate of her capacities is revealed in the minister's exhortation to the Puritan husband not only to instruct his wife in religion but "to make it easy to her." She was the weaker vessel in both body and mind, and her husband ought not to expect too much from her. . . .

The proper conduct of a wife was submission to her husband's 6 instructions and commands. He was her superior, the head of the

---

prodigally: wastefully;

family, and she owed him an obedience founded on **reverence.** He stood before her in the place of God: he exercised the authority of God over her, and he furnished her with the fruits of the earth that God had provided. . . . She should therefore look upon him with reverence, a mixture of love and fear, not however "a slavish Fear, which is nourished with hatred or aversion; but a noble and generous Fear, which proceeds from Love." She was not his slave or servant. When Daniel Ela told his wife Elizabeth that "shee was none of his wife, shee was but his Servantt," neighbors reported the incident to the authorities, and . . . the Essex County Court fined him forty shillings. . . .

Her husband's authority was strictly limited. He could not law-   7
fully strike her, nor could he command her anything contrary to the laws of God. . . . In one respect she was almost his equal, for she had "A joint Interest in governing the rest of their Family." . . .

In describing the husband's authority and the wife's submission   8
it has been necessary again and again to use the word "love." Love was indeed, as one minister put it, "the Sugar to sweeten every addition to married life . . ." but it was more than sugar. The minister did not mean to imply that love was a luxury, a happy more than a fortunate accident to the Puritans. It was a duty imposed by God on all married couples. It was a solemn obligation that resulted directly from the marriage contract. If husband and wife failed to love each other above all the world, they not only wronged each other, they disobeyed God.

Morgan, *The Puritan Family*

[The Puritan woman] was responsible for the care, clothing, and   1
feeding of her family, whatever her social status. If she had servants, she had to direct them, see that they did their work properly, show them how to do certain things, look after them when they were ill, and maintain a watchful eye at all times. If she did not have servants, as was the case with most of the women in the early settlements, she had even less leisure, for she not only had to bear and care for children, but she had to cook and wash for the whole family without benefit of any labor-saving device; she not only had to make garments for all the family, including the menfolk, but she had to spin the thread and weave the yarn into the cloth for these garments. She also had to knit socks and stockings.

Louis B. Wright, *Everyday Life
in Colonial America*

_____

reverence: respect

THE ROLE OF CHILDREN IN COLONIAL NEW ENGLAND

It was the obligation of Puritan parents to make sure that their chil- 1
dren learned how to make a living and play their own part in adult
life when they grew up. Since girls in colonial times were expected
to become wives and mothers, they normally began learning how to
do household chores when they were very young, as early as five
years old. In most families, the oldest son would be expected to take
up his father's business while the others became **apprentices** in
some other trade or profession. Usually they began their training at
about ten to fourteen years old.

Every Puritan child was taught to reverence his parents. . . . 2
Thomas Cobbett advised children to "Present your Parents so to your
minds, as bearing the Image of Gods Fatherhood, and that also will
help on your **filial** awe and Reverence to them." According to Cobbett, filial reverence consisted of a holy respect and fear both of a
parent's person and of his words; a reverent child . . . feared to lose
[his parents'] favor, feared to cross their just interests, feared to grieve
them or fall short of their expectations. Moreover, he displayed these
fears in his outward actions. When he spoke to his parents, he stood
up. . . . If he saw his parents approaching him, he went to meet them
and bowed to them; he spoke reverently to them and of them, and
to express his sense of shame for his faults, he blushed and confessed
his unworthiness when they corrected him. . . .

Since the training for almost every trade was gained through an 3
apprenticeship of seven years to some master of the trade, if a child
wished to be free and able to earn his living by the time he became
twenty-one, he had to begin his apprenticeship not later than his
fourteenth year. . . . Of course if he was so fortunate as to go to college, he might put off the choice of a calling until later; for the mere
fact of possessing a college degree narrowed the choice: anyone with
a "liberal" education would adopt a "liberal" calling, that is, a calling
which required no manual labor and no long period of apprenticeship. About half the graduates of Harvard College in the seventeenth
century entered the ministry. . . .

When a child became an apprentice, he went to live with his 4
master and could not "absent himself day nor night from his Mas-

---

apprentices: those who, in return for food and lodging, work for others to
learn a trade;   filial: pertaining to son or daughter

ter's service without his leave." . . . The removal of a child from his parents when he was only fourteen years old or less seems a little strange, in view of the importance which the Puritans attached to family relations. The mere force of custom must have been partly responsible: apprenticeship was the only known way of learning a trade, and since the Middle Ages it had been customary for an apprentice to live with his master, even if his own home stood next door. . . . Not only were boys put out to learn a trade, but girls were put out to learn housekeeping. . . .

I suggest that Puritan parents did not trust themselves with their 5 own children, that they were afraid of spoiling them by too great affection. The custom of placing children in other families already existed in England in the sixteenth century. Foreigners visiting the country attributed it to lack of parental affection, but Englishmen justified it on the grounds that a child learned better manners when he was brought up in another home than his own. The Puritans in continuing the practice probably had the same end in view. Certainly some parents were not fit to bring up their own children . . . [and their] children became over-familiar, "as if hail-fellow well met (as they say) and no difference twixt parent and child"; there were too many children, the ministers said, "who carry it proudly, disdainfully and scornfully towards parents."

Such conduct was inexcusable, for by the laws of God an **incor-** 6 **rigibly** disobedient child deserved death. New England laws provided that punishment for a rebellious son and for any child who should **smite** or curse his parents; but rather than apply this extreme penalty, the courts directed another law against parents whose affections blinded them to their children's faults. When children were allowed to become "rude, stubborn and unruly," the state might take them from their parents "and place them with some masters for years (boyes till they come to twenty one, and girls eighteen years of age compleat) which will more strictly look unto, and force them to submit unto government. . . ."

Psychologically this separation of parents and children may have 7 had a sound foundation. The child left home just at the time when parental discipline causes increasing friction, just at the time when a child begins to assert his independence. By allowing a strange master to take over the disciplinary function, the parent could meet the

---

incorrigibly: incapable of being corrected or reformed;   smite: hit child upon a plane of affection and friendliness. At the same time the child would be taught good behavior by someone who would not forgive him any mischief out of affection for his person.

Morgan, *The Puritan Family*

MEN ASSUMING BIGGER SHARE AT HOME, NEW SURVEY SHOWS
Tamar Lewin

Working men have begun to shoulder a far greater share of responsi- 1 bility for child care and household chores, according to a new survey.

The study, by the Families and Work Institute, a nonprofit re- 2 search group based in New York, suggests that since 1977, when the Department of Labor conducted a similar study, there has been a gradual **convergence** in the way men and women in the work force use their time.

"You look through all these numbers and you begin to hear a 3 theme song about men and women," said Ellen Galinsky, president of the Institute. "There are real changes in what men and women are doing. For example, men put in 30 percent as much time on workday chores as women in 1977, but now it's up to 75 percent. We see that gap closing in lots of different areas."

One surprising result of the survey, the largest and most com- 4 prehensive of its kind in recent years, is that despite the rise in the number of dual-income families, children under 18 are getting some- what more attention from their working parents than they did 20 years ago, mostly because of the change in fathers' behavior.

Ever since the 1970's, when large numbers of women entered 5 the work force, working mothers have complained that they bore far too much of the load for the second shift, the hours of child care and household chores it takes to keep a family going.

What particularly irritated many working mothers was that while 6 they were frantically cooking, cleaning and arranging play dates, working fathers were spending more time on themselves than on caring for their children, a perception borne out by the data from 1977. But the new survey shows that has changed: working fathers now spend more time doing things with their children than they spend on themselves.

---

convergence: coming together from different directions

The survey authors caution that the time estimates are self- 7
reported, and may be biased by workers' view of what the socially
desirable response would be; the extent to which that bias may have
changed, or been magnified, since 1977 is unknown. The authors
also point out that time spent caring for children may overlap with
time doing chores, like when a parent is talking to a child while doing
the dishes.

But, they say, the data do seem to indicate a real shift in how 8
much attention children of working parents are getting—although
no effort was made to consider what parents actually do with their
children in that time.

Still, 70 percent of working mothers and fathers say they do 9
not have enough time to spend with their children. Despite the increased time men are putting in, 56 percent of employed mothers
said they wished the fathers would spend more time with their children, and 43 percent wished the men would do more household
chores.

The Families and Work Institute survey found that working fa- 10
thers spent an average of 2.3 workday hours caring for, and doing
things with, their children, a half-hour more than the average reported in the Department of Labor survey 20 years ago. Working
mothers spend more time with their children but their time commit-

Life with Father

A new survey shows that working men are spending more time with
their children . . .

Time (hours) for children for married employees working 20 or more hours a week
with children under 18.

WORKDAYS				NON-WORKDAYS		
	MEN	**WOMEN**			**MEN**	**WOMEN**
1977	1.8	3.3		1977	5.2	7.3
1997	2.3	3.0		1997	6.4	8.3

. . . and more time on chores.

WORKDAYS				NON-WORKDAYS		
	MEN	**WOMEN**			**MEN**	**WOMEN**
1977	1.2	3.3		1977	4.0	6.7
1997	2.1	2.8		1997	4.9	5.8

Source: Families and Work Institute, cited in *The New York Times* ment has not changed much since 1977. On their days off, both working men and women are spending about an hour more with their children than they did 20 years ago, with women devoting about 8 hours, and men 6.

Men are also spending more time, and women less, on house- 11 hold work than they did 20 years ago—and both sexes spend less time on personal activities than they used to. Over the last 20 years, women's workday time on chores has decreased by about half an hour a day, to 2.8 hours, while men's time has increased by nearly an hour to 2.1 hours in 1997.

Men spend about an hour and a half on personal activities on an 12 average workday, half an hour less than 20 years ago. And women have about an hour and a quarter of personal time a day, down a little less than a half hour since 1977.

Elder care was a widespread responsibility. A quarter of those 13 surveyed had provided care to an elderly relative during the preceding year. More than one-third of them had reduced their work hours or taken time off to provide that care, and men were just as likely as employed women to have done so. Workers with elder care responsibility spend an average of nearly 11 hours a week providing assistance, with men and women putting in equal time. . . .

The survey found that 85 percent of American wage and salaried 14 workers lived with family members and had day-to-day family responsibilities. Nearly half have children under 18 living with them, and nearly 1 in 5 employed parents is single. Among employed single parents, about 27 percent are men. . . .

The rise in dual-income couples since 1977 has been dramatic: 15 two-thirds of the married male employees with children under 18 now have employed spouses, compared with slightly under half in 1977. . . .

SINGLE PARENTS STRUGGLE WITH POVERTY
Jonathan Marshall

Recent evidence points to high and still growing rates of divorce and 1 births out of wedlock as major causes of poverty in America. With six of every 10 children born in the past decade destined to grow up at some point with a single parent, many experts argue that the economic impact of changing family structure has become a critical national problem.

Single parenting is a struggle, regardless of whether the head of 2
household is a man or a woman, but mothers still overwhelmingly
bear that hardship. They almost always end up caring for their children after divorce or abandonment and also face more hurdles in
the job market.

"The rise of female-headed families has had dire social and eco- 3
nomic consequences because these families are far more vulnerable
to poverty than are other types of families," University of Chicago
sociologist William Julius Wilson wrote in a landmark 1987 study.
"Sex and marital status of the head (of household) are the most important determinants of poverty status for families, especially in
urban areas."

Secretary of Health and Human Services Louis Sullivan under- 4
scored that message earlier this year when he called the rise of single-
parent families "the most important family challenge of the '90s."

Recent U.S. Census data tell a depressing story about the rela- 5
tionship between family structure and economic distress:

- Between 1960 and 1990, the share of families with children
  headed by women tripled to 25 percent.
- Households headed by women make up a rising share of the
  poor, soaring from 23.7 percent in 1960 to 53.1 percent of the
  total number of families living in poverty in 1990.
- In 1990, 45 percent of all families with children headed by a
  single woman were mired in poverty, compared with only 8
  percent of those headed by a married couple.
- From 1983 to 1986, the average poor family stayed on welfare
  less than four months—but the average single mother stayed
  on welfare more than 23 months.

Family breakup may be as hazardous to mental health and social 6
adjustment as it is to material aspirations, according to recent research by Princeton sociologist Sara McLanahan and other scholars.
Even though most single mothers cope heroically, they have less time
and money to bestow on their children, making it tougher to help
with schoolwork, enforce discipline and otherwise guide their children's development.

National surveys show that children living with a single parent 7
are 62 percent more likely to drop out of high school, three times as
likely to be treated for emotional or behavioral problems and more

than twice as likely to give birth out of wedlock than are children living with both parents.

Loss of Paycheck

Economists cite several reasons for the high rate of poverty among   8
single-parent families. The most obvious is the terrible blow to the
household budget from the sudden loss of one paycheck through
death or divorce.

Single mothers are at a special disadvantage, because women   9
generally make only about two-thirds as much as men. Not only do
some face discrimination, many have little work experience when
they are suddenly forced into the job market.

"We have too many homemakers in America who got fired from   10
that job," says Leslie Wolfe, executive director of the Center for
Women Policy Studies in Washington, a women's advocacy organization. "They didn't develop a work life because they thought raising children was their job."

Displaced Homemaker

That profile fits Conni Dean, a divorced mother of three who now   11
works at a kitchen design firm in Albany [California]. When her
marriage ended nine years ago, the best work she could find in
Shasta County was as a secretary earning $5 an hour, not enough
to cover expenses. Eventually, she applied for welfare to pursue a
college degree. Dean graduated last month from San Francisco State
University.

"I had a high school education and lots of training to be a house-   12
wife and mother," Dean recalled. "I had no real job training or salable
skills. Where I came from, women were not trained to take care of
themselves."

Dean also found that the high cost of child care was a "huge ob-   13
stacle" to supporting her family through work. California's GAIN program—Greater Avenues for Independence—made her schooling and
new job possible by paying for that service.

Other welfare programs may even have accelerated the trend   14
toward single parenting by giving poor mothers an escape hatch out
of unhappy relationships and less incentive to remarry. In many
states, women used to be eligible only if they lived with no husband
present, giving them a reason to split up or never marry.

Loss of Jobs

A more significant cause of single parenting, in the view of most ex-   15
perts, is the declining economic status of unskilled men. During the
past two decades, as many blue-collar jobs vanished, wages for these
jobs plummeted. Deprived of a stable job and significant income,
these men make less desirable marriage partners for women whose
own job opportunities have grown during the same period.

"It's wrong to suggest that marriage is an easy thing to do," Wolfe   16
said. "It assumes there is a whole bunch of great guys around to marry."

Prescriptions for coping with these trends are much more open   17
to dispute than the diagnosis. Most programs to aid the poor run up
against the dilemma that increased benefits tend to reduce the incentive to work and increase dependency, not to mention raising the
ire of many taxpayers.

Consensus gives way to furious debate when anyone . . . sug-   18
gests reversing family trends of the past three decades through reaffirmation of "traditional values."

Yet a wide spectrum of commentators, from Jesse Jackson to Pat   19
Buchanan, agrees that some change in attitudes is needed on the
part of teenage girls who get pregnant and young men who proudly
escape their responsibilities as fathers.

Supplying more economic opportunities for teenagers at risk of be-   20
coming parents may be a powerful force in shaping attitudes, according to recent research by economists Greg Duncan and Saul Hoffman.

Or as Nicholas Zill, executive director of Child Trends, a Wash-   21
ington-based research organization, put it, "You want to make it easier to be good."

Essay Assignment

**Drawing your support from your class discussion notes, the in-
formation in the preceding excerpts, and your own knowledge
of the past and the present, write an essay in which you compare and/or contrast family life in Colonial New England with
family life in present-day America and show the importance of
these similarities and/or differences.**

(continued)

This assignment is broad enough to result in a book, so you'll have to limit your discussion to one or at most two aspects of the topic. Perhaps you'll want to focus on the role of mothers only, or fathers, or children. You could also look at female roles in general or male roles. Concentrate on some aspect of the subject that particularly interests you.

For more discussion of this issue and suggestions about organizing your essay, log on to http://devenglish.wadsworth.com.

Pre-writing

In class, discuss the roles assumed by typical family members in seventeenth-century New England. Who did what? What was expected of the father, the mother, the children? *What do their roles and expectations show us about their values?* Be sure to keep track of the main points that come out of this discussion by taking notes; otherwise when it comes time to write, you will have forgotten much of what was said.

The next step will be to exchange information about your family organization with your classmates, perhaps in small groups. There probably will be a lot of variety in how present-day families organize themselves; and it will be important for you and your classmates to exchange information in order to get a clear picture of what some of the key differences (and similarities) are.

Based on the reading assignment and class discussions, come up with a description of what seems to be a typical late twentieth-century American family. It probably won't look exactly like any of your individual families, but it should reflect present-day trends. For example, you might discover that most students' mothers work outside the home, that many parents are divorced, or that some fathers do the majority of the cooking.

With all this information in hand, you will be ready to examine the ways modern American families' organizations and values differ from and are similar to those of New England during the seventeenth century. Again, you may find it useful to make a chart to help in your comparisons, listing characteristics under headings like "Colonial New England" and "Present-Day United States."

Writing

Your introductory paragraph should give a brief overview of the similarities and/or differences you perceive, mention what aspect of the subject you are discussing, and point to the direction your comparison/contrast essay will take. Will you emphasize the differences, the similarities, or both?

The body of the essay should give examples from the seventeenth century and the present to support your discussion. Review the opening section of this chapter for suggestions about organizing the essay. The conclusion of your essay should mention the importance of what you have learned about the changing or unchanging values of American families. Be sure to review the Writer's Checklist on pages 231–233.

EXAMINING AMERICAN AND ASIAN EDUCATIONAL METHODS

There is much concern today that American education is not meeting the challenge of today's world, that we are not educating our children to be competitive in the future with those of other nations and cultures. A study of American education found the system so poor that the study was entitled "A Nation at Risk."

While there has been criticism of American education at all levels below graduate school, the focus of most of the concern has been on what we do, or don't do, in our elementary and secondary schools. At the same time, studies have shown a much higher achievement rate in many aspects of education, particularly mathematics, among children in other countries and especially in Asia. The Associated Press reported in February 1992 that "13-year-olds from the United States scored lower in science than top-ranked South Korea, Taiwan, Switzerland, the former Soviet Union, Hungary, France, Italy, Israel, Canada, Scotland, Slovenia, and Spain" and that math results were similar. In January 1993, Reuters news agency released a study showing that US students in the first, fifth, and eleventh grades ranked behind Japanese and Taiwanese students in math, though they led in "general knowledge" questions. The math gap, however, got worse as the students got older. A *New York Times* report in April 1993 indicated improvement in American students' math scores in some states, but 75 percent of the students studied were still "below standard."

Reading Assignment

Pre-reading

Although you may not know a great deal about Asian methods of education at this moment, you know a huge amount about American methods of education in elementary and secondary schools. As a way of beginning to think about this topic, ask yourself questions like the following: How long is the usual school year? How many students are in an average first- or third-grade class? How large is a typical high school class? Roughly, how many hours of homework are assigned weekly in elementary or high school? What subjects are taught? How do teachers teach—by lecture or discussion? What do American teaching methods suggest about the values of this society? Which values appear to be more important? Which ones less important? Remember to take notes as you come up with answers to these questions.

Reading

In the following series of articles, writers examine various aspects of the differences between Asian and American educational methods and accomplishments. Be sure to read actively, taking notes in the margins or on a sheet of paper.

POOR MATH PERFORMANCE OF U.S. STUDENTS PROMPTS CALL FOR REFORM
Kim McDonald

Pre-college students in the United States are "underachievers" in   1 mathematics, compared to their **peers** in other industrialized nations, and their poor performance demonstrates an urgent need for a renewal of the U.S. mathematics curriculum, a study of international mathematical achievement has concluded.

The report, *The Underachieving Curriculum: Assessing U.S. School*   2 *Mathematics from an International Perspective*, presents the findings of the Second International Mathematics Study, a survey of the achievement of eighth and twelfth graders in the United States and 17 other countries that was conducted in the early 1980s.

According to the 125-page report, the mathematical achieve-   3 ment of U.S. eighth graders declined slightly compared to other countries in the 20 years since the first international study was conducted, while the achievements of twelfth-grade students enrolled in advanced mathematics classes showed only modest improvement.

Among those at the eighth-grade level, students in Japan turned   4 in the best performance, scoring among the highest in all categories tested—algebra, arithmetic, geometry, measurement, and statistics.

U.S. eighth graders were slightly above the international aver-   5 age in computational arithmetic, average in algebra, and well below the average in geometry and problem solving.

_____

peers: equals

Students in college-preparatory mathematics courses in Hong 6
Kong achieved the highest scores among twelfth graders, while
those in Japan were a close second in each of the six categories
tested—number systems, sets and relations, algebra, geometry, elementary functions and calculus, and probability and statistics.

WHY ARE U.S. KIDS POOR IN MATH?
Barbara Vobejda

A study to determine why American children lag behind those in 1
many other countries in mathematics has found that the attitudes of
U.S. mothers toward their children's performance in school differ
dramatically from those of Japanese and Chinese mothers.

While American mothers are likely to believe their children's 2
achievement is determined more by ability than effort, Japanese and
Chinese mothers stress effort as an explanation for achievement. The
Asian mothers demand more of their children and spend more time
helping them with homework, according to a study released today
by a National Research Council panel.

"In other countries, [the belief is] if you work hard, you're going 3
to do well," University of Michigan Professor Harold W. Stevenson
said. "The mother thinks that by helping, she can improve performance. In America they say, `The kid just isn't good in math.'"

In addition to the study of attitudes toward math among moth- 4
ers and children in Japan, Taiwan and the United States, researchers
compared mathematics teaching techniques in those countries. They
found that the Asian children spend more time in school, more time
in math classes and, in those classes, more time working on math
activities.

American children, for example, were out of their seats an aver- 5
age of 21 percent of the period set aside for math, compared with 4
percent for the Chinese students and 2 percent for Japanese students.

Together, the studies provide more clues to what researchers say 6
is the complex question of why American children fare poorly in international comparisons. "The classrooms are radically different,"
said University of Chicago Professor James Stigler. Stigler pointed to
a number of important differences, including a relative lack of coherence in American math classes.

In a typical American first grade, a teacher will run through a se- 7
ries of math activities, moving, for example, from measurements to
addition to telling time. "There's nothing that ties it together for the
child," Stigler said.

By comparison, a Japanese teacher begins the class by stating 8
the day's goal, then rarely varies from that topic, often spending an
entire class on one problem, but tackling it with different activities.

American teachers also spend more time working with individu- 9
als. In Japan and Taiwan, where the size of an average class is much
larger than in this country, teachers usually work with the whole class.

JAPAN'S SCHOOL SYSTEM
James Kilpatrick

Imagine, if you will, the first day of school in Japan. The 6-year-olds, 1
entering the first grade, are scrubbed and shining. This week's report
from the U.S. Department of Education on "Education in Japan"
paints the picture: "Entrance into elementary school is a major step
in a child's life, and Japanese culture goes to some lengths to dramatize this.

"Preparation begins several months in advance. A mother at- 2
tends meetings sponsored by the school that her child will attend.
The school specifies what it expects the child to know and be able to
do upon entry. Well-organized personal habits, polite use of language and traffic safety are among the matters emphasized."

Japanese children then settle down to an academic regime 3
that would scare the daylights out of most American families. In
the United States, the school year extends to 180 days of teaching. In Japan, the school year runs to 220 days. Students attend
classes all day Monday through Friday and half a day on Saturday.
After formal classes end in the afternoon, most students stay at
school for an hour or two of club activity or sports; a fourth of the
students take supplementary or remedial classes at private schools
called "juku."

What does the typical third-grader study? He gets eight hours a 4
week of Japanese, five of arithmetic, three of science, social studies
and physical education, and two hours each of music and art. The
Japanese language has two 48-character phonetic systems. First-
graders are expected to read and write both of them and to learn a
few Chinese characters as well. Each year thereafter they must mas-

ter an additional 200 Chinese characters. Formal training in **calligra-phy** begins in the third grade.

Children are expected to behave, and such is the **veneration** 5 paid in Japan to learning that the children do in fact behave. Moral education begins in the first grade, where the pupils are instructed in "the importance of order, regularity, cooperation, thoughtfulness, participation, manners and respect for public property." They are taught "endurance, hard work and high **aspirations**." Parents are expected to attend PTA meetings. Parents also are expected to rein-force the schools' training in "punctuality, neatness and respect for authority."

With few exceptions, all elementary schools in Japan follow the 6 same daily schedule and use the same textbooks and teaching mate-rials. All fifth-grade classes in arithmetic, for example, will be intro-duced to decimals and fractions at the same time. Children are promoted automatically from one grade to another. If a child has not mastered the work, tough luck. Slow learners are expected to catch up in "juku" or to be tutored by their parents.

The Japanese theory is that all children have the same potential 7 for learning. Therefore all children are required to learn large quanti-ties of new material and to proceed rapidly from one new concept to the next. "The plight of children who have fallen seriously behind is much discussed in Japan."

Not everything in the Japanese system seems to me admirable 8 or desirable, but some elements are impressive. Does the elementary program strike you as too tough? The high schools are even tougher.

WE SHOULD CHERISH OUR CHILDREN'S FREEDOM TO THINK
Kie Ho

Americans who remember "the good old days" are not alone in com- 1 plaining about the educational system in this country. Immigrants, too, complain, and with more up-to-date comparisons. Lately I have heard a Polish refugee express dismay that his daughter's high school has not taught her the difference between Belgrade and Prague. A German friend was furious when he learned that the mathematics

---

calligraphy: elegant handwriting;   veneration: profound respect;
aspirations: aims

test given to his son on his first day as a freshman included multiplication and division. A Lebanese boasts that the average high-school graduate in his homeland can speak fluently in Arabic, French, and English. Japanese businessmen in Los Angeles send their children to private schools staffed by teachers imported from Japan to learn mathematics at Japanese levels, generally considered at least a year more advanced than the level here.

But I wonder: If American education is so tragically inferior, why   2
is it that this is still the country of innovation?

I think I found the answer on an excursion to the Laguna Beach   3
Museum of Art, where the work of schoolchildren was on exhibit. Equipped only with colorful yarns, foil paper, felt pens and crayons, they had transformed simple paper lunch bags into, among other things, a waterfall with flying fish, Broom Hilda the Witch, and a house with a woman in a skimpy bikini hiding behind a swinging door. Their public school had provided these children with opportunities and direction to fulfill their creativity, something that people tend to dismiss or take for granted.

When I was 12 in Indonesia, where education followed the   4
Dutch system, I had to memorize the names of all the world's major cities, from Kabul to Karachi. At the same age, my son, who was brought up a Californian, thought that Buenos Aires was Spanish for good food—a plate of tacos and burritos, perhaps. However, unlike his counterparts in Asia and Europe, my son had studied *creative* geography. When he was only 6, he drew a map of the route that he traveled to get to school, including the streets and their names, the buildings and traffic signs and the houses that he passed.

Disgruntled American parents forget that in this country their   5
children are able to experiment freely with ideas; without this they will not really be able to think or to believe in themselves.

In my high school years, we were models of dedication and obe-   6
dience; we sat to listen, to answer only when asked, and to give the only correct answer. Even when studying word forms, there were no alternatives. In **similes**, pretty lips were *always* as red as sliced pomegranates, and beautiful eyebrows were *always* like a parade of black clouds. Like children in many other countries in the world, I simply did not have a chance to choose, to make decisions. My son, on the contrary, told me that he got a good laugh—and an A—from his

---

disgruntled: discontented;   similes: comparisons of two unlike things teacher for concocting "the man was as nervous as **Richard Pryor** at a **Ku Klux Klan** convention."

There's no doubt that American education does not meet high standards in such basic skills as mathematics and language. And we realize that our youngsters are ignorant of Latin, put **Mussolini** in the same category as **Dostoievski,** cannot recite the Periodic Table by heart. Would we, however, prefer to stuff the developing little heads of our children with hundreds of geometry problems, the names of rivers in Brazil, and 50 lines from *The Canterbury Tales*? Do we really want to retard their impulses, frustrate their opportunities for self-expression? 7

When I was 18, I had to memorize Hamlet's "To be or not to be" **soliloquy** flawlessly. In his English class, my son was assigned to write a love letter to Juliet, either in Shakespearean jargon or in modern lingo. (He picked the latter; his Romeo would take Juliet to an arcade for a game of Donkey Kong.) 8

Where else but in America can a history student take the role of Lyndon Johnson in an open debate against another student playing Ho Chi Minh? It is unthinkable that a youngster in Japan would dare to do the same regarding the role of Hirohito in World War II. 9

Critics of American education cannot grasp one thing, something that they don't truly understand because they are never deprived of it: freedom. This most important measurement has been omitted in the studies of the quality of education in this century, the only one, I think, that extends even to children the license to freely speak, write and be creative. Our public education certainly is not perfect, but it is a great deal better than any other. 10

STRENGTHS, WEAKNESSES, AND LESSONS OF JAPANESE EDUCATION
James Fallows

As Asian societies excel in coping with modern technology and schooling people to deal successfully in the world—we need to ask ourselves how they do it. Japan's achievements are comparable to ours, but its culture is so different that it makes a useful, revealing mirror. In Japanese education, there are aspects we should choose to emulate, and others that we would not want to adopt. There are real 1

Richard Pryor: famous black comedian;   Ku Klux Klan: white supremacist organization;   Mussolini: Italian dictator, 1922–1943;   Dostoievski: nineteenth-century Russian novelist;   soliloquy: speech, monologue problems in the Japanese system, and these should point us in the opposite direction. The problems fall into four main categories.

1. **Excessive pressure**—There is unrelenting pressure on Japan-   2
ese children, due to the *all or nothing* impact that school success has on their futures. School success means university admission test scores. Test scores are virtually the only factor that determines which students get into which universities. University admission, as opposed to grades earned in university, determines what kind of career you can have in Japan.

Getting into the right university is so lastingly important that   3
many students (especially boys) who fall short on one year's test become *ronin,* wandering warriors, taking off one to four years for full-time cramming for the test. It is obviously more desirable to start preparation earlier, so students at age 8 or 10 begin the famous afternoon and evening cram schools. It is no wonder Japanese students have so little room in their lives for anything but studying, or why the motto for so many is "Pass with four, fail with five"—referring to the hours of sleep they permit themselves. Japanese parents and teachers, to say nothing of students, complain bitterly about this system but feel powerless to change it.

2. **Sexual discrimination**—Japan's school system rests on a divi-   4
sion of labor between the sexes that would be completely unacceptable to us. With minor exceptions, men carry out economic and political work. Women are completely responsible for the families, including their children's education. Women are expected to have professional commitment to their children's welfare and are honored for their success. Although, from the Japanese perspective, this approach has worked, the country loses the benefit of female talent in the business and professional worlds and male talent in child rearing.

3. **Conformity**—Much of the strict conformist mold into which   5
so many children are forced has to do with the almost total centralization of schools. On any given day, you can walk through schools anywhere from Hokkaido in the Siberian north to Kyushu in the tropical south and find students reading the same chapters in the same classes from the same books. Written Japanese is taught in a way that requires students to use their right hands.

The emphasis on standardization leads to a high, consistent level   6
of competence throughout the nation, but it also constricts the

breathing space for children who do not fit or are not comfortable in this rigid mold. Japanese educators and parents urge us not to forget the benefits our diversity and individualism bring to American education, as they lament this weakness in their own system.

4. **Separateness and isolation**—Japan's teachers, policemen, 7 politicians, and business managers willingly point out that their society is relatively easy to run because "We are all Japanese." Today's Japanese population includes people whose ancestors came from Mongolia and Polynesia; there are also several distinct minority groups. But for more than a century, political leaders and intellectuals have promoted the idea that to be a Japanese citizen is to be part of one pure race, separate from any other, and automatically bound together.

The cost of this engineered unity is that the differences between 8 "we Japanese" and everyone else may be viewed as negatives. For instance, it certainly does not engender friendly feelings throughout the rest of Asia. I often felt while living there that every white American should spend a few years in Japan, not only to experience the culture, but to learn how it feels to be judged according to a stereotype a hundred times a day. If my children were late for school, I knew what was going through everyone's mind, because Americans are thought to be **indolent.**

Americans must embrace the opposite virtue. A multiracial soci- 9 ety is harder to run than a more racially unified one, but it allows us to use talents no matter what their origin. The American multiracial ideal (which is, of course, not fully achieved) seems far more precious after you see how much of the world runs on racial or tribal lines.

The Japanese system has truly remarkable strengths that we 10 should try to imitate or approximate in our own cultural setting. Some of them are the following.

1. **Emphasis on effort**—We should learn from Japanese and 11 other East Asian schools the cardinal importance of stressing effort. American educators complain that schools are burdened with moral and social missions that get in the way of real teaching. But the moral burden on Japanese schools is much heavier and more explicit, especially in the elementary years. The primary element of most courses

---

indolent: lazy

is how to be a proper Japanese, with the most important and consistent lesson being, "Try your best."

Japanese emphasis on effort and persistence in overcoming 12 hardship, however, may go too far by our standards. Efforts toward these goals include "Nude Kindergartens," in which students attend school shirtless all year to build endurance, and the practice of sending boys to school in short pants throughout the winter.

Do not be misled into enthusiasm for the Japanese six-day school 13 week out of belief that its purpose is principally academic. If Japanese society regarded a shorter school week desirable, the course content could easily fit into five days. *Length* is the point; it is part of an endless process of reinforcing effort. Nonetheless, we should learn from the radical idea that lies beneath this system. The more you talk about effort and the less you talk about raw ability, the more you build up the idea that all are capable of succeeding if they really try.

Much of America's school system focuses on early detection of 14 differences in **innate ability.** We give tests, classify, and track students in the belief that this will help them obtain instruction that is best for them. The Japanese system spends no time at all this way. During elementary school, there is no tracking. Classes are typically 40 or 45 students per teacher, and they all move through the same books together. No one skips a grade; no one is held back. There is ruthless separation later by exams, but selection is made as late as possible, *after everyone has had a chance to try.*

The need for this approach is a concept so radical that we can 15 barely grasp it here. The Japanese school system acts as though intellectual ability does not matter, assuming that just about everyone has enough ability to succeed. Japanese educators know that there are differences in ability, but they regard them as trivial.

The Japanese system contends that in normal life, determination 16 and grit will always matter more than theoretical, upper-bound potential. Differences in raw ability will keep most of us from being Albert Einstein or winning Nobel prizes, but they do not necessarily bar us from achieving most possibilities in life.

The full consequence of this view is that *the key factor in success* 17 *is within everyone's grasp.* Emphasis on effort encourages everyone to try and gives society a stake in developing everyone's potential. If we

---

innate ability: ability one is born with

took this lesson seriously, we would ask why we measure differences in theoretical potential, when societies that care so little about these differences do so well.

2. **High value placed on education**—Japan views the moral and 18
academic formation of children as the fundamental act of social survival, economic investment, and even national defense. Mothers and
teachers are viewed as soldiers are viewed in their homeland during
war. This devotion to education exists even though the Japanese
teachers' union is one of the few **strident** left-wing groups in the
country. Teachers are somewhat better paid than in America, but the
real difference is in prestige. To call someone *sensei,* or teacher, is the
ultimate honorific.

Students reflect this emphasis in a different way. A recent poll 19
compared high school students' attitudes in the U.S. and Japan.
When asked what they worried about most, Japanese students said
exams and study; American students said sex.

Of course, it is easier to say that Japan has done all this right than 20
to say how the U.S. could do the same. Japan values education partly
because of the **Confucian** tradition of rule by scholars, but also because of the shocks administered by **Commodore Perry** and **General MacArthur,** which taught the Japanese that they had to school
themselves to survive. We could use a similar shock to our system,
some modern counterpart to *Sputnik.*

3. **Collective responsibility**—Japanese education deliberately 21
builds a sense of collective responsibility and group well-being in
classrooms, communities, corporations, and the nation. The spirit is
easier for Japan to evoke than for America; Japan can fall back on
racial unity, along with broader emphasis on traveling, working, playing, and living in groups. However, the Japanese system takes deliberate steps that could be used in any society. Each class is graded as a

---

strident: loud, noisy, shrill;   Confucian: coming from Confucius, an ancient
Chinese philosopher;   Commodore Perry: US naval officer who forced
Japan to open its doors to international trade;   General MacArthur: US
general in charge of Japan after its defeat in World War II;   *Sputnik:* name of
the first satellite to orbit the earth, launched by Russia at a time when
American rockets failed to fly—the success of *Sputnik* prompted a major
funding of education programs in the United States

class; teachers talk to students every day about their group welfare. It would not be easy for American schools to develop this attitude, but the Japanese system goes out of its way to try, and the American system could too.

4. **Fairness**—By some measures of social equity and social   22 democracy, Japanese education and society may strike us as snobbish and unfair. **Hierarchy** runs through every aspect of Japanese life. Moreover, money has begun to distort the Japanese school system as it has ours. Because the cram schools are so important and so expensive, an increasing number of students who enter Tokyo University are children of the rich.

However, the fairness of the Japanese system has a different   23 philosophical base than that of Western societies. The most important fact about Japan's educational success is that average performance is so good not because the *best* scores are so high, but because the *worst* ones are. Principals and teachers are rotated from school to school every few years in an attempt to keep achievement levels uniform throughout Japan. This central control keeps one school, region, or class of people from falling too far behind.

Americans can learn about this kind of fairness from Japanese   24 education. We may have the most fortunate upper and middle classes in the world, but Japan has the most fortunate lower class. As our two systems have competed, the best bottom has proven more important than the best top.

Although I am not an educational specialist, I would like to offer   25 some personal suggestions gleaned from Japan's success.

- First, the effects of school and family are difficult to separate. In the short term, there is little to do about the high incidence of broken families in America, but something *can* be done about the economic harm that divorce often inflicts on children. Currently, the federal government **garnishees** our wages to cover the obligations we owe our parents through Social Security. Similarly, we could use the IRS to garnishee divorced parents' wages to make sure they carry out their obligations to their children.

---

hierarchy: ranking of people according to wealth or power;   garnishee: government seizure of all or part of one's wages to pay a debt; here, the social security tax is meant

- Second, we could **temper** the power and autonomy of local school boards. Every other major society has decided that all its students need to know certain things and meet national standards. I think America has to do the same.
- Third, we need to even out the funding extremes that make our best and worst schools so different from each other. We need to find fairer ways to pay for schools.
- Fourth, we need to focus on the real school problem—not lack of perfection at the top, but real failure at the bottom. Every time we talk about saving the schools, we should define the task as making the worst 30 to 40 percent much better, rather than adding Advanced Placement courses and further enriching schools that already perform very well. One way to do this is to expand Head Start; another is to generate a national spirit of service and crusade with a Peace Corps or National Service Corps that would bring talented young Americans or even foreign volunteers to work in our worst schools.

Although many U.S. analysts hold up Japanese education as an   26 ideal, a closer look reveals that the solution to America's education problem is not so simple. Because American schools are part of American society, they will always differ from Japanese schools—and so they should. In closing, I would like to offer American educators the challenge I addressed to American cultural, political, and economic leaders in *More Like Us: Making America Great Again*:

"Many of the practices that make Japan so efficient would sim-   27 ply stifle us. If, for some reason, America really tried to make itself like Japan . . . it could never be more than a second-rate version of the real thing. If it tried that, America would also give up the values that not only are crucial to its success but constitute its example to the world. American society is the world's purest expression of the individualist belief—the idea that a society can flourish if each person is freed to pursue happiness as he or she sees fit. If we think these values are worth defending, we need to show that a society based on them can continue to succeed. Fundamentally, we owe it to ourselves, not to the Japanese . . . , to make our society as flexible, decent, and democratic as it can be. But **chastening** examples from outside can help us concentrate on our task."

---

temper: reduce;   chastening: correcting or making better

SCHOOL HERE IN THE UNITED STATES
AND THERE IN VIETNAM
Student Essay

In the West, the educational system teaches students to think and to   1
experiment with ideas that are important. In the East, it teaches students facts and self-discipline.

In Western countries, people have more freedom, which means   2
that some students are not concerned about their education. Yet, to
look on the bright side, the instructors teach students the thinking
process and to experiment with ideas. The problem in Eastern countries is that teachers always force students to do what they tell them
to do; but the students respect themselves and learn more.

In Vietnam if the teacher assigns the student homework to do   3
but the student forgets to do it, that student will get in big trouble.
Not only will his grade be lowered but he will be suspended or his
parents will be called. Sometimes grade-school children will be
spanked in front of the class. In the United States, the teachers don't
care. If the students do the work, it's fine with them; if they don't,
it's okay. When I was just in the United States for a few weeks, my junior high school teacher gave us homework that was very hard for
me, and I got stuck. On the following day, I was almost crying because I was thinking that the teacher was going to punish me. When
I entered the class, the teacher noticed that I hadn't done my homework, but she said it was okay, not to worry about it. When she said
that, I felt as though I was in heaven. Since then, if I don't understand my homework, I just put it aside. As a result, I'm getting lazier
every day. It's like I don't care about my education.

In the United States, the important point is that the instructor   4
teaches students to think and to experiment with ideas. This is very
different from Vietnam, where we never do experiments by ourselves. In high school, I took an Introduction to Physical Science class,
and the teacher gave us a partner to work with on experiments.
Whenever it was time to do an experiment, I just depended on my
partner. While she mixed all the substances together, I just stood
there, and if she needed anything, I got it for her. Toward the end of
the semester, the teacher announced that the final would include an
experiment, and we had to do it ourselves without a partner. So during the last week, I kept asking my partner questions about how to
finish our experiment, and she took lots of her time to show me. But
during the final I was "dead meat." I flunked it.

Inventing the New World

One indicator of future wealth is the value of the patents a nation holds. It has long been assumed that the United States had nearly an insurmountable lead in basic scientific research, and therefore an ultimate advantage in the world's industrial competition. Recent studies have shown, however, that while the United States is strong in a variety of academic fields like environmental studies, agricultural sciences, and clinical medicine and life sciences, it is behind in areas necessary for supporting industrial advances: engineering, computer science, electronics, communications, robotics and instrumentation. Several studies have attempted to measure not just the overall number of patents, but also the number of important and influential ones—those that will most likely generate wealth and growth for a nation. These studies show a new world in which Japan is rapidly overtaking the United States. U.S. spending on research and development has only nominally increased over the past 10 years, holding between 1.5 and 2 percent of the gross national product. In Japan, R&D spending has reached 3 percent of GNP.

Source: World Rank Research Team

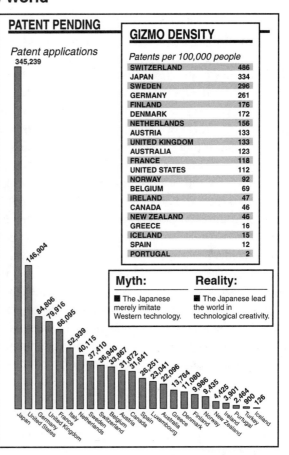

PATENT PENDING

Patent applications

GIZMO DENSITY

Patents per 100,000 people

SWITZERLAND	486
JAPAN	334
SWEDEN	296
GERMANY	261
FINLAND	176
DENMARK	172
NETHERLANDS	156
AUSTRIA	133
UNITED KINGDOM	133
AUSTRALIA	123
FRANCE	118
UNITED STATES	112
NORWAY	92
BELGIUM	69
IRELAND	47
CANADA	46
NEW ZEALAND	46
GREECE	16
ICELAND	15
SPAIN	12
PORTUGAL	2

Myth:	Reality:
■ The Japanese merely imitate Western technology.	■ The Japanese lead the world in technological creativity.

Patent applications: 345,239; Japan 146,904; United States 84,806; Germany 79,916; United Kingdom 66,095; France 52,939; Italy 40,115; Netherlands 37,410; Sweden 36,940; Switzerland 33,867; Austria 31,872; Belgium 31,641; Canada 26,251; Spain 23,041; Luxembourg 22,096; Australia 13,764; Greece 11,080; Denmark 9,986; Finland 9,435; Norway 4,425; New Zealand 3,901; Ireland 2,464; Portugal 900; Turkey 126; Iceland

SOME PUBLIC SCHOOLS DON'T MAKE THE GRADE
Richard Morin

What grade do America's public schools deserve? Depends on who's   1
doing the grading. Public school teachers and parents give high marks to the schools—but college professors and employers say the schools fail to give their graduates the skills they need to succeed in college or the workplace.

More than nine out of 10 public school teachers and two out of   2
three parents say the schools in their areas are doing an "excellent" or "good" job educating children, according to a series of surveys

released [in January 1999] by the Public Agenda foundation and Education Week Magazine.

But the people who deal directly and most immediately with the 3 products of the public school systems disagree—strongly. Only a third of all employers and slightly more college professors say that today's public high school students have the skills necessary to succeed in the working world or in college, the polls found.

Employers are particularly critical. Levels of dissatisfaction on 4 some key measures of performance declined dramatically from results of a similar poll conducted just one year ago.

Three out of four employers—77 percent—say recent job appli- 5 cants rate only fair or poor in terms of "their work habits, such as being organized and on time," up from 58 percent in early 1998. A majority of those employers interviewed—54 percent—grade recent applicants low in terms of "being respectful and polite"; just 32 percent offered a similarly negative assessment one year ago.

Perhaps it's unfair to hold schools accountable for students with 6 dismal social skills or bad manners. But it's quite fair to ask about the **3 R's**—and again, public school students were graded low by employers. Big majorities say young applicants are inadequate in terms of basic math skills (64 percent) and their grammar and spelling (80 percent), both up, but only significantly, from last year's poll. . . .

Post-reading

After having read the passages above and using your pre-reading notes, list the characteristics of Asian and American educational systems. You might use two sheets of paper—one each for Asian and American methods—and make two columns:

American   **Asian**

Another way would be to put all the advantages for both systems on one sheet and all the disadvantages on another:

Advantages   **Disadvantages**

As you do this, be sure to think further about educational methods, and don't hesitate to include your own ideas. For instance, an advantage of one system might seem to you to involve a corresponding disadvantage. When you read, for example, that Asian children get less individual attention than

---

3 R's: reading, writing, and arithmetic

American children and so their classes can move faster and cover more material, you might recognize a disadvantage—slower children are more likely to be left behind and feel defeated. Also, as you make your lists, be sure to identify which writer talks about which advantages and which disadvantages so that when you are ready to write, you will be able to find your references easily and to use quotations.

Essay Assignment

Because of years of declining test scores and behavioral problems, the American educational system has come under attack for failing to provide students with the basic skills needed for college and the work force. As a result, some people have suggested that we use the Asian model of education in our schools, while others argue that we need to retain our own system but merely implement it better. Write an essay in which you examine American and Asian educational methods, noting the advantages and disadvantages of each. Come to a conclusion about *either* which system you think is best for the United States and why *or* what combination of the two systems you think should be instituted.

For more discussion of this issue and suggestions about organizing your essay, log on to http://devenglish.wadsworth.com.

Pre-writing

Since the assignment asks you to examine the advantages and disadvantages of the two systems, your first step should be to study and evaluate your lists. Remember that you can go in two directions with this assignment. Either you can decide which system seems superior or you can pick out elements of each and recommend a combination of the best of both systems.

In the first case, remember that a system can be superior without being perfect. As a result, you may find yourself writing sentences acknowledging both strengths and weaknesses, for example, "*Although* the Asian system has X weaknesses, it still seems better in Y and Z ways." Because issues like this are rarely black and white, there is almost always much to be said on both sides. When you have decided which way you want to deal with the assignment, go back over your lists, grouping your points as you think you will want to use them in your paper, and make a brief outline. Also jot down a working thesis to help direct and focus your essay.

Writing

Although the basic organization of the comparison section of the essay might be pretty much the same regardless of your final goal, keep in mind a point about the actual writing of this section. If, for instance, you plan to argue that the American way is better, you will want your comparison paragraphs to focus as much as possible on the strengths of the American system. Don't ignore or leave out the weaknesses, but focus on the strengths.

The concluding section of an essay in which you try to say that one system is better will require some argument. For example, suppose you read a review comparing two restaurants. Let's say the writer had much to say about the relative good and bad points of each in terms of service, atmosphere, salads, meat and poultry dishes, desserts, and prices. Suppose the review claimed that one place had wonderful salads and low prices, but that the other one was really just about as good or even better in every other respect. Then the writer concludes, "And so I recommend the Bug-Eyed Lobster on Main Street over the Great Dirt on 24th because of its superior salads." You'd think, "Whoa! How did salads suddenly get so important? What about the other place's better meat dishes, great chicken, and only slightly higher prices?" And so on. A conclusion in a comparison/contrast essay really has got to take everything into consideration—not just one or two of the writer's favorite points. The real conclusion of the essay, then, might not be a single paragraph; it might be several paragraphs.

If, on the other hand, you plan to write about the best of both systems, you should focus about equally on their strengths and weaknesses: the strengths and weaknesses of the American system are such-and-such and why; those of the Asian system are such-and-such and why. Or the strengths of both are such-and-such and why; their weaknesses are such-and-such and why.

No matter what organization you use, the concluding section of an essay on the best system or the best of both systems should simply summarize what you think *is* the best. For suggestions about organizing your essay, review the opening section of this chapter. Be sure to review the Writer's Checklist on pages 231–233 for reminders to help you complete this assignment.

DISCOVERING INHERITED VERSUS LEARNED DIFFERENCES BETWEEN BOYS AND GIRLS

We have all heard people make general observations about one sex or the other: "Being more aggressive than women, men are better at business" or "Because they are more nurturing than men, women should choose careers in which they care for other people, like nursing or waitressing." Such generalizations are examples of sexual stereotyping—attributing certain characteristics or traits to *all* members of one sex or the other.

Like any kind of stereotyping (racial, religious, etc.), sexual stereotyping has both positive and negative effects. On the positive side, it allows us to understand quickly something about a person and to make decisions accordingly. For example, let's say a baker is asked to decorate two birthday cakes—one for a ten-year-old boy and one for a ten-year-old girl. The baker is far more apt to put a football player or a bicycle on the boy's cake and a ballerina or roses on the girl's cake than vice versa. Why? The stereotype of young girls suggests that they like to dance and smell flowers and dislike organized sports and other physical activities. The stereotype of young boys, on the other hand, suggests that they like sports and other physical activities, *hate* ballet, and have no appreciation for the beauty of nature. The baker's stereotypical response is a practical one. It saves her the time it would take to find out about the individual children, their likes and dislikes, and the chances are pretty good that the girl would prefer a ballerina to a linebacker on her cake and the boy a 10-speed to a rose.

On the other hand, the baker might be absolutely wrong. The boy might have a great career ahead of him as a dancer and choreographer, the girl might be a future millionaire tennis ace. This is where stereotypes, sexual or otherwise, become problematic at best and dangerous at worst—especially if they are so ingrained in society's belief system as to blind us to their fallacies. Not all girls like ballet; not all boys dislike flowers. What if the parents of Chris Evert, one of the greatest tennis players in the history of the game, had forbidden her to play on the grounds that girls aren't supposed to excel in sports? What if the parents of Mikhail Baryshnikov, one of the greatest dancers of the twentieth century, had refused to allow him to study dance because ballet dancers are "sissies"?

Clearly the "nature" versus "nurture" question and the resulting argument as to the benefits and detriments of sexual stereotyping are complex, multifaceted issues. We must hesitate to draw *absolute* conclusions on so complex an issue. We must instead think long and hard about the arguments because they affect us and our children, the next generation of men and women.

Even now we can look back at the treatment of women in Western societies and other parts of the world as late as the 1970s and see appalling discrimination, based always on the assumption that men are *naturally* more capable of performing most difficult physical and mental tasks than are women. Even in, say, 1960, the idea that women could become police officers, firefighters, executives of major corporations, or soldiers would have been considered ridiculous. Despite the fact that Elizabeth I of England and Catherine the Great of Russia, to name only two, were among the greatest national leaders in European history, it would have been impossible in 1960 to find more than a tiny handful of women in important political positions—and none as heads of state.

During the 1960s, women in the United States were going to college in great numbers, about as many as men, but when they finished their educations, they disappeared into the kitchens of suburbia. Some went on to graduate school, a few of these even finished and became scholars, a still smaller number entered the fields of medicine and still fewer of law, but the overwhelming majority of even the best educated simply became mothers. They were doing what they were expected to do.

The trouble here is that when you remove half of the talent from your talent pool, you get a society that is half as capable as it ought to be. Would American industry have made the catastrophic mistakes it did in the 1950s, 60s, and 70s, mistakes that resulted in economic domination by Japan, if all the women with brains and creativity enough to compete with men in business had been allowed to do so? We will never know, but the question is a reasonable one.

In our pluralistic society, one other matter arises having to do with this question. Many of our citizens are not far removed in time, and thus in cultural attitudes, from cultures other than North American. The United States remains a nation of immigrants, and immigrants always bring with them the ways of their native countries. In respect to the treatment of women, for instance, most Asian, Middle-Eastern, and Central and South American societies still treat women as inferiors, as people incapable of doing "men's work." In other words, there is not a single way in this country in which women are regarded or treated but a variety of ways.

Nevertheless, the question now is how to enable *everyone*, male and female, to realize his or her abilities and talents, without being stifled in some way or other by gender stereotyping.

Despite its potential for damage, sexual stereotyping has historical precedent. Throughout our history, women have assumed the role of caretaker and nurturer, and a lot more girls than boys take ballet lessons. By the same token, more men than women have succeeded in the business world, and flipping channels on any Sunday afternoon reveals the obvious—far more men than women participate in professional sports. These realities point to an extraordinarily complex and fascinating question: Do men and women behave differently because they are biologically predisposed to do so (the result of their heredity) or because their parents and society at large expect them to do so (the result of their environment)—the question of "nature" versus "nurture"?

There persists a considerable controversy over whether sex differences are learned (the result of environment) or genetically determined (the result of heredity). However, advances in the study of our biological makeup continue to reveal a much more complicated reality.

For example, scientists have discovered that men and women use different parts of their brains for different tasks, such as math, reading, or being sad. In addition, behavioral geneticists have concluded that about half of all personality differences are the result of heredity, with the rest coming from environment. To complicate things even more, the question arises, "Can environment create heredity?" (Can nurture become nature?) In some cases, the answer might be yes. In the March 27, 1995, *Newsweek,* Geoffrey Cowley writes,

> Men tend to excel at spatial reasoning, women at spotting stationary objects and remembering their locations. . . . Archeological findings suggest that men hunted and women foraged throughout vast stretches of evolutionary time. And psychologists Irwin Silverman and Marion Eals have noted that "tracking and killing animals entail different kinds of spatial problems than does foraging for edible plants."

Men and women may have developed these different abilities as a result of their environment thousands of years ago. Or they may have performed their different hunting and foraging roles because they already had these different abilities. We don't know the exact relationship between nature and nurture, or whether these are even the right categories for discussing the problem.

We do know that boys and girls differ in many ways because of hormonal differences. Boy fetuses, for example, receive a lot of the hormone testosterone while most girl fetuses receive relatively little. Testosterone, in fact, is what turns a fetus into a boy. But a professor of psychology at UC Berkeley, Marc Breedlove, reminds us of the central question when he stated: "There's one thing I know that testosterone does to masculinize [babies'] brains. It causes them to be born with a penis. And everybody treats the baby differently. I'm sure that affects the development of the brain. Is that a biological effect or a social effect? It's both." (*Newsweek,* March 27, 1995.)

In other words, psychology, environment, and biology are closely intertwined, and we still don't know the sources of most male/female differences. So as you read the following articles, keep in mind that none of these authors (and none of the scientists) has command of all the facts, yet.

Reading Assignment

Pre-reading

As a way of beginning to think about this topic, consider your own ideas about this complex issue. How much of who you are is the result of your being born a woman or a man? How much is the result of the way you were brought up—your family's training and expectations? How much is the result of your friends and acquaintances in school and in the neighborhood where you lived as a child? In what ways do young boys differ from young girls and vice versa? To what do you attribute the differences—genetic determination or socialization? (You may attribute certain differences to one and certain differences to another.)

Reading

As you read the following articles and essays, which address the "nature" versus "nurture" issue, keep an open mind and listen to what the writers have to say. Also, remember to read actively, taking notes in the margins or on a separate sheet of paper.

BIOLOGY INFLUENCES SEX ROLES
Tim Hackler

In the following excerpts from an essay appearing in United Airlines' Mainliner *magazine, the author, a free-lance journalist, gives an overview of the "nature" versus "nurture" issue, admitting to the influence of environment while acknowledging the importance of heredity. He uses for his primary example the relationship between the hormone testosterone (the "male" hormone) and levels of aggression in both men and women.*

Recent research has established beyond a doubt that males and fe- 1 males are born with a different set of "instructions" built into their **genetic code**. Science is thus confirming what poets and parents have long taken for granted.

Studies at Harvard University and elsewhere show that marked 2 differences between male and female baby behavior are already obvious in the first months of life. Female infants are more oriented toward people. Girls learn to recognize individual human faces and to distinguish between individual voices before male babies of the same age. By four months, a female infant is socially aware enough to distinguish between photographs of familiar people. Girls learn to talk earlier than boys; they articulate better and acquire a more extensive vocabulary than boys of a comparable age. They also begin to smile earlier than boys. . . .

Male infants, on the other hand, are more interested in *things*. 3 At four months a boy will react to an **inanimate** object as readily as to a person. Given the choice between a mother's face and a bright geometric object hanging over his crib, the boy, unlike the girl, will just as frequently babble at the inanimate object as at his mother. A

---

genetic code: inherited human makeup;   inanimate: not living few months later he will begin trying to take it apart. When boys and girls of pre-elementary-school age are asked to manipulate three-dimensional objects, boys overwhelmingly out-perform girls. Boys also show more rough-and-tumble play than girls—as almost any parent can attest—and tend to explore away from their mothers earlier and more often. Stanford psychologists Karl Pribram and Dianne McGuinness conclude that women are "communicative" animals and men are "manipulative" animals.

But to what extent are these sex differences learned, and to what 4
extent are they genetically determined?

Until recently it was widely assumed that most human behavior 5
could be explained by "socialization." In the heredity versus environment argument—sometimes phrased as nature versus nurture—environment was considered of overwhelming importance in determining human behavior. To suggest that any human behavior could even remotely be compared to the instinctive behavior that we see in animals was dismissed as barbarian. Indeed, extreme environmentalists remain committed to the idea that mankind is unlike all other animal species by insisting that heredity has nothing to do with the difference in the ways males and females act and think. If boys and girls were brought up in exactly the same way, they contend, then all behavioral differences between men and women would evaporate. . . .

In most animal species, and in all **primate** species, males are 6
more active, exploratory, and aggressive than females. The primate species *Homo sapiens* is no exception. In no human culture ever studied has the female been found more aggressive than the male. The argument that parents tolerate aggression in boys but discourage it in girls, and that therefore aggression is not genetically determined, but culturally taught does not stand up to recent evidence linking aggression specifically to the male hormone testosterone.

Numerous studies have shown that when testosterone is admin- 7
istered to pregnant laboratory animals, the female offspring show an increase in the incidence of rough-and-tumble play and a decrease in the tendency to withdraw from threats and approaches of other animals.

---

primate: animal group including monkeys, apes, and humans;
Homo sapiens: humankind

In a famous decade-long series of studies at Johns Hopkins Uni- 8
versity, Drs. Anke Ehrhardt and John Money demonstrated that the
same phenomenon seemed to be true for human beings as well. . . .

We have already seen that one of the most pronounced differ- 9
ences between men and women (a difference already present in the
first months of life and continued through adulthood) is that women
show verbal superiority, while men show "spatial superiority," a quality that shows up in such tasks as map reading, solving mathematical problems, and perceiving depth.

Researchers have found that this sex difference in skills appar- 10
ently has something to do with the organization of the brain. It has
been known for a decade that the two **cerebral hemispheres** of the
brain are functionally different, and that in the large majority of individuals, the left hemisphere specializes in verbal tasks, while the right
hemisphere specializes in spatial perception. It is only recently, however, that neuropsychologists have noticed that males and females
differ in their tendencies to use these hemispheres.

Dr. Sandra F. Witelson of McMaster University in Hamilton, On- 11
tario, was among the first to show that males tend to specialize in use
of the spatially oriented right hemisphere, while females tend to use
their left and right hemispheres about equally, thus implying a relatively greater usage of the linguistically oriented left hemisphere. . . .

It bears repeating that all of the sex differences described here 12
represent differences *on the average.* That is to say a minority of
women will be found to be more interested in "masculine" pursuits
than the average man, and vice versa. Also, there is some evidence
that the more creative the individual, the more he or she tends to include both typically male and female behavior in his or her personality. Finally, no experts suggest that the culture in which we live is
unimportant in shaping male and female behavior; indeed it is probably more important than genetic considerations.

It does seem certain, however, that the extreme environmental- 13
ist explanation for behavior, which has been so dominant in political
and academic thought for the past few decades, is no longer **tenable**. Males and females may, in fact, be marching to the beat of a
different drummer. . . .

The most commonly offered explanation for these differences is 14
that such a division of skills had survival value for our ancestors, when

cerebral hemispheres: halves of the brain;   tenable: defensible men were specialized for skills involved in hunting, and women were specialized for skills involved in rearing children and tending to domestic tasks. (There is some evidence that women may have invented pottery, and it is almost certain that in most cultures they tended to the sewing. This is reflected today in the fact that women are able to perform better at manual dexterity tasks involving fine finger coordination than men.) Even though such division of tasks may have less survival value today than for our ancestors, such specialization has, to some extent, found its way into our genes, since mankind existed in a hunter/gatherer state for the first 99 percent of his history.

SOCIETY DETERMINES SEX ROLES
Janet Saltzman Chafetz

In the following excerpts from an essay that appeared in Masculine/Feminine *or Human?, the writer argues that the influence of the environment (culture) begins at birth and determines how men and women perceive themselves throughout life.*

A baby is born knowing nothing, but full of potential. The process   1
by which an individual becomes a creature of society, a socialized human being reflecting culturally defined roles and norms, is complex and as yet imperfectly understood. It is evident, however, that most individuals eventually reflect societal definitions more or less well; most males born and raised in America will someday think and behave like other American males in many important ways and not, for instance, like their Japanese counterparts. Through the **socialization** process humans come to more or less completely **internalize** the roles, norms, and values appropriate to the culture and subculture within which they function. . . .

The first crucial question asked by the parents of a newborn baby   2
is "what is it? A boy or a girl?" Only later will they be concerned with any other attribute of the infant, even its physical condition; the first priority is to establish its sex.

. . . When the proud father lifts his infant he might jostle it just a   3
little if it's a boy; he will pet and cuddle it if it's a girl. In the months that follow, mother will speak to the infant more if it happens to be

---

socialization: adaptation to the needs of society;   internalize: make a part of one's own thinking female—and later everyone will wonder why it is that young girls show greater linguistic skills than boys. Father will continue to play a bit rough with the infant if the child is male. Both parents will discourage a male toddler from "clinging"—but not his sister. Research shows that up to six months of age, male infants receive more physical contact from their mothers than do female babies . . . while after that males are more quickly and totally discouraged from such contact. . . .

From the beginning of life, the objects that surround an infant, 4 including the clothes in which it is dressed, reflect its sex. Laurel Walum (*The Dynamics of Sex and Gender: A Sociological Perspective*) points out that "there are different styles and colors for male and female babies in such basics as cribs, potty seats, comforters, changing tables, diaper pins, and toys. . . ." A little later in life, parents will devote hours to combing *her* hair and putting decorations in it and will **bedeck** *her* with jewelry, but they will look with horror on *his* games with mother's lipstick or clothes. Jane will often be attired in dresses and told not to get dirty and not to do anything that will let her "underpants show"; Dick will be in trousers with no such restrictions—and later everyone will say that girls are **innately** less well physically coordinated and weaker than boys. And so begins the life and training of these new human beings. . . .

The parents of the little girl relate to her as a breakable object to 5 be carefully tended, protected and beautified; the little boy's parents treat him as self-reliant, physically active, even "tough," and not very emotionally expressive. These images are undoubtedly learned by the children. In addition, children are verbally instructed and **sanctioned** for doing or refraining from certain things according to sex. . . . These restrictions and encouragements serve to "define reality" for children in self-fulfilling ways. If little Jane is assumed to be weak, in need of protection, and an ornamental thing, she will be clothed in apparel reflecting these attributes and informed not to do anything out of keeping with her attire. Unable to swing on the jungle gym and still live up to her parents' image of her and the **strictures** they impose, she will most certainly fail to develop her muscles; ultimately, she will indeed be weak, in need of protection, and engrossed in her own appearance.

---

bedeck: adorn;   innately: possessing at birth;   sanctioned: given approval; strictures: restrictions, limitations

THE OTHER DIFFERENCE BETWEEN BOYS AND GIRLS
Richard M. Restak

In the following essay, the author, a neurologist, discusses the biological evidence supporting the idea that boys think differently than girls. We must admit these differences, his thesis goes, because if we don't, we will increase—rather than decrease—social inequality between the sexes.

There is no denying it: Boys think differently from girls. Even though 1 recent brain-research evidence is controversial, that conclusion seems inescapable. I know how offensive that will sound to feminists and others committed to overcoming sexual stereotypes. But social equality for men and women really depends on recognizing these differences in brain behavior.

At present, schooling and testing discriminate against both 2 sexes, ignoring differences that have been observed by parents and educators for years. Boys suffer in elementary-school classrooms, which are ideally suited to the way girls think. Girls suffer later, when they must take scholarship tests that are geared for male performance.

Anyone who has spent time with children in a playground or 3 school setting is aware of differences in the ways boys and girls respond to similar situations. For example, at a birthday party for five-year-olds it's not usually the girls who pull hair, throw punches or smear each other with food.

Typically, such differences are explained on a cultural basis. Boys 4 are expected to be more aggressive and play rough games, while girls are presumably encouraged to be gentle and nonassertive. After years of exposure to such expectations, the theory goes, men and women wind up with widely varying behavioral and intellectual **repertoires**. As a **corollary**, many people believe that if child-rearing practices could be equalized and sexual stereotypes eliminated, most of these differences would eventually disappear. The true state of affairs is not that simple.

Undoubtedly, many differences traditionally believed to exist be- 5 tween the sexes are based on stereotypes, but evidence from recent brain research indicates that some behavioral differences between men and women are based on differences in brain functioning that

---

repertoires: ranges of skills and accomplishments;   corollary: result, effect

are biologically inherent and unlikely to be changed by cultural factors alone.

One clue to brain differences between the sexes came from ob-   6
servation of infants. One study found that from shortly after birth,
females are more sensitive to certain types of sounds, particularly to
a mother's voice. In a laboratory, if the sound of the mother's voice
is displaced to another part of the room, female babies react while
males usually seem oblivious to the displacement. Female babies are
also more easily startled by loud noises. . . .

Female infants speak sooner, have larger vocabularies and rarely   7
demonstrate speech defects. . . . Girls exceed boys in language abilities, and this early linguistic bias often prevails throughout life. Girls
read sooner, learn foreign languages more easily and, as a result, are
more likely to enter occupations involving language mastery.

Boys, in contrast, show an early visual superiority. They are also   8
clumsier, performing poorly at something like arranging a row of
beads, but excel at other activities calling on total body coordination. Their attentional mechanisms are also different. A boy will react
to an inanimate object as quickly as he will to a person. A male baby
will often ignore the mother and babble to a blinking light, **fixate**
on a geometric figure and, at a later point, manipulate it and attempt
to take it apart. . . .

There is evidence that some of these differences in performance   9
are differences in brain organization between boys and girls. Overall,
verbal and spatial abilities in boys tend to be "packaged" into different hemispheres: the right hemisphere for nonverbal tasks, the left
for verbal tasks. But in girls nonverbal and verbal skills are likely to be
found on both sides of the brain. The hemispheres of women's brains
may be less specialized for these functions. . . .

We now have the opportunity, based on emerging evidence of   10
sex differences in brain functioning, to restructure elementary grades
so that boys find their initial educational contacts less stressful. At
more advanced levels of instruction, teaching methods could incorporate verbal and linguistic approaches to physics, engineering and
architecture (to mention only three fields where women are conspic-
uously underrepresented).

The alternative is to do nothing about brain differences. There is   11
something to be said for this approach, too. In the recent past, en-

---

fixate: concentrate

hanced social benefit has usually resulted from stressing the similarities between people rather than their differences. We ignore brain-sex differences, however, at the risk of confusing biology with sociology, and wishful thinking with scientific fact.

GROWING UP FREE: RAISING YOUR CHILD IN THE 80'S
Letty Cottin Pogrebin

In this excerpt from her book, Letty Cottin Pogrebin discusses the sex role stereotypes children have acquired at different stages of their development.

The Preschool Child

Because children have to decode two sex roles—the one to play and 1 the one to avoid—each sex must be familiar with the approved "norms" for the other sex.

This is an acquired talent. Before age two, there is little evidence 2 of sex-typed awareness or preferences, but by two-and-a-half or three, both girls and boys know which toys "belong" to each sex and which tools, appliances, clothing, and activities go with mommies or daddies.

Between infancy and early adolescence, research shows that 3 more boys than girls feel heavily pressured by sex role standards. For example, to protect their "masculine" image, tiny little boys will assiduously deny themselves a highly attractive "feminine" toy and choose to play with an unappealing sex-neutral toy instead, whereas girls feel free to pick the "opposite" sex toy if it is more attractive, and they don't give the boring neutral toy a second glance.

In nursery school, boys who cross the sex line to play with dolls, 4 dress-up clothes, kitchen toys, or art materials are criticized by their classmates six times as often as other children, while girls who try out such "masculine" activities as blocks, hammers, transportation toys, or sandbox play may be ignored by their peers but are not criticized.

Kids don't just know sex linkages, they have a pretty clear pic- 5 ture of the power differences involved. A child between about three and five knows enough to say, "Mommy never really has things belong to her." Or "He's the daddy so it's his but he shares nice with the mommy."

Preschoolers' ideas about adult occupations are already **ossified** 6 stereotypes. I often tell the story of a friend who took a childrearing

---

ossified: become set in a rigid pattern

leave of absence from her job as a newspaper reporter. One day, when her three-year-old, Sarah, expressed interest in a TV story about a crime reporter, my friend decided to explain her own career: "Before you were born, I used to have a job like that," the mother said, building to a simple but exciting description of journalism. "I went to fires or to the police station and the stories I wrote were printed in the newspaper with my name on them."

After listening attentively, Sarah asked, "Mommy, when you had   7
this job before I was born, did you used to be a man?"

What necessitated the magical thinking that turned her mother   8
into a man was Sarah's inability to associate the exciting job of a newspaper reporter with the female sex.

Seventy Wisconsin children, ages three to five, had much the   9
same problem. When asked "What do you want to be when you grow up?" the boys mentioned fourteen occupations: fireman, policeman, father/husband, older person, digger, dentist, astronaut, cowboy, truck-driver, engineer, baseball player, doctor, Superman, and the Six-Million-Dollar Man. Girls named eleven categories: mother/sister, nurse, ballerina, older person, dentist, teacher, babysitter, baton-twirler, iceskater, princess, and cowgirl.

Next, the children were polled on their more realistic expecta- 10
tions: "What do you think you *really* will be?" they were asked. The girls altered their choices toward even more traditional roles—changing from ballerina, nurse, and dentist, to mother—while the boys changed to *more* active, adventurous futures—for instance, from husband to fireman.

Pittsburgh children of the same ages were asked "What do you 11
want to be when you grow up?" followed by "If you were a boy (girl), what would you be when you grow up?" For the first question, most chose stereotyped careers: policeman, sports star, cowboy, and one "aspiring spy" for the boys; nursing and the like for the girls. To the second—what they would be if they were the "opposite" sex—the children answered with stereotyped other-sex occupations as well. But their *reactions* to that second question were striking: The boys were shocked at the very *idea* of being a girl. Most had never thought of it before, some refused to think about it, and one "put his hands to his head and sighed. 'Oh, if I were a girl I'd have to grow up to be nothing.'"

The girls, on the other hand, obviously had thought about the 12
question a great deal. Most had an answer ready. "Several girls mentioned that this other-sex occupational ambition was their *true* ambi-

tion, but one that could not be realized because of their sex." More **poignantly**, the gender barrier had become so formidable that it even blocked out fantasies and dreams. "Thus, one blond moppet confided that what she really wanted to do when she grew up was fly like a bird. 'But I'll never do it,' she sighed, 'because I'm not a boy.'"

Stereotypes According to Five- to Eleven-Year-Olds

When kindergarten children were asked to imagine a typical day in 13 their futures, the girls talked about getting up to clean house and feed the baby; the boys talked about performing an operation and being on a space ship.

To find out whether children increase their knowledge of sex 14 stereotypes between kindergarten and fourth grade, researchers showed children pictures of a man and a woman and asked which one would match a range of behaviors or characteristics. For example, "One of these people is a bully. They are always pushing people around and getting into fights. Which person gets into fights?" Or, "One of these people is emotional. They cry when something good happens as well as when everything goes wrong. Which is the emotional person?"

Additional questions elicited information about which person 15 daydreams, owns a store, talks a lot, says bad words, is confident, and so on. Comparing the age groups, examiners found an increase in the number of items stereotyped between kindergarten and second grade, but no change between second and fourth grade—which suggests that with the basic stereotypes under their belts, children need little additional elaboration.

One more intriguing result: *Both girls and boys learn the male* 16 *stereotype earlier than the female one. The male ideal obviously demands greater attention.*

By age five or six, almost all children claim (in their own vocabu- 17 laries, of course) that every male is more powerful, invulnerable, **punitive**, aggressive, fearless, and competent than every female.

Eight- to eleven-year-old boys say that adult men need to make 18 decisions, protect women and children in emergencies, do hard labor and dirty work, fix things, support their families, get along with their wives, and teach their children right from wrong. Men are the boss, control the money, get the most comfortable chair and the daily papers, get mad a lot but laugh and make jokes more than women do and are more fun to be with.

---

poignantly: emotionally appealing, touchingly;   punitive: punishing

The boys say that female adults are indecisive, afraid of many   19
things, get tired a lot, need help often, stay home most of the time,
are **squeamish**, don't like adventure, are helpless in emergencies, do
things the wrong way, and are not very intelligent. Women always
"have to keep things neat and tidy, take the pep out of things, easily
become jealous and envy their husbands, feel sad more often than
men, and are pests to have along on an adventure."

Eight- to eleven-year-old girls have similar stereotypes in their   20
repertoire: child care, the interior of the house, clothes and food are
"feminine"; manipulation of the physical environment, machines,
transportation, the structure of the house, most recreation, and most
occupations are "masculine."

Primary school children also classify being good at games as   21
"masculine," being quiet as "feminine." Trucks, cars, and **boisterous**
self-assertion are "masculine"; jump ropes, dolls, cuddling, and dependency are "feminine." Arithmetic and athletic, spatial and mechanical skills are "masculine"; reading and artistic and social skills
are "feminine." School objects, such as a blackboard and a book, are
"feminine"; chess is "masculine."

Stereotypes According to Twelve- to Seventeen-Year-Olds

Many of the tensions of adolescence are attributable to one unfortu-   22
nate misconception, which begins here and persists into maturity:
the confusion of sex role standards with sexual competence.

Lack of experience and a frame of reference for their developing   23
sexuality lead teenagers to equate extremes of "femininity" and
"masculinity" with the ultimate in sexiness. They are anxious about
everything: their physical appearance, hormonal changes, popularity, desirability as a romantic and sexual partner, academic standing,
and destiny in life. Understandably, many adolescents therefore seek
an identity within the clearcut outlines of stereotype. At this age, di-
gressions from the "norm" are imagined to bring social **ostracism**
and worse.

Sex-typed interests peak for girls at thirteen and for boys at six-   24
teen, years that roughly correspond to the peak transformations of
puberty. Take, for example, the **montages** created from magazine
pictures by some eighth graders. The boys were asked to express

---

squeamish: oversensitive, easily sickened;   boisterous: loud, noisy;
ostracism: banishment or exclusion;   montages: pictures made from other
pictures or images glued together

"Boys' Ideas of Their Maleness"; the girls "Girls' Ideas of Their Fe-maleness"; and then each group did "opposite" sex evaluations.

One group of boys plastered a large number 2 on their montage 25 about femaleness and a number 1 on their maleness poster. Seeing this, the girls' group immediately pasted a big zero on their "Girls' Ideas of Maleness" montage. In later discussions, the girls poured out their resentment of men and boys: "They think they're superior because they bring home all the money; boys are inferior and always in trouble; they are lazy; they act like animals."

Verbally, the boys characterized girls and women as being bossy, 26 nosy, self-centered, talkative, and interested in their looks, breasts, menstruation, birth control, getting married, and having babies.

The "Girls' Ideas of Their Femaleness" montage concentrated on 27 beauty, marriage, love, sex, make-up, cooking, money, dieting, cleanliness, perfume, jewelry, clothes, and skin. Yet the girls objected to the boys' idea of their femaleness because "all it is is sex, sex, sex, sex, making love, bust developers, work, cooking, children and cleaning. They think we're their slaves."

On their own maleness montages, the thirteen- and fourteen- 28 year-old boys pictured sports, hunting, cars, cycles, muscle develop-ment, military service, careers, and work. In some posters, family scenes appeared minimally; in others not at all.

These posters, and their creators, depict two different worlds 29 and the brand of male-female alienation that is all too familiar among adults.

As the plot thickens on the adolescent social scene, an aboutface is 30 happening in the intellectual sphere: Children stop stereotyping school achievement as "feminine" and start stereotyping the whole academic package as "masculine." To test this finding, I asked some thirteen-year-old girls which gender label they would put on mathematics:

"Math is a girl's thing because all the girls are better at it."

"No, it's a boy's thing when you think of how boys need it when they grow up."

"Women need it too—for adding up prices and budgets."

"Yeah, maybe if you think of arithmetic, it's female. But when you think of a mathematician, it's male."

Sex role standards for achievement become more definite and 31 extreme with age. By the time they are seventeen, both sexes almost unanimously stereotype athletics and arithmetic as male, and read-ing and social skills as female.

High school seniors are also relentlessly judgmental about what   32
is inappropriate for adults. In one national survey, 30 percent of them
said a woman's place is in the home and 4 percent think women are
totally incapable of working outside the home.

Post-reading

Some of the preceding selections discuss innate differences between male
and female children, while others reflect on ways in which children are
treated differently according to their gender. To prepare for this assignment,
you will need to go through these pieces, first listing the actual differences
between males and females and then listing differences in the ways boys and
girls are treated at home and at school. Add to your lists your own observations about how boys and girls were treated differently at the schools you attended and in the homes, yours and others, you are most familiar with.

Now compare what you know about the actual, innate differences between males and females and how they are treated. Does the treatment tie
in with the actual differences? Is it partially or totally unrelated to the differences? Think about and make notes on your views on how we could treat
boys and girls at school and at home that would make more sense in terms
of the actual differences between the genders.

When you have finished this work, you should have notes on the following topics:

1.   Innate differences between boys and girls
2.   Ways boys and girls are treated at school
3.   Ways they are treated in homes you are familiar with

Essay Assignment

**Write an essay in which you use the readings above and your
own experience to indicate the extent to which you think there
are actual or innate differences between males and females and
the extent to which you think male and female behavior is produced by environment. Since we cannot control our heredity
but we can control our environment, discuss changes you think
should be made in the way we raise children in order to ensure
that boys and girls will both get the best chance to develop
their individual talents.**

**For more discussion of this issue and suggestions about orga-
nizing your essay, log on to http://devenglish.wadsworth.com.**

Pre-writing

Since the assignment asks you to weigh *the extent to which* you think observable differences in male and female behavior are innate (nature) or learned (nurture), the first thing you need to do is weigh the points made in the readings carefully. Be sure to examine the different arguments to see how well they are backed up with specific evidence or whether they seem to be based more on personal opinion. You will find that not every argument is equally good. Notice also that while all the essays cover childhood, childhood represents a pretty long range of ages. Be sure to weigh carefully the evidence for nature and nurture at the different ages studied. If you write a conclusion in which you recommend changes in the raising of children, you will want to be fairly specific about what ages you are talking about. Remember also that there are at least three important influences on the formation of children: the family, of course, but also school and the media, such as television programs children are exposed to. You might not be able to cover all three of these influences, though you should be aware of them.

Start with an outline of the points made in the readings and add to these anything from your own experience that you feel is relevant. Then write a working thesis to help you focus and direct your essay. Remember that a working thesis is one that you can change if you change your mind as you are writing.

Writing

Your introduction should briefly outline the issue and state your thesis. Your paragraphs will probably pretty much follow the points listed in the post-reading section that you decide to cover. Your conclusion, of course, should make one or more recommendations. For suggestions about organizing your essay, see the opening section of this chapter.

THE WRITER'S CHECKLIST

The Idea Draft

1. Does your idea draft *respond fully* to the assignment?
2. Are your ideas *organized* in the way you want?
3. Does your *introduction* explain what the essay will be about and what its purpose is?
4. Do you have a *thesis* that states your point or indicates the issue the essay will address?
5. Do the *body paragraphs* each have a *topic sentence*? Do they develop the main points by giving *specifics and examples* to support those points?

6. Does your *conclusion* make one or more recommendations?
7. Have you *collaborated* with at least one trusted friend or fellow student who has read your draft *critically*, looking for lapses in logic or other weaknesses in content?

Sentence Combining

When you revise your idea draft, remember to use coordinators and subordinators when possible. Be especially alert for sentences *or pairs of sentences* in which you are comparing two things. In such cases, words like *while, whereas,* and *but* will usually help you show the relationship you have in mind.

In the assignment about sexual stereotyping, notice how Richard M. Restak, in "The Other Difference Between Boys and Girls," uses *while* and *but* to make his ideas clear:

> Boys are expected to be more aggressive and play rough games, <u>while</u> girls are presumably encouraged to be gentle and nonassertive.

> Undoubtedly, many differences traditionally believed to exist between the sexes are based on stereotypes, <u>but</u> evidence from recent brain research indicates that some behavioral differences between men and women are based on differences in brain functioning. . . .

In "Biology Influences Sex Roles," Tim Hackler uses *while* for the same purpose. Notice that although a very long sentence is the result, it is not at all hard to read:

> We have already seen that one of the most pronounced differences between men and women (a difference already present in the first months of life and continued through adulthood) is that women show verbal superiority, <u>while</u> men show "spatial superiority," a quality that shows up in such tasks as map reading, solving mathematical problems, and perceiving depth.

When making major transitions—those between paragraphs or even between sections of an essay—writers often use *but* or other phrases; Hackler uses the following sentence to make just such a major transition:

> <u>But</u> to what extent are these sex differences learned, and to what extent are they genetically determined?

After a paragraph on the areas of superiority of female infants, Restak starts his next paragraph this way:

> Boys, <u>in contrast,</u> show an early visual superiority.

After a paragraph about the primary interests of female babies, Hackler begins his next paragraph like this:

Male infants, <u>on the other hand</u>, are more interested in *things*.

And remember that when you wish to make a concession between two ideas, the words *although* and *even though* are essential, as in this passage from Restak's essay:

> There is no denying it: Boys think differently from girls. <u>Even though</u> recent brain-research evidence is controversial, that conclusion seems inescapable.

Later Drafts

1. Taking into account the constructive criticism you have received, have you *revised* accordingly—that is, reorganized, if that was a problem, or given additional support, if that was?
2. Have you read your essay *aloud*, listening closely to what it *actually says*, not just what you think it says? (This is another good place to work with a trusted fellow student or friend. Have him or her read your essay aloud and both of you listen closely to what it says.)
3. Have you *revised your sentences* if they seemed unclear or awkward as you read them aloud?
4. Have you checked for those *mechanical difficulties* that you know you sometimes have? Have you used the dictionary to check words that you think may be *misspelled*?

Final Draft

If you have followed this assignment step by step, you have worked exceedingly hard on this essay. Therefore, make sure your final draft reflects your care and effort by being as professional looking as possible.

1. Type it neatly, using the format your instructor has assigned.
2. Proofread slowly and carefully, word by word, line by line. (One last time, ask a trusted friend to proofread it *after* you have, or exchange your essay with another student and proof each other's.)

Sentence Combining

JOINING IDEAS TO SHOW CONTRAST AND CONCESSION

One of the most common writing tasks you are likely to encounter in college, in almost any classes you take, is that of making comparisons between two ideas or things, to show their similarities, or making contrasts between them to show their differences. An allied task—one that is even more common than comparisons and contrasts—is to show relationships of concession.

Here is a short comparison passage:

> I have here two objects. Both are round and about three inches in diameter. Both grow on trees, and both are edible. The one in my left hand is considered a fruit, and the one in my right hand is also. So both are normally found in the same section of the supermarket.

Here is a short contrast passage:

> I have here two objects. The one in my left hand has a smooth red skin and a stalk on one end, but the one in my right hand has a slightly pebbled orange skin and no stalk. The one in my left hand has a firm texture and sweet flavor, while the one in my right hand is pulpy and juicy and has a slightly acidic taste. The red one is grown in northern climates in the summer, whereas the orange one grows in southern, warmer climates all year round.

Notice the connecting words in the two passages:

In the first: *and, and, and, so.*
In the second: *and, but, and, and, while, and, and, whereas.*

While both passages make liberal use of the most common joining word in the language, *and*, the contrast passage employs three other words in central places: *but, while,* and *whereas.*

Here is another short passage; what joining words does it use?

> Mary is faced with a dilemma, which of two cars to buy. The red one is sleek and attractive, and it has been newly painted, but it leaks oil and smokes slightly, and its brakes and tires are in poor condition. The green one is rather dingy, but it is in excellent mechanical condition. Although Mary finds the red one much more attractive, she decides that the green one is a better purchase.

Up until the last sentence, we have the familiar words of comparison and contrast: *and* and *but.* Then we find a new word, *although.* This word enters because the last sentence does something none of the other sentences does; it shows a relationship of concession between the two parts of the sentence. You will remember from studying subordinators that these words indicate opposition between ideas: *although, though, even though, while,* and *whereas.* It is now time to qualify that statement. It is true that all of those words do show opposition, but three of them—*although, though,* and *even though*—also show concession, and in fact that is their main function.

WHAT IS CONCESSION?

To concede a point is to admit that it is true. In argument or discussion, we often must admit that some of the things our opponent says are true. For instance, John argues that oranges are better than apples, while Mary argues the opposite. Mary points out that the skin of apples is more pleasant to the touch than the skin of oranges. John has to admit that this is true, so he says,

Although apples have more pleasant skins, oranges are superior in many other ways.

John has used *although* to concede a point. He could also have used *though* (more informal) or *even though* (more emphatic). He might even have used *while* or *whereas*, although these words are better at showing contrasts than at showing concession.

You will remember the mention of *transition words* at the end of Chapter 3. Two common transition words that you may want to use occasionally in writing comparison/contrast essays are *however* and *on the other hand*.

SUMMARY OF COMPARISON/CONTRAST WORDS

We have now looked at a number of joining words that you will need to use in writing essays, paragraphs, or sentences involving comparison, contrast, and concession. These words fall into three categories:

Coordinators	Subordinators	Transition Words
and	although	however
but	though	on the other hand
	even though	
	while	
	whereas	

Remember the differences among these words: Coordinators may join independent sentences; when they do, put a comma in front of the coordinator. Coordinators may also introduce sentences:

Mary likes handball, but John prefers jogging.
Mary likes handball. But John prefers jogging.

Subordinators join dependent clauses to sentences; when the dependent clause comes first, put a comma after it; when it follows the sentence, do not use a comma.

While Mary likes elephants, John prefers penguins.
John prefers penguins while Mary likes elephants.

Transition words do not join sentences and may be placed within or at the end of a sentence instead of at the beginning of it.

Mary likes a good time; however, John mopes.
Mary likes a good time; John, however, mopes.

USING JOINING WORDS TO SHOW EMPHASIS

There is one final difference between coordinators and subordinators that you need to know. When the coordinator *but* joins two sentences, the ideas in the two sentences get equal emphasis. But when the subordinators such as *although, whereas,* and *while* join sentences, the idea following the subordinator gets played down somewhat.

Here you are trying to sell your battered old car, which you have taken beautiful care of. It doesn't look very good, but it runs like a whiz. You have two customers, A and B, who have looked it over and taken it for a test drive. They now speak:

A: "Well, although it doesn't look very good, it certainly runs well."
B: "Well, although it runs well, it certainly doesn't look very good."

Who do you think is most likely to buy it?

As it turns out, neither A nor B buys it. (A would have, but at the last moment, she got a phone call telling her that her rich uncle Fred had just given her a Mercedes-Benz.) So here you are again, facing two prospective customers along with the friend of one of them, who is not in the market for a car. The three people make the following comments. Who is leaning toward buying the car, who is leaning toward not buying it, and who is the neutral observer?

C: "Although it's rather ugly, it's in excellent condition."
D: "It's rather ugly, but it's in excellent condition."
E: "Although it's in excellent condition, it's rather ugly."

In all of the examples above, the subordinate clause (the *although* clause) has come at the beginning of its sentence, but, as you know, such clauses can just as easily come at the end of sentences:

It's in excellent condition although it's rather ugly.

EXERCISE: JOINING TO SHOW EMPHASIS—1

The following exercises will give you practice in using *although, while,* and *whereas* to join ideas and to give emphasis. Remember that all of these words can show contrast or opposition, but only *although* (or its friends *even though* and *though*) can show concession. Example:

Showing contrast/opposition:

> *While* Jamaal was a stellar math student, his English was just barely passing.

> Kevin was terrible at sports *whereas* his sister Athena got a scholarship to play basketball.

Showing concession:

> *Although* I love meeting new people, I hate blind dates.

> Maria would not sell her old car *even though* it was costing her too much money to run.

Remember that the contrast/concession words play down the part of the sentence they are attached to and emphasize the part of the sentence they are *not* attached to. Example:

Show contrast/opposition; emphasize second sentence:

> *Whereas* my pet tarantula does helpful things around the house such as eating bugs, my cat just spreads fleas everywhere.

Show concession; emphasize first sentence:

> Marlissa knows that she studies best in the mornings *although* she'd rather go jogging then.

Although Most women like to shop.
Men generally go to the store just to buy something they want.
  a. Show opposition; emphasize first sentence.
  b. Show concession; emphasize second sentence.
  c. Which version do you prefer? Why?

While 2. For women, it's the process that counts.
For men, it's the results.
  a. Show opposition; emphasize second sentence.
  b. Show opposition; emphasize first sentence. (Don't use the same joining word you used in *a.*)
  c. Which version do you prefer? Why?

although 3. This idea may be generally true.
There are many complications and exceptions to it.
  although a. Show concession; emphasize second sentence.
  b. Show concession; emphasize first sentence.
  Whereas, While c. Which version do you prefer? Why?
  4. Women do seem to shop more than men.
They don't shop just for anything.
  a. Show opposition; emphasize second sentence.
  b. Show concession; emphasize second sentence.

5.   A woman may spend several hours shopping with a friend.
     They will probably not, for example, shop in a hardware store.
whereas   a.   Show opposition; emphasize second sentence.
where   b.   Show concession; emphasize first sentence.
     c.   Join the two sentences in another way of your choice.
     d.   Which version do you prefer? Why?

6.   Men rarely go out just to shop.
     It is possible to find men wandering around aimlessly in hardware or auto-
     motive stores.
whereas   a.   Show opposition; emphasize first sentence.
     b.   Show opposition; emphasize second sentence.
Eventhough   c.   Show concession; emphasize the sentence of your choice.
     d.   Which version do you prefer? Why?

EXERCISE: JOINING TO SHOW EMPHASIS—2

You have practiced using the subordinators that indicate opposition and concession. In these exercises, you will continue to use these words, but you will now also practice using the word *but* to show contrast. Remember that while the subordinators give differing emphasis to the two parts of a sentence, the word *but*, a coordinator, gives the *same* emphasis to the two parts. Examples:

Mary's python, Filbert, died.
Mary was not particularly sad.
   Show concession; emphasize sentence two.

Solution: *Although* Mary's python, Filbert, died, Mary was not particularly sad.

Mary preferred fairly independent pets, like cats.
She found Filbert to be rather clinging.
   Show opposition; emphasize sentence one.

Solution: Mary preferred fairly independent pets, like cats, *while* she found Filbert to be rather clinging.

Filbert was a well-behaved python.
He didn't seem to have much personality.
   Show opposition; give equal emphasis.

Solution: Filbert was a well-behaved python, *but* he didn't seem to have much personality.

Musical Tastes

1.   John liked rock and roll.
     Mary preferred classical music.
        Show opposition; give equal emphasis.

2.   Rock and roll is the music of today.
     Classical music has retained its popularity over generations.

    a.   Show concession; emphasize sentence one.
    b.   Show concession; emphasize sentence two.

3.   Lovers of rock and roll often like classical music too.
      Those who prefer classical music usually hate rock and roll.
while a.   Show opposition; emphasize sentence one.
whereas b.   Show opposition; emphasize sentence two.

4.   Jazz came from popular black sources in the South.
      Some of it has since developed in the direction of classical music.
    a.   Show opposition; give equal emphasis.
    b.   Show opposition; emphasize sentence one.
    c.   Show opposition; emphasize sentence two.

5.   Jazz in its original forms was an African-American art form.
      It influenced many white musicians, even including the French composer
      Maurice Ravel.
    a.   Show opposition; give equal emphasis.
    b.   Show concession; emphasize sentence two.
    c.   Show concession; emphasize sentence one.

6.   Tastes in popular music change every generation or so.
      Those who like the new music always heap scorn on the music that
      preceded them.
    a.   Show concession; emphasize sentence one.
    b.   Show concession; emphasize sentence two.

EXERCISE: JOINING TO SHAPE SENTENCES

In the following exercises, you are asked to "shape" the sentences, joining them to show a particular point of view or emphasis. As an example, look at the following two sentences:

Strikes are an essential part of the labor-management bargaining process.
They are very costly and disruptive to both management and workers.

If the president of General Motors were going to write these two sentences as one sentence, he would surely want to "shape" it in such a way as to emphasize the bad aspects of strikes, and so he might write this:

Although strikes are an essential part of the labor-management bargaining process, they are very costly and disruptive to both management and workers.

The head of a labor union, on the other hand, would probably "shape" the sentence this way:

Strikes are an essential part of the labor-management bargaining process although they are very costly and disruptive to both management and workers.

To do the following exercises, you need to know, if you don't already, that two baseball teams in the American League, the New York Yankees and the Boston Red Sox, are unusually fierce rivals. As a result, Red Sox fans usually hate the Yankees, and Yankee fans usually hate the Red Sox.

The Yankees and the Red Sox

1. In 1978, the Boston Red Sox led the Eastern Division of the American League almost all year.
   The New York Yankees won the championship on the last day.
   a. Show opposition; join the sentences as you would if you were a neutral sportswriter.
   b. Show opposition; join them as you would if you were a New York Yankees fan.
   c. Show opposition; join them as you would if you were a Boston Red Sox fan.

2. Recently, the Yankees have spent great amounts of money trying to buy the best players available.
   They had little success in winning championships until recently.
   a. Show concession; join the sentences as you would if you were a solid supporter of the Yankees.
   b. Show concession; join the sentences as you would if you disliked the Yankees.

3. In 1986, the Red Sox won the American League championship.
   The New York Mets beat them in the World Series.
   a. Show opposition; join the sentences as you would if you were merely reporting the facts.
   b. Show opposition; join the sentences as you would if you were a Red Sox fan.
   c. Show opposition; join the sentences as you would if you were from New York.

4. The 1986 Red Sox had many great hitters, such as Wade Boggs and Jim Rice.
   They were a very slow team.
   a. Show concession; join the sentences as you would in a paragraph about the strengths of the Red Sox.
   b. Show concession; join the sentences as you would in a paragraph about their weaknesses.

5. Until the late 90's, the Yankees had excellent hitters.
   Their pitching was rather poor.
   a. Join the sentences as you would in a paragraph about the weaknesses of the Yankees.
   b. Join the sentences as you would in a paragraph about the strengths of the Yankees.

6. The Red Sox have excellent players.
   We Yankee fans can't stand them.
   Join these two sentences.

7. We Red Sox fans have had to admire the numerous great teams the Yankees have had over the years.
    They still drive us crazy.
      Join these two sentences.

REVIEW

In the following exercises, you will practice using modifiers and showing relationships of opposition and concession. The places where you should use a subordinator have been indicated (as in sentence 2 below).

What Carolyn Did on Her Summer Vacation

1. The previous summer, Carolyn had a job.
    The job was boring.
    The job was low paying.
    The job was working in the stockroom.
    It was the stockroom of a department store.
    The department store was small.
    The department store was local.
2. This summer, she hoped to find a job.
    The job would be more stimulating.
    The job would be with a better salary.
      [join: equal emphasis]
    For six weeks, she could find nothing.
    The weeks were long.
    The weeks were anxious.
    The weeks were in March and April.
3. She was discouraged by her search.
    Her search was fruitless.
    Her search was for a summer job.
      [join: emphasize second sentence]
    She kept up her effort.
    Her effort was painstaking.
4. Her patience and her searching were rewarded when she found two jobs.
    Her searching was careful.
    Her searching was scrupulous.
    The jobs were interesting looking.
5. One was a job.
    The job was standard.
    The job was moderately exciting.

The job was in sales.

The job was in a women's store.

The store was in town.

>   [join: equal emphasis]

The other was a position.

The position was extremely interesting.

The position was in an advertising agency.

The agency was in a distant city.

6. Carolyn liked the idea of a job.

    The job was well paying.

    The job was selling women's clothes.

    >   [join: emphasize second sentence]

    She did not like the idea of staying in town.

7. She was not excited about a position.

    The position was an internship.

    The position was with low wages.

    >   [join: emphasize second sentence]

    She was excited about a job.

    The job was glamorous.

    The job was in an advertising agency.

    The job was in a large city.

8. Carolyn's mother hoped she would take the job.

    Her mother was worried.

    The job was in sales.

    The job was near home.

    >   [join: decide whether to emphasize the first or second sentence or to give them equal emphasis.]

    Her father thought the internship was an opportunity.

    The internship was in advertising.

    The opportunity was great.

    The opportunity was to get experience.

    The experience was practical.

    The experience was in the business world.

9. Carolyn loved her home and the town where she grew up.

    >   [join: decide whether to emphasize the first or second sentence or to give them equal emphasis]

    She wanted to have the experience of living in a city and working at a kind of job.

    The experience was novel.

The experience was challenging.

The city was big.

The kind of job was completely new.

10. The internship required work and hours.

The work was very hard.

The hours were very long.

The hours were at low pay.

> [join: decide whether to emphasize the first or second sentence or to give them equal emphasis]

Carolyn found it very rewarding.

The Black Death

1. Modern medicine has almost eliminated the danger.

The danger is to humans.

The danger is from plague.

> [join: emphasize second sentence]

It still does not understand some forms.

The forms are of this disease.

This disease is terrifying.

This disease is deadly.

2. The plague wiped out millions.

The millions were of people.

The millions were in China.

The millions were in India.

The millions were in the Middle East.

> [join: equal emphasis]

Most Europeans had never heard of it.

[subord] It struck them in the fourteenth century.

3. It is believed that people died.

The people were between forty and fifty million.

The people were in Europe.

They died of plague.

They died by the end of the century.

4. There are three forms of plague.

[coord] Each form has different symptoms.

5. The form produces lymph nodes, blotches, destruction, and blackening.

The form is the most famous.

The lymph nodes are swollen.

The blotches are purple.

The blotches are caused by blood hemorrhaging.

The hemorrhaging is under the skin.

The destruction is of the nervous system.

The blackening is of the body.

The blackening is just before death.

6. Many historians believe that the rhyme refers to the blotches.

The rhyme is sung by children.

The rhyme is "Ring Around the Rosey."

The blotches are under the skin.

The blotches are caused by plague.

[coord] They think that the last line, "All fall down," refers to the death of the victim.

7. The fourteenth-century Europeans tried cures and methods.

The methods were preventive.

The cures and methods were of every kind.

   [join: emphasize second sentence]

They were unsuccessful.

[subord] They did not know the virus was carried by fleas.

8. The victims were cared for.

The victims were the very first.

The caring was by their fellow citizens.

Their fellow citizens were goodhearted.

   [join: emphasize second sentence]

Victims were left to die.

The victims were later.

The dying was on their own.

[coord] The entire social order collapsed.

The social order was of Europe.

The collapse was total.

9. People killed strangers.

People killed gypsies.

People burned Jews to death.

The strangers were innocent.

The burning was in many European cities.

   [join: emphasize first sentence]

The Jews were dying.

The dying was of plague.

The dying was just as rapidly as anyone else.

10. The black death should teach us lessons.

    The black death was of the fourteenth century.

    The black death was in Europe.

    The lessons are about the effects.

    The effects are of fear.

    The effects are of ignorance.

    The effects are of superstition.

CHAPTER 5

Arguing

FACTS AND OPINIONS

We all hold opinions about almost any subject. For example, Janet might believe that "Netty's Neighborhood" (a television show about a divorced black woman with three children who lives in Beverly Hills) realistically portrays the life of the black, single mother. Her neighbor, Anna, who is black, might believe that "Netty's Neighborhood" is about as close to being representative of a black family as Bill Cosby is to being the average American father.

Okay. There's no harm in either opinion. Janet and Anna can sit on their front steps on an evening and have the following dialogue.

JANET: Netty's family sure represents the average American black family.

ANNA: No, they don't.

JANET: Yes, they do.

ANNA: No, they don't.

And this dialogue can drag boringly on—and might if Janet and Anna were small children. ("That's my toy." "No, it isn't." "Yes, it is." "No, it isn't.") But they're not. Therefore, a more predictable turn for the discussion is that one woman starts supporting her position—often by citing facts.

ANNA: According to the 1985 Census Report, black female heads of families have a median family income of $9,574. As a divorce lawyer to some of Hollywood's most affluent stars, Netty makes at least $135,000 annually.

JANET: Oh. Then they aren't representative financially?

ANNA: No, they are not.

Both women hold opinions. The difference between their viewpoints, however, is that Anna possesses facts upon which to base her opinion; Janet doesn't. This is a vital difference.

On a daily basis, most of our opinions are relatively unimportant. Who, for example, really cares whether or not Janet thinks Netty's family is an average American family? Besides Anna, no one. However, if Janet were writing a term paper on the status of American black families with a single head of household and, relying solely on her opinion, cited Netty and her children as the average family, her professor might very well fail the paper. And for good reason; she would be wrong. Her opinion, to which she is entitled, would be unsupported by facts.

Many people think that because they are entitled to hold opinions on any subject they want, those opinions are just as good as anyone else's. But they aren't. An opinion is only as good as the facts behind it. Basic to critical thinkers and writers is the ability to distinguish between facts and opinions.

Fact versus Opinion

A fact can be verified. We can find out whether it is true or not, at least theoretically. Is it a fact that the moon is 568 feet from Earth? We can check it. Is it a fact that New York City is the largest city in the United States? Again, we can find out. Is it a fact that Ohio is the best state of all fifty? How would one check that out? It is a matter of opinion.

An opinion can be the result of a number of factors: a knowledge of facts, an unexamined acceptance of others' opinions (those of our parents, our friends, or the nightly news anchorperson), a bias (often unconscious), a "gut response" (it just feels "right"), or a combination of these and other factors. One of the goals of a college education is to help students form opinions founded upon an examination of the facts.

EXERCISE

Based on your own knowledge, decide which of the following statements are facts and which are opinions:

- The Los Angeles Lakers won the 1987 National Basketball Association championship.
- Chicago is situated on the southwest shore of Lake Michigan.

- The United States Navy is the finest fighting force in the world today.
- Cats are a lot more fun than dogs.
- The Constitution of the United States was approved in Philadelphia, Pennsylvania.
- As a result of the Watergate investigations, President Nixon resigned from office.
- Sacramento, California, possesses as many Mexican restaurants as a porcupine has quills—they're everywhere.
- In July 1987, the world's population grew to 5 billion.
- The movie *Full Metal Jacket* was rated R.
- It should have been rated NC17 because of all the violence in it.
- William Shakespeare is the world's greatest playwright.
- Ted Williams, of the Boston Red Sox, was the finest hitter in baseball in the 1940s and 1950s.

Distinguishing Fact from Opinion

As you can see, it is not always easy to distinguish fact from opinion. Let's look at the case of Ted Williams. We know that he was the last player to bat .400 for a season and that he had a higher lifetime batting average and hit more home runs than any other player of the 40s and 50s. Those statistics make it sound like he was the best hitter of the time. But Joe DiMaggio was also an extremely good hitter, and he got hits in fifty-six consecutive games, a record most baseball people think is the greatest hitting feat ever. So is Williams still the greatest hitter of the time?

Sometimes whether we consider a statement to be a fact or an opinion will depend upon its source. In Williams's case, we would probably accept it as a fact that he was the best batsman if a number of respected authorities on baseball said he was. If, however, your roommate, who is a diehard Boston Red Sox fan, said Williams was the greatest, then you might question whether it was fact or opinion; it still might be a fact, or it might be the opinion of an overly enthusiastic fan.

Another, perhaps more difficult aspect of distinguishing fact from opinion has to do with interpretation. Take, for example, the statement, "Shakespeare is the world's greatest playwright." In order to determine whether that's fact or opinion, we must determine not only the source of the statement ("Said who?") but also what the source meant by "greatest." Is a great playwright designated so by the number of plays he or she wrote? By the quality of the plays? (And how do we determine a play's quality?) Is the best play the funniest and most entertaining? The most thought provoking? The list of questions we need to answer in order to determine whether that statement is fact or opinion goes on and on and on. Finally, because we cannot answer with any certainty all the questions, we must assume that the statement, "Shakespeare is the world's greatest playwright," is an opinion, perhaps a reasoned and thoughtful opinion, but an opinion nonetheless.

Facts and "Facts"

That a fact is a fact does not mean necessarily that it is correct. It may appear to be so. However, if it is based on false or inaccurate information, it may be downright wrong. Remember that for centuries, it was a fact that the Earth was flat. Or take our friends Anna and Janet. Anna convinced Janet that "Netty's Neighborhood" did not represent a typical black family by using a statistic, the fact that in 1985, the median family income of a single-parent, female-headed black family was $9,574. Anna got that figure from the 1985 US Census Report, a fairly reliable source for that kind of information.

However, Anna might have remembered the figure incorrectly, inverted the numbers ($9,754?), gotten the information from a supermarket rag like the *National Enquirer,* or just made it up to win her point. Janet, however, believed in Anna's honesty, respected the statistic's source, and had faith in her friend's memory. But if Janet were assigned to write a term paper on the status of single-parent, black families in America in the 1980s, she'd be well advised to check the Census Report herself to make sure her friend did have the fact right.

EXERCISE

Relying on your own knowledge and judgment, determine which of the following are statements of fact and which statements of opinion, and discuss with your classmates the reasons why:

- The sun rises in the east.
- Teenagers spend more money on renting home videocassettes than they do on going to movie houses.
- Agatha Christie's play *The Mousetrap* has been playing longer in London than any play in the history of English theater.
- It is by far the best play of the modern English stage.
- More people have enjoyed this play in the past twenty years than have enjoyed everything written by Shakespeare put together.
- According to a 1986 Yale University study, a single woman of thirty has a 20 percent chance of marrying.
- By the time she is thirty-five, her chances are only 5 percent.
- Anything is fair in love and war.

- People who own pit bull terriers have the same moral values as drug runners and thieves.
- The Golden Gate Bridge was fifty years old in 1987.
- It is the most beautiful bridge in the world.
- It is one of the main tourist attractions in San Francisco.

EVALUATING EVIDENCE AND SHAPING YOUR ARGUMENT

A lot of the problems students and professional people face are issues in which it is important to sort out facts from opinions and, in the case of the opinions, decide how much they can be trusted. A group of people may think that capital punishment deters crime and ought to be the mandatory sentence for murder. In order to convince the state of this view, they would try to prove that the death penalty is a greater deterrent to crime than life imprisonment is. They might examine homicide rates in states that had capital punishment and in those that didn't, they might look at the before-and-after homicide rates in a state that abolished the death penalty, or they might study the rates of homicide in a state before and after a much publicized execution.

In fact, scholars have done just that, and this group might cite the work of Isaac Ehrlich, who published a study in 1975 which shows that a decline in executions in the United States led to a corresponding increase in murders. Unhappily for Ehrlich, a group of other social scientists found his work seriously flawed. Ehrlich's findings were based entirely on evidence he gathered from 1962 to 1974, a time when, it is true, the number of executions declined and the number of homicides rose. The trouble is that the increase in the number of homicides was part of an overall rise in crime—of all sorts—a fact that Ehrlich didn't take into consideration in his study. Therefore, his findings were debunked because there was no reason to think that the rise in murders was the result of the decline in executions.

Professional people are often asked to offer suggestions, give reports, choose between possible options, or make recommendations. A grocer might have to decide from which of two vegetable distributors to buy; a broker might have to advise a client on investment options; a city manager might have to report to the city council on whether or not to allow a twenty-story Holiday Inn to be built downtown. The quality of all such decisions depends entirely on how well the issue is examined and how carefully the various facts, opinions, and inferences are examined and used.

Preparation

There are four important things to remember in dealing with arguments:

1. *Don't make up your mind about the issue ahead of time.* You may have believed for years that X was true and Y was false, and your family

or your friends may still believe it, but that doesn't mean they're right. If you're smart, you'll be aware that such beliefs are often based on weak or biased information (or no information at all, just prejudice). Wait until you've examined all the evidence. Remember that you may have just as many prejudices and groundless opinions as the next person.

2. *Don't fall for the fallacy of "common sense."* Common sense leads to all sorts of erroneous conclusions. For instance, legislatures have learned that increasing criminal punishments for particular crimes doesn't always lead to a reduction in those crimes, as common sense would suggest it would. Why not? For one thing, a jury will often hesitate to convict a person of a particular crime if the penalty for it seems disproportionately severe. When the crime then goes unpunished, where is the deterrent value of the severe penalty? And severe penalties for lesser crimes may lead to more severe crimes. For instance, if we instituted the death penalty for dealing certain dangerous drugs, then drug dealers would realize that they might as well kill in order to prevent being caught, since the penalty would be the same anyway. Common sense once told us that the world was flat, that the sun rotated around the Earth. Common sense isn't always wrong, but it often is.

3. *When examining an issue, sort out the facts from the opinions.* In the case of opinions, ask yourself whose opinions they are. Are they likely to be biased for some reason? Are they likely to be based on self-interest? Are they "expert" opinions, ones that should be given strong consideration?

4. *When "facts" contradict each other, consider who has produced the contradictory "facts" and which side has the greater weight of "facts."* For instance, in the 1970s and 80s, numerous studies carried out by independent researchers consistently showed that cigarette smoking and other forms of tobacco use were extremely harmful to people's health. A much smaller number of studies commissioned by the tobacco industry showed that smoking was not very harmful. These two sets of "facts" clashed with each other, but the anti-smoking studies were more credible because they came from independent researchers and were more numerous than the others.

Arranging Your Argument

When you write, don't ignore the other side. The writer who argues only his or her own point is much less effective than the writer who takes his or her opponent into consideration. How do you feel about someone who doesn't seem to listen to your side in a dispute and just keeps arguing his or her own views? How, on the other hand, do you feel about a person who says, "Yes, I see what you mean, and I agree with you about so and so" before going on to give his or her own opinions?

When you organize the paragraphs of an argument essay, you may be tempted to write an introduction, a paragraph covering the pro side, a paragraph covering the con side, and a conclusion. On the face of it, this seems to make a lot of sense, but it is usually not a good idea.

Pro or con paragraphs usually feature two problems. One is that they are like sacks. You can throw everything into one of them, but then there's no order inside it; within the sack everything is a hodgepodge. The other problem is that the length of such paragraphs often fools the writer into thinking the paragraph is well developed when it isn't.

Suppose, for instance, that in 1948 an executive for a major American railroad was preparing a paper in which he was going to argue that his company should immediately begin replacing its steam locomotives with diesels. This would be a pro/con issue, and he would have plenty of opposition. Suppose he wrote a paragraph like the following:

> Diesel locomotives offer numerous advantages over steam. They are easier to maintain. They create less wear on tracks, ties, and roadbed. They offer greater flexibility in use. And they are cheaper to run.

He would certainly get nowhere because he has failed to explain *why* they are easier to maintain, *why* they create less wear on tracks, *how* they are more flexible, and finally, *why* they are cheaper to run and *how much* cheaper they are. His argument would be completely vulnerable to attack. In short, rather than one paragraph of advantages, he would need at least four—and possibly more if any of these points was sufficiently complex.

Generally speaking, there are three ways to organize pro/con arguments. One is to begin with all the points on one side and then to conclude with all the points on the other side. In cases like this, most writers like to start with the position they oppose, the one they think is the weaker, and conclude with the side they favor, the stronger one in their view. Let's say you want to argue that all grading systems should be abolished in college. You might organize your essay as follows. *Remember that this outline does not indicate the paragraph divisions of an essay, only the sequence of the argument.*

Introduction
Arguments in favor of grading systems
Arguments against grading systems
Conclusion

If the argument involves more than one issue, the organization will naturally be less straightforward. Suppose you wanted to argue that a credit/no credit grading system should be instituted instead of the letter-grade system. You would have to deal with the arguments for and against each of these systems. So your organization might look like this (again, the outline does not indicate the paragraphing):

Introduction

Arguments in favor of letter grades

Arguments against letter grades

Arguments against credit/no credit grades

Arguments in favor of credit/no credit grades

Conclusion

A third way of handling these kinds of arguments is to argue each issue point by point instead of in separate paragraphs or sections of the paper.

Writing Your Argument

While you are analyzing your information, try to decide which side has the better arguments. You may, of course, decide that A is correct and X is wrong and then realize, while writing, that X is really right. There's nothing wrong with that; it happens to writers all the time. But it is certainly inconvenient. It's much better to think everything through as carefully as possible first so you don't surprise yourself.

When you're sure about what you think, try to write your essay in such a way that you emphasize the point you will finally want to make. For example, suppose you are writing on the topic "Bananas should be outlawed." You have read the relevant documents and have the following list of points:

Facts

Last year 136 people were injured in banana-related accidents.

Medical studies have shown that bananas are high in potassium, a preventative of heart disease.

A survey by the Banana Institute showed that 96.7 percent of cereal eaters believe that sliced bananas improve the taste of their cereal.

Since most bananas come to the United States from foreign countries, they have a slight negative effect on our trade balance.

Opinions

Herbert Clutch believes that the yellow color of bananas causes jaundice.

The Mothers Opposed to Seductive Stuff (MOSS) argue that bananas have an immoral shape. (This group also opposes flagpoles.)

After nearly choking to death on a banana, Arcana Wedgefeather reports that she and others like her grow nauseated in the produce section of supermarkets.

You decide that the opinions are weak and the facts are on the side of bananas. Mr. Clutch and Ms. Wedgefeather have no medical credentials to support their views, while the potassium studies were undertaken by impartial researchers. In a population of well over 250 million, 136 injured people isn't very many. The Banana Institute survey is suspicious (96.7 percent of people never agree on anything), but in your experience most people do like bananas. Meanwhile, MOSS seems to be a group of cranks.

While you want to report the arguments for banning the banana, you should word your paragraphs in such a way that you try to affect how the reader will view this material. You might write your essay in this way:

> While a move to outlaw the sale of bananas has sprung up in some parts of the country, the proponents of this view have little credibility. For instance, a group calling itself Mothers Opposed to Seductive Stuff argues that the very form of the banana tends to undermine our morals, but no other group concerned with morals has ever found the shape of the banana offensive or indecent, and MOSS would even like to get rid of flagpoles. It has also been argued that bananas can have a sickening effect in the supermarket on those who have had accidents with them, but no medical evidence supports this view.
>
> Some statistics indicate that bananas do create some problems. In the United States last year, 136 people were injured in banana-related accidents, and since most of our bananas come from foreign countries, they have a slight negative effect on our trade balance. But 136 accidents in a population of over 250 million is very few, and the trade balance problem is too small to be important.

Writing your argument in this way, you will not have to review every single point in detail when you get to your conclusion because you have already shown that the anti-bananas arguments have little merit.

In the event that you don't feel the case is so one-sided, you should, of course, write the pro and con points in a more balanced way. Then your conclusion will have to sum up the main points on both sides. You may even decide—and write your conclusion to show—that you aren't able to make up your mind on this issue with the evidence you have. That is a perfectly reasonable and intelligent conclusion to come to in many cases.

*A*ssignments and Readings

DECIDING CARMEN HERRERA'S FUTURE

Difficult pro/con issues can come up in our personal lives just as they emerge at the local or national level. Often these personal issues involve values that are just as important as those behind the big public issues, and they usually involve passions and prejudices as well. It is essential for our happiness and well-being that we try to resolve our own problems as objectively as we can, for our prejudices and feelings—and those of our friends and relatives—can often lead us into trouble, or at least lead our lives in undesirable directions. The following case is such an issue.

Carmen Herrera's family emigrated from El Salvador to the United States ten years ago when Carmen was in the second grade. Carmen got excellent grades in elementary school and did so well in high school (she has maintained a 3.8 GPA) that Ms. Aguilar, her guidance counselor, is encouraging her to continue her education by attending the University of Mountainfield, a prestigious state university, in New Berryford, a city two hundred miles away. Although Carmen has no specific career goals, she enjoys school and would like to continue.

As the oldest of five children, she also feels a responsibility to her family. Since their move to the United States, they have been living in a three-bedroom apartment, saving for a down payment on a house. Carmen has been contributing some of the money she makes working part time as a clerk-typist to the house fund, but she realizes that she will not be able to work during the academic year if she attends school full time and must meet the grade-point average required of a scholarship student.

Ms. Aguilar feels that because of her high school record, test scores, and financial need, Carmen has an excellent chance of being awarded a scholarship that would cover her tuition, books, and room and board.

A friend, Alicia Casillas, is planning to attend a small private business school in town, Radcliffe Business College, which guarantees job placement at the end of an eight-month training program in secretarial skills, including word processing. Although the program would take some initial investment from her parents, Carmen thinks that she could easily pay this back and in a few years contribute enough to the house fund so that her family could purchase their own home. Then she could still go to college if she wanted to.

Reading Assignment

Pre-reading

Before you read the following recommendations from Carmen's family and acquaintances, think about her dilemma. Although you know little about her situation, you should consider the differences between liberal arts and vocational educations. In general, what are the benefits of a liberal arts education? What are those of vocational education? As you think about this issue, remember to take notes so you won't forget your thoughts as you read other people's.

Reading

Carmen has been talking to people about her problem and has gotten the following reactions. Remember to read actively, taking notes in the margins or on another sheet of paper.

VARIOUS COMMENTS ON CARMEN'S DILEMMA

Ms. Aguilar (her high school counselor): "It doesn't matter that you don't know what you might major in at college. Most majors require only two years to complete, so you have plenty of time to find out what you like. Meanwhile, you'll be taking courses in a number of disciplines and getting the kind of liberal education you're going to need in order to succeed in whatever field you decide to enter. You know, hardly anyone from this school ever goes to college, except perhaps to the community college, or even thinks about getting a scholarship. You would set a wonderful example to the younger students if you made it."   1

Mr. and Mrs. Herrera (her parents): "*When* we get a house or even *whether* we get a house is not your worry. You are young. You have to live your life and do what is best for you. One of the reasons we moved from El Salvador was so that you children could have opportunities that we were denied, and the biggest one is education. You must get the best education you can."   2

Victor Oquendo (her boyfriend): "You can't afford to go away to college even if you get a scholarship. Where are you going to get spending money for clothes, movies, things like that? Are you going to hit your parents up every time you want to go shopping? Every time you want a hamburger? I think you're being unrealistic. You should stay here, go to Radcliffe, and get a good job, help your parents, and save for the future."   3

Mr. Hansen (her employer at ABC Clerical Services): "You're a terrific typist. If you go to Radcliffe and learn to use a word processor, I'd be happy to hire you full time. In fact, I'll keep the position open for you. It's guaranteed. And, if you want, you can keep your part-time job here. We'll make arrangements to fit your schedule at Radcliffe."   4

Alicia Casillas (her friend): "I'd be scared of college, a place like Mountainfield or something. It's different. The people are different.   5

You wouldn't know anybody. Besides, if you go to Radcliffe you can keep your job at ABC and start making *big* money in eight months instead of maybe four years from now. Remember Dwana Brown, who graduated two years ago? She's working for Bechtel now and makes $24,000 a year. She's even got her own apartment!"

Maria Herrera (her fourteen-year-old sister): "I'd give anything to go 6 to Mountainfield. Think of all the new people you'll meet. Think of the courses you could take—music, dance, drama—not like in this school where you have to sit through boring classes where the teacher reads from the textbook. At Mountainfield you'd really get good teachers. Plus, if you go and do well, then Mom and Dad might help me go to someplace like that. I don't think I'll be able to get the scholarships you can."

Thomas Herrera (her sixteen-year-old brother): "Our parents will 7 never get a house with the prices what they are around here unless we both keep helping them. And you really could help them out if you were earning a decent salary and living at home. I think we owe it to them. They gave up a lot to get us out of El Salvador and give us a chance. We should help them out now."

Post-reading

Go over the background to Carmen's problem, listing the most important facts. Then go through the opinions of her friends and relatives. In each case, ask yourself whether each one is expressing a fact or an opinion and list the facts and opinions separately. In the case of the facts, you will want to indicate how important each one is. (You could use a star system, as in rating the movies, with four-star facts, three-star facts, and so on.) With the opinions, it will be important to note not just what they are but also who holds them. Which opinions seem to be based on a genuine concern for Carmen and which seem based more on the concerns of the people holding the opinions? You could then rate the opinions in order of value also.

In examining the opinions, it is important for you to think about each one yourself. It is perfectly possible for a person with no axe of his or her own to grind to have a pretty worthless opinion of a matter, just as it's possible that an opinion based on self-interest might really express an important point. You will need to think for yourself about the financial realities and future consequences for Carmen's life that are involved in either of her two possible courses of action.

Essay Assignment

Write an essay in which you examine the evidence for and against Carmen's attending the University of Mountainfield and Radcliffe Business College. Carefully considering both options, come to your own conclusion about which school she ought to attend.

For more discussion of this issue and suggestions about organizing your essay, log on to http://devenglish.wadsworth.com.

Pre-writing

Before you begin organizing your essay, review the section "Evaluating Your Evidence and Shaping Your Argument." In particular, keep in mind the following four points:

1. Be sure to include the strongest arguments of both sides.
2. Don't make "sack paragraphs," with all the arguments on one side in one paragraph and all the arguments on the other side in a second one.
3. Remember that a statement isn't an argument; statements are often like topic sentences—that is, sentences that have to be explained or backed up.
4. Make sure your conclusion is based solidly on the arguments preceding it. It should reflect the strengths and weaknesses of the arguments covered in your essay, not be merely your own unsupported opinion tacked on at the end.

Writing

Your introduction should briefly outline the issue and state your thesis, which may well be your recommendation. Your paragraphs will probably pretty much follow the essay assignment itself, and your conclusion, of course, will either make a recommendation or restate your thesis. Be sure to review the Writer's Checklist on pages 339–340 as you work on this assignment.

SHOULD HIGH SCHOOL STUDENTS WORK?

In an earlier age, it was rare for high school students to work, unless they had to do so in order to help support their families. Those who did work part time usually did so only for two or three hours after school, leaving the evenings and the weekends for study and socializing. The relatively small amounts of money teenagers made at these jobs generally went toward financing dates or into a college-saving fund.

Now, however, the proliferation of franchise businesses, particularly fast-food outlets, that seek inexperienced, easily trained young people to do repetitious work at the minimum wage has created many job opportunities for teens. At the same time, teenagers have become a prime target for advertisers, who bombard them with glossy inducements to buy the latest in clothes, in electronics, in hit records. The pressure is on, particularly among teens who come from working- and middle-class families, to get jobs and to work long hours in order to get as much of their own disposable income as possible.

As a result, the issue of whether—or how much—teenagers who don't have to work should work has gradually become a major concern to parents, educators, psychologists, and sociologists, who worry about the effects of part-time work on the physical, educational, psychological, and social well-being of teenagers. However, other professionals, especially those employers who benefit from the low wages awarded to teenagers, maintain that teenagers profit, more than just financially, from working because they learn responsibility and become accustomed to adult life.

Reading Assignment

Pre-reading

As a way of beginning to think about this topic, you might consider these questions on the basis of your own experience or that of others you know: What is positive about high school students holding jobs during the school year? What is negative about it? What are the issues involved besides the problem of work interfering with school? Take notes that you can refer to after you've read what others have to say on the subject.

Reading

Remember to take notes in the margins or on a separate sheet of paper as you read the following four essays.

PART-TIME WORK ETHIC: SHOULD TEENS GO FOR IT?
Dennis McLellan

The author is a staff writer for the Los Angeles Times. *This article appeared in that newspaper.*

John Fovos landed his first part-time job—as a box boy at Alpha   1
Beta on West Olympic—the summer after his sophomore year at
Fairfax High School in Los Angeles. "I wanted to be independent,"

he said, "and I felt it was time for me to see what the world was really like."

Now an 18-year-old senior, Fovos works the late shift at the su- 2 permarket stocking shelves four nights a week. He saves about $50 a week, but most of his paycheck goes to his car payment and membership at a health spa. "The rest is for food—what I don't eat at home—and clothes."

Shelley Staats went to work part time as a secretary for a Cen- 3 tury 21 office when she was 15. Since then, she has worked as a cashier for a marine products company, scooped ice cream at a Baskin-Robbins, cashiered at a Video Depot and worked as a "floater" at May Co.

The Newport Harbor High School senior currently works about 4 25 hours a week in the lingerie department at the new Broadway in Costa Mesa. Although she saves about $200 a month for college, she said she works "to support myself: my car and clothes and just stuff I do, like going out."

Working also has helped her to learn to manage both her time 5 and money, Staats said, and her work in the department store is providing experience for a future career in fashion merchandising.

But, she acknowledged, there are times when working while 6 going to school has taken its toll.

"Last year I was sleeping in my first-period class half the time," 7 admitted Staats, who occasionally has forgone football games and school dances because of work. "After a while, it just wears you out."

Nathan Keethe, a Newport Harbor High School senior who 8 works more than 20 hours a week for an exterminating service, admits to sometimes feeling like the odd man out when he sees that fellow students "are out having a good time after school and I'm working. But then I think there's a lot of other kids out there working, too, and it doesn't seem so unusual."

Indeed, what clearly was the exception 40 years ago is now the rule. 9

Fovos, Staats and Keethe are riding the crest of a wave of part- 10 time student employees that began building at the end of World War II and has steadily increased to the present. In 1981, according to a study by the National Center for Education Statistics, 80% of high school students had held part-time jobs by the time they graduated.

Part-time work during the school years traditionally has been 11 viewed as an invaluable experience for adolescents, one that builds character, teaches responsibility and prepares them for entering the adult world.

But the authors of a **provocative** new book challenge conven- 12
tional wisdom, contending that an over-commitment to work during the school years "may make teenagers economically wealthy but
psychologically poor. . . ."

The book, *When Teenagers Work: The Psychological and Social* 13
Costs of Adolescent Employment, is by Ellen Greenberger, a developmental psychologist and professor of social ecology at the University
of California, Irvine, and Laurence Steinberg, a professor of child and
family studies at the University of Wisconsin.

Based on national research data and on the authors' own study 14
of more than 500 working and non-working students at four Orange
County [California] high schools, the book reports that:

- Extensive part-time employment during the school year may
  undermine youngsters' education. Students who work long
  hours are more likely to cut back on courses at school, taking
  easier classes and avoiding tougher ones. And, say the authors,
  long hours of work begun early in the school years increase the
  likelihood of dropping out.
- Working leads less often to the accumulation of savings or
  financial contributions to the family than to a higher level of
  spending on cars, clothes, stereos, concerts and other luxury
  items.
- Working appears to promote, rather than deter, some forms
  of delinquent behavior. About 30% of the youngsters in
  their first part-time job have given away goods or services;
  18% have taken things other than money from work; 5½%
  have taken money from work; and 17% have worked under
  the influence of drugs or alcohol, according to the Orange
  County study.
- Working long hours under stressful conditions leads to
  increased alcohol and marijuana use.
- Teen-age employment—typically in dull or monotonous jobs for
  which the sole motivation is the paycheck—often leads to increased **cynicism** about working.

Moreover, the authors contend that adolescents who work long 15
hours may develop the superficial social skills of an adult, but by
devoting too much time to a job they severely curtail the time

---

provocative: challenging, stimulating; cynicism: scornful, sneering attitude needed for **reflection, introspection** and identity experimentation that is required to develop true maturity.

Such findings lead Greenberger and Steinberg to conclude 16 "that the benefits of working to the development of adolescents have been overestimated, while the costs have been underestimated."

"We don't want to be read as saying that kids shouldn't work 17 during the school year," Greenberger said in an interview. "Our argument is with over-commitment to work: That working long hours may interfere with other very important goals of the growing years."

The authors place the blame partly on the types of jobs avail- 18 able to young people today. By working in unchallenging, monotonous jobs in fast-food restaurants or retail shops, they contend, teen-agers learn few new skills, have little opportunity for meaningful contact with adults and seldom gain work experience that will lead to future careers.

"Parents and schools," Greenberger said, "should wake up from 19 the dream that having a kid who works 30 hours a week is promoting his or her transition to adulthood."

Greenberger and Steinberg's findings, not surprisingly, do not 20 sit well with the fast-food industry.

"The fast-food industry is probably the largest employer of 21 young people in the United States," said Paul Mitchell, spokesperson for Carl Karcher Enterprises, which employs thousands of teen-agers in its Carl's Jr. restaurants.

"For most of those young people," Mitchell said, "it's their first 22 job, the first time they are told that you make a product a certain way, the first time they work with money, the first time they are made aware to be there on time and do it right . . . and it's just a tremendous working experience."

Terry Capatosto, a spokeswoman for McDonald's, calls Green- 23 berger and Steinberg's findings "absurd, to say the least."

"Working at McDonald's contributes tremendously to [young 24 people's] personal development and work ethic," said Capatosto, noting that countless McDonald's **alumnae** have gone on to professional careers and that about half of the people at all levels of McDonald's

---

reflection: thoughtfulness;   introspection: self-examination;
alumnae: graduates

management, including the company's president and chairman of the board, started out as crew people.

"The whole idea of getting students out in the community dur- 25 ing the time they're also a student is a very productive thing to do," said Jackie Oakes, college and career guidance specialist at Santa Ana High School.

Although she feels most students work "for the extras kids 26 want," Oakes said they worked for a variety of reasons, including earning money to go on a trip with the school band and saving for college.

As for work taking time away from studying, Oakes said, "I think 27 if a kid isn't interested in studying, having a job doesn't impact that."

Newport Harbor High School's Nathan Keethe, who usually 28 earns Bs, doesn't think he'd devote more time to schoolwork if he weren't working. "Not really, because even when I wasn't working I wasn't too devoted to school," he said, adding that "for somebody who is, I wouldn't recommend working too much. I do think it would interfere."

Fairfax High's John Fovos, who works about 27 hours a week, 29 however, said his grade-point average actually has risen since he began working part time. The motivation? "My parents told me if my job hindered my grades, they'd ask me to quit," he said.

Although she acknowledges that some teen-age workers may 30 experience growth in such areas as self-reliance and improved work habits, Greenberger said, "It's not evident that those things couldn't be **realized** in other settings as well. There's no evidence that you have to be a teen-age drone in order to grow in those areas."

As for the notion that "it would be great to get kids out into the 31 workplace because they'll learn," Greenberger said that "the news is not so good. On the one hand we find that relatively little time on the job is spent using anything resembling higher-order **cognitive** skills," she said. "Computation nowadays is often done automatically by the cash register; so much for practicing arithmetic. Kids do extremely little writing and reading [on the job]. There's also very little job training. In fact, most of the youngsters in our survey reported their job could be done by somebody with a grade-school education or less."

---

realized: made real or actual;   cognitive: process of acquiring knowledge

MCJOBS
Ben Wildavsky

The following article was published in an issue of Policy Review.

According to the standard lament, the 18 million jobs created in 1
America since the 1982 recession are an **illusory** measure of economic expansion; a nation of hamburger-flippers, goes the argument, is a nation in decline.

As the **archetypal** fast food establishment, serving close to 7 per- 2
cent of the U.S. population every day and employing a remarkable 1
out of 15 first-time job seekers, McDonald's has been a frequent target for those **expounding** the "dead-end jobs" thesis. . . .

While the typical complaints critics voice about McDonald's cer- 3
tainly have some basis in reality—annual turnover often surpasses
100 percent, and it is not difficult to find crew members who complain of high pressure and low wages—the overall picture is more
positive. A closer look at the people who work at McDonald's shows
that a surprising number of burger-flippers advance through the
ranks and enjoy the benefits that go with managerial responsibility
in a demanding business. More important, most employees who
pass through McDonald's gain the kinds of skills that help them get
better jobs. . . .

Marion Foran started working at McDonald's in July, 1973, a 4
month after graduating from high school in Helena, Montana. She
planned to attend the University of Northern Arizona at Flagstaff,
and her mother told her to go out and get a job. "In my family," says
Foran, "there were five kids, and it was assumed that if you wanted
to go to college you'd have to pay your own way." She was hired at
$1.60 an hour, intending only to stay until she had financed her first
year of college. . . .

Soon, Foran was awarded the first in a series of promotions. She 5
became a second assistant manager, working six days a week supervising employees, hiring and training crew members, taking inventory, and helping with the financial reports, all for the grand sum of
$350 a month.

By the time she was 18, Foran was first assistant manager, had 6
purchased a new Volkswagen bug with her own money, and had
trained two new second assistants. . . .

---

illusory: deceptive;   archetypal: original model or type
expounding: arguing for

At age 20 . . . she moved to Las Vegas and started work as a man- 7
ager trainee at a McDonald's in a poor section of town, a far cry from
small-town Montana. By 1978, Foran was promoted to restaurant
manager and was asked to open a brand new outlet on the Las Vegas
Strip. . . .

After managing another Las Vegas store for one and a half years, 8
Foran was promoted to area supervisor in 1982 at age 26; she over-
saw operations at five or six stores and earned $24,000 a year, with
the added benefits of a company car and weekends off. After two
more years, she became a field consultant, then a training assistant,
running the Basic Operations Course that all would-be McDonald's
managers must take. . . .

In April, 1988, she started her current job as a professor at Ham- 9
burger University, the McDonald's manager-training center at company headquarters in Illinois, famous for issuing each graduate of its
one- and two-week intensive courses a degree in Hamburgerology
with a minor in Fries. . . .

A less spectacular but perhaps more typical example of some- 10
one who has progressed through the ranks is David Fisher. Fisher was
recently promoted to second assistant at a McDonald's in a suburb
of Washington. The average salary nationally for those in his position
is $19,500, with full medical benefits. . . .

Fisher disagrees with people who think McDonald's jobs lead 11
nowhere. He is exasperated by the high turnover that plagues
the tight D.C.-area labor market—"some kids just hop from job
to job"—and thinks that too many employees expect something
for nothing: "There's an amazing amount of opportunity available, but no one's going to hand it to you." He cites three successful second assistants, all in their early 20s, who started at
the bottom—one from Korea, one from Nigeria, and one from
Jamaica. Apparently, recent immigrants, who may find few other
jobs as easily available, can achieve considerable mobility at Mc-
Donald's. . . .

Not everyone paints as rosy a picture of McDonald's as those 12
who have made it. In addition to low wages and a hot, high-speed
work environment, some employees complain of poor treatment
by managers. Mark Kershaw, a 33-year-old manager from Ogden,
Utah, who started at McDonald's in high school and came back as
a manager when a back injury caused him to lose his railroad job,
agrees that "there are some managers who treat them like
slaves." He tries to avoid this, and has gotten to know his employees

well, to the point of advising them about problems outside the
workplace. . . .

Lou DeRosa, the 29-year-old manager of a Connecticut McDon- 13
ald's, grew up in a tough New Haven neighborhood. He offers a
blunt assessment of McDonald's jobs that seems realistic for many of
those who take them: "This is a survival job. A lot of people can't
handle it. This is something that shows you if you can work or not.
It's not like a department store where you can lay back." DeRosa
stresses the time constraints and high standards crew members must
work to: "It separates the men from the boys." . . .

While the number of success stories to be found within McDon- 14
ald's belies the notion that jobs there are **irredeemably** worthless,
these examples are not intended to suggest that such career paths
are typical, only that they are possible. The vast majority of those
who work at McDonald's come and go with great frequency, and
not everyone sees anything wrong with this. "*All* jobs are dead-end,"
says Walter Williams, professor of economics at George Mason University. "We as a nation suffer from the Horatio Alger myth, where a
guy comes in as a porter and becomes president of the company."
The typical person, according to Williams, achieves upward mobility
across jobs, not within a job. This process involves working at a particular job, gaining experience, finding out about other jobs, and
moving on. . . .

What exactly do fast food jobs teach? A 1984 study by Ivan 15
Charner and Bryna Fraser . . . attempted to answer that question.
. . . As might be expected, high percentages of employees reported learning such directly job-related skills as operating a cash
register (80 percent) and operating food preparation machines (85
percent). Seventy percent of employees believed they had learned
"some" or "a great deal" about training other workers, 50 percent
learned supervisory skills, and 40 percent learned inventory control, while fewer than 20 percent developed bookkeeping or accounting skills.

More important than the specific skills learned are what Charner 16
and Fraser call "general employability skills," the kinds of qualities an
employee—particularly a young person with limited work experience—must possess to be successful in any job. Ninety-four percent
of employees said their jobs helped them learn teamwork, 89 per-

---

irredeemably: hopelessly

cent learned how to deal with customers, and 69 percent developed an awareness of how a business runs. Respondents learned such crucial work skills as taking directions (73 percent), getting along with coworkers (75 percent), being on time (57 percent), finishing an assigned task (64 percent), taking responsibility for mistakes (65 percent), coming to work regularly (59 percent), and being well groomed (44 percent). . . .

The not-so-hidden secret of McDonald's success lies in the **meticulous** operating procedures for food preparation and service that all its stores follow. Before being shown the ropes by a crew trainer, new employees watch an orientation video that stresses neatness and hygiene. Employees are told they must bathe daily, have clean hair and teeth, keep moustaches and sideburns trimmed, wear only neutral nail polish, and wash their hands with soap before and after using any work station.   17

Another video, "Counter 1: The Six Steps," teaches the fundamentals of customer service. Crew members are told to be at the counter before the customer arrives, to look him or her in the eye, and to smile. A beaming teenager is shown greeting a customer with an upbeat "Good afternoon! May I take your order please?" The narrator instructs crew people, "Vary the greeting and the tone of your voice from customer to customer—you don't want to sound like a robot." . . .   18

Training tapes with titles like "Fries," "Opening the Store," and "A Study in Breakfast" are used to teach various stations and responsibilities, with detailed station observation checklists used both as a reference point for crew people and a performance assessment tool for managers. No point is too small to be left out—making french fries involves 15 separate steps, with seven more to be followed for bagging—though a number of tasks require more human initiative than a checklist can spell out. If counter people are not busy, for example, they should help their coworkers, clean the counter, and replenish supplies. Those working the grill are guided by a timer, but must rely on visual inspection to decide exactly when to turn the patties. And counter people have standing instructions to replace any items dropped by customers at no cost, informing the manager afterwards so the product can be accounted for in the store's inventory. . . .   19

---

meticulous: extremely careful and precise;

By looking at the qualities that large employers of entry-level   20
personnel say they are looking for, it becomes clear that these closely
coincide with the employability skills taught in fast food jobs. Alan
Wurtzel, chairman of Circuit City, a chain of electronics stores based
in Richmond, Virginia, says that when his stores hire new cashiers
and stock clerks, specific skills are unimportant. "The most important thing we're looking for is attitude and energy. We want people
who are reliable, presentable, clean shaven, honest, can get along
with coworkers, and can follow directions." When a new store
opens, Wurtzel says, 10 applicants have to be screened for every
one hired; people with these basic work skills are apparently not
easy to find.

Ninety percent of Mike O'Shea's new employees have fast food   21
experience, mostly at McDonald's. While the 20-year-old assistant
manager of a downtown Chicago shoe store says he is unimpressed
by applicants with a string of short-term hitches at fast food restaurants, he understands people who rise to a certain level and decide
it's not worthwhile to continue. . . .

As senior human resources coordinator at the Washington-   22
area Capital Centre entertainment complex, Kim Whittington considers fast food experience a plus in a candidate for entry-level
positions: "For me it shows the motivation, the initiative, especially if they've been there over a year. They learn people skills,
cash handling, getting people in and out quickly; they could even
learn some management skills if they're training other people."
Whittington stresses the importance of "basic, basic work skills,"
adding, "we have problems with dependability, especially among
young people." . . .

Evidently, the kinds of skills learned at McDonald's are the kinds   23
of skills employers are looking for. This does not mean that the jobs
are a **panacea** whose abundance offers a magic solution to the nation's problems. Although McDonald's jobs undeniably fulfill various
people's needs for part-time and seasonal employment, they are just
as undeniably plain hard work. Like all jobs that are easily available
to many different people, what they can do and are doing . . . is to
give people a chance to work hard and get ahead, even—perhaps
especially—those whose lack of skills and advantages might seem to
limit their prospects enormously.

---

coincide: correspond exactly;   panacea: cure-all

WHY FAST-FOOD JOINTS DON'T SERVE UP GOOD JOBS FOR KIDS
Amitai Etzioni

The author, a distinguished scholar and academician, wrote this article for the Washington Post.

McDonald's is bad for your kids. I do not mean the flat patties and 1 the white-flour buns; I refer to the jobs teenagers undertake, mass-producing these choice items.

As many as two-thirds of America's high-school juniors and se- 2 niors now hold down part-time jobs, according to studies. Many of these are in fast-food chains of which McDonald's is the pioneer, trend-setter and symbol.

At first, such jobs may seem right out of the Founding Fathers' 3 educational manual for how to bring up self-reliant, work-ethic-dri-ven, productive youngsters. But in fact, these jobs undermine school attendance and involvement, impart few skills that will be useful in later life, and simultaneously skew the values of teenagers—espe-cially their ideas about the worth of a dollar.

It has been a longstanding American tradition that youngsters 4 ought to get paying jobs. In folklore, few pursuits are more deeply revered than the newspaper route and the sidewalk lemonade stand. Here the youngsters are to learn how sweet are the fruits of labor and self-discipline (papers are delivered early in the morning, rain or shine), and the ways of trade (if you price your lemonade too high or too low . . .).

Roy Rogers, Baskin-Robbins, Kentucky Fried Chicken, et al., may 5 at first seem nothing but a vast extension of the lemonade stand. They provide very large numbers of teen jobs, provide regular em-ployment, pay quite well compared to many other teen jobs and, in the modern equivalent of toiling over a hot stove, test one's **stamina**.

Closer examination, however, finds the McDonald's kind of job 6 highly uneducational in several ways. Far from providing opportuni-ties for **entrepreneurship** (the lemonade stand) or self-discipline, self-supervision and self-scheduling (the paper route), most teen jobs these days are highly structured—what social scientists call "highly routinized."

---

stamina: strength, endurance;   entrepreneurship: organizing a business

True, you still have to have the gumption to get yourself over to 7
the hamburger stand, but once you don the prescribed uniform,
your task is spelled out in minute detail. The franchise prescribes the
shape of the coffee cups; the weight, size, shape and color of the
patties; and the texture of the napkins (if any). Fresh coffee is to be
made every eight minutes. And so on. There is no room for initiative,
creativity, or even elementary rearrangements. These are breeding
grounds for robots working for yesterday's assembly lines, not tomorrow's high-tech posts.

There are very few studies of the matter. One of the few is a 1984 8
study by Ivan Charner and Bryna Shore Fraser. The study relies mainly
on what teenagers write in response to questionnaires rather than
actual observations of fast-food jobs. The authors argue that the employees develop many skills such as how to operate a food-preparation
machine and a cash register. However, little attention is paid to how
long it takes to acquire such a skill, or what its significance is.

What does it matter if you spend 20 minutes to learn to use a 9
cash register, and then—"operate" it? What "skill" have you acquired? It is a long way from learning to work with a **lathe** or carpenter tools in the olden days or to program computers in the
modern age.

A 1980 study by A. V. Harrell and P. W. Wirtz found that, among 10
those students who worked at least 25 hours per week while in
school, their unemployment rate four years later was half of that of
seniors who did not work. This is an impressive statistic. It must be
seen, though, together with the finding that many who begin as
part-time employees in fast-food chains drop out of high school and
are gobbled up in the world of low-skill jobs.

Some say that while these jobs are rather unsuited for college- 11
bound, white, middle-class youngsters, they are "ideal" for lower-
class, "non-academic," minority youngsters. Indeed, minorities are
"over-represented" in these jobs (21 percent of fast-food employees). While it is true that these places provide income, work, and
even some training to such youngsters, they also tend to per-
petuate their disadvantaged status. They provide no career lad-
ders, few marketable skills, and undermine school attendance
and involvement.

The hours are often long. Among those 14 to 17, a third of fast- 12
food employees (including some school drop-outs) labor more than

---

lathe: a wood-working machine

30 hours per week, according to the Charner-Fraser study. Only 20 percent work 15 hours or less. The rest: between 15 and 30 hours.

Often the stores close late, and after closing one must clean up 13 and tally up. In affluent Montgomery County, Md., where child labor would not seem to be a widespread economic necessity, 24 percent of the seniors at one high school in 1985 worked as much as five to seven days a week; 27 percent, three to five. There is just no way such amounts of work will not interfere with schoolwork, especially homework. In an informal survey published in the most recent year-book of the high school, 58 percent of the seniors acknowledged that their jobs interfere with their schoolwork.

The Charner-Fraser study sees merit in learning teamwork and 14 working under supervision. The authors have a point here. However, it must be noted that such learning is not automatically educational or wholesome. For example, much of the supervision in fast-food places leans toward teaching one the wrong kinds of compliance: blind obedience, or shared **alienation** with the "boss."

Supervision is often both tight and woefully inappropriate. 15 Today, fast-food chains and other such places of work (record shops, bowling alleys) keep costs down by having teens supervise teens with often no adult on the premises.

There is no father or mother figure with which to identify, to 16 **emulate,** to provide a role model and guidance. The work-culture varies from one place to another. Sometimes it is a tightly run shop (must keep the cash registers ringing); sometimes a rather loose pot party interrupted by customers. However, only rarely is there a master to learn from, or much worth learning. Indeed, far from being places where solid adult work values are being trans-mitted, these are places where all too often delinquent teen values dominate. Typically, when my son Oren was dishing out ice cream for Baskin-Robbins in upper Manhattan, his fellow teen-workers considered him a sucker for not helping himself to the till. Most youngsters felt they were entitled to $50 severance "pay" on their last day on the job.

The pay, oddly, is the part of the teen work-world that is most 17 difficult to evaluate. The lemonade stand or paper route money was for your allowance. In the old days, apprentices learning a trade from a master contributed most, if not all, of their income to their par-ents' household. Today, the teen pay may be low by adult standards,

---

alienation: being apart from, outside of;   emulate: copy, imitate but it is often, especially in the middle class, spent largely or wholly by the teens. That is, the youngsters live free at home, ("after all, they are high-school kids") and are left with very substantial sums of money.

Where this money goes is not quite clear. Some use it to support 18 themselves, especially among the poor. More middle-class kids set some money aside to help pay for college, or save it for a major purchase—often a car. But large amounts seem to flow to pay for an early introduction into the most trite aspects of American consumerism, flimsy punk clothes, trinkets, and whatever else is the last fast-moving teen craze.

One may say that this is only fair and square; they are being 19 good American consumers and spending their money on what turns them on. At least, a cynic might add, these funds do not go into illicit drugs and booze. On the other hand, an educator might bemoan that these young, yet unformed individuals, so early in life are driven to buy objects of no intrinsic educational, cultural or social merit, learn so quickly the dubious merit of keeping up with the Joneses in ever-changing fads, promoted by mass merchandising.

Many teens find the instant reward of money, and the youth sta- 20 tus symbols it buys, much more alluring than credits in calculus courses, European history, or foreign languages. No wonder quite a few would rather skip school—and certainly homework—and instead work longer at a Burger King. Thus, most teen work these days is not providing early lessons in work ethic; it fosters escape from school and responsibilities, quick **gratification** and a short cut in the consumeristic aspects of adult life.

Thus, **ironically,** we must add youth employment, not merely 21 unemployment, to our list of social problems. And, like many other social ills, the unfortunate aspects of teen work resist easy correction.

Sure, it would be much better if corporations that employ 22 teens would do so in conjunction with high schools and school districts. Educators could help define what is the proper amount of gainful work (not more than "X" hours per school week); how late kids may be employed on school nights (not later than 9 P.M.); encourage employer understanding during exam periods, and insist on proper supervision. However, corporations are extremely unlikely to accept such an approach as that, which in effect, would

---

gratification: satisfaction of desires;   ironically: in contrast to expectations curb their ability to draw on a major source of cheap labor. And, in these **laissez-faire** days, Congress is quite disinclined to pass new social legislation forcing corporations to be more attentive to the education needs of the minors they so readily employ.

Parents who are still willing to take their role seriously may 23 encourage their youngsters to seek jobs at places that are proper work settings and insist that fast-food chains and other franchises shape up or not employ their kids. Also an agreement should be reached with the youngsters that a significant share of teen earnings should be dedicated to the family, or saved for agreed-upon items.

Above all, parents should look at teen employment not as auto- 24 matically educational. It is an activity—like sports—that can be turned into an educational opportunity. But it can also easily be abused. Youngsters must learn to balance the quest for income with the needs to keep growing and pursue other endeavors that do not pay off instantly—above all, education.

Go back to school. 25

WHY NOT ASK THE STUDENTS? URBAN TEENAGERS MAKE THE CASE FOR WORKING
Katherine Cress

For many of today's urban minority high school students from low- 1 income families, the future looks bleak. In their neighborhoods, violence is a fact of life. Some teenagers face pressure to join gangs and get involved in drug activity, and 50% or more of all inner-city students drop out of high school. For these and other reasons, such teenagers are considered to be "at risk" for various problems, including unemployment. The question is, How can minority high school students in urban areas be helped to make a successful transition from school to higher education or to the adult world of work?

The business community has long endorsed one popular answer. 2 Business believes that jobs are "good" for young people. More specifically, business claims that jobs help disadvantaged students make a successful transition from school to work. According to the Committee for Economic Development, part-time work during high school can give at-risk youth

---

laissez-faire: let (business) alone;   at-risk: likely to fail a sense of purpose and an important connection with the outside world. Young people from disadvantaged homes often lack knowledge about the world of work, have few positive adult role models, and have limited access to the job market. Businesses can offer valuable real-world experiences for these youths and offer the role models they lack. In addition, appropriate job experience can help teach or reinforce the basic skills in which disadvantaged youth are so often deficient.

Others, however, doubt whether working can perform this link- 3 ing function. William Behn, John Ogbu, Michelle Fine, and others suggest that the experience of working cannot by itself magically provide the access to opportunity that poor minority students in urban areas lack. Rather, they fear, if students take on employment, it may simply serve to train them earlier in life to accept a **subservient** place in a society that remains **intractably** discriminatory. In effect, jobs may reproduce inequality rather than break down barriers.

At the same time, others have begun to worry about how working 4 affects students' performance in school. Brooke Workman maintains that students in the midwestern college-prep high school where he teaches work simply because it is "the thing to do" and then suffer as a result from fatigue, falling grades, and a diminished interest in schooling. Linda McNeil, who studied students from four midwestern high schools, found that working students tended to feel tired in class, to take easier electives, and to avoid upper-level courses. McNeil summed up her findings by commenting that "increased student employment has become one of the factors which has caused teachers and students to expect less from each other." While both Workman and McNeil studied populations in the Midwest rather than the urban minority students on which I focus here, their warning must be considered: some jobs, for some students, have been shown to diminish commitment to schooling.

What do the students themselves think? Missing from the re- 5 search is any attempt to find out from urban students what working means to them. There are two good reasons to pursue this question. The first is an **ethnographic** one: if we want to conduct thorough analyses of programs that are being implemented in schools, we need to begin to listen to what students themselves think. Second, as businesses begin to play an increasing role in the **socialization** of

---

subservient: inferior, subordinate;   intractably: stubbornly;   ethnographic: cultural, social;   socialization: adjustment to the values of society the young, we need to find out if their youth programs accomplish what they claim. Surprisingly, little or no **evaluation** has accompanied the raft of business-led employment programs that have sprung up in recent years, and this lack of accountability must be corrected.

In 1989 I interviewed high school juniors and seniors in Boston 6 regarding the nature of their work experiences. These students were working part-time under the auspices of the Boston Compact, a school/business/university partnership that has been admired and **replicated** across the country. Such initiatives represent a key component in the business community's renewed commitment to public education. Focusing on an all-urban, predominantly at-risk population made it possible to understand for the first time the work experiences of the group most in need of any positive benefits employment may provide.

The interviews explored three interrelated questions. How do 7 part-time jobs in Boston businesses affect students' understanding of the adult world of work? How do these jobs affect students' sense of their potential access to that world? And how do these jobs influence the way students view their future? In interviewing a sample of at-risk high school students, I found that work can offer such students a valuable growth experience when the conditions and the relationships in the workplace are right. Prior research suggests that work does more harm than good; the results of my study suggest that the reverse *can* be true.

Findings on five central issues emerged from the interviews and 8 shed light on the questions of how at-risk students experience work and how they plan for the future. The issues were: (1) the role of work relationships in students' lives, (2) students' conscious acquisition of skills and work habits on the job, (3) work as an alternative to "the street," (4) the way students regard money, and (5) whether work during high school affects the way students plan for college and careers. There seems to be a great deal about the work experience that educators and businesspeople must strive to understand better—and to do so, they need information that only working students themselves can provide.

The most significant finding of my study was that relationships 9 on the job, especially relationships with adults, matter a great deal to students. Students spoke again and again about their interactions,

---

evaluation: testing;   replicated: copied

both positive and negative, with adult supervisors. Kevin's description of his relationship with his supervisor was positive:

> I used to be cold-hearted and ruthless. If I wanted something, I'd take it. But I look at my boss . . . he's nice. He does things, you know? He travels the world, he owns his own plane, he flies across country and to Europe and stuff, he's a nice guy, you know? He doesn't fight anybody for something. That's what I'd like to be.

Students look up to their supervisors and admire their clothes, 10 speech, office skills, and behaviors. Students also value their accessibility, warmth, and personal ethics. When Kevin vowed to model himself after his boss, who taught him that you can succeed without "stomping on people to get to the top," he was showing that he had learned from this man a new way of *being* in the world.

On the negative side, some students described adults who were 11 inconsiderate and even cruel. Jeffrey, who led a team of environmental service workers at one of the city's large hospitals, was falsely accused by a nurse with whom he worked of shirking his duties. As it turned out, she had forgotten to tell him about the assignment in question. Before the situation was resolved, however, Jeffrey felt that she was wrong. "And then she didn't talk right [to me], the way she was supposed to. Even if she was angry, she shouldn't have talked down to us. She said we don't want to work there, [that] all the kids who work there won't do anything on the weekends—things she felt inside about some of the other workers, this was the time she let it all come out." In the end the nurse apologized to Jeffrey, which he says made him feel "relieved. Because it was my trust that was on the line. My dependability."

Students' experiences on the job vary by race. Interviews 12 brought to light a difference in the frequency with which white and nonwhite students experienced positive and negative relationships with adults in the workplace. White students were more likely than nonwhite students to talk about positive experiences with adults on the job; nonwhite students spoke more often than whites about negative experiences with adults on the job. Because the ability to relate well to adults in positions of power enhances students' opportunities in the adult world of work, white students may experience a smoother entry into the working world.

The literature on student work suggests that many student work- 13
places are segregated by age (at least in the naturally occurring
student job market), and the literature characterizes this segregation
as a negative phenomenon. However, the students I interviewed saw
both advantages and disadvantages to age-segregated workplaces. A
positive aspect of working with peers was being with college-age
co-workers who served as role models. "They tell you what to expect when you get to college," Richard explained, "and we kind of
want to be like them when we get there." Ivonne agreed: "Being
around college students—that sort of made me want to broaden
my mind."

On the negative side, students described age-segregated work- 14
places gone wild, with little or no adult supervision. Stephen called
the insurance company in which he worked "the zoo," and, at
Jacques' job at a hospital cafeteria, a fight broke out when another
student worker slapped Jacques' girlfriend. In his words, "I just got
in a fight because she got smacked and was on the floor crying."

Significant differences existed between white and nonwhite stu- 15
dents' attitudes concerning the experience of working with peers.
The most striking difference was that twice as many nonwhite students as white students talked about both the advantages and the
disadvantages of working with peers. Males were more likely than
females to see disadvantages to working with peers. The reasons
for these differences are unclear. The findings simply raise questions
about relationships between students on the job and draw attention to the particular importance of peer relationships for students
of color.

None of the previous studies of students who work mentioned 16
the finding of my study that some urban students clearly recognize
and consciously seek the future-oriented benefits of working. While
Ellen Greenberger and Laurence Steinberg observed that improved
work habits develop on the job, Milfred Dale's study of inner-city
youth showed no connection between working and the development of more mature work habits. None of the prior research has revealed the belief of some working students that they are gaining
valuable job skills and work habits. However, the students in my
study made it clear that they wanted, valued, and sought out these
skills and habits. James stated that he worked to acquire the skills
that he "would need in a job in the future," explaining that, thanks

to his work in a record store, "by senior year I'll be able to run the whole store, because they're showing me everything right now. These skills will really help in the future—like managing, marketing, stocking—so I will be able to do all that." James' goal is to own and operate his own business after college. Akeem stressed the prestige of having a "respectable" job during high school: "You tell people you have a job at a bank, and they say, 'Yeah, that boy's real clever.'"

Cultivating good work habits was also important to these stu-   17
dents. Matt said that working had helped him learn to control his temper: "I've learned not to snap the gun when my boss tells me something. Not that it's wrong, but he'll be picking something out so the next time I won't do it, and I tend to get a little snappy. I tend to get a little bent out of shape about it sometimes. So I don't think it would be good to have an attitude like that down the line."

Career counselors who work with students see the acquisition of   18
job skills and good work habits as the key to opportunities in the adult world of work, especially for at-risk students. One counselor explained that urban students, many of whom come from "chaotic backgrounds," operate on impulse. When their desires are thwarted, they get angry and go off. They need to learn, this counselor continued, that "there are ways to deal with your frustrations in a responsible manner."

It is encouraging to note that nonwhite students more so than   19
whites said that they valued gaining job skills and appropriate work habits through their jobs. This may mean that jobs help at-risk students put together the pieces that will secure them access to success in the adult world of work.

Work can also serve as an important alternative to "the street."   20
Students reported that school demanded little of them and that the only alternatives to working after school were going home to watch television or getting into trouble. Male students were particularly aware of the lure of the street, where drugs were bought and sold and gang activity lent structure to life. Reggie talked about the teenagers who chose the street over jobs:

> Oh yeah, there's kids out there—stealing cars, selling drugs, and
> all that. This kid in my class, he goes and pulls out his money and
> flashes $850, in 50s and 20s. And he says, "I have money—
> mucho moolah." And I say, "Well, I have money too, it may not
> be as much as yours, but it's cleaner than yours." And he looked

at me and didn't even talk. It's like he thought about it, and there was nothing he could say.

However, previous research does not suggest that jobs can pro- 21 vide an escape from delinquency and dangerous environments. Among the students sampled by Steinberg and his colleagues, working caused an increase in cigarette and marijuana use; the researchers also found that other work-related behaviors—such as **materialism, cynicism,** and acceptance of unethical business practices—could push students toward delinquency. The studies by Denise Gottfredson and by Milfred Dale did not present evidence that working increased delinquent behavior in students, but neither did they show work as a way out of delinquency or as protection against a dangerous and **pervasive** youth culture. They did not find what seemed to be true for some of the students interviewed here— that work was often the safest place to be.

It is generally assumed that high school students work "for the 22 money." However, the above revelations about how important it is to students to establish good working relationships, to acquire productive job skills and work habits, and to avoid the street clearly show that work means more to students than simply making money.

Even when they do talk about the financial benefits of working, 23 students speak in relatively unselfish terms. For example, many students mentioned that, before they had jobs, they were constantly forced to ask their parents for money—but once they became moneymakers themselves, they could use their income to take pressure off their families. As James put it, "I used to ask my mother for money. Then I had to get a job. I'm getting too old to ask my mother for money. I like to be my own person." Laronda actually lent her mother money; Kevin paid for his family's groceries. Seventeen-year-old Carmen, already married, worked to pay household expenses. Kevin, J. T., and Matt paid their own room and board. Contributing to their own support—and thereby contributing to the welfare of the family as a whole—was a significant way students found to connect with their families. It made students feel useful and independent at the same time. . . .

Overall, schools and businesses should take steps to enhance 24 students' work experiences. Schools should integrate work into the

---

materialism: belief that only material goods are important; cynicism: belief that people are motivated by selfishness; pervasive: spread everywhere curriculum, recognize work as a powerful after-school intervention, and help students reflect on and learn from their workplace experiences. Businesses should ensure that students' work experiences are carefully structured and supervised. In addition, they should establish mentoring and college-preparation programs to help students plan realistically for the future. Finally, businesses should begin to evaluate their efforts; up to this point, jobs programs have seldom been carefully evaluated. If schools and businesses put their efforts into improving young people's experience of working, then the energy, enthusiasm, and skills that students gain from it will not be wasted.

Post-reading

These reading selections raise numerous questions bearing on the issue of whether high school students should work. The most obvious one is whether part-time work tends to interfere with school, including both social and homework time, but there are several others. Before you can get very far with the planning of this essay, you will, therefore, have to make notes in two separate areas: (1) What are the issues involved besides the problem of work interfering with school and (2) What facts and opinions in these articles bear on each of these issues?

It is going to be essential to list the issues, and it will certainly be a good idea to work with others in your class to make sure you have identified all of them. Then you will need to list the facts and opinions under each of the issues (unless some of the facts and opinions apply equally to several issues at the same time).

As always in the case of opinions, it is essential to look at where they come from (does the person have some reason to be biased in favor of one view?) and at how they are backed up. For instance, which of the following two opinions do you think has better support?

"I think horror movies are bad. They show all kinds of terrible things happening to people."

"I think horror movies are bad. They cheapen human life by making murder, the worst act a human being can commit against another, merely a form of entertainment."

Now is also the time to go back to your pre-reading notes or any of the other thoughts you had while reading these articles. In the same way that you test those of others, you need to test your own ideas. Write them down under the appropriate issue headings, and look as objectively as you can at how well supported *your* opinions are.

People often make the mistake of thinking that their own experiences are representative—that is, that what they have gone through proves something is true for everyone. Individual experiences rarely *prove* anything. If they did, scientists investigating this or almost any other issue could simply study one person, find out how he or she was affected, and write up a report. But, of course, they can't do that. They have to study many people who are as representative as possible of the whole population being examined. Keep in mind, then, that while your own experiences are important, they are probably not conclusive.

Essay Assignment

Write an essay in which you examine the evidence for and against high school students working part time. Carefully consider both sides of the question and, weighing the pro and con arguments, come to your own conclusion on this issue.

Pre-writing

Before you begin organizing your essay, review the section "Evaluating Evidence and Shaping Your Argument." Be sure to keep in mind these four points:

1. Include the strongest arguments of both sides.
2. Don't put all the arguments on one side in one paragraph and all the arguments on the other side in a second one.
3. Remember that a statement isn't an argument. Statements often resemble topic sentences—that is, sentences that have to be explained or supported.
4. Make sure your conclusion is based solidly on the arguments preceding it. It should reflect the strengths and weaknesses of the arguments covered in your essay, not be merely your own unproven opinion tacked on at the end.

Jot down a working outline, organizing your main points and citing your support, and a working thesis.

Writing

Your introduction should briefly outline the issue and state your thesis. Your paragraphs should support your thesis while dealing with the complexity of the problem as you see it. Your conclusion, of course, should either summarize your essay's main points or make a recommendation.

Be sure to review the Writer's Checklist on pages 339–340 to help you complete this assignment.

SHOULD PEOPLE KEEP HANDGUNS AT HOME?

It has often been said that the United States is a country built upon guns. Our Revolutionary War began when some ordinary farmers in Massachusetts went home, got out their hunting guns, and attacked a unit of the British army. And, of course, the frontiersmen who explored and gradually opened up the North American continent for settlement all carried guns of one kind or another. During the nineteenth century, our old west was famous for its gun-toting cowhands, criminals, and lawmen. This long tradition has resulted in a society that today is more heavily armed than any other in the world.

Although many people favor outlawing guns of all kinds and others would legalize weapons of every type, the argument in recent years has centered primarily on handguns and assault rifles—weapons of use primarily to kill human beings, though some kinds of handguns are used in target shooting.

Although the United States has the highest homicide rate by firearms of any country in the world, other countries have shown concern about guns. After a massacre of schoolchildren and their teacher in Scotland, Britain declared all firearms illegal and collected every gun in the nation under penalty of prison sentence. In 1997, Australia, responding to a similar massacre, declared all semiautomatic weapons and pump-action shotguns illegal and spent more than $260 million to pay citizens to turn in their weapons. Canada has tightened its already very tight gun-control laws.

The American response to numerous massacres, both of school children and adults, has been less drastic. In 1994, Congress passed the Brady Bill, which requires a five-day waiting period and background check of anyone seeking to buy a gun from a licensed dealer. In 1998, a new FBI computerized check system went into effect that blocked 11,584 gun sales during its first 41 days. But 1,030,606 gun sales went through. Laws have been passed both locally and nationally to bar the sales of assault rifles, but these laws exempted the most popular models and permitted gun manufacturers to make "copycat" models that can be sold legally. Finally, 31 states have no laws banning the private sale of guns, and in most states dealers at gun shows can sell whatever they want to whoever wants to buy it.

But more important than whether we have national or local legislation to make it more difficult to own guns, in particular handguns, is the decision by individuals to buy a gun. Many feel that with handguns in the hands of criminals, it makes no sense for law-abiding citizens not to be armed. Others argue that since handguns are useful for only one purpose, to kill human beings, it is unwise and perhaps even immoral to own them.

Reading Assignment

Pre-reading

Before you read the following articles and essays, ask yourself how you stand on this issue and why. Write down your position and the reasons for it so you can refer to them after you've finished reading what other people have to say about handguns.

Reading

Read actively, making notes in the margins or on a separate sheet of paper.

THE SECOND AMENDMENT TO THE U.S. CONSTITUTION

The argument over whether handguns should be outlawed or strictly licensed often begins with the Second Amendment to the Constitution of the United States, part of the Bill of Rights. One side points to it as their Constitutional sanction to own handguns; the other argues that owning handguns has little to do with maintaining a militia—that is, a citizen army or a reserve military force.

A well regulated militia being necessary to the security of a free state, the right of the people to keep and bear arms shall not be infringed.

FIREARM-RELATED DEATHS IN THE UNITED STATES AND 35 OTHER HIGH- AND UPPER-MIDDLE-INCOME COUNTRIES
E. G. Krug, K. E. Powell, and L. L. Dahlberg
Division of Violence Prevention, National Center for Injury Prevention and Control, Centers for Disease Control and Prevention.

Background. The Forty-Ninth World Health Assembly recently de- 1
clared violence a worldwide public health problem. Improved understanding of cross-national differences is useful for identifying risk
factors and may facilitate prevention efforts. Few **cross-national**
studies, however, have explored firearm-related deaths. We compared the incidence of firearm-related deaths among 36 countries.

Methods. Health officials in high-income (HI) and upper-middle- 2
income (UMI) countries with populations greater than one million
were asked to provide data . . . on firearm-related homicides, suicides, unintentional deaths and deaths of undetermined intent, as
well as homicides, and suicides, for all methods combined. Thirty-six
(78%) of the 46 countries provided complete data. We compared
age-adjusted rates per 100,000 for each country and pooled rates by
income group and geographical location.

Results. During the one-year study period, 88,649 firearm deaths 3
were reported. Overall firearm mortality rates are five to six times
higher in HI and UMI countries in the Americas (12.72) than in Europe (2.17), or Oceania (2.57) and 95 times higher than in Asia
(0.13). The rate of firearm deaths in the United States (14.24 per
100,000) exceeds that of its economic counterparts (1.76) eightfold
and that of UMI countries (9.69) by a factor of 1.5. Suicide and homicide contribute equally to total firearm deaths in the US, but most
firearm deaths are suicides (71%) in HI countries and homicides
(72%) in UMI countries.

Conclusions. Firearm death rates vary markedly throughout the 4
industrialized world. Further research to identify risk factors associated with these variations may help improve prevention efforts.

Keywords. Firearms, violence, suicide, homicide, cross-cultural com- 5
parison, developed countries, epidemiology. . . .

In 1990, self-directed and interpersonal violence caused 2.7% of the 6
world's disability adjusted life years (DALY) lost—the numbers of
years of life lost from premature death combined with the loss of
health from disability. This percentage is projected to increase to
4.2% in 2020. In view of what it described as a dramatic increase in
the incidence of intentional injuries, the Forty-Ninth World Health

---

cross-national: across national boundaries, international

Assembly recently adopted a resolution declaring violence a leading worldwide public health problem and urged member states to assess and develop science-based solutions to the problem.

Violence can be defined as the intentional use of physical force— 7
against another person or against oneself—which results in or has a high likelihood of resulting in injury or death. Much of the previous research conducted on violent deaths has focused on homicide or suicide. In some countries, firearms are the most frequently used weapons in homicide and suicide. This is particularly true in the United States, where 71% of homicides and 61% of suicides are firearm-related. In 1993, a firearm was involved in the deaths of 39,595 people in the US (15.6 per 100,000), making firearm injuries the seventh leading cause of death. . . .

International comparisons of firearm-related fatality rates are 8
not common. . . . International comparisons, however, may provide important insights into the magnitude of and risk factors for a health problem. These risk factors can be further studied and may lead to new prevention strategies. In this report, we describe firearm-related deaths in 36 countries and address several questions: How do firearm-related death rates in the US compare with rates in other countries of similar and lower economic status? Are firearm-related death rates similar among geographical regions? Do sex- and age-specific firearm death rates vary across income groups? We also place firearm death rates into the broader context of violent deaths by presenting overall homicide and suicide rates. . . .

Results
Homicide and Suicide Rates

During the one-year study period, the 36 countries combined re- 9
ported 82,465 homicides (6.9 per 100,000) and 130,546 suicides (10.9 per 100,000). Homicide rates for individual countries range from 0.55 in England and Wales to 25.12 in Estonia. Suicide rates range from 1.46 in Kuwait to 34.05 in Estonia (Table 5.1). Some countries reported extremely high violent death rates. . . . The highest rates for homicide are mainly found in Estonia, Mexico, Brazil and the US. The highest suicide rates were reported by Estonia, Hungary and Slovenia, the only countries from Eastern Europe that are included in our study.

Table 5.1   Violent Death Rates per 100,000 Population for 36 Selected High-Income and Upper-Middle-Income Countries

	Year	Population	Firearm total	Firearm homicide	Firearm suicide
High-income countries					
United States	1993	257,783,004	14.24	7.11	6.30
Northern Ireland	1994	1,641,711	6.63	5.07	1.32
Finland	1994	5,088,333	6.46	0.84	5.39
Switzerland	1994	7,021,000	5.31	0.57	4.53
France	1994	57,915,450	5.15	0.40	4.08
Canada	1992	28,120,065	4.31	0.68	3.33
Norway	1993	4,324,815	3.82	0.26	3.44
Austria	1994	8,029,717	3.70	0.37	3.25
Israel	1993	5,261,700	2.91	0.70	1.78
Belgium	1990	9,967,387	2.90	0.53	2.07
Australia	1994	17,838,401	2.65	0.41	2.10
Italy	1992	56,764,854	2.44	1.47	0.81
New Zealand	1993	3,458,850	2.38	0.15	1.88
Denmark	1993	5,189,378	2.09	0.22	1.74
Sweden	1993	8,718,571	1.92	0.18	1.65
Kuwait	1995	1,684,529	1.84	0.34	0.03
Germany	1994	81,338,093	1.24	0.20	0.88
Ireland	1991	3,525,719	0.97	0.03	0.75
Spain	1993	39,086,079	0.78	0.19	0.36
Netherlands	1994	15,382,830	0.70	0.30	0.31
Scotland	1994	5,132,400	0.54	0.18	0.30
England/Wales	1992	51,429,000	0.41	0.08	0.28
Taiwan	1994	21,086,686	0.37	0.12	0.11
Singapore	1994	2,930,200	0.21	0.05	0.15
Hong Kong	1993	5,919,000	0.14	0.09	0.05
Japan	1994	124,069,000	0.05	0.02	0.03
Upper-middle-income countries					
Brazil	1993	160,737,000	12.95	9.59	0.72
Mexico	1994	90,011,259	12.69	10.35	1.01
Estonia	1994	1,499,257	12.26	7.73	2.86
Argentina	1994	34,179,000	8.93	2.10	2.89
Portugal	1994	5,138,600	3.20	1.17	1.00
Slovenia	1994	1,989,477	2.60	0.30	2.13
Greece	1994	10,426,289	1.29	0.52	0.71
Hungary	1994	10,245,677	1.11	0.22	0.80
Mauritius	1993	1,062,810	0.19	0.00	0.12
South Korea	1994	44,453,179	0.12	0.04	0.02

A firearm was involved in over half of the deaths classified as   10
homicides in Northern Ireland (86%), Italy (74%), the US (71%),
Brazil (56%), Mexico (56%) and Greece (51%). In the remaining
countries a firearm was involved in less than half the homicides reported. A firearm was involved in almost one-quarter (24%) of the
deaths classified as suicides in all of the countries. A firearm was involved in less than half the suicides reported by each of the countries
individually, with the exception of the US (61%).

Firearm-Related Deaths

Variations by country
During the one-year study period, 88,649 firearm deaths were re-   11
ported by the 36 countries, for a pooled rate of 7.4 deaths per 100,000.
. . . Firearm homicide rates range from a low of 0.00 in Mauritius to
10.35 in Mexico. Firearm suicide rates range from 0.02 in South Korea
to 6.30 in the US. Unintentional firearm death rates range from 0.00 in
Hong Kong, Japan, Kuwait, and Singapore to 1.32 in Mexico.

Variations by geographical region
When responding countries are grouped by region, firearm mortal-   12
ity is highest in the Americas and lowest in Asia (Figure 5.1). In fact,
the overall firearm mortality rate is five to six times higher in the
Americas (12.72 per 100,000) than in Oceania (2.57) or Europe
(2.17), and it is 95 times higher than in Asia (0.13). In the Americas
most (58%) firearm deaths are homicides. Suicides make up most
of the firearm deaths in Europe (69%) and Oceania (80%). In Asia,
35% of the firearm deaths are reported as homicides, 37% as suicides, 20% as unintentional deaths and 8% as deaths of undetermined intent.

Rates by income group
The rate of firearm death in the US (14.24 per 100,000) is eight times   13
the pooled rate for the other HI countries (1.76) and is 1.5 times the
pooled rate for the UMI countries (9.69) (Figure 5.2). Firearm homicide rates are about 19 times higher in the US (7.11) and UMI
countries (6.89) than in HI nations (0.37). In comparison, the US
firearm suicide rate (6.30) is five times higher than the rate for HI
nations (1.21) and is nearly seven times higher than the rate for UMI
nations (0.91).

Comparing the proportion of homicides and suicides that in-   14
volve a firearm, the US emerged as having a far greater proportion
than either HI or UMI countries. Seventy-one percent of homicides in

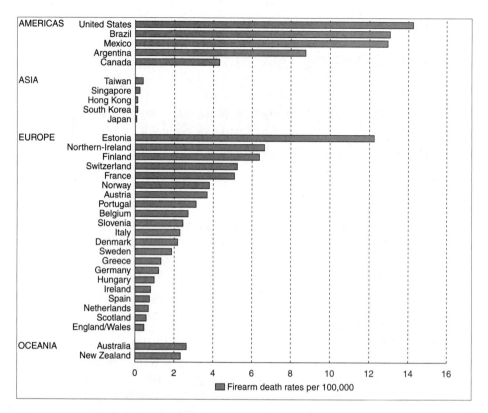

Figure 5.1   Firearm death rates, by country and region, in 36 high- and upper-middle-income countries

the US involve a firearm, compared with 33% in HI countries and 54% in UMI countries. Sixty-one per cent of suicides in the US involve a firearm, compared with 11% in HI countries and 17% in UMI countries.

When we assessed the proportion of firearm deaths that are homi-   15
cides and suicides, we observed marked variations in the income groups. . . . In the US, the proportion of firearm deaths that are homicides (46%) is almost equal to the proportion that are suicides (48%). In the HI countries, however, the proportion of firearm deaths that are suicides is much greater (71%) than the proportion of such deaths that are homicides (19%). The reverse is true for UMI countries, where most firearm deaths are homicides (72%) rather than suicides (9%).

Variations by age and sex
Age and sex patterns of firearm mortality in HI and UMI countries are   16
similar, differing only in magnitude. Firearm homicide and uninten-

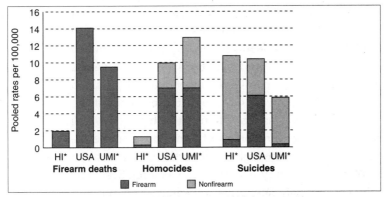

*HI indicates high-income countries, and UMI indicates upper-middle-income countries.

Figure 5.2 Firearm death, homicide, and suicide rates, by income, in 36 high- and upper-middle-income countries

tional death rates are higher in younger age groups and firearm sui-cide rates are higher for older adults. However, when compared with their counterparts in the HI and UMI groups, the young people (15–24 year age group) in the US stand out in several ways. In the US, the 15–24 year age group has the highest age-specific rate of firearm homicide, whereas the rate is higher in the 25–34 year age group in HI and UMI countries. . . . The 15–24 year age group in the US also has the highest age-specific rate of unintentional firearm deaths, but this is not the case in HI countries. . . . Finally, in the US, firearm sui-cide rates among people 15–24 years old are higher than for those 25–54 years old. . . . The reverse is true in the HI and UMI groups.

Although firearm mortality rates among males uniformly exceed 17 rates among females, the rates among females are relatively closer to the rates among males in the US than in either the HI or UMI group. The male/female firearm mortality ratio in the US (6.0) is two-thirds to almost one-half the ratio in the HI (9.7) and UMI (10.9) countries. Five countries, however, have a lower male/female firearm mortality ratio than the US: Hong Kong (1.9), Kuwait (2.3), South Korea (3.2), Portugal (4.4) and Argentina (4.9).

Discussion

Our study explores the incidence of firearm-related deaths among 18 36 wealthier nations of the world. It is, to our knowledge, the first cross-national comparison of firearm death rates among males and females of all ages. During a one-year period, a firearm was involved in almost 90,000 deaths in the 36 countries included in our study. We observed marked variations in firearm deaths among these nations whether considered individually or grouped by income or geographical location. Among these 36 countries, the US is unique in several aspects. It has the highest overall firearm mortality rate, a high proportion of homicides that are the result of a firearm injury, and the highest proportion of suicides that are the result of a firearm injury. The US also has a relatively low male/female firearm mortality rate ratio—a finding which indicates that the difference between the rates for males and females is smaller in the US than in most other countries. Finally, the age-specific patterns indicate that the impact of all causes of firearm mortality—homicide, suicide, and unintentional injuries—is more pronounced in the younger age groups (<**25 years old**) in the US than in other nations.

Particularly high firearm mortality rates were noted among   19
four nations in the western hemisphere (the US, Mexico, Brazil and Argentina). In contrast, firearm mortality among the five participating Asian countries (Japan, South Korea, Hong Kong, Singapore and Taiwan) was very low. Higher rates of homicide in general and firearm homicide in particular were noted among UMI countries. HI countries reported low firearm suicide rates, but overall rates of suicide were otherwise comparable with the US rate.

The explanations for these observations [are] undoubtedly com-   20
plex and in need of further study. A few areas worthy of pursuit have been identified, and future research is likely to expand the list. For the purposes of discussion, factors influencing firearm injury mortality can be separated into three general areas that are not mutually exclusive: factors that influence the use of a firearm, factors that influence the homicide rate, and factors that influence the suicide rate. Factors that have been suggested to influence the use of firearms include the social norms concerning the use of firearms, the availability of firearms in general, and the types of firearms that people choose to use. Social norms may play a role in forearm-related mortality, homicide and suicide, in part by influencing if a weapon is used and what type of weapon is used. The use of

---

<25 years old: 25 years old and under

firearms should be low in places where strong social norms inhibit people from using firearms. Social norms, for example, may be part of the reason for the very low rates of firearm mortality in all five Asian countries participating in our study.

Firearm availability varies greatly among nations: among the 14   21 countries in our study for which such data are available, the proportion of households possessing a firearm ranges from <1% in Japan to 48% in the US. A positive association between firearm ownership and rates of firearm homicide, firearm suicide, and overall suicide has been reported. Research findings are mixed, however, about the relationship between firearm ownership and overall homicide rates. Because firearms are more lethal than other weapons, such as knives, choosing a firearm as a weapon increases the likelihood of a fatal outcome. The types of firearms available may also influence mortality rates, because some models are more likely to be lethal than others.

Firearm mortality rates may also be influenced by underlying   22 causes of homicide and suicide that operate independently of the firearm-related factors just described. Social factors that may influence homicide rates include income inequality, low funding for social programs, divorce, the proportion of households with working women, ethnic-linguistic **heterogeneity,** and social acceptance of violence. Factors that may influence suicide rates include economic instability, unemployment, breakdown of the family group structure, **intergenerational** pressures and competition, **secularization,** and substance use and misuse. . . .

We should strive to improve our understanding of the factors   23 that account for cross-national variations in violent and firearm death rates. For example, in most HI countries, suicide rates are high, but firearms play a relatively small role. In most UMI countries, firearms are involved in more than half of all homicides. In some nations, such as the US and Estonia, firearm death rates of all types are high, whereas in other nations, such as the five Asian nations in our study, firearm death rates of all types are low. A better understanding of the economic, socio-cultural and other factors that underlie these differences will help in the design and implementation of national or regional interventions. The low rates in Asia show that such deaths can be prevented and provide hope that other nations may achieve similar levels.

---

heterogeneity: differences;   intergenerational: between the generations; secularization: drawing away from a religious orientation

HANDGUN REGULATIONS, CRIME, ASSAULTS, AND HOMICIDE: A TALE OF TWO CITIES

Drs. J. H. Sloan, A. L. Kellermann, D. T. Reay, J. A. Ferris, T. Koepsell, F. P. Rivara, C. Rice, L. Gray, and J. LoGerfo

The following study examines the effect of handgun ownership on homicide rates in two cities similar in every respect but one: their handgun control laws. One city, Vancouver, British Columbia, has very strict handgun ownership laws, as does Canada as a whole. The other city, Seattle, Washington, has very loose handgun ownership laws. The study appeared in the November 10, 1988, issue of The New England Journal of Medicine, *a highly respected medical journal.*

Approximately 20,000 persons are murdered in the United States   1
each year, making homicide the 11th leading cause of death and the 6th leading cause of the loss of potential years of life before age 65. In the United States between 1960 and 1980, the death rate from homicide by means other than firearms increased by 85 percent. In contrast, the death rate from homicide by firearms during this same period increased by 160 percent.

Approximately 60 percent of homicides each year involve   2
firearms. Handguns alone account for three fourths of all gun-related homicides. Most homicides occur as a result of assaults during arguments or **altercations**; a minority occur during the commission of a robbery or other felony. S. P. Baker has noted that in cases of assault, people tend to reach for weapons that are readily available. Since attacks with guns more often end in death than attacks with knives, and since handguns are disproportionately involved in intentional shootings, some have argued that restricting access to handguns could substantially reduce our annual rate of homicide.

To support this view, advocates of handgun control frequently   3
cite data from countries like Great Britain and Japan, where the rates of both handgun ownership and homicide are substantially lower than those in the United States. . . .

Opponents of gun control counter with statistics from Israel and   4
Switzerland, where the rates of gun ownership are high but homicides are relatively uncommon. However, the value of comparing data from different countries to support or refute the effectiveness of gun control is severely **compromised** by the large number of poten-

---

altercations: heated, noisy quarrels;   compromised: made suspicious tially **confounding** social, behavioral, and economic factors that characterize large national groups. To date, no study has been able to separate the effects of handgun control from differences among populations in terms of socioeconomic status, aggressive behavior, violent crime, and other factors. To clarify the relation between firearm regulations and community rates of homicide, we studied two large cities in the Pacific Northwest: Seattle, Washington, and Vancouver, British Columbia. Although similar in many ways, these two cities have taken decidedly different approaches to handgun control.

Study Sites

Seattle and Vancouver are large port cities in the Pacific Northwest. 5 Although on opposite sides of an international border, they are only 140 miles apart, a three-hour drive by freeway. They share a common geography, climate, and history. Citizens in both cities have attained comparable levels of schooling and have almost identical rates of unemployment. When adjusted to U.S. dollars, the median annual income of a household in Vancouver exceeds that in Seattle by less than $500. Similar percentages of households in both cities have incomes of less than $10,000 (U.S.) annually. . . . The two communities also share many cultural values and interests. Six of the top nine network television programs in Seattle are among the nine most watched programs in Vancouver.

Firearm Regulations

Although similar in many ways, Seattle and Vancouver differ 6 markedly in their approaches to the regulation of firearms. In Seattle, handguns may be purchased legally for self-defense in the street or at home. After a 30-day waiting period, a permit can be obtained to carry a handgun as a concealed weapon. The recreational use of handguns is minimally restricted.

In Vancouver, self-defense is not considered a valid or legal rea- 7 son to purchase a handgun. Concealed weapons are not permitted. Recreational uses of handguns (such as target shooting and collecting) are regulated by the **province,** and the purchase of a handgun requires a restricted-weapons permit. A permit to carry a weapon must also be obtained in order to transport a handgun, and these weapons can be discharged only at a licensed shooting club. Hand-

---

confounding: confusing;   province: Canadian equivalent of U.S. state guns can be transported by car, but only if they are stored in the trunk in a locked box.

Although they differ in their approach to firearm regulations, 8 both cities aggressively enforce existing gun laws and regulations, and convictions for gun-related offenses carry similar penalties. . . . Similar percentages of homicides in both communities eventually lead to arrest and police charges. In Washington, under the Sentencing Reform Act of 1981, murder in the first degree carries a minimum sentence of 20 years of confinement. In British Columbia, first-degree murder carries a minimum sentence of 25 years, with a possible judicial parole review after 15 years. Capital punishment was abolished in Canada during the 1970s. In Washington State, the death penalty may be invoked in cases of aggravated first-degree murder, but no one has been executed since 1963.

Rates of Gun Ownership

Because direct surveys of firearm ownership in Seattle and Vancou- 9 ver have never been conducted, we assessed the rates of gun ownership indirectly by two independent methods. First, we obtained from the Firearm Permit Office of the Vancouver police department a count of the restricted-weapons permits issued in Vancouver between March 1984 and March 1988 and compared this figure with the total number of concealed-weapons permits issued in Seattle during the same period. . . . Second, we used Cook's gun prevalence index, a previously **validated** measure of intercity differences in the **prevalence** of gun ownership. This index . . . **correlates** each city's rates of suicide and assaultive homicide involving firearms with survey-based estimates of gun ownership in each city. Both methods indicate that firearms are far more commonly owned in Seattle than in Vancouver. . . .

Ownership of Firearms in Seattle and Vancouver

	Seattle	*Vancouver*
Long guns (rifles, shotguns)	Not registered	Not registered
Total concealed-weapons permits issued 1984–1988	15,289	——
Total restricted-weapons permits issued 1984–1988	——	4,137
Cook's gun prevalence index	41%	12%

---

validated: proven;   prevalence: existence;   correlates: relates to each other

Results

Over the whole seven-year study period, 388 homicides occurred in   10
Seattle (11.3 per 100,000 person-years). In Vancouver, 204 homicides occurred during the same period (6.9 per 100,000 person-
years). . . .

When homicides were subdivided by the mechanism of death,   11
the rate of homicide by knives and other weapons (excluding
firearms) in Seattle was found to be almost identical to that in
Vancouver. . . . Virtually all of the increased risk of death from homicide in Seattle was due to a more than **fivefold** higher rate of homicide by firearms. Handguns, which accounted for roughly 85
percent of the homicides involving firearms in both communities,
were 4.8 times more likely to be used in homicides in Seattle than
in Vancouver. . . .

Discussion

In order to exclude the possibility that Seattle's higher homicide rate   12
may be explained by higher levels of criminal activity or aggressiveness in its population, we compared the rates of burglary, robbery,
simple assault, and aggravated assault in the two communities. Although we observed a slightly higher rate of simple and aggravated
assault in Seattle, these differences were relatively small—the rates in
Seattle were 16 to 18 percent higher than those reported in Vancouver during a period of comparable case reporting. Virtually all of the
excess risk of aggravated assault in Seattle was explained by a seven-
fold higher rate of assaults involving firearms. Despite similar rates of
robbery and burglary and only small differences in the rates of simple and aggravated assault, we found that Seattle had substantially
higher rates of homicide than Vancouver. Most of the excess mortality was due to an almost fivefold higher rate of murders with handguns in Seattle.

Critics of handgun control have long claimed that limiting access   13
to guns will have little effect on the rates of homicide, because persons who are intent on killing others will only work harder to acquire
a gun or will kill by other means. If the rate of homicide in a community were influenced more by the strength of intent than by the availability of weapons, we might have expected the rate of homicides
with weapons other than guns to have been higher in Vancouver than
in Seattle, in direct proportion to any decrease in Vancouver's rate of

---

fivefold: five times

firearm homicides. This was not the case. During the study interval, Vancouver's rate of homicides with weapons other than guns was not significantly higher than that in Seattle, suggesting that few would-be assailants switched to homicide by other methods.

Ready access to handguns has been advocated by some as an important way to provide law-abiding citizens with an effective means to defend themselves. Were this true, we might have expected that much of Seattle's excess rate of homicides, as compared with Vancouver's, would have been explained by a higher rate of **justifiable** homicides and killings in self-defense by civilians. Although such homicides did occur at a significantly higher rate in Seattle than in Vancouver, these cases accounted for less than 4 percent of the homicides in both cities during the study period. When we excluded cases of justifiable homicide or killings in self-defense by civilians from our calculation of relative risk, our results were almost the same.   14

It also appears unlikely that differences in law-enforcement activity accounted for the lower homicide rate in Vancouver. Suspected offenders are arrested and cases are cleared at similar rates in both cities. After arrest and conviction, similar crimes carry similar penalties in the courts in Seattle and Vancouver. . . .   15

Our analysis of the rates of homicide in these two largely similar cities suggests that the modest restriction of citizens' access to firearms (especially handguns) is associated with lower rates of homicide. This association does not appear to be explained by differences between the communities in aggressiveness, criminal behavior, or response to crime. Although our findings should be **corroborated** in other settings, our results suggest that a more restrictive approach to handgun control may decrease national homicide rates.   16

CRIME IS THE BASIC PROBLEM, NOT GUNS
Wayne LaPierre

Wayne LaPierre is executive director of the National Rifle Association's Institute for Legislative Action.

America has a crime problem, not a gun problem. Misguided attempts to control crime by restricting the law-abiding only serve to divert attention and resources from direct action against the criminal.   1

---

justifiable: proven right, valid;   corroborated: supported

Advocates of further gun restrictions are making the U.S. a much 2
more dangerous place in which to live.

More than 20,000 laws regulate the rights of peaceful, honest 3
citizens to buy and use firearms—and yet the crime rate continues to
rise. When will we stop kidding ourselves? Do we really believe law
No. 20,001 will make any difference?

How many more people will die before we realize it's time to de- 4
vote our resources and public debate toward a direct confrontation
with violent criminals?

The nearly 3 million members of the National Rifle Association 5
are leading the fight to deal with the insanity of our plea-bargaining
system, the tragedy of early-release programs for violent criminals
and the failure to enforce minimum mandatory sentences.

It's a tragedy that we don't enforce a law already on the books. 6
This stipulates that a criminal dealing drugs on the street who carries
a gun is subject to a five-year-to-life mandatory sentence. The streets
of Los Angeles and Washington would be safer tomorrow if this law
were enforced tonight.

When we begin swift and sure prosecution we may finally send 7
the message that people who commit violent crimes will be behind
bars for a long time.

The NRA has consistently supported programs like the McCollum- 8
Staggers amendment and legislation passed last week in Virginia establishing an instant identification system—similar to checks done
for credit card purchases—that stops felons from trying to circumvent the law to buy guns.

The technology and information are in place to make such 9
checks a reality. But most criminals do not purchase firearms over
the counter. They buy them on the black market or steal them and
never enter our system of regulatory law.

The NRA is advocating a plan of attack called Project Crime Con- 10
trol. It's designed to get criminals off the streets for good, and that's
the only way to curb crime. Project Crime Control calls for the following immediate steps:

- Prosecute and jail felons found in possession of firearms.
- Create new prison space. We can no longer afford the system's
  standard excuse, "There's no place to put these criminals."
- Establish a federal death penalty for killing a police or correc-
  tions officer.
- Deny probation and parole to violent felons who misuse deadly
  weapons.

- Stop the travesty of plea bargaining by enacting a tough federal law that allows only one felony in a five-year period to be bargained down to a misdemeanor. This will keep lawbreakers such as Patrick Purdy, the Stockton [Calif.] schoolyard gunman, off our streets and in jail.
- Require a 10-year sentence for using kids in a trafficking crime. Let drug kingpins know we're going to protect our kids.

From Los Angeles to Washington, drugs and violent crime are 11 making our cities increasingly unlivable. Problems that were once only associated with the "big city" are infecting other areas. With each felon committing over 187 felonies per year, the $430,000 it costs to let one roam free makes the $20,000 per year spent to keep one behind bars seem like a bargain.

We have some hard choices to make right now. Will we create 12 more political placebos, laws that add nothing to public security and only regulate the law-abiding?

Or will we finally begin fixing a criminal-justice system that 13 would set a Patrick Purdy loose on society seven times? Our limited supply of human, monetary and time resources cannot be wasted in even beginning to follow the wrong course. We must decide right now whether to fight crime, or freedom.

SHOULD YOU CARRY A GUN? A NEW STUDY ARGUES FOR CONCEALED WEAPONS
Romesh Ratnesar

Is a gun-carrying nation a safer nation? Fearful of being victimized 1 by indiscriminate violence, many Americans are gnawed by a dilemma: Should I or shouldn't I carry a gun? The question is a real one for a growing number of Americans because the tally of states with "right to carry" laws has gone from eight to 31 since 1985. These states will issue a concealed-weapon permit to any citizen without a criminal record who wants one—no questions asked.

But here's one: Do those laws really protect people and cut 2 crime? A study published in 1995 showed that guns were used defensively about 2.5 million times a year and that in only 5% of cases were defenders harmed after they **brandished** their gun. But such findings were based on narrow surveys whose scope, upon re-exam-

---

brandished: waved menacingly

ination by gun-control advocates, could easily have been exaggerated. Thus, discerning the benefits of packing heat has largely remained a matter of conscience, not science.

Now, however, the author of a new book, *More Guns, Less Crime: 3 Understanding Crime and Gun Control Laws,* has analyzed crime rates in the 10 states that passed right-to-carry laws from 1977 to 1992. He contends that after more relaxed concealed-carry laws were enacted, murders fell an average of 8%, rapes 5% and aggravated assaults 7%. (For the same period in the entire country, the number of murders went up 24%, and rapes 71%. Assaults more than doubled.) The **purported** reason: would-be criminals were deterred from choosing victims who just might have a pistol tucked in their purse. Increases in accidental deaths by handguns—on the whole relatively rare—were barely noticeable, fewer than one death a year. With the National Rifle Association **flacking** the book to members, it sold out its first printing in three weeks.

More Guns, Less Crime has touched off furious protests from gun- 4 control lobbyists and criminologists, who call the book's research **spurious**, its statistics **suspect** and its conclusion—that "allowing law-abiding citizens to carry concealed handguns will save lives"— dangerous. Part of what's threatening about the book is its author: John Lott, a **wonkish** University of Chicago economist who has never been an N.R.A. member and prior to writing the book did not own a gun. (He has since bought a .38-cal. pistol.) "If I had really strong views about guns," he says, "I wouldn't have waited until I was 40 to write this."

The book claims to be the most comprehensive look ever at the 5 effect of gun laws on crime, examining data from all 3,054 U.S. counties over a span of 18 years. The findings are **startling**. Not only did violent crime drop after states relaxed concealed-weapon laws, but it tumbled more **precipitously** the longer the laws were on the books: after five years, murder was down 15%, rape 9%. The two groups most vulnerable to violent crime—women and blacks—benefit the most after the easing of the laws. And in right-to-carry states, the average death rate from mass public shootings dropped 69%. After the school shooting in Springfield, Ore., in May, Lott argued that teachers should be allowed to tote guns to school.

---

purported: claimed; flacking: advertising; spurious: false; suspect: suspicious; wonkish: slang word meaning studious or scholarly
startling: very surprising; precipitously: steeply

It all sounds a bit **apocalyptic** to critics. "A heavily armed pub- 6
lic," says Duke University public-policy professor Philip Cook, "could
easily lead to a more heavily armed army of robbers and assaulters
who will fire first and ask questions later." Jens Ludwig, a professor
of public policy at Georgetown University, contends that the book
does not account for **fluctuating** factors like poverty levels and
policing techniques, which might affect crime rates even more than
gun laws.

Other critics raise questions about whether Lott **massaged the** 7
numbers. One **arcane** quarrel: for statistical purposes, Lott dropped
from his study sample any counties that had no reported murders
or assaults for a given year. Researchers from Carnegie Mellon University took Lott's figures and analyzed crime rates only in counties
with populations above 100,000. Using this yardstick, right-to-carry
laws reduced aggravated assaults 67% in Maine—but increased
murders 105% in West Virginia. Still other critics note that in concealed-carry states, only about 2% of people have even bothered
to get a permit, and they tend to be white males in suburban counties, hardly the population most at risk. After Philadelphia passed a
concealed-carry law in 1995, the number of people with such permits rose by 10,000 in two years. But the murder rate remained as
high as it had been for the previous decade. Despite all these in-
conveniences, Lott stands by the thoroughness of his research: "No
study on crime has attempted to control for anywhere near as many
factors as I have."

However debatable their effectiveness in practice, concealed- 8
carry laws appeal to citizens grown **skittish** over lethal violence—if
only because measures to restrict access to weapons don't seem
to have ended the bloodbaths. Last month the Missouri legislature
put a concealed-carry referendum on next April's ballot, and law-
makers in Michigan are scheduled to vote on a similar measure
soon [1999]. "Carrying a gun does not guarantee you won't get
hurt," says Suzanna Gratia Hupp, a Texas legislator who crusaded
for her state's law, "but it changes the odds." Many Americans will
take them.

---

apocalyptic: divine revelation (rather than a scientific discovery)
fluctuating: varying;   massaged the numbers: used statistics to prove a
point rather than to reveal the truth;   arcane: understood only by those
with special knowledge;   skittish: nervous

TAKING ANOTHER LOOK AT RIGHT TO BEAR ARMS
Neil A. Lewis

These 12 words were engraved in red stone near the entrance to the 1
National Rifle Association headquarters, which used to be near the
White House: "THE RIGHT OF THE PEOPLE TO BEAR ARMS SHALL
NOT BE INFRINGED." . . .

The language is from the Second Amendment to the Constitu- 2
tion and serves as a **mantra** to people who insist that the government may not take away their guns.

Yet the basic flaw in relying on those words alone is that they 3
constitute only half an amendment. The full text says: "A well regulated Militia, being necessary to the security of a free State, the right
of the people to keep and bear Arms, shall not be infringed."

It is the first clause that has been used by opponents of a broad 4
reading of the amendment to assert that the Constitution does not
guarantee each citizen the right to own a gun.

So, what is a well-regulated militia? More important, does the 5
language of the Second Amendment mean that the right to bear
arms exists only in conjunction with such a militia? In other words, is
it a right guaranteed to individuals by the Constitution?

It is an issue that now has a special **piquancy** with the increased 6
attention to private armed groups who style themselves militias and
are fervent in their belief in the right to arm themselves.

Ignored for decades, there is now a flourishing scholarly trade in 7
the Second Amendment, almost all of it from opponents of gun-control laws.

Much of the work is devoted to analyzing the amendment's first 8
clause dealing with a well regulated Militia. Some of the academic
analyses delve into the definitions and duties of militias at the time
of the Constitution's framers. Others are **recondite** journeys into the
precise wording of the amendment and comparisons with the language of other amendments.

Some of the scholarship is finely reasoned, some far less so. And 9
some of the authors are subsidized by the NRA through its Legal Defense Fund.

Yet all the scholarly journals taken together have less firepower 10
than this simple and straightforward fact: The nation's courts have
uniformly rejected an expansive interpretation of the Second Amend-

---

mantra: Hindu word meaning a sacred formula;   piquancy: pleasantly
disturbing;   recondite: not easily understood by most people

ment. Never in the history of the United States has a federal court invalidated a law regulating the private ownership of arms on Second Amendment grounds.

And, for the most part, the NRA has shied away from pressing courts to adopt its view of the Second Amendment. 11

The prevailing judicial view has long been that the Second Amendment guarantees the right to bear arms only in the context of maintaining a well-regulated—that is state-sponsored—militia. 12

The late Erwin Griswold, the former U.S. solicitor general and dean of the Harvard Law School, said the amendment was unique among those in the Bill of Rights because its purpose is clearly expressed in the text. 13

"This was explicitly recognized by the Supreme Court in its 1939 opinion in United States vs. Miller, where it said that the 'obvious purpose' of the amendment was to 'assure the continuation and render possible the effectiveness' of state militias, and that it 'must be interpreted and applied with that end in view,'" Griswold once said. 14

State militias, also mentioned in Article I of the Constitution, are generally taken to mean the forces that have since become state-run groups of the National Guard. 15

Since the Miller case, the Supreme Court has twice reaffirmed that the Second Amendment protects only state militias, not private ownership of guns, most recently in 1980 when it said that legislative restrictions on the use of firearms did not **"trench upon** any constitutionally protected liberties." 16

The rifle association seems to recognize this judicial reality. For example, all the NRA inspired challenges to the Brady law, which imposes a waiting period for handgun purchases, are based on the notion that it is an undue burden on local officials to enforce a federal statute. 17

Tom Wyld, a senior NRA official, said his group had been sparing in citing the Second Amendment for tactical reasons. 18

Most of the recent scholarly work favors the NRA view, Wyld said, and there has to be a gradual shift in the jurisprudence as there was in civil rights over the decades. 19

But Dennis Henigan, the legal director of Handgun Control Inc., said the NRA was hypocritical because it promotes a broad Second Amendment philosophy in the political arena but "leaves it outside the courthouse door." 20

---

trench upon: restrict or cut into

That may explain why the NRA has a brief filed in U.S. District 21
Court in Michigan challenging the ban enacted by Congress last year
on the manufacture and possession of some assault-type weapons.
The brief argues that the law is unconstitutionally vague and moves
the federal government too deeply into local law enforcement. But
nowhere does it raise the issue of the Second Amendment.

WHY I BOUGHT A GUN
Gail Buchalter

*A woman explains why she owns a gun, but comes to an uneasy conclusion,
in this essay published in* Parade *(a Sunday newspaper magazine with a
large and varied distribution).*

I was raised to wear black and cultured pearls in one of Manhattan's 1
more desirable neighborhoods. My upper-middle-class background
never involved guns. If my parents felt threatened, they simply put
another lock on the door. . . .

Today, I am typical of the women whom gun manufacturers 2
have been aiming at as potential buyers—and one of the millions
who have succumbed: Between 1983 and 1986, there was a 53 percent increase in female gun-owners in the U.S.—from 7.9 million to
12.1 million, according to a Gallup Poll paid for by Smith & Wesson,
a gun manufacturer. . . .

I began questioning my beliefs one Halloween night in Phoenix, 3
where I had moved when I was married. I was almost home when
another car nearly hit mine head-on. With the speed of a New
York cabbie, I rolled down my window and screamed curses as the
driver passed me. He instantly made a U-turn, almost climbing my
back bumper. By now, he and his two friends were hanging out
of the car windows, yelling that they were going to rape, cut and
kill me.

I already had turned into our driveway when I realized my hus- 4
band wasn't home. I was trapped. The car had pulled in behind me.
I drove up to the back porch and got into the kitchen, where our
dogs stood waiting for me. The three men spilled out of their car and
into our yard.

My adrenaline was pumping faster than Edwin Moses' legs clear- 5
ing a hurdle. I grabbed the collars of Jack, our 200-pound Irish
wolfhound, and his 140-pound malamute buddy, Slush. Then I
kicked open the back door—I was so scared that I became aggressive—and actually dared the three creeps to keep coming. With the

dogs, the odds had changed in my favor, and the men ran back to the safety of their car, yelling that they'd be back the next day to blow me away. Fortunately, they never returned.

A few years and one divorce later, I headed for Los Angeles with 6 my 3-year-old son, Jordan (the dogs had since departed). When I put him in preschool a few weeks later, the headmistress noted that I was a single parent and immediately warned me that there was a rapist in my new neighborhood.

I called the police, who confirmed this fact. The rapist had no 7 **modus operandi**. Sometimes he would be waiting in his victim's house; other times he would break in while the person was asleep. Although it was summer, I would carefully lock my windows at night and then lie there and sweat in fear. Thankfully, the rapist was caught, but not before he had attacked two more women.

Over some time, at first imperceptibly, my suburban neighbor- 8 hood became less secure. A street gang took over the apartment building across from my house, and flowers and compact cars gave way to graffiti and low-riders.

Daytime was quiet, but these gang members crawled out like 9 cockroaches after dark. Several nights in a row they woke me up. It was one of the most terrifying times in my life. I could hear them talk-ing and laughing as they leaned against our fence, tossing their empty beer cans into our front yard. I knew that they were drinking, but were they also using violence-inducing drugs such as PCP and crack? And if they broke in, could I get to the police before they got to me?

I found myself, to my surprise, wishing that I had a loaded pistol 10 under my pillow. In the clear light of day, I found this reaction shock-ing and simply decided to move to a safer neighborhood, although it cost thousands of dollars more. Luckily, I was able to afford it.

Soon the papers were telling yet another tale of senseless horror. 11 Richard Ramirez, who became known as "The Walk-In Killer," spent months crippling and killing before he was caught. His alleged crimes were so brutal and bizarre, his desire to inflict pain so intense, that I began to question my beliefs about the **sanctity** of human life—his, in particular. The thought of taking a human life is repug-nant to me, but the idea of being someone's victim is worse. And how, I began to ask myself, do you talk pacifism to a murderer or a rapist?

---

modus operandi: consistent method of operating;   sanctity: sacredness

Finally, I decided that I would defend myself, even if it meant 12
killing another person. I realized that the one-sided pacifism I once
so strongly had advocated could backfire on me and, worse, on my
son. Reluctantly, I concluded that I had to insure the best option for
our survival. My choices: to count on a cop or to own a pistol. . . .

I . . . called [a] friend. He was going to the National Rifle Associ- 13
ation convention that was being held in Reno and suggested I tag
along. . . . The next day at the convention center, I saw a sign announcing a seminar for women on handguns and safety. I met pis-
tol-packing grandmas, kids who were into competitive shooting and
law-enforcement agents. I listened to a few of them speak and then
watched a video, "A Woman's Guide to Firearms." It explained everything from how guns worked to an individual's responsibilities as a
gun owner.

It was my kind of movie, since everything about guns scares me— 14
especially owning one. Statistics on children who are victims of their
parents' handguns are overwhelming: About 300 children a year—almost a child a day—are killed by guns in this country, according to
Handgun Control, Inc., which bases its numbers on data from the National Safety Council. Most of these killings are accidental.

As soon as I returned to Los Angeles, I called a man I had met a 15
while ago who, I remembered, owned several guns. He told me he
had a Smith & Wesson .38 Special for sale and recommended it,
since it was small enough for me to handle yet had the necessary
stopping power.

I bought the gun. That same day, I got six rounds of special am- 16
munition with plastic tips that explode on impact. These are not for
target practice; these are for protection.

For about $50 I also picked up the metal safety box that I had 17
learned about in the video. Its push-button lock opens with a touch
if you know the proper combination, possibly taking only a second
or two longer than it does to reach into a night-table drawer. Now I
knew that my son, Jordan, couldn't get his hands on it while I still
could. . . .

Today he couldn't care less about the gun. Every so often, when 18
we're watching television in my room, I practice opening the safety
box, and Jordan times me. I'm down to three seconds. I'll ask him
what's the first thing you do when you handle a gun, and he looks
at me like I'm a moron, saying for the umpteenth time: "Make sure
it's unloaded. But I know I'm not to touch it or tell my friends about
it." Jordan's already bored with it all.

I, on the other hand, look forward to Mondays—"Ladies' Night"   19
at the target range—when I get to shoot for free. I buy a box of bul-
lets and some targets from the guy behind the counter, put on the
protective eye and ear coverings and walk through the double doors
to the firing lines. . . . I am keeping my promise to practice. Too
many people are killed by their own guns because they don't know
how to use them.

It took me years to decide to buy a gun, and then weeks before   20
I could load it. It gave me nightmares.

One night I dreamed I woke up when someone broke into our   21
house. I grabbed my gun and sat waiting at the foot of my bed. Finally, I saw him turn the corner as he headed toward me. He was big
and filled the hallway—an impossible target to miss. I aimed the gun
and froze, visualizing the bullet blowing a hole through his chest and
spraying his flesh all over the walls and floor. I didn't want to shoot,
but I knew my survival was on the line. I wrapped my finger around
the trigger and finally squeezed it, simultaneously accepting the intruder's death at my own hand and the relief of not being a victim. I
woke up as soon as I decided to shoot.

I was tearfully relieved that it had only been a dream.   22

I never have weighed the consequences of an act as strongly as I   23
have that of buying a gun—but then again, I never have done anything with such deadly **repercussions**. Most of my friends refuse
even to discuss it with me. They believe that violence begets violence.

They're probably right.   24

MAN SHOOTS OWN SON

The following story appeared in the San Francisco Chronicle, *dateline Los Angeles.*

A North Hollywood man, victimized by burglars two months ago,   1
shot and killed his 3-year-old son early yesterday when he mistook
the boy's shadow for that of an intruder, police said.

Manuel Sesmas, 30, told police that he and his wife, Nely, were   2
awakened by the opening and closing of their bedroom door at
3:45 A.M.

Mrs. Sesmas told her husband, "Here they come," said police   3
Detective Kevin Harley.

---

repercussions: results

Sesmas said he jumped out of bed, grabbed a pistol and opened 4
the bedroom door. He said he saw a shadow and fired downward to
avoid seriously hurting anyone.

The shadow turned out to be that of his son, Victor Manuel 5
Sesmas, just days away from his fourth birthday.

Post-reading

Controversial issues always rouse people's passions strongly on one
side of the question or another; the more controversial the issue, the
stronger the passions. And the question of handgun control is one of the
most controversial in American society. In cases like this, it is particularly
important to sort out facts from opinions and, when dealing with opinions, to decide which seem to be the best-founded ones.

With these matters in mind, take the following steps in the analysis
stage of your writing process. First, go back over the reading assignments
above and make notes about what is fact and what is opinion in each. In
the case of articles that are entirely or almost entirely opinions, evaluate
and make brief notes about how well founded the opinions are. Are they
the opinions of someone who has actually studied the issue? Or are they
opinions based on personal experience? In the latter case, you should ask
whether the person's experience has been the same as yours or as that of
many people or only a few. You might want to keep separate sets of notes
in some or all of the following categories:

Very important facts

Less important facts

Well supported opinions

Poorly supported opinions

Be sure to make notes about *why* you consider some facts or opinions more
important than others.

Essay Assignment

**Study the information above and write an essay in which you
examine this issue and come to a conclusion as to whether
handguns should be banned or licensed on a national basis.**

**For more discussion of this issue and suggestions about orga-
nizing your essay, log on to http://devenglish.wadsworth.com.**

Pre-writing

If you have taken all the steps outlined above, you are now ready to let the facts and opinions argue with each other, to decide which side of the issue seems to have the stronger case. And you will also need to decide *how much* stronger the stronger case is. Is it very much stronger or only marginally stronger? In the former instance, you may decide that it is so strong that there is no question about the issue. In the latter instance, you may decide that one side has a slightly stronger case but that the issue is really still open to question.

As you think about organizing your essay, remember four important points from the section "Evaluating Evidence and Shaping Your Argument":

1. Be sure to include the strongest arguments of both sides. You may not wish to include weak ones, particularly ones based on poorly supported opinions.

2. Don't make "sack paragraphs," with all the arguments against gun control in one paragraph and all the arguments for it in another.

3. Remember that a statement isn't an argument; statements are often topic sentences, in effect—that is, sentences that have to be explained or backed up.

4. Make sure your conclusion is based solidly on the arguments preceding it. It should reflect the strengths and weaknesses of the arguments you cover in your essay, not be your own unsupported opinion tacked on at the end.

Create a working outline, with supporting examples, plus a working thesis.

Writing

Your introduction should probably acknowledge the controversial nature of this topic, as well as introducing your topic and stating your thesis. The body paragraphs should deal with the strongest opposing arguments, either by rebutting them or by acknowledging their validity. (Note how Buchalter ends her essay, "Why I Bought a Gun.") However, your arguments and their support should be more compelling than those of your opposition. The conclusion should either make a recommendation or summarize your main points in order to emphasize your thesis. Be sure to review the Writer's Checklist on pages 339–340.

CENSORSHIP OF HIGH SCHOOL NEWSPAPERS

Censorship in a democracy such as the United States is an extremely controversial issue. Do people in power have the right to restrict what others say and write within a system of government that professes freedom of expression? For example, should even a democratic government have the power to forbid certain kinds of information from being reported to the public on the grounds that it might endanger the safety of the nation? Similarly, should certain books be taken off public library shelves because they may corrupt the country's youth—for instance, *Catcher in the Rye* or *Lady Chatterley's Lover*—as some have argued? When, if ever, is censorship in the best interests of a group of people?

So concerned with this issue were the men who wrote the Constitution of the United States of America that they added an amendment to it—the First Amendment, ratified December 15, 1791:

> Congress shall make no law respecting an establishment of religion or prohibiting the free Exercise thereof; or abridging the freedom of speech, or of the press; or the right of the people peaceably to assemble, and to petition the Government for a redress of grievances.

Clearly this amendment guarantees our right to freedom of speech—or does it? The next question that arises is who is guaranteed the freedom of expression and under what conditions? Do all of us have equal rights? Do high school students, for example, have the same rights as adults?

In 1983, the principal of Hazelwood East High School, in a suburb of St. Louis, ordered two pages of the *Spectrum,* the student newspaper, to be deleted because he found two articles objectionable—one on teenage pregnancy and one on the impact of divorce on students. Cathy Kuhlmeier and two other students who worked on the *Spectrum* brought suit because they thought their First Amendment right to freedom of expression had been violated.

The case, *Hazelwood School District, et al., v. Cathy Kuhlmeier, et al.,* was tried first at the District Court, which upheld the rights of the principal to censor the paper. The students then appealed to the Court of Appeals, which reversed the District Court's decision and said the First Amendment had been violated. The case ended up in the Supreme Court, which, on January 13, 1988, ruled in favor of Hazelwood School District and against the students.

However, not all of the Supreme Court justices agreed. Justices White, Rehnquist, Stevens, O'Connor, and Scalia were in the majority, but Justices Brennan, Marshall, and Blackmun dissented, and did so strongly—proving that even some of the finest legal minds in this country disagree on this issue.

Reading Assignment

Pre-reading

As a way of beginning to think about this topic, ask yourself what your position is. Do high school students have the same rights as adults? Why or why not? Discuss this issue with your classmates and others. And remember to take notes so you won't forget their positions and arguments.

Reading

PREGNANCY AT HAZELWOOD HIGH
Christine de Hass

The following excerpts are from a lengthy article on teenage pregnancy. The article discusses teenage sexuality, birth control, parents' ability to discuss sex with their teenage children, abortion, and the squeal law (which would require doctors or clinics to notify the parents of anyone under eighteen years of age who requested any form of birth control). The article then presents three accounts by Hazelwood East High School students who became pregnant—the part of the article the principal found objectionable even though the names were changed to protect the students' privacy. Here are parts of those accounts.

Terri: I am five months pregnant and very excited about having my   1
baby. My husband is excited too. We both can't wait until it's born.

After the baby is born, which is in July, we are planning to move   2
out of his house, when we save enough money. I am not going to be coming back to school right away (September) because the baby will only be two months old. I plan on coming back in January when the second semester begins.

When I found out I was pregnant, I really was kind of shocked   3
because I kept thinking about how I was going to tell my parents. I was also real happy. I just couldn't believe I was going to have a baby. When I told Paul about the situation, he was really happy. At first I didn't think he would be because I wasn't sure if he really would want to take on the responsibility of being a father, but he was very happy. We talked about the baby and what we were going to do and we both wanted to get married. We had talked about marriage before, so we were both sure of what we were doing.

I had no pressures (to have sex). It was my own decision. We 4
were going out four or five months before we had sex. I was on no
kind of birth control pills. I really didn't want to get them, not just so
I could get pregnant. I don't think I'd feel right taking them.

At first my parents were upset, especially my father, but now 5
they're both happy for me. I don't have any regrets because I'm
happy about the baby and I hope everything works out.

Patti: I didn't think it could happen to me, but I knew I had to start 6
making plans for me and my little one. I think Steven (my boyfriend)
was more scared than me. He was away at college and when he
came home we cried together and then accepted it.

At first both families were disappointed, but the third or fourth 7
month, when the baby started to kick and move around, my
boyfriend and I felt like expecting parents and we were very excited!

My parents really like my boyfriend. At first we all felt sort of un- 8
comfortable around each other. Now my boyfriend supports our
baby totally (except for housing). . . . After I graduate next year,
we're getting married. . . .

I want to say to others that it isn't easy and it takes a strong, will- 9
ing person to handle it because it does mean giving up a lot of things.
Secondly, if you're not going to give your child all the love and affection around, you won't be a good parent. Lastly, be careful because
the pill doesn't always work. I know because it didn't work for me.

This experience has made me a more responsible person. I feel 10
that now I am a woman. If I could go back to last year, I would not
get pregnant, but I have no regrets. We love our baby more than
anything in the world (my boyfriend and I) because we created him!
How could we not love him??? . . . He's so cute and innocent. . . .

Julie: At first I was shocked. You always think, "It won't happen to 11
me." I was also scared because I did not know how everyone was
going to handle it. But then I started getting excited.

There was never really any pressure (to have sex). It was more of 12
a mutual agreement. I think I was more curious than anything.

I had always planned on continuing school. There was never any 13
doubt about that. I found that it wasn't as hard as I thought it would
be. I was fairly open about it and people seemed to accept it. Greg
and I did not get married. We figured that those were the best circumstances. So we decided to wait and see how things go. We are

still planning on getting married when we are financially ready. I also am planning on going to college at least part time.

My parents have been great. They could not have been more 14 supportive and helpful. They are doing everything they can for us and enjoy being "grandma and grandpa." They have also made it clear it was my responsibility. . . .

DIVORCE'S IMPACT ON KIDS MAY HAVE LIFELONG EFFECTS
Shari Gordon

This is the other article the principal of Hazelwood East High School censored from the May 13, 1983, edition of the Spectrum.

In the United States one marriage ends for every two that begin. The 1 North County percentage of divorce is three marriages end out of four marriages that start.

There are more than two central characters in the painful drama 2 of divorce. Children of divorced parents, literally millions of them, are torn by the end of their parents' marriage.

What causes divorce? According to Mr. Ken Kerkhoff, social stud- 3 ies teacher, some of the causes are:

• Poor dating habits that lead to marriage.

• Not enough variables in common.

• Lack of communication.

• Lack of desire or effort to make the relationship work.

Figures aren't the whole story. The fact is that divorce has a psy- 4 chological and sociological change on the child.

One junior commented on how the divorce occurred. "My dad 5 didn't make any money, so my mother divorced him."

"My father was an alcoholic and he always came home drunk 6 and my mom really couldn't stand it any longer," said another junior.

Diana Herbert, freshman, said, "My dad wasn't spending 7 enough time with my mom, my sister, and I. He was always out of town on business or out late playing cards with the guys. My parents always argued about everything."

"In the beginning I thought I caused the problem, but now I re- 8 alize it wasn't me," added Diana.

"I was only five when my parents got divorced," said Susan Kiefer, 9
junior. "I didn't quite understand what the divorce between my parents really meant until about the age of seven when I understood that
divorce meant my mother and father wouldn't be together again."

"It stinks!" exclaimed Jill, a junior. "They can, afterwards, remarry 10
and start their lives once again, but their kids will always be caught
in between."

Out of the 25 students interviewed, 17 of them have parents 11
that have remarried.

The feelings of divorce affect the kids for the rest of their lives, 12
according to Mr. Kerkhoff. The effects of divorce on the kids lead to .
the following:

- Higher rate of absenteeism at school.
- Higher rate of trouble with school, officials and police.
- Higher rate of depression and insecurity.
- Run a higher risk of divorce themselves.

All of these are the latest findings in research on single parent 13
homes.

A LIMIT ON THE STUDENT PRESS
Jean Seligmann and Tessa Namuth

This article, published in Newsweek, *discusses the Supreme Court's decision
on the* Hazelwood *case.*

Abortion, teen suicide, AIDS, runaway kids. They're all standard fare 1
on local television news shows and the stuff about which teenagers
endlessly chatter. But when these topics begin making headlines in
high school newspapers, local school boards and high-school principals often feel compelled to ban them. Such juvenile prior restraints
are not rare: last year the Student Press Law Center in Washington received more than 500 reports of censorship battles from student editors around the country. Now these youthful editorialists have few
weapons left. Last week, in a 5–3 ruling, the U.S. Supreme Court gave
school administrators broad latitude to suppress controversial stories.
"A school need not tolerate student speech that is inconsistent with its
'basic educational mission'," Justice Byron White wrote for the majority. "School officials may impose reasonable restrictions on the speech
of students, teachers and other members of the school community."

Last week's decision arose from a suit by journalism students at   2
Hazelwood East High School in Missouri. They went to court after
their principal, Robert E. Reynolds, deleted two pages from the May
13, 1983, issue of the *Spectrum,* a student newspaper produced as
part of an elective course called Journalism II. Reynolds pulled the
pages because of two stories about teen pregnancy and divorce. In
his view, the articles did not adequately disguise the identities of girls
who had been pregnant or [protect] the **anonymity** of a parent who
was getting divorced. Further, he said, references in the first story to
sexual activity and birth control were inappropriate for younger students to read. Because of a printer's deadline, he says he had no
chance to ask students to make revisions.

In a stinging dissent, Justice William Brennan (joined by Justices   3
Thurgood Marshall and Harry Blackmun) charged that Reynolds had
"violated the First Amendment's prohibitions against censorship of
any student expression that neither disrupts classwork nor invades
the rights of others." The decision, Brennan warned, could convert
public schools into "**enclaves** of **totalitarianism** . . . that strangle
the free mind at its source."

Reaction at Hazelwood East High was mixed. "I think the princi-   4
pal should have some say in what stories the paper does," says Tammy
Hawkins, current editor of the *Spectrum,* "but he should have con-
sulted the students." Cathy Kuhlmeier, one of those who filed the suit,
was disturbed by the decision, which she said might "turn kids off to
journalism." Principal Reynolds felt **vindicated.** "We're glad the court
gave us local control over the curriculum," he said. Reynolds didn't
wait for judicial permission: last semester he vetoed a proposed story
on AIDS, telling a faculty adviser that "the climate wasn't right."

The ruling, which does not affect private schools because their   5
administrators are not state officials, is also not expected to have
much impact on college newspapers. At that level, where most students are not minors, the courts have almost always extended full
First Amendment protections. But all student newspapers financed
and supervised by the public schools would seem to come under the
new ruling, not only those that are produced as part of a journalism
curriculum. The school could be considered the newspaper's pub-

---

anonymity: the state of remaining unknown or unrecognized;
enclave: an area within the boundaries of another;
totalitarianism: authoritarian rule of many by one person or one group;
vindicated: cleared of blame or accusation, justified

lisher, explains Ivan B. Gluckman, legal counsel for the National Association of Secondary School Principals, and thus has the authority
to veto articles on subjects it doesn't approve of. "But I don't think
the court means for principals to have absolute rights to censor," he
says. The rights they do have "are meant to be exercised within reason, for example, when something is obscene, indecent or just bad
journalism."

   Unfortunately that may prove a murky standard in practice. The   6
court vigorously defended the **prerogatives** of high-school officials.
But the justices might have prevented another round of disputes if
they had also urged administrators to use their power cautiously. Can
a student paper, for instance, run a story about a local anti-abortion
center that works with high-school girls or the formation of a
teenage gay-rights group? It will now depend on the principal's
views. "The papers will be more **orthodox** and bland," predicts Alan
Levine, a New York lawyer and author of a book called *The Rights of
Students*. "The only alternative will be leaflets and an underground
press." That's an unlikely route, although, in this age of home computers, not impossible. The Constitution may no longer extend very
far into the schoolhouse, but surely it protects desktop publishing by
editors of all ages.

HIGH SCHOOL PAPERS GROW UP

Jerry Carroll

*Carroll, a reporter, writes about topics being covered in some California high
school newspapers. Unlike most of the country, the* Hazelwood School
District v. Kuhlmeier *decision will have little effect in California because an
amendment to the State Education Code says that school authorities will
have no say in what the newspapers print with the exception of materials
that are libelous, obscene or slanderous, that "create a clear and present
danger of unlawful acts . . . [or that] cause substantial disruption to the
orderly operation of the school." Nonetheless, people in California feel
strongly about the decision.*

San Lorenzo journalism teacher Richard Lloyd remembers when high   1
school newspapers did not deal with anything more weighty than
cars, sock hops and football games. OK, maybe the lousy food at the
cafeteria.

---

prerogatives: exclusive rights or privileges;   orthodox: following accepted
traditions or beliefs

How times have changed. . . . "Right now, my students are writ- 2
ing in-depth feature stories about alcoholism in the home, AIDS and
a sociological study of our school," said Lloyd.

The gradual but startling shift in high school journalism—from 3
covering campus high jinks to reporting on such serious issues as date
rape and teenage pregnancy—is such that last week the Supreme
Court gave school administrators greater powers of censorship.

Justice Byron White wrote in the majority opinion that school 4
officials "must be able to take into account the emotional maturity of the intended audience in determining whether to **disseminate** student speech on potential sensitive topics, which might
range from the existence of Santa Claus in an elementary school
setting to the particulars of teenage sexual activities in a high
school setting."

The case involved a Missouri high school where a principal re- 5
fused a student newspaper permission to publish an article about
teenage pregnancy and the effect of divorce on students.

The ruling has no effect in California, where Lloyd and a few 6
other high school journalism teachers successfully lobbied in the
early 1970s for an amendment to the State Education Code that en-
sured broad press freedom for students. . . . The education code language prompted the principal at Homestead High School in
Cupertino last week to reverse a decision to stop publication of an
article in the newspaper there about a 17-year-old student who
tested positive to HIV virus, which can lead to AIDS. . . .

Written by Kathryn Pallokoff, 17, the article is a careful and re- 7
sponsible account of the problem, giving figures on the spread of
the disease and warning of the importance of "safe sex."

Other articles in the newspaper detailed complaints about stu- 8
dents being harassed by Army recruiters, Governor George Deukme-
jian's spending plan for schools, and the risks involved in drinking
and driving. . . .

The AIDS article wouldn't raise a brow if seen in another publi- 9
cation. But reports like it will not be seen in high school newspapers in most of the rest of the country after the Supreme Court
decision.

Even though it doesn't apply in California, high school journal- 10
ists and their newspaper advisers view the ruling with scorn.

---

disseminate: spread around, distribute

"My students are very much offended by the idea they are   11
not considered mature enough to handle these topics," said Steve
O'Donoughue, the newspaper adviser at Fremont High School in
Oakland. "They feel in general—and I'm sure it's just not my students—that it is hypocritical, especially when the two topics in the
original case, divorce and teen pregnancy, are common topics in the
lives of these kids.

"I don't know when it changed, but I'd say certainly in the '80s,   12
despite the image of students being wrapped up in their Esprit outfits and MTV, that a lot of the high school press has been covering
what you might call the hard topics, the topics they feel affect them.
These include AIDS, teenage pregnancy—the topics the Supreme
Court ruled the principal had the right to censor. . . .

"I think students are more aware of topics that earlier genera-   13
tions wouldn't even talk about. They can talk a lot more clinically
about sexual topics. Just listening to student discussions about AIDS
amazes me how detached and informed they are." . . .

Donal Brown, faculty adviser to the Redwood *Bark* at Lark-   14
spur's Redwood High School, said the switch from fluff to substance in student newspapers coincided with "the awareness of
young people that they have to do something about the problems
they are facing."

He said the Redwood *Bark* last spring did an article about the   15
rape of a 16-year-old girl who had become drunk at a party.

"It was extremely important for our community that this come   16
out. It increased the awareness of students of how evil this was. We
had an editorial talking about how students should give each other
support and not allow these things to happen. There were a lot of
people at the party who could have been more aware and protective of the girl who let herself get drunk," Brown said. . . .

He said allowing students to come to grips with the real prob-   17
lems that lie beyond the campus gives them the sense "they can improve things, help shape the society. They don't have to be passive
robots taking their place in some sort of totalitarian enclave."

Said Rebecca Jeschke, 17, one of the editors in chief: "If you give   18
kids responsibility, they rise to the occasion."

HIGH COURT GIVES A CIVICS LESSON

Fred M. Hechinger

Some people argue that the schools have the duty, indeed an obligation, to introduce students to only the highest values and morals with the hopes that the students will emulate them. Others argue that schools must also introduce students to the "real world" with the hopes that the students will be prepared to deal with the social and political problems that exist outside the high school walls; not doing so, they argue, amounts to repressing students' minds. In an essay published in the New York Times, *Hechinger discusses these two theories about the role of schools that underlie the* Hazelwood School District v. Kuhlmeier *decision.*

In 1969, the Supreme Court ruled that students "do not shed their   1
constitutional rights to freedom of speech or expression at the schoolhouse gate."

Last week, in a 5 to 3 ruling, the court put some limits on this   2
broad view of the Bill of Rights when it decided that a student newspaper was part of a high school's curriculum and subject to censorship of any content that conflicted with a "valid educational purpose."

The case, *Hazelwood School District v. Kuhlmeier,* grew out of a   3
long-standing conflict between two theories of education. The court sided with the traditionalists, who see the school as a molder of values for the immature. In the words of Justice Byron R. White, who wrote the majority opinion, schools must set "standards that may be higher than those demanded by some newspaper publishers or theatrical producers in the 'real' world."

On the other side of the controversy is a view of schools set forth   4
by Horace Mann, the 19th-century patron saint of universal public education, and, more recently, by John Dewey, the philosopher of progressive education. These men, though not rejecting limits on students' rights, held that schools are not enclaves apart from the "real world." Dewey described them instead as "embryonic" versions of society in which students learn to act as citizens in a democracy.

In a dissent that was solidly in the tradition of Dewey, Justice   5
William J. Brennan Jr. wrote that the mere claim by school officials that student expression is incompatible "with the school's pedagogical message" does not justify suppression. Otherwise, he wrote, school officials could convert public schools into "enclaves of totalitarianism."

Justice Brennan conceded that educators have an "undeniable, and 6
undeniably vital, mandate to **inculcate** moral and political values" but
[argued] that this is "not a general warrant to act as thought police."

"The young men and women of Hazelwood East," he wrote, 7
"expected a civics lesson, but not the one the Court teaches them
today." . . .

In the Supreme Court's reversal of the appellate court, Justice 8
White upheld the school authorities' right to censor speech that is
"ungrammatical, poorly written, inadequately researched, biased or
prejudiced, vulgar or **profane**, or unsuitable for immature audiences," none of which (with the possible exception of the last point)
was at issue in the Hazelwood case. . . .

The Hazelwood ruling is not likely to put an end to the controversy. 9
There is much agreement, shared by the dissenting Justices . . . that
limits exist to student rights, in particular those of the student press.
But there is no consensus about how far school administrators can
go in imposing their own views, or those of the political mainstream.

On this point the disagreement is clear-cut: Justice White be- 10
lieves that principals may reject any student expression that could
"associate the school with any position other than neutrality on matters of political controversy." Justice Brennan emphasizes the importance of "teaching children to respect the diversity of ideas that is
fundamental to the American system."

For decades the student press has taken a zig-zag course be- 11
tween **docile** publications that attract little attention and the more
enterprising or provocative ones that are read and debated. During
the campus upheavals of the late 1960's, students came to equate
supervision with suppression, and rebelled by creating an underground press that eluded adult influence altogether. . . . With last
week's ruling, the principals have regained lost ground, but they will
be under an even greater burden to draw the difficult distinction between instilling values and repressing developing minds.

CENSORSHIP: A FACT OF LIFE
STUDENTS ARE FORCED TO FACE
Jonathan Yardley

Yardley, the book critic of the Washington Post, *addresses the theory that
schools have a traditional mission and the Supreme Court's decision supports*

---

inculcate: teach by frequent repetition;   profane: contemptuous,
blasphemous;   docile: ready to be taught, submissive

just that. High school students do not have, he argues, the same rights as adults. His conclusion, however, points not to the ease with which school authorities should censor students but to the complexity of the tasks that teachers and administrators face.

Apart from teenage newspaper editors, self-appointed guardians of journalistic rights and First Amendment extremists, few Americans are likely to take serious exception to the Supreme Court's ruling last week on censorship of high-school newspapers. Its support for a principal in Missouri who had deleted stories from a student newspaper is sound both constitutionally and educationally. But the decision should not be interpreted as **carte blanche** for censorship, and it must not be taken as an excuse to sweep under the rug the serious issues with which the student journalists were attempting to deal. . . . 1

The Hazelwood student paper is not an independent publication, but a teaching instrument of its journalism department. Had the students chosen to express themselves in an independent publication—an underground or counter-culture newspaper, perhaps—Reynolds would have had no authority to censor or discipline them, and presumably would have had the good sense not to try. But stories published in the student newspaper are another matter altogether. . . . As Justice Byron White put it in his majority opinion . . . 2

"A school must be able to take into account the emotional maturity of the intended audience in determining whether to disseminate student speech on potentially sensitive topics, which might range from the existence of Santa Claus in an elementary school to the particulars of teenage sexual activity in a high school setting. A school must also retain the authority to refuse to sponsor student speech that might reasonably be perceived to advocate drug or alcohol abuse, irresponsible sex or conduct otherwise inconsistent with the shared values of a civilized social order." 3

In conclusion, White wrote that Reynolds "could reasonably have concluded that the students who had written and edited these articles had not sufficiently mastered those portions of the Journalism II curriculum that pertained to the treatment of controversial issues and personal attacks [and] the need to protect the privacy of individuals. . . ." Or, to put it another way, high school isn't the real world, and the rules of the real world do not always apply there. 4

---

carte blanche: full permission, ability to do what you want

To Justice William Brennan, writing in dissent, the majority deci-   5
sion is "brutal censorship," but even as one who usually agrees with
Brennan on questions of civil liberties and rights, I think in this instance he goes too far. The decision does not, as he contends, over-
turn a 1969 ruling denying that students "shed their constitutional
rights to freedom of speech or expression at the schoolhouse door";
the majority quite specifically reaffirmed that broad principle, qualifying it only by the observation, also based in precedent, that "a
school need not tolerate student speech that is inconsistent with its
'basic educational mission,' even though the government could not
censor similar speech outside the school."

This seems to me a matter of simple common sense. Even though   6
the legal rights of children have gained broader recognition in recent
years, it remains that children are not adults and that they have no
explicit or **implicit** right to behave with the full freedom granted to
adults. Freedom entails the responsibility to exercise it with mature
judgment, and this neither young children nor adolescents possess.
One of the most important functions of the schools is to prepare them
for that exercise; the principal of Hazelwood High School, in restricting the contents of an issue of *Spectrum,* was attempting among other
things to teach his journalism students a lesson about what is and is
not a responsible exercise of journalistic freedom.

But it was also an act of censorship, no question about that, and   7
no doubt the court's endorsement of it will be interpreted in some
quarters as license to clamp down on other, less offensive forms of
student expression. Should that lead to heavy-handed restraints on
student publications, performances and other activities—especially
any restraints involving the expression of political or ideological sen-
timent—the result would be a bad civics lesson for the students and
an **abrogation** of sound educational practice by the schools.

But this isn't likely to happen, at least on a widespread basis; the   8
initial reaction to the decision was measured, except among the few
alarmists who see it as the death **knell** for student rights, and no principals seemed to be in a great hurry to haul out the scissors and red
pencils. Most school authorities probably agree with the Hazelwood
school superintendent, who said the decision "reaffirms our position
that the board of education has authority to establish curricula."

---

explicit: directly expressed, clearly defined, explained;   implicit: indirectly
expressed, not clearly defined, implied;   abrogation: abolishment by
authority, nullification;   knell: slow, solemn sounding of a bell

What nobody seemed to be saying, though, is that the ruling 9
gives school administrators no help in dealing with the questions
that the *Spectrum* articles raised. Like it or not, reality at the high
schools is very different from what it was only a generation ago, and
reality is what school administrators have to contend with. Sexual
promiscuity, teenage pregnancy, drug and alcohol abuse: These and
"conduct otherwise inconsistent with the shared values of a civilized
social order" are scarcely new to the schools, but they are present
now to an extent without precedent and they simply cannot be scis-
sored away by censorship or other forms of escape.

However clumsily and immaturely, the editors and writers of 10
Spectrum were trying to discuss these questions in a manner that
they hoped would help their fellow students; their journalistic quali-
fications may have been limited, but their intentions were good. The
court's reaffirmation of the schools' disciplinary powers certainly is
welcome, but if the schools now use those powers to push reality
out of sight, they will be doing no one any good, least of all the students. A society that expects its educational system at all levels to act
in loco parentis cannot insist that this same system willfully ignore
the facts of its students' lives. Somehow the schools have to reconcile their traditional educational mission with the responsibility we
have **foisted** on them to teach students how to live in the real world;
it's a tough assignment.

Post-reading

As you are now aware, if you weren't already, the question of students'
rights and the problems of censorship are extremely complex. As in all really
tough arguments, intelligent and educated people disagree vehemently, and
their arguments are frequently well reasoned and thoughtful. Now, it's your
turn.

Go back to the pieces above and ask yourself the following:

- Who is the author?
- Who is the audience?
- What does the author hope to accomplish?

In the margins or on a separate sheet of paper, write brief summary notes of
each article, including in them the author's position and his or her main

---

in loco parentis: in the place or position of a parent (Latin);
foisted: imposed

support. Also note any questions you think the article raises and doesn't answer and/or any places you disagree with the author. In the latter case, make sure you jot down *why* you disagree. (The articles by Hechinger and Yardley are particularly important for the purposes of this assignment.)

Now, make lists of the arguments for the censorship of high school publications and the reasoning behind them (noting the circumstances when censorship may be justified) and of the arguments against it and the reasoning behind them. After having carefully evaluated the lists, you are ready to write the paper.

Essay Assignment

Write an essay in which you discuss not just the *Hazelwood* case but also the broader issue of censorship in high school publications. You may want to take a firm position on this issue, or you may wish to explain the arguments surrounding the issue without taking a firm position.

For more discussion of this issue and suggestions for organizing your essay, log on to http://devenglish.wadsworth.com.

Pre-writing

As you think about organizing your essay, remember these important points:

1. Give your readers sufficient background to understand the complexity and importance of the issue.
2. Cite the strengths, as well as the weaknesses, of the arguments you mention, including your own.
3. Support statements with facts and/or well-founded opinions to strengthen your argument.

For further ideas on structuring your essay, refer to the section "Writing Discussion Essays." Then jot down a working thesis and outline.

Writing

Although you may feel strongly one way or the other on this issue, remember that there's no right or wrong answer. There are, however, stronger and weaker arguments. In order to compose the strongest one you can, keep an open mind while you write and use the most compelling support you can muster. Be sure to review the Writer's Checklist on pages 339–340.

SHOULD ENGLISH BE THE OFFICIAL LANGUAGE OF THE UNITED STATES?

Currently, an organization named U.S. English, located in Washington, D.C., wants to amend the Constitution so that it names English the official language of the United States. In this effort, U.S. English has mounted campaigns in a number of states to have English declared the official language of those states. The results of these efforts have so far been successful. Many states—some, such as North Dakota, with virtually no non-English-speaking populations, and others, such as California and Florida, with large numbers of people whose native language isn't English—have now passed laws or constitutional amendments making English their official language.

Many countries have populations divided among speakers of different languages. Some of these countries have such large multilingual populations that more than one language is considered official and is used by the government. To name only those in the democratic West, there are Canada (English and French), Switzerland (German, French, Italian, and Romansch), Belgium (French and Flemish), Finland (Finnish and Swedish), and Ireland (English and Gaelic). There are also countries in which minority populations speak languages or dialects other than the dominant one, though only the dominant one is considered official and used by the government. Among those countries are France, Spain, and Italy.

In some of these countries, notably Canada and Belgium, there have been serious conflicts and even physical clashes between members of the different linguistic populations, though the sources of these conflicts have not been the languages themselves but ethnic, historic, economic, or political differences. In none of these cases were members of minority language groups recent immigrants to the country. In some Asian and European countries, fairly large immigrant populations did bring with them their original languages. This happened, for instance, in France, where many workers from North Africa have taken up residence, and in Japan, which has a large Korean population, but in neither case were efforts made to establish the new language on the same footing as the dominant one.

According to a report issued by the US Census Bureau in 1993, 31,844,979 people, or about one out of every fourteen residents of the United States, speak a language other than English at home, but the report also notes that only 21 percent of these speak English poorly or not at all. The largest number speaking another language at home speak Spanish,

17,339,172, with French coming in a distant second at 1,702,176. Of those who speak English poorly or not at all, most speak Spanish or an Asian language. The census report also indicates that there are severe economic penalties for not being able to speak English. Those who speak only Spanish typically earn one-third to one-half as much as Spanish speakers who also speak English.

California makes an interesting case study of the issues involved in an election in which a constitutional amendment was on the ballot to make English the state's "official" language. In 1986 California voters were asked to vote for or against a state proposition (Proposition 63) that would make English the official language of the state. Proposition 63 was drafted by U.S. English.

Reading Assignment

Pre-reading

Before you read Proposition 63 and the arguments for and against it, reflect on your own experience: What are your thoughts on making English the official language of California or of the whole country? What would be the benefits of doing so? What would be some of the problems? Who would benefit? Who would be hurt and to what extent, do you think?

This is an extremely complex topic, so discuss it in class and with friends and acquaintances outside of class, making note of the arguments you hear and registering whether they are based on fact or opinion. Consider whether the opinions are ill founded or well founded.

Reading

Following is the text of Proposition 63, followed by the arguments for and against the proposition that were printed in the voters' handbook published by the State of California. Included after that are several articles and letters to the editor concerning Proposition 63 and the issues it raises. Remember to read actively, taking notes in the margins or on a separate sheet of paper.

PROPOSITION 63

(a) *Purpose*
English is the common language of the people of the United States of America and the State of California. This section is intended to preserve, protect and strengthen the English language, and not

to **supersede** any of the rights guaranteed to the people by this Constitution.

(b) *English as the Official Language of California*

English is the official language of the State of California.

(c) *Enforcement*

The Legislature shall enforce this section by appropriate legislation. The Legislature and officials of the State of California shall take all steps necessary to insure that the role of English as the common language of the State of California is preserved and enhanced. The Legislature shall make no law which diminishes or ignores the role of English as the common language of the State of California.

(d) *Personal Right of Action and Jurisdiction of Courts*

Any person who is a resident of or doing business in the State of California shall have **standing** to sue the State of California to enforce this section, and the Courts of record of the State of California shall have jurisdiction to hear cases brought to enforce this section. The Legislature may provide reasonable and appropriate limitations on the time and manner of suits brought under this section.

ARGUMENT IN FAVOR OF PROPOSITION 63

The State of California stands at a crossroads. It can move toward 1 fears and tensions of language rivalries and ethnic distrust. Or it can reverse that trend and strengthen our common bond, the English language.

Our immigrants learned English if they arrived not knowing the 2 language. Millions of immigrants now living have learned English or are learning it in order to participate in our culture. With one shared language we learn to respect other people, other cultures, with sympathy and understanding.

Our American heritage is now threatened by language con- 3 flicts and ethnic separatism. Today there is a serious erosion of English as our common bond. This amendment reaffirms California's oneness as a state, and as one of fifty states united by a common tongue.

This amendment establishes a broad principle: English is the official 4 language of California. It is entitled to legal recognition and protection as such. No other language can have a similar status. This amendment recognizes in law what has long been a political and social reality.

---

supersede: take the place of;   standing: the right

Nothing in the amendment prohibits the use of languages other 5
than English in unofficial situations, such as family communications,
religious ceremonies or private business. Nothing in this amendment
forbids teaching foreign languages. Nothing in this amendment re-
moves or reduces any Californian's constitutional rights.

The amendment gives guidance to the Legislature, the Gover- 6
nor and the courts. Government must protect English:

- by passing no law that ignores or diminishes English;
- by issuing voting ballots and materials in English only (except
  where required by federal law);
- by ensuring that immigrants are taught English as quickly as
  possible (except as required by federal law);
- by functioning in English, except where public health, safety
  and justice require the use of other languages;
- by weighing the effect of proposed legislation on the role of
  English; and
- by preserving and enhancing the role of English as our common
  language.

Californians have already expressed themselves decisively. More 7
than a million Californians asked to place this measure on the ballot, the third largest number of petition signatures in California history. In 1984, 70+ percent of California voters, 6,300,000, approved
Proposition 38, "Voting Materials in English ONLY."

This amendment sends a clear message: English is the official 8
language of California. To function, to participate in our society, we
must know English. English is the language of opportunity, of government, of unity. English, in a fundamental sense, is US.

Every year California's government makes decisions which ig- 9
nore the role of English in our state; some may cause irreversible
harm. Government's bilingual activities cost millions of taxpayers'
dollars each year. This amendment will force government officials to
stop and think before taking action.

The future of California hangs in the balance—a state divided or 10
a state united—a true part of the Union. YES is for unity—for what is
right and best for our state, for our country, and for all of us.

S. I. Hayakawa, Ph.D.
United States Senator, 1977–1982

J. William Orozco
Businessman

Stanley Diamond
Chairman, California English Campaign

ARGUMENT AGAINST PROPOSITION 63

This summer we celebrated the 100th anniversary of the Statue of 1
Liberty. That glorious 4th of July brought all Americans together.
Now, four months later, Proposition 63 threatens to divide us and
tarnish our proud heritage of tolerance and diversity.

This proposition, despite its title, does not preserve English as our 2
common language. Instead, it undermines the efforts of new citizens
of our state to contribute to and enter the mainstream of American life.

English is and will remain the language of California. Proposition 3
63 won't change that. What it *will* do is produce a nightmare of expensive **litigation** and needless resentment.

Proposition 63 could mean that state and local government 4
must eliminate multilingual police, fire, and emergency services such
as 911 telephone operators, thereby jeopardizing the lives and safety
of potential victims.

It could mean that court interpreters for witnesses, crime vic- 5
tims, and defendants have to be eliminated.

It could outlaw essential multilingual public service information 6
such as pamphlets informing non-English-speaking parents how to
enroll their children in public schools.

Even foreign street signs and the teaching of languages in pub- 7
lic schools could be in jeopardy.

We can hope that sensible court decisions will prevent these con- 8
sequences. But Proposition 63 openly invites costly legal attempts to
seek such results. It is certain to set Californian against Californian
with tragic consequences.

What makes this especially troubling is that the overwhelming 9
majority of immigrants *want* to learn English. In fact, a recent study
shows that 98% of Latin parents say it is essential for their children
to read and write English well.

Asians, Latinos, and other recent immigrants fill long waiting lists 10
for English courses at community colleges and adult schools. But this
initiative does nothing positive to help. For instance, it provides for
no increase in desperately needed night and weekend English
classes.

The Los Angeles County Board of Supervisors, when faced with 11
a negative local measure like this one, firmly and wisely rejected it by
a unanimous, **bipartisan** vote. On April 21, 1986, they said in part:

---

litigation: legal action;   bipartisan: two party

"English as the official language resolutions will not help anyone 12
learn English. They will not improve human relations, and they will
not lead to a better community. They will create greater intergroup
tension and ill will, encourage resentment and bigotry, pit neighbor
against neighbor and group against group. They reflect our worst
fears, not our best values.

"In many areas . . . non-English-speaking persons have some- 13
times represented a problem for school teachers, service providers,
law enforcement officers, who are unable to understand them. The
problem will be solved over time as newcomers learn English. It has
happened many times before in our history. In the meanwhile . . .
common sense . . . good will, sensitivity, and humor will help us
through this challenging period."

Well said by public officials representing both sides of the politi- 14
cal spectrum.

Proposition 63 is unnecessary. It is negative and counterproduc- 15
tive. It is, in the most fundamental sense, un-American.

> John Van De Kamp
> Attorney General
>
> Willie L. Brown, Jr.
> Speaker, California State Assembly
>
> Daryl F. Gates
> Police Chief
> Los Angeles Police Department

ENGLISH-ONLY PROPOSITION
DRAWS LOTS OF HOT WORDS
John Wildermuth

*This article and the next one by John Wildermuth, concerning Proposition
63, both appeared in the* San Francisco Chronicle *on October 20,
1986.*

In San Francisco's heavily Hispanic Mission District, there are many 1
stores where English words are seldom heard.

On the 30-Stockton bus, which makes the slow trip through the 2
narrow, crowded streets of Chinatown, drivers chat with riders in
Cantonese.

In the Tenderloin, only Vietnamese characters mark many small 3
shops and businesses. Tagalog is the language of choice in large parts
of Daly City.

This increasing use and visibility of foreign languages in the state   4
is one of the reasons voters will be faced with a decision on Proposition 63 on November 4.

The measure would proclaim English as the official language of   5
California and ban any law "which diminishes or ignores the role of
English as the common language of the State of California."

In rallying support for the English-only attempt, former Senator   6
S. I. Hayakawa speaks in near-**apocalyptic** terms. "What is at stake in
the long run is our unity as a nation," said Hayakawa, honorary chairman of U.S. English, the Washington-based group backing Proposition 63. "For the first time in our history, our nation is faced with the
possibility of the kind of linguistic division that has torn apart Canada
in recent years."

Lined up against the proposition is a loose-knit coalition of His-   7
panic, Asian, religious and liberal organizations, backed by most of
the state's best known politicians.

So far, the campaign has generated plenty of hot words but not   8
much to enlighten voters. The two sides do not even agree on what
Proposition 63 will do.

Supporters say the measure's major effect will be symbolic,   9
"strengthening the ties that bind us all together through the magic
bond of a common language," according to Hayakawa.

Stanley Diamond, director of the state campaign, said the   10
proposition would simply eliminate bilingual ballots in San Francisco
and Los Angeles, where they are not required by federal law, and
end any requirements that nonemergency government services be
provided in foreign languages.

Opponents, however, argue that Proposition 63 could require a   11
complete dismantling of all government bilingual services and declare open season on other attempts to aid non-English-speaking immigrants. "We're trying to let people know that this initiative is a can
of worms," said Marcello Rodriguez of Californians United Against
Proposition 63. "If passed, this proposition will create a legal nightmare," said Louise Renne, San Francisco city attorney. "It is so open-
ended that it will lead to countless lawsuits."

Bilingual operators on 911 emergency lines, interpreters in   12
courts and hospitals and disaster information printed in Spanish and
Chinese all may have to go if Proposition 63 is passed, opponents

---

apocalyptic: like the sayings of a prophet

charge. One legislator even suggested that the Latin motto on the wall of the state Senate chamber might have to be painted over.

Such charges are all part of a "planned campaign of deceit, dirty 13 tricks and **unconscionable** lies," campaign director Diamond said. But he argued that the charges will not make much of a difference because Californians already have shown they overwhelmingly support the English-only effort.

More than one million signed petitions to qualify the initiative 14 for the ballot. And a California Poll released last week showed the measure leading 57 percent to 13 percent, a whopping 4-to-1 margin.

Even opponents admit the measure has plenty of appeal. "If vot- 15 ers think this proposition is only going to name English the official language of California, certainly it's going to pass," said John Trasvina, an attorney for the Mexican-American Defense Fund. "We have to make them look beyond that to the other potential effects."

The claim that English is in danger of becoming less important 16 in California or the United States is ridiculous, said Geoffrey Nunberg, a linguist associated with the Xerox Palo Alto Research Center and Stanford University. "English needs about as much special protection as the Chicago Bears do," he said. "The children of immigrants want to learn English. The problem is getting them to learn their parents' or grandparents' language."

English-language classes are jammed throughout California, with 17 more than 40,000 students turned away from classes in Los Angeles County alone. In San Francisco, 18,000 students are studying English as a Second Language in adult education classes run by the community college district, said Christine Bunn, a spokeswoman for the program.

The anti-initiative forces cite studies they say prove the English- 18 only measure is unnecessary, including one showing that 95 percent of first-generation Mexican Americans born in the United States are proficient in English and more than half of the second generation speak no Spanish at all.

"The notion that non-English speaking residents are propagat- 19 ing a new generation of non-English speakers is bunk," said Henry Der of Chinese for Affirmative Action.

Diamond, Hayakawa and other supporters of the initiative say it 20 is not anti-immigrant, anti-minority or anti-Hispanic, and they dis-

---

unconscionable: excessive, unrestrained

miss most of the complaints and charges aimed at Proposition 63. What is important, Diamond says, is the message that passage of the proposition will send to California and its people. "This constitutional amendment is a great big neon sign saying if you want to succeed, you have to learn English."

HOW MIAMI ADJUSTED TO ITS BILINGUAL BAN
John Wildermuth

In 1980, voters in Dade County, Fla., banned the use of county   1
money for "utilizing any language other than English or promoting any culture other than that of the United States." The effect was not as bad as opponents had predicted.

"In a nutshell," said Murray Greenberg, first assistant county at-   2
torney, "it hasn't prohibited the use of Spanish the way its support-   *NSo*
ers had hoped, and it hasn't had as negative an effect as its opponents feared."

Opponents of Proposition 63, which would proclaim English   3
to be California's official language, continually cite the Dade County experience as an example of what will happen if the initiative passes in November. Backers of the proposition, who include some groups involved in the Florida campaign, deny that there is any similarity.

After the vote, Dade County publications and newsletters no   4
longer were sent out in Spanish and welfare and hospital forms were printed only in English. Government jobs were no longer advertised in Spanish-language newspapers, and Dade County stopped financing the annual Spanish Heritage Festival.

But the county, which includes the city of Miami, did not end its   5
bilingual emergency health and safety services. Hurricane warnings still were broadcast in Spanish and English, and Spanish-speaking residents still could use the 911 emergency number to get an ambulance or report a fire.

In Miami's Metrorail subway system, warnings about the electri-   6
fied rails are printed in Spanish, although foreign-language signs about how to use the system were taken down. "We were not going to interpret the law to endanger the life, health and safety of citizens," Greenberg said.

In 1984, the County Commission modified the bilingual ban, al-   7
lowing the county to use other languages where health, safety or tourism are involved. . . .

[U.S. English], which claims more than 200,000 members, con- 8
tends that multilingual ballots and bilingual education keep people
with limited English proficiency from getting ahead. . . .

THE CASE FOR BILINGUAL BALLOTS
Joaquin G. Avila

The following excerpts are from an article in the San Francisco Sunday
Examiner and Chronicle. *The author is an activist for non-English speakers'
rights.*

In 1975 Hispanics and Asians went before Congress to document 1
decades of blatant discriminatory practices that had kept us from
an equal vote. Prime among the issues raised was an urgent appeal
for oral and written help for citizens who cannot understand all-
English voting materials. Since almost 10 percent of U.S. Hispanics
are monolingual in Spanish and 41 percent speak Spanish mostly,
that need is particularly acute among Latinos. Congress responded
by providing for bilingual elections in places where any given for-
eign-language-speaking group forms more than 5 percent of the
total population and has high illiteracy and low voter-registration
rates.

Some Hispanics and Asians have poor English skills because they 2
went to inferior schools. Some, raised by parents who were **migrant**
workers, suffered frequent interruptions in their studies. Some **naturalized** very late in life. The language barrier already limits these
people's chances to gain jobs, to live in decent neighborhoods, to
gain good educations. . . .

No one feels the need to learn English more than foreign-lan- 3
guage speakers. If they don't learn the language, it is more for lack
of time and access to classes than for lack of desire. San Francisco
Community College Centers had about 3,000 names on waiting
lists for English as a Second Language (ESL) classes in Asian and Hispanic areas last year. The motivation is there; the ESL classes are
not. . . .

In 1982, the Mexican American Legal Defense and Education 4
Fund commissioned a group of scholars to find out how bilingual
voting help was used. About one-third of the Hispanics studied said
they would be less likely to vote without Spanish-language help. The

---

migrant: traveling;   naturalized: became citizens

group also found that those most likely to use Spanish aids were people over 65, people with poor educations and people with low incomes. . . .

Some charge that bilingual ballots waste taxpayers' money. The 5 numbers tell a different story. Asians and Hispanics together form 33 percent of San Francisco's citizenry. Yet bilingual elections consume only about 5 percent of our election budget. In November, 1980, San Francisco spent over $58,000 to send English-language pamphlets to San Franciscans who never voted. Bilingual elections, by contrast, cost from $25,000 to $40,000 per election. With Asians and Hispanics forming about one-third of the city, we can be sure their taxes cover those costs. . . .

From the 1976 to 1980 presidential elections, Hispanic voter 6 registration jumped 64 percent in Texas and 38 percent in California. Those leaps were largely due to Voting Rights Act reforms—including bilingual elections. . . .

LIBERTY AND LANGUAGE FOR ALL
Andy Rooney

You'll probably be surprised to hear that English is not the official 1 language of the United States. I was surprised. The story is, we don't have an official language, and Senator Walter Huddleston of Kentucky has just proposed a constitutional amendment to declare one. The language he proposes, of course, is English.

By the time most of us are 30, we've been faced with the **incon-** 2 **trovertible** evidence of our own shortcomings and prejudices so often that we can't deny them, even to ourselves. I'm not proud of myself for it, but I notice I'm intolerant of people who have lived in this country for years and can't or don't speak English.

Luckily for me, I don't have to rely on prejudice alone to argue 3 the case for people learning English if they live in this country. It's for their own good. The Spanish-speaking people who have chosen to abandon their native land to come here to live are never going to get jobs as good as the English-speaking people have. English-speaking Hispanics are going to get better jobs than those who don't speak English. It's that simple. If they came to this country to get in on the good things it has to offer, one of the best ways to get in on them is to learn English.

---

incontrovertible: unquestionable

Arnoldo Torres, a spokesman for the League of United Latin   4
American Citizens, says that if English were declared the official language here, we'd be "creating a monster" that could lead to the op-
pression of Spanish-speaking people and other citizens who speak
foreign languages.

To be able to speak only Spanish in an English-speaking country   5
is already a monster in their lives. It limits what they can do, where
they can go and what jobs they can get. It makes them less than
equal, and no one can bestow that kind of equality. They'll have to
earn it by learning.

In 30 states, the ballots in the election booths are printed in Eng-   6
lish and Spanish. Many official government forms also are printed in
both languages. That kind of translating help isn't like providing wheel-
chair access to public places for the handicapped. By printing a few important things in Spanish for people who don't read or speak English,
we're giving young Hispanics the impression they'll always be able to
make out here. It makes it seem unnecessary for them to learn English.

I can understand older people having a hard time picking up a   7
new language, but there's no excuse for not making the younger
Hispanic generation learn English. Any foreign language is best
learned young in a natural setting. Anyone who's ever spent time in
a foreign country knows that if you have an interpreter around all
the time, you never learn the language. If, on the other hand, you're
thrown out among the people on your own with no help, you damn
well better start learning some words just to survive. First thing you
know, you're learning the language.

Spanish-speaking kids shouldn't be encouraged to keep speak-   8
ing Spanish outside their homes. There's a growing division in this
country between the great number of Spanish-speaking people
who've come here in the last 10 years and the rest of us, most of
whose ancestors came from Europe generations ago. The new immigrants seem less willing to give up their native tongue. They gave up
their homeland; why do they resist giving up their language? A little
intolerance is good for the soul. If you go around tolerating everything all the time, you get walked all over. I personally enjoy being
intolerant once in a while. I'm intolerant of people who come here
to live and don't want to learn to speak English.

Puerto Rico has a non-voting delegate to Congress, Baltasar Cor-   9
rada. He says that imposing English on all citizens of the United
States would violate their guarantees of free speech.

How do you say "Hogwash!" in Spanish, Mr. Corrada?   10

LETTERS TO THE EDITOR ABOUT PROPOSITION 63

These letters to the editor present opinions on the issue of making English the official language of California or the United States.

Editor:

The Congress has realized that it would be unwise to prevent the use 1
of languages other than English in helping the government communicate with its citizens and the citizens communicate with each other.
Accordingly, it has shown no interest in the efforts of Hayakawa's organization, U.S. English, to get a constitutional amendment mandat-
ing English only as the "official language" of the United States.

It looks now as though the strategy of U.S. English is to achieve 2
the same results state by state. This effort should be stopped now.
Vote no on Proposition 63.

                                                        Harrison E. Woodbury

Editor:

The supporters of Proposition 63 claim that English is under attack, 3
but they offer no evidence that it is. Nor does Proposition 63 offer
any help to new citizens who want to learn English. All it does is penalize them.

Those penalties include: abolishing bilingual ballots and voter 4
materials, abolishing bilingual education, possibly eliminating social,
health, and emergency services in languages other than English.

My question is: why?   5

                                                        Marlene Winslow

Editor:

It would be nice if some of the writers to this column (Marlene 6
Winslow) would inform themselves before spouting off. Proposition 63 merely makes our language official, like the rose, the
eagle, the anthem. It cannot eliminate most bilingual ballots or
education because those are controlled by federal laws. It will
not eliminate 911 emergency services or court interpreters or private business signs or languages spoken in the home or marketplace.

                                                        Eugene S. Cottage

Editor:

Did you ever try to live in Germany without learning German? France 7
without learning French? Japan without learning Japanese? Mexico
without learning Spanish? Get serious. We seem to be the only country in the world that allows new immigrants to settle here without
learning our language. I think it's time to change that.

Mary Peters-Wilson

Post-reading

As always in the case of arguments, the important thing is to get the
facts and the opinions in the case sorted out, and that's essential here too.
But when you are dealing with materials with political implications, such as
California's Proposition 63 and the materials printed in the voters' handbook, you also have to clear away the hot air, the propaganda techniques
both sides will trot out to sway the voters.

You will find a number of standard techniques of political propaganda
here. Always watch out when politicians or others start draping themselves
in the flag, trying to make themselves look like patriots, while by implica-
tion the other side seems to be vaguely un-American. Look out for phrases
like "American heritage" and "glorious 4th of July." When someone wraps
the flag around himself to make himself look ultra-patriotic, we usually
wonder what he's hiding. Keep alert for dire predictions such as "The future of California hangs in the balance," particularly when they are also
stale, overused expressions. It is easy to predict that the very best or the
very worst will take place should a program or bill pass. Rarely does either
one happen.

Beware of scare tactics, often signaled by the verb "could." When people start telling you what *could* happen, you may want to look into the
likelihood of that *could* coming true. If it *could* happen, then it also *might
not* happen. Finally, watch out for the tactic called the "bandwagon"—the
one in which someone tries to sell you something or convince you of
something by telling you how many others have bought it or believe it. Is
it a good sign that seventy-six zillion people have eaten Gumsludge's hamburgers? No. The best food is eaten by a small number of people. Large
numbers of people are often wrong; many would argue they are usually
wrong.

Go back over the reading assignments and any notes you have taken,
being especially alert to political propaganda—clichés as well as inflated
language. Once the political propaganda is put aside, what do the arguments look like? How strong are they without their political "bells and
whistles"?

Essay Assignment

Write an essay in which you argue for or against the movement to make English the official language of the United States.

For more discussion of this issue and suggestions about organizing your essay, log on to http://devenglish.wadsworth.com.

Pre-writing

In this case, after sorting out fact from opinion, it is important to measure the results of Proposition 63 as forecast by its supporters and its opponents against the text of the law itself. And you will also want to look at the results produced by essentially the same law in another part of the country, which Wildermuth addresses in "How Miami Adjusted to Its Bilingual Ban." They should tell you something about the likely impact of this law, and the results of this analysis could produce the last section of your essay.

Remember to jot down an outline of your main points in the order you plan to present them and the support you intend to use. Also, compose a working thesis to help focus and direct your essay.

Writing

Review the section "Evaluating Evidence and Shaping Your Argument." In particular, keep in mind the following four points:

1. Be sure to include the strongest arguments of both sides; however, in this instance, you may have to mention and then discount any propaganda techniques such as flag waving, scare tactics, or bandwagon appeals.

2. Don't lump all the arguments on one side in one paragraph and all the arguments on the other side in a second paragraph.

3. Remember that a statement alone isn't an argument; statements are often like topic sentences—that is, sentences that have to be explained or backed up.

4. Make sure to base your conclusion on the arguments preceding it. It should reflect the strengths and weaknesses of the arguments covered in your essay; avoid merely tacking on your own unproven opinion at the end.

THE WRITER'S CHECKLIST

The Idea Draft

1. Does your idea draft *respond fully* to the assignment?

2. Are your ideas *organized* in the way you want?

3. Does your *introduction* explain what the essay will be about and what its purpose is?

4. Do you have a *thesis* that states your point or indicates the issue the essay will address?

5. Do the *body paragraphs* each have a *topic sentence*? Do they develop the main points by giving *specifics and examples* to support those points?

6. Does your *conclusion* express your view on the issue and is it based on the argument in the body of your essay?

7. Have you *collaborated* with at least one trusted friend or fellow student who has read your draft *critically*, looking for lapses in logic or other weaknesses in content?

Sentence Combining

In revising your idea draft, keep in mind the possibility of using appositives, if you have studied them. Generally, you will probably use adjective clauses automatically because we use them in speech a great deal, but appositives are constructions that writers, not speakers, use. One of the most common uses of appositives is to identify someone or something, as in these instances from Dennis McLellan's article on part-time work for teenagers. (Note that the appositive in the first example contains an adjective clause too.)

Nathan Keethe, a Newport Harbor High School senior who works more than 20 hours a week for an exterminating service, admits to sometimes feeling like the odd man out. . . .

John Fovos landed his first part-time job—as a box boy at Alpha Beta on West Olympic—the summer after his sophomore year at Fairfax High School in Los Angeles.

The book, *When Teenagers Work: The Psychological and Social Costs of Adolescent Employment,* is by Ellen Greenberger, a developmental psychologist and professor of social ecology at the University of California, Irvine, and Laurence Steinberg, a professor of child and family studies at the University of Wisconsin.

Often professional writers use appositives to develop their ideas, as in this case from Amitai Etzioni's essay:

> But in fact, these jobs undermine school attendance and involvement, impart few skills that will be useful in later life, and simultaneously skew the values of teenagers—especially their ideas about the worth of a dollar.

McLellan does the same thing but uses a common appositive + adjective clause construction starting with the word *one*:

> Part-time work during the school years traditionally has been viewed as an invaluable experience for adolescents, one that builds character, teaches responsibility and prepares them for entering the adult world.

Later Drafts

1. Taking into account the constructive criticism you have received, have you *revised* accordingly—that is, reorganized, if organization was a problem, or given additional support, if support was?

2. Have you read your essay *aloud,* listening closely to what it *actually says* (not just what you think it says)?

3. Have you *revised your sentences* if they were unclear or awkward? (This is another good place to work with a trusted fellow student or friend. Have him or her read your essay aloud, and both of you should listen closely to what it says.)

4. Have you checked for those *mechanical difficulties* that you know you sometimes have? Have you used the dictionary to check words that you think may be *misspelled?*

Final Draft

If you have followed this assignment step by step, you have worked exceedingly hard on this essay. Therefore, make sure your final draft reflects your care and effort by being as professional looking as possible.

1. Type it neatly, using the format your instructor has assigned.

2. Proofread slowly and carefully, word by word, line by line. (One last time, ask a trusted friend to proofread it *after* you have, or exchange your essay with another student and proof each other's.)

Sentence Combining

SHAPING SENTENCES TO SHOW
RELATIONSHIPS: APPOSITIVES

Among the words that can modify nouns are nouns themselves. In English, we can use nouns to add to the meaning of other nouns in ways that some other languages cannot do. For instance, in some languages, if you want to specify what kind of hunter someone is, you have to add a prepositional phrase to the noun meaning hunter. In these languages you would have a hunter of deer or a hunter of alligators. In English we simply put the qualifying noun in front of the main noun, thus: deer hunter, alligator hunter. Similarly, we speak of office buildings instead of buildings for offices or student union buildings rather than buildings for the union of students.

In addition to these common usages, in which we put nouns in front of other nouns, we also put noun modifiers behind the nouns they modify. Studies show that experienced writers use this kind of noun construction very frequently while inexperienced writers do not. Thus, learning this construction will take you a long way toward making your writing like that of writers in the academic and professional worlds.

Noun modifiers that follow the nouns they modify normally rename or identify or describe in different words the nouns they refer to. Two other points are worth mentioning here. First, these noun modifiers often have modifiers of their own, sometimes very long strings of them. Second, writers usually set these modifiers (together with their modifiers) off with commas. Here is an example:

Everyone looked up to George, the tallest <u>student</u> in the freshman class.

In this case, the noun *student* is the main modifier of George, but it has other words modifying it—*the tallest* and *in the freshman class.* All of those words together are a *noun phrase* modifying *George,* telling something about him. Here are a few more examples:

I'm going to make one of my favorite dishes tonight, <u>chicken Marengo.</u>

The street I live on, *a noisy, dirty, busy <u>thoroughfare,</u>* is not a pleasant place to be.

He had yet another idea for solving all our problems, *the third <u>one</u> that evening.*

Mary's car, *a dreadful <u>clunker</u> due to fall apart any day,* was purchased by a friend of hers, *a <u>guy</u> who was sure he could fix anything that ran on wheels.*

Punctuating Noun Phrases in Sentences

1. Single phrases are set off by commas. Remember to put a comma *after* the phrase as well as in front of it:

    Martha Goggle, a retired airline pilot, lives next door.

    I love her house, a redecorated 747.

2. Series of nouns or noun phrases are set off by dashes when they occur in the middle of sentences:

    My favorite forms of entertainment—concerts, movies, books, and records—are all fairly expensive.

3. Series of noun phrases at the ends of sentences are most often set off with a comma or a dash, less often with a colon:

    There are several dangers involved in skiing—broken legs, wind-burned skin, and death by avalanche.

EXERCISE

Combine the following sentences using noun phrases whenever you can, as in this example:

Melvin hated his cage.
Melvin was an oversized Indian elephant.
His cage was an undersized cell with poor room service.

Solution: Melvin, an oversized Indian elephant, hated his cage, an undersized cell with poor room service.

Rashaad and Gloria

1. Rashaad was dedicated to his studies.

    He was a nineteen-year-old math major.

2. Until she met him, Gloria studied hard but also enjoyed the good times.

    She was his girlfriend.

    The good times were parties.

    The good times were movies.

    The good times were concerts.

3. Rashaad could rarely be dragged to anything.

    He was the ultimate nerd.

4. He told her his idea of a great evening.

    It was dinner.

It was calculus until 11:00.

It was a glass of wine.

It was her to snuggle with.

5. After she missed three of her favorite events, Gloria decided to dump Rashaad.

One event was the Fifties Sock Hop.

One event was the Homecoming Dance.

One event was the Butchers' Meat Ball.

6. One night a mysterious object came crashing through Rashaad's window.

It was a calculator with a note wrapped around it.

7. The note said, "Dear Rashaad. Here is my idea of a good time.

It is dinner with Fred.

Fred is an art major I have just met.

It is dancing with Fred until 1:00.

It is snuggling with Fred."

8. The note concluded with these words.

These words were, "Use this to count on, from now on, because you can't count on me."

EXERCISE

Following are three sample sentence-combining exercises using noun phrases:

1. They bought some furniture.

    The furniture was a new sofa.

    The furniture was a bookcase.

    Solution: They bought some furniture, a new sofa and a bookcase.

2. He won the grand prize at the big raffle.

    The grand prize was a set of dishes purchased at a secondhand store.

    Solution: He won the grand prize at the big raffle, a set of dishes purchased at a secondhand store.

3. David and Martha pulled the roast out of the oven.

    David and Martha are my favorite cooks.

    The roast was a piece of meat big enough to feed the First Infantry Division.

Solution: David and Martha, my favorite cooks, pulled the roast out of the oven, a piece of meat big enough to feed the First Infantry Division.

In the first four exercises below, the noun phrases are underlined to help you identify them.

Albert's Pets

1. Albert Lee moved into a new place.
   Albert is an old friend of mine.

2. His apartment is attractive, but Albert had a problem.
   His apartment is a condominium not far from here.
   Albert is a man newly divorced.

3. Albert had a love-hate relationship with his condominium.
   His condominium was an attractive, sunny, two-bedroom apartment.

4. He loved the place but hated being there because nobody else was around.
   The place was the first apartment he had ever had all to himself.
   Nobody else was no other creature of any kind.

5. In short, Albert was lonely.
   Albert was a gregarious man from a large family.

6. That's why Albert decided to get a couple of pets.
   The pets were a dog and a cat.

7. The dog was a mutt he got from the pound, and the cat came from a friend of his.
   The dog was a puppy he named Animal.
   The cat was a kitten he called Kitty.

8. Animal quickly ate a major portion of his wardrobe.
   Animal was a frisky and untameable little beast.
   His wardrobe was his slippers, a shoe, several socks, and the leg of a pair of trousers.

9. Kitty used her claws to produce shredded furniture when she tired of chasing Animal.
   The shredded furniture was a shredded couch, a shredded chair, and a handsome set of shredded drapes.

10. Albert's expensive new condominium was a wreck, but Albert was happy as a clam.
    The wreck was nothing but a large playground for Animal and Kitty.

Creating Noun Phrase Modifiers

Because these noun phrases are so important to good writing and so useful to anyone who has to write much, some additional exercises follow to assist you in actively using them to express information you have. In each case, you are given a short sentence with an underlined noun and a blank to be filled in:

She bought the car she had been longing for _____

_____.

Your task is to fill in the blank with a noun referring to the underlined noun:

She bought the car she had been longing for, a Ford _____

_____.

Of course, since specific writing is usually better than general writing, it would be better to be more specific than that, to add a whole noun phrase:

She bought the car she had been longing for, an almost new maroon and gray Ford convertible.

Start with thinking first of a single noun, like *Ford,* and build on it since you are working here with using noun phrases. In the following exercises, questions follow the first four sentences to help you find first a noun and then a whole noun phrase that will work. Be sure to provide the normal punctuation used to set off appositives.

1. I saw a movie the other day _____.
   (What kind of movie? A comedy? A horror film? What was it about?)

2. I visited her house last week_____.
   (What kind of house? A mansion? A cottage? Or was it just a normal residence with some particular characteristics?)

3. A new store just opened in the mall _____
   _____.
   (What kind of store? A store selling what? A store you want to visit? Why?)

4. Mary observed the monster through her binoculars _____
   _____.
   (What kind of monster? A huge beast of some sort? A creature from outer space? Your younger brother dressed in an outlandish costume? Your younger brother dressed in his normal way?)

5. I play my current favorite record all the time _____.

6. My homework _____ is going to keep me up all night.

7. My current job _____ is taking up too much of my study time.

8. The birthday present I got last year _____ was just what I wanted.

9. There are four things that I wish I could afford to buy myself now _____

   _____

   _____.

10. Of my three favorite TV shows _____

   _____ I think I enjoy the last one the most.

EXERCISE

The following exercises are similar to the ones you have just done. In the first five, you are given a model sentence to imitate. Use the model word for word but instead of copying the noun phrases of the model, use your own, drawing on your own thoughts and experiences.

1. **Model:** I get a lot of enjoyment out of my car, an aging 280Z that gets me where I want to go about as fast as I want to get there.

   Your sentence: I get a lot of enjoyment out of my car [or some other object], _____.

2. **Model:** I went to an interesting high school, a place where basketball was more important than American history and you were graded according to how much money your parents had.

   Your sentence: I went to an interesting high school,_____

   _____

   _____.

3. **Model:** I really enjoyed a book I read last week, an odd novel about a man living in New York City with three women.

   Your sentence: I really enjoyed [or hated] a book I read last week,

   _____.

4. **Model:** There is one teacher I always remember fondly, a high school speech teacher who took us to see Broadway musicals.

   Your sentence: There is one teacher I always remember fondly,

   _____.

5. **Model:** I could eat one of my favorite dishes, chicken and vegetables cooked in apple brandy, just about every week.

Your sentence: I could eat one of my favorite dishes, _____

_____ .

just about every week.

6. Write a sentence in which you use a noun phrase to describe a television show you enjoy.

7. Write a sentence in which you use a noun phrase to describe one or more members of your family.

8. Write a sentence in which you use a noun phrase to describe a job you have or once had or would like to have.

9. Write a sentence in which you use a noun phrase to describe your room or your house.

10. Write a sentence in which you use a noun phrase to describe a hobby of yours or an activity you enjoy.

REVIEW

In the following exercises, you will practice using modifiers and joining words. In the first three, noun phrases are underlined, but in the rest, you will have to find them on your own. As in previous exercises, places where you should use joining words have been indicated.

Note : When you use a noun phrase to modify a noun that already has a prepositional phrase following it, your noun phrase modifier should always follow the prepositional phrase. For example, if you wanted to use the noun phrase *my mother* to modify any of the following nouns + prepositional phrases, you would write them this way:

The woman of the house, my mother
The doctor in charge, my mother
The person with the best idea, my mother
The speaker on the platform, my mother

The Statue of Liberty

1. The most famous statue was the creation of a sculptor.
   The statue is in the United States.
   The statue is the Statue of Liberty.
   The sculptor was French.
   The sculptor was with grandiose ideas.
   The sculptor was Frédéric-Auguste Bartholdi.

2. He was assisted by an engineer.

    The engineer was celebrated.

    The engineer was Alexandre-Gustave Eiffel.

    Eiffel was the designer and builder of the Eiffel Tower.

    The Eiffel Tower is famous.

    The Eiffel Tower is in Paris.

3. The world associates the Statue of Liberty with New York.

    New York is the main American center for finance and the arts.

    [join to show concession]

    Bartholdi originally created a series of models.

    The series is fascinating.

    The models are of the statue.

    The models were designed for the Suez Canal in Egypt.

4. These models of female figures were part of Bartholdi's plan.

    The female figures were holding a torch aloft.

    The plan was for a lighthouse.

    The lighthouse was in the shape of an enormous female figure.

    The figure was standing at the entrance to the canal.

5. The light would come from the figure's torch and from a crown on her head.

    The light was shining from the lighthouse.

    The torch and the crown are both features of the Statue of Liberty.

6. His Suez statue rejected, Bartholdi came to the United States and proposed a statue.

    Bartholdi was a believer in freedom in an age of European despotism.

    The statue was dedicated to liberty.

7. Many Americans of the time were suspicious of Europeans.

    [join to show opposition or concession]

    His idea gained support in America, and he even secured a location.

    His idea was unique.

    His idea was grandiose.

    The location was for the proposed statue.

    The location was Bedloe's Island in New York harbor.

8. The statue was made of copper.

    The copper was beaten into shape over plaster forms.

The copper was mounted on a steel skeleton.

The skeleton was designed by Eiffel.

9. Americans of the time were apprehensive that the statue might not be fully clothed.

   The Americans were a prudish bunch.

10. The man who swung public opinion in favor of the statue was Joseph Pulitzer, who drummed up support through his two newspapers.

    Pulitzer was an immigrant from Hungary.

    The newspapers were the *New York World* and the *St. Louis Post-Dispatch*.

In the following exercise, you will practice using modifiers, including appositives, and joining words. To assist you with the joining words, places in which coordinators and subordinators should be used are marked.

Cold Comfort

1. [subord] The first caveman had the first case of sniffles.

   We have begun to understand the cold only in years.

   The cold is common.

   The years are recent.

2. A cold results.

   [subord] A virus enters our upper respiratory tract and begins to kill the cells there.

   The virus is a microscopic organism.

   Our upper respiratory tract is our nose and throat.

   It kills the cells there in order to reproduce.

3. The symptoms of a cold are the results of the body.

   The symptoms are most frequent.

   The symptoms are congestion.

   The symptoms are a drippy nose.

   The symptoms are coughing and sneezing.

   The body is attempting to get rid of the virus.

   The virus is invading.

4. Many of our cold remedies really interfere with our bodies' attempts.

   The attempts are to kill the virus.

The virus is causing the cold.

[coord] We should take as few such remedies as possible.

5. One would think we could develop drugs.

   The drugs are to kill the cold viruses.

   [coord] There is one complication.

   The complication is little.

   The complication prevents us from doing that.

6. [subord] Scientists have so far identified more than two hundred different cold viruses.

   These are only a fraction of the ones.

   The ones are harmful.

   The ones are in existence.

   [coord] It would require a different drug to kill each different virus.

7. [subord] You could get shots against every cold virus.

   The virus is known.

   You could still catch a cold.

   The cold would be every year of your life.

   The cold would be from an unknown virus.

8. Linus Pauling believed that vitamin C can prevent colds.

   He was a famous scientist.

   He won the Nobel Prize in chemistry.

   [coord] Scientists have concluded that vitamin C has little or no effect.

   The effect is deterrent.

9. The only thing that has prevented people from catching each other's colds is a facial tissue.

   The tissue is impregnated with iodine.

   The tissue is called "the killer Kleenex."

10. [subord] Most people believe that kissing is an easy way to transmit a cold virus.

    Fortunately, it is not.

11. [subord] You wish to catch a cold.

    The cold is good.

    The cold is annoying.

    The cold is sneezy.

    The cold is drippy.

Simply shake hands with someone or touch an article.

The article belongs to that person.

SHAPING SENTENCES TO SHOW RELATIONSHIPS: ADJECTIVE CLAUSES

So far you have worked with adding individual words or phrases to nouns to amplify their meanings. In this lesson, you will add clauses to nouns. Unlike a phrase, a clause contains both a subject and a verb. Following, for example, are phrases of the kinds you have been working with. Note that although some of them contain forms of verbs, none of them contains both a subject and a verb; that is, none of them could be changed into a sentence.

a groaning monster
groaning loudly
bored by the company of frogs
at the local shopping center
with all kinds of clothes
in violent reds, luminescent blues, blazing yellows
the tallest student in the freshman class
a piece of meat big enough to feed Godzilla

Length has nothing to do with whether a group of words is a phrase or a clause; the only thing that counts is whether there is a subject and a verb in the group of words. Here are some common clauses; their subjects and verbs are underlined:

because <u>he had eaten it</u>

while the <u>wind blew</u>

how <u>nobody</u> in the house <u>knows</u> about the leak

what the <u>woman</u> with the new coat <u>will want</u>

The clauses that modify nouns are different from the four above. Noun-modifying clauses—which, you will not be surprised to hear, are called *adjective clauses*—generally begin with the word *who, that,* or *which.* They begin with *who* if the noun the clause modifies is a person word, and they begin with *that* or *which* if it is a word referring to anything that isn't a person.

The woman / who took the plane to Paris

The coat / that I wore to the concert last night

In the exercises below, you will find pairs of short sentences. You are to make the second sentence of each pair into an adjective clause modifying the underlined noun in the first sentence. In each case, find the word in the second sentence that either repeats or refers to the underlined noun and change it into *who* if the underlined noun is a person word or *that* or *which* if it is a thing word. Here are some examples:

1. The <u>woman</u> is my aunt.

   She bought me a new kangaroo.

   Solution: The woman <u>who bought me a new kangaroo</u> is my aunt.

   Explanation: The word in the second sentence that refers to *woman* is *she. She* is a person word, so it is replaced by *who.*

2. The <u>box</u> contained the birthday present.

   It fell off the table.

   Solution: The box <u>that fell off the table</u> contained the birthday present.

   Explanation: The word in the second sentence that refers to *box* is *it. It* is a thing word and so is replaced by *that* or *which.*

3. The <u>plan</u> is really interesting.

   You proposed it.

   Solution: The plan <u>which you proposed</u> is really interesting.

   Explanation: The word in the second sentence that refers to *plan* is *it. It* is a thing word and so is replaced by *that* or *which.* But one cannot say *The plan/ you proposed which / is really interesting,* and so one must move the word *which* to the front of the clause.

EXERCISE

In the first five pairs of sentences below, the noun in the first sentence that the adjective clause is to modify is underlined, and the noun or pronoun in the second sentence that refers to it and must be changed to *who, that,* or *which* is also underlined.

Cars and the Environment

1. George bought a used <u>car</u>.

   <u>It</u> gave him endless problems.

2. He took it to a <u>mechanic</u>.

   <u>He</u> told him it would cost $450 to fix it.

3. George bought a <u>car</u>.
   He thought he would like <u>it</u>.

4. But now he owns <u>one</u>.
   He hates <u>it</u>.

5. However, he has found a <u>mechanic</u>.
   <u>He</u> does excellent work.

6. A problem is the harmful effect of automobiles on the environment.
   We have to face this problem.

7. Cars have a particularly damaging effect.
   The cars are not maintained properly.

8. But the gases still create serious atmospheric problems.
   Even new cars emit these gases.

9. The cars are primarily responsible for the smog in most of our cities.
   People drive these cars to and from work and around town on errands.

10. However, the pollution comes from other sources as well.
    We suffer from this pollution.

SPECIAL RULES

Using adjective clauses can involve some rules that you and your instructor may or may not want to get into. Here are two special rules.

Adjective Clauses: Special Rule 1

Sometimes adjective clauses should have commas around them and sometimes they should not. Although most of the time it does not matter whether a particular adjective clause is set off with commas or not, sometimes it does, at least in American (as opposed to British) usage.

Let us begin by calling these clauses *comma clauses* (for those with commas around them) and *no-comma clauses* (for those without). Most adjective clauses are no-comma clauses, and whenever you are in doubt about whether to put commas around an adjective clause, follow one simple rule—don't.

Whether or not we put commas around adjective clauses has *nothing whatever to do with the content of the clause, with what the clause says*. It is the noun the clause modifies that determines whether the clause will be a comma clause or a no-comma clause. If the noun requires no further identification for us to know who or what it refers to, the clause following it will

be a comma clause. Here are some typical kinds of nouns that usually produce comma clauses after them:

Proper nouns:

<u>Mary Smith</u>, who works night and day, is an excellent lawyer.

<u>The Golden Gate Bridge</u>, which spans the entrance to San Francisco Bay, is
by no means the longest bridge in the world.

Any noun indicating all members of a class of things or group of people
or other living creatures:

<u>Copper</u>, which has numerous important uses, is growing scarce.

Homeowners hate <u>crabgrass</u>, which spoils the appearance of their lawns.

<u>Japanese automobiles</u>, which are very well built, have captured an impor-
tant share of the American market.

Let us salute the <u>crocodile</u>, which has survived from the Age of Reptiles.

<u>The English</u>, who have produced some of the world's greatest writers, have
not produced many first-rate painters.

Nouns preceded by possessive words usually will produce comma
clauses following them:

<u>George's houseboat</u>, which is a wreck, is no place to bring people you like.

Sometimes we do or do not use commas around a clause depending on
whether we want to indicate that the information in the clause refers to all
the members of the class indicated by the noun or only to some of those
members:

<u>American lawyers</u>, who charge outrageous fees, are a disgrace. (indicates
that all American lawyers charge outrageous fees)

<u>American lawyers</u> who charge outrageous fees are a disgrace. (indicates that
only some charge outrageous fees and that only those are a disgrace)

EXERCISE

In the following exercise, decide whether the adjective clauses, which
are underlined, should have commas around them and, if so, why:

1. Mark Twain <u>who is probably America's greatest humorist</u> came from a small
    town in Missouri.

2. Wolverines <u>which live only in the far north</u> are generally considered to be
    among the most intelligent of animals.

3. Many animals <u>which are not as intelligent as the wolverine</u> have adapted better to living near human beings.

4. Most people enjoy the paintings of Winslow Homer <u>which are rich in color and often quite dramatic.</u>

5. The boulevards of Paris <u>which are spacious and tree lined</u> are among the most beautiful streets in the world.

6. These broad straight boulevards are surrounded by narrow little streets <u>that twist and turn.</u>

7. My neighborhood <u>which has both broad and narrow streets</u> does not quite have the same charm as most of Paris.

8. The *Journal of Unforeseeable Disasters* <u>which I subscribe to</u> provides my favorite bed-time reading.

9. I am a great admirer of women athletes <u>who are as dedicated to their sports as men without, on the whole, getting the same monetary rewards.</u>

10. I have become a fan of lightly flavored mineral water <u>which is both thirst quenching and tasty.</u>

Adjective Clauses: Special Rule 2

When the noun an adjective clause modifies is a personal one and when the clause is a comma clause, good writers must decide whether to use *who* or *whom* in the clause. It isn't necessary to make this decision in no-comma clauses. To tell whether you should have *who* or *whom,* you need to see your adjective clause as a sentence, like this:

John, who ate the cake, wore a big smile.

    who ate the cake (clause)

    he ate the cake (sentence)

John, whom the alligator ate, was missed by all.

    whom the alligator ate (clause)

    the alligator ate him (sentence)

You can see that when the subject of the clause (*who, he*) refers to the noun the clause modifies, you use *who,* but when some word that is not the subject of the clause refers to the noun (*whom, him*), you use *whom.*

The following exercises involve choosing between *who* and *whom;* in the first five, the clause has been rewritten for you so you can see which word, the subject or some other word, refers to the noun the clause modifies.

1. Mary, (who/whom) loves parties, gave one last week.
   she loves parties

2. John, (who/whom) Mary can't stand, found out about it.
   Mary can't stand him

3. John came to the party with Jane, (who/whom) he had dated once.
   he had dated her once

4. Jane, (who/whom) liked Mary, was happy to be there.
   she liked Mary

5. Mary, (who/whom) nothing could faze, tossed John out.
   nothing could faze her

6. John, (who/whom) was fazed by everything, went home alone.

7. Jane, (who/whom) Mary invited to stay, did so.

8. Jane danced a great deal with Fred, (who/whom) Mary was secretly interested in.

9. Mary scowled a great deal at Fred, (who/whom) Jane was dancing with.

10. Fred, (who/whom) was having a great time, wondered what Mary was scowling about.

11. At that point, George, (who/whom) was madly in love with Jane, entered the room.

12. Now George, (who/whom) no one wanted to dance with, started scowling at Jane.

13. Jane and Fred, (who/whom) all the dark looks were being directed at, just wanted to have a good time.

14. Jane and Fred said good night to the others, (who/whom) were disappointed, and left.

15. But Mary and George, (who/whom) Jane and Fred had run away from, got over it and lived happily ever after anyway.

REVIEW

To do the following exercises, you will need to remember the difference between adjective clauses, which you have just been studying, and noun phrases, which you studied in the previous lesson. They can be easy to confuse since both do essentially the same thing—modify nouns.

> George bought the camera of his dreams, an expensive new Japanese model
>   (noun phrase modifying *camera*)

George bought the camera <u>that he had always wanted</u>. (adjective clause
   modifying *camera*)

As you can see, these two constructions do the same general kind of
thing but do it in ways that are often quite different. For instance, we could
use both our noun phrase and our adjective clause in the same sentence,
modifying the same word.

George bought the camera that he had always wanted, an expensive new
Japanese model.

Remember: Adjective clauses begin with *who, which,* or *that.* Noun
phrases do not.

In the following exercises, you will practice using modifiers and joining words. To help you with adjective clauses, sentences that should be
changed into adjective clauses are marked with the appropriate clause
word—*who, which,* or *that.* When a sentence is not marked with an adjective clause word, it should not be turned into an adjective clause; try to
use a noun phrase instead. As in previous exercises, places where you
should use joining words have been indicated. *IMPORTANT: Before doing
this exercise, review the punctuation of noun phrases on page 342,* just before
the exercises.

Don't Go Near the Water

1. Until well into the nineteenth century, men wore nothing in the water
    and swam only with other men.

    (*who*) The men swam for pleasure and exercise.

2. Women wore gowns with weights.

    The weights were sewn into their hems.

    [join]

    They bathed only with other women.

    (*who*) Women got into the water only to get wet.

3. Sea bathing did not begin until around the 1830s.

    The sea bathing was sexually mixed.

    The sea bathing was an American invention.

4. Women wore a number of clothes.

    (*who*) Women intended to go into the sea.

    The number of clothes was incredible.

    The clothes were a long dress.

    The clothes were long, full undergarments.

The clothes were gloves.

The clothes were a bathing cap.

The clothes were overshoes.

The drawers were under the dress.

The bathing cap was with a straw hat over it.

5. By the second half of the nineteenth century, baths encouraged mixed bathing and even swimming.

   The baths were public.

   The baths were built in most cities.

   The cities were American.

   The swimming was by women.

6. Of course, the clothes had to give way to attire.

   (*which*) The clothes had made swimming impossible.

   The clothes were the dresses, gloves, and overshoes.

   The attire was more practical.

   The attire was less bulky.

   The attire was for bathing.

7. The 1920s was a time.

   The 1920s was the "jazz age."

   The time was characterized for women by skirts.

   The time was characterized for women by the right to vote.

   The time was characterized for women by the first great woman swimmer.

   The skirts were short.

   The swimmer was Gertrude Ederle.

   (*who*) Gertrude Ederle swam the English Channel faster than any man had ever done.

8. Men's and women's swimsuits now looked similar.

   The swimsuits were tank tops.

   The swimsuits were shorts.

   The tank tops and shorts were woolen.

   The shorts were belted.

   [join]

   Most communities made rules.

   The rules were foolish.

   The rules applied only to women.

   (*which*) The rules said that only a few inches of skin could show above the knee.

9. In the 1940s, bathing suits covered less body, and the swimsuit came in.
   The bathing suits were for both men and women.
   (*who*) The men and women were now beginning to seek tans.
   The swimsuit was two-piece.
   The swimsuit was for women.

10. The bikini made its initial impact in France in the 1950s, and the famous string bikini seems to have been an invention.
    The bikini was named after an island.
    The island was in the Pacific.
    (*that*) The United States destroyed the island in an atomic bomb test.
    (*which*) The string bikini leaves almost nothing to the imagination.
    The invention was Brazilian.

Cats That Love the Water

1. Catfish are found in large numbers in almost every part of the world.
   They come in more than two thousand species.
   The parts of the world are North and South America.
   The parts of the world are Africa.
   The parts of the world are Asia.
   The parts of the world are Europe.
   The species range from gigantic to tiny and from harmless to dangerous.

2. The biggest catfish can weigh more than five hundred pounds and will eat virtually anything.
   The biggest catfish is the wels.
   The wels is huge.
   The wels is voracious.
   The wels lives in eastern Europe and western Asia.
   Anything swims in its waters.

3. Many varieties of catfish are found in the United States.
   [join]
   The largest species are the flathead cat and the blue fulton.
   The flathead cat is ugly.
   These live in the Mississippi River and its tributaries.
   These can weigh over one hundred pounds.

4. Among the oddest catfish are the electric cat of Africa and a South American catfish.
   The electric cat is dangerous.

It can give an 800-volt shock.

The South American catfish is tiny.

It swims into the gills of other fish.

It lodges there.

It feeds on their blood.

5. The "walking" catfish can stay out of water for hours and slither across land.

It is a variety.

The variety is from southeast Asia.

It was brought to Florida.

6. American catfish will not shock you or drink your blood.

    [join]

Many have spines.

The spines are sharp.

The spines are sawlike.

The spines are behind their heads.

The spines are covered with a substance.

The substance is slightly poisonous.

The substance can produce a sharp sting.

The sting can last for several hours.

7. Catfish come in such a variety.

The variety is astonishing.

It is a variety of sizes.

It is a variety of shapes.

    [join]

All catfish have at least two characteristics in common.

These characteristics are the "whiskers."

The "whiskers" give them their name.

These characteristics are the fact that none of them has scales.

8. Among the tales are those about the wels.

The tales are astonishing.

The tales are told about catfish.

The wels is gigantic.

The wels is Eurasian.

The wels is said to eat birds.

The birds are swimming on the water's surface.

The wels is said to have swallowed a small child.

The child was playing near the shore.

9. Equally amazing is the description of "noodling."

   "Noodling" is a method of catching catfish.

   The catfish are large.

   The catfish are in backwaters of the Mississippi.

10. The fisherman wades into the water, gropes under logs and in holes, feels around until he finds a fish, then puts his hand in its mouth and pulls it out into the open.

    The water is muddy.

    The logs are old.

    The holes are deep and dark.

    The holes are the places that big catfish like to hide in.

    Its mouth is huge.

CHAPTER 6

Discussing

ARGUMENT AND DISCUSSION
IN SCHOOL AND ON THE JOB

One of the words you are likely to find most often on essay examinations and written assignments is *discuss*. When teachers use this word, they want you not to ramble on about a matter, writing whatever comes into your head, but to formulate a carefully organized, complete argument or discussion of the issue.

We are all used to arguing a point. We often try to convince someone else, or a great many other people, to accept our position on an issue. As parents, we may want to convince our children to get good grades at school; as children, we may want to convince our parents that a C+ in chemistry really is a good grade given the difficulty of the course.

In college and in the professional world, argumentation is often a little different. One kind of argument may be intended to produce a decision—change a university's admissions policies, for example. Another kind may be intended to describe or explain something—what the university's admissions policies are, how they developed historically, and what results they are currently having on society, to continue our example. This kind of argumentation, which we will call "discussion" from now on, may involve considering which of all the causes of World War I are the most significant or trying to find a relationship between economic and voting patterns in a particular place at a particular time. Academic and professional discussion sometimes leads to a clear-cut preference for one position over another, but it often seeks instead to help us gain a better understanding of an issue or a situation.

The assignments that follow do not have "right" answers or solutions. For instance, one examines the availability, cost, and quality of child care for the small children of women who work outside the home. While the problems surrounding quality child care have no simple solutions, just as obviously any question that bears on child care is extremely important and one we should try to understand as well as we can.

The best way of trying to understand such a complex issue is to examine it from as many points of view and with as much information as possible. Then when we discuss the necessity of increased funding to support day care, we can support our position with thoughtful and well-founded discussion.

Opinion, as you have already learned, can be well founded or ill founded. We all have opinions, some based on fact (well founded), some solely on gut response (ill founded). As you have also already learned, opinions based on feelings alone are out of place in an academic or professional discussion. Only the most simple-minded audience—one you are not apt to find in the academy or the professions—will accept an argument whose support is based solely on its author's emotional reaction. "We should impeach President X because his position toward women annoys me." Well, it might. But that won't convince the House of Representatives to initiate the impeachment process. "We should impeach Richard Nixon because we have hundreds of feet of recorded tape that prove he encouraged his subordinates to conceal illegal activities and so committed a criminal offense." Once the House members hear the tapes (the support for this opinion) and if those tapes do indeed convince them of Nixon's involvement, then the argument to impeach him acquires some basis.

All of the following assignments are issues about which reasonable, intelligent, well-intentioned people disagree. Although they have no "right" answer, each issue has evoked thoughtful and compelling arguments. Read the articles and essays with an open mind—one which acknowledges that *your* opinions, as well as those of the writers you read, may be well or ill founded.

WRITING DISCUSSION ESSAYS

In discussion essays, the first paragraph should *introduce* the subject and *acknowledge* its complexity. It may also *present* your position, or you may save that for your conclusion. The next paragraph (or paragraphs) should give your readers as much background as you think they will need to understand the issue. Then the organization may start to look somewhat like that of a typical argument essay.

As in argument essays, you must show that you understand the arguments on the other side in order to successfully convince readers of your views. If you appear to have looked at only one side of an issue, readers might very well conclude that you are only partially informed and don't understand the entire issue. Understandably, they might then simply dismiss your essay as being one-sided.

Therefore, you have to discuss opposing positions, acknowledging their strengths and/or pointing out their weaknesses. Some writers do this first, saving their own arguments for last. Additionally, they will show that they know what their weak points are (and may even concede their weakest ones) as well as make sure they cover their strong ones. As in the case of argument outlines, remember that the outlines here do not represent paragraph divisions.

> Approach 1 (address opposition first)
>   Introduction
>   Background
>   Opposing arguments and their reasoning
>   Writer's arguments and their reasoning
>   Conclusion

Other writers take up the opposition point by point. This is easier to do if the number of points to be considered is relatively small. Here are typical outlines for these two approaches. Again, remember that these do not represent paragraph divisions.

> Approach 2 (discuss issue point by point)
>   Introduction
>   Background
>   Argument 1
>   Opposing argument and reasoning
>   Writer's argument and reasoning
>   Argument 2
>   Opposing argument and reasoning
>   Writer's argument and reasoning
>   Arguments 3, 4, 5, and so on, as above
>   Conclusion

Another way to deal with a complex and thorny issue, particularly when you aren't necessarily trying to argue for one side or the other, is to spend the body of the essay discussing the various aspects of the issue. Then, in the conclusion, either summarize the whole issue or, if it is appropriate, make a recommendation about what should be done. This is really not very different from the approaches above except that rather than taking a position on one side or another, the writer is merely trying to clarify the whole issue, to show what is involved in it and what its implications are. Such an essay might have this kind of organization:

Introduction

Background

Explanation of aspect 1 (including arguments for and against)

Explanation of aspect 2 (including arguments for and against)

Explanations of aspects 3, 4, 5, and so on, as above

Summary conclusion or recommendations

*A*ssignments and Readings

WHO SHOULD CARE FOR THE CHILDREN?

Biologically and historically, women have been the family members primarily responsible for raising the children, at least the young ones. But now two trends that have been developing for some time are beginning to catch up with our old assumptions about child care. One is that an increasing number of women are deciding to enter the workforce, either out of financial necessity or for personal gratification. The other is that a high rate of divorce and a high rate of pregnancy out of wedlock have produced single mothers in unprecedented numbers, and for the most part, these women are young and poor. In both cases, the result is children with no one to take care of them.

Yet society needs children to grow up as healthy, happy, productive human beings who will be able to run things when their turn comes. It also needs women who can use their education and training in the workforce and women who can get the training they need to get off welfare. For all of these things, it needs people who can bring up children to be physically, psychologically, and emotionally healthy adults. The question is: Who's going to do it?

Reading Assignment

Pre-reading

As a way of beginning to think about this topic, ask yourself questions like the following and jot down your answers.

Should biological mothers be the ones to care for children? Why?

Should child care be available for women who want or need to work? If so, who should pay for it?

What role should married fathers play in child care?

Should society penalize unmarried fathers who contribute nothing to child care?

What role should government play in child care?

How many families do you know in which either both parents work or only one parent is present? In these cases, how is child care managed? Is it managed well? As far as you know, are the children adequately supervised? Do they tend to get into trouble? Do you see or have you heard of any problems with juvenile delinquency or criminality as a result of inadequate child care?

Reading

WHO'S TAKING CARE OF THE CHILDREN?
Michael Ryan

Energetic and outspoken, Angela Roffle, at 31, is halfway toward her   1
college degree and fulfilling her dream of climbing out of welfare. Nothing has come easily to her. She is a single mother with a 10-year-old and 2-year-old twins living on the economic brink in a crime-ridden area. But for Roffle, those are not the biggest obstacles to achieving her goal. Child care is.

"This is a bad day to talk about child care," she told me the af-   2
ternoon we met in St. Louis. "A neighbor usually takes care of my kids while I'm in school, but she had to take today off. I have two backups, but my second babysitter is in the hospital, and I couldn't get to the third because my car broke down." Because of her difficulties, Roffle missed several classes and lost precious study time. Still, she is not defeated. "You know," she said, "there are plenty of women who go through this, just like me, at least once a week. You just have to."

Every day in America, millions of parents struggle to find ways   3
and means to provide care for their children while they go to work or school. Today, two-thirds of mothers work outside the home. One-quarter of the kids in this country live with only one parent. An estimated 23 million children require child care.

Of those kids, 8.3 million go to licensed day-care settings that   4
are inspected and required to meet minimum standards for health, safety and educational content. That leaves 14.7 million children in unlicensed settings. Some will get first-rate care with highly motivated caretakers. But others will go to substandard settings where

they may run the risk of fire or accident and, in some cases, abuse. Still others have no regular child care. Their parents must depend on a shifting network of friends and relatives, and sometimes, in desperation, even leave their children unsupervised.

Child-care experts report that obtaining good day care is a na- 5 tionwide problem. It is frequently either in short supply, not up to standards or out of reach financially. "I call it a 'trilemma,'" said Arlyce Currie of Bananas, an Oakland, Calif., resource center for parents.

For many parents, the cost is the biggest problem. "Affordability 6 is the big issue," said Nancy Travis of Atlanta's Save the Children agency. "Child-care costs here range from $46 to $160 a week." Even for many in the middle class, such costs are prohibitive.

As Kathy Doellefeld-Clancy discovered, however, even having a 7 good income does not guarantee quality care. She and her husband both have good jobs, and she took great care in choosing a day-care center for her son Jonathan. Almost immediately, though, she started to worry.

"One day, I went in and there were about 40 kids with only four 8 teachers watching them," Doellefeld-Clancy said. "I had to stop a piece of equipment from falling on one of the children. I called the director, and she said it was just a fluke. But I went back another time and found one teacher supervising 14 kids."

The last straw came when Jonathan, then 16 months, bit an- 9 other child. A trained child-care worker would have understood that this behavior can occur at a certain stage. Instead, Jonathan was left in a playpen for an entire day without toys or human contact. One teacher, appalled by this "punishment," reported it to Doellefeld-Clancy. She quickly moved her son to another center.

There are other problems. In some states and localities, the back- 10 grounds of child-care workers are checked. In Georgia, owners of day-care centers are **vetted** by the Georgia Bureau of Investigation. But in states such as Missouri, church-related day-care centers are exempt from virtually all regulation—as a parent we will call "Dave" discovered to his horror.

Dave thought he had solved the day-care problem when he 11 found a responsible-looking church-affiliated center for his son, then 2. "Then one day when I suggested we go outside and play," Dave recalled, "my son said, 'Are we going to play Pull Your Pants Down?'

---

vetted: checked

I said, 'What do you mean?' and he said, 'That's a game we play at school.'"

Dave and his wife sat down with their son and elicited the infor-   12
mation that an adult at the day-care center involved the children in "games" that included taking their pants down and touching them. They reported their findings to state authorities, who questioned their son, found him credible, and said they would investigate.

"They went to the center and asked, 'Is there someone here who   13
abuses children?'" Dave recalled with indignation. "What do you think the answer was? No action was taken against the center."

Dave and his wife have since put their son in another day-care   14
center, and they have taken him to a counselor. "We think we found out in time," Dave said. "We hope that no permanent damage was done."

Most children, of course, probably will never be injured or mo-   15
lested in child care. But, as Barbara Reisman, Executive Director of the Child Care Action Campaign (CCAC), an advocacy group, points out, "Of course you want children to be in a place where they're not in danger, but that's not enough. All children should be cared for in a bright, engaging space by well-trained, well-qualified people who love children."

That kind of child care is not a luxury but a practical necessity   16
for the economy, Reisman argues. Some studies show that early childhood education of the kind provided in quality day-care settings can help keep kids from dropping out of school later.

Advocates argue that good child care can also benefit employ-   17
ers. Richard Stolley, president of CCAC, was instrumental in the de-velopment of a day-care center at Time, Inc., the large media company where he is editorial director. "It's a productivity issue," he explained. "The number of employees who don't show up or who show up **harried** because child-care arrangements have fallen through is enormous. Child care is not a women's issue. It has an effect on productivity of men and women, on the whole working family."

Angela Roffle, Kathy Doellefeld-Clancy and Dave are three faces   18
of the national problem of child care. Each has struggled to find qual-ity care—each is, somehow, finding a way to solve the problem.

Other countries take a different approach. If Angela Roffle had   19
been born in France, she would have received free pre-natal health

---

harried: disturbed

care, been granted maternity leave and her children would have been eligible for government-sponsored preschools. In more than 100 countries, Dave and Kathy Doellefeld-Clancy would be entitled to parental leave from their jobs to ensure their children were properly cared for.

In the United States, parents can get a tax credit of up to $1,440 20 annually for child care (which, typically, can cost two times that). Can our government afford to do more?

"The real question," Reisman argued, "is, 'Can it afford not to?'" 21 One study shows that 25% of mothers on welfare can't take jobs because they can't find adequate child care. The social costs of not having good preschool and after-school care, Reisman said, may be far greater than the expense of providing them.

Some communities and businesses are working to find solutions 22 to the day-care dilemma. The Hilltop Day Care Center in Florissant, Mo., was begun a generation ago by the School of Social Work of Washington University. It was designed to provide educationally enriched day care for low-income children. Today, Hilltop—headquartered in an old bank building—is a subsidiary of Lutheran Family and Children's Services and has about 90 children, mostly from low- and middle-income families, enrolled.

"It's a place where our kids can interact with other children," Va- 23 lerie Joyner told me when she and her husband, Thomas, stopped by the center. "They prepare kids for reading and learning." Two of the Joyners' three children attended Hilltop, and their 6-year-old is thriving in kindergarten after a year there.

Not far away, in an old public-school building in St. Louis, is Mc- 24 Care, a day-care center for employees of McDonnell Douglas, the aircraft manufacturer. "We are completely self-supporting," Steve Zwolak, the center's director, told me proudly. "We charge from $85 to $145 a week, and we have 61 staff members for 186 kids." At McCare, infants get personal attention; older kids get educational play and parents are encouraged to stop in during their breaks.

When I visited, Ann McMahon Piening was dropping off her two 25 kids. Formerly an engineer, she was laid off by the company, but her husband still works there. She says that McCare has helped her establish herself in a new career. "I couldn't do it without McCare," she said. "I wouldn't be willing to leave my children unless I was sure they were safe and getting the kind of attention I would give them myself. My husband and I can go to work ready to do our best, happy that our children are well taken care of."

REPORT HIGHLIGHTS NEED FOR BETTER CHILD CARE
Monica Gyulai

Children's advocates want America's parents to have it all: Better   1
child care at lower cost.

Calling for increased government subsidies and corporate partici-   2
pation to offset child care costs to parents, a nationwide report released [May 5, 1998] also cites a need for better-paid, better-educated
child care workers.

According to the Annie E. Casey Foundation's ninth annual "Kids   3
Count" children's data book, while the demand for day care is growing, its availability is inadequate and the quality provided often poor.

"We know how important and how influential child care is on a   4
child," said Amy Dominguez-Arms, policy director at Children Now,
an Oakland-based advocacy group. . . . "Any space (in a day care
center) isn't good enough—that isn't what we're looking for. Quality
child care is costly to provide."

On average, child care workers in California earn $7 an hour, or   5
less than half the wages of automotive mechanics in the state, according to the U.S. Bureau of Labor Statistics.

In Bay Area counties, however, child care costs to parents are con-   6
siderable, according to a 1997 report by Children Now. Monthly infant
care costs average $690 and care for pre-schoolers averages $480.

"It's a real difficult issue," said Bill O'Hare, the Kids Count coor-   7
dinator and a father of two children in day care. "When you pay it
out, it seems like a lot of money, but when you look at what care
workers are getting, it's peanuts." . . .

The report states that finding good and affordable child care is a   8
challenge for working parents of all income levels in the country, but
emphasized that the problem is significantly greater for low-income
households.

"Data suggest it's typically people who are eking out a meager   9
standard of living—people who are not quite comfortable yet, but
who are not on welfare, that have the roughest time," said Isabel
Sawhill, a senior fellow at the Brookings Institution in Washington, D.C.

HOME DAY CARE PROVIDERS FACE INCREASING DEMAND
Tammy Hansen

Lynne Lyberger drops her twin sons off at the Livermore Laboratory   1
Employee Children's Center on her way to work. Her boys, who
have been going to the lab-sponsored day care facility since they

were 3 months old, spend their weekdays there at a monthly cost of $900 each.

Across town, Janette Billingsley starts her day by saying good- 2 bye to her husband and two teenage children as they head for work and school.

Parents begin dropping their children at her family home day 3 care, where she is licensed to care for 14 children, ages 2 to 10. A former preschool teacher, Billingsley opened her day care 10 years ago to be more available to her own children.

Lyberger and Billingsley represent just two pieces of the increas- 4 ingly complex puzzle of child care. It's a puzzle everyone is trying to solve—from President Clinton to local referral agencies. No one, however, is more interested in solutions than the working parents who face vexing choices about who will care for their children. And there are a lot of them.

In Alameda County, 54 percent of children under 5 years old and 5 64 percent of children ages 6 to 13 live in homes where both parents or a single parent works, according to the California Child Care Resource and Referral Network. Of the estimated 157,430 children with working parents, about 52,337 are in child care outside the family. The majority of those—34,303—are under the age of 5. . . .

Nationally, there are more than 50 million working mothers, ac- 6 cording to U.S. Census data. Most of these women return to work in their child's first three to five months, according to the National Institute of Child Health and Human Development. Parents across the country face what first lady Hillary Rodham Clinton has called the "silent crisis" of finding good, affordable child care.

Providers fear things may get worse in the wake of welfare re- 7 form. With an anticipated increase in demand from welfare parents going to work, competition for . . . child care spots . . . will increase. Infant and odd-hours care are especially hard to find.

Only 1 percent of the county's licensed and license-exempt day 8 care homes and centers provide evening, overnight or weekend care. Forty percent offer before- and after-school care. Five percent accept children under the age of two. Yet, 40 percent of calls to the state resource and referral network are about infant care, 14 percent ask about before- and after-school and 5 percent seek weekend or overnight care.

Care providers also worry about an influx of untrained workers 9 because some former welfare recipients may see in-home child care as a source of income. Without training, such new providers could lower the bar for child care. Child care providers in homes and centers must have some schooling, be trained in CPR and first aid and pass a tuberculosis test. But anyone can care for the children of one other family without any such training. . . .

Training, however, is only part of the story, according to child 10 care activist Marcy Whitebook, co-director of the Center for The Child Care Work Force, Berkeley. The center is a nonprofit group lobbying for better wages and training for providers.

"Eighty-five percent of the child care in this country is mediocre 11 or poor," she claimed. Child care providers are some of the nation's lowest paid employees.

That translates into a lot of turnover in a profession that relies on 12 stability. Research has proven that the key elements to good child care are trained teachers who stay at one job, and low teacher-to-child ratios. Changing faces in a child care setting takes a toll on children in slower development of language and other skills.

Some children may even become more aggressive. 13

"If people are coming and going all the time, that really takes its 14 toll on children," Whitebook said.

Assistants in Alameda County child care centers made an aver- 15 age $6.70 an hour, with an average high of $7.63 in 1995. The national average wage was $7. "Teachers," with more college credits, made $8.52 to $10.97 an hour, Whitebook said. Home day care providers often earn less. Child care providers make $20,000, compared to the approximately $27,000 a grammar school teacher earns annually.

Child Care Links reports that 34 percent of those child care 16 providers who leave do so for another job or to go back to school. . . .

Whitebook, who attended President Clinton's recent child care 17 summit, said only public and corporate investment will close the revolving child care door. Clinton has pledged to throw $300 million at the problem, but she said that isn't enough.

Tax breaks for families don't help either, because the money 18 never goes toward improving facilities or wages.

"It's easier to get money for your child to go to college than to 19 get help for child care," she said. "There needs to be public and private investment in child care."

Single parent Lyberger said parents also should be willing to 20 pay for what they get. She could have gotten care for less than half the $1,800 a month she pays at the lab, but decided to invest more.

"I honestly think that my two are better off in the day care situa- 21
tion they're in, and I'm at work. You work better when you are confident and secure that your kids are taken care of," Lyberger said.

AN INTERVIEW WITH MARY S.

The speaker, a twenty-six-year-old woman with two small children, discusses
why she chose to return to her job as a county social worker, even though
she didn't have to for financial reasons.

I stayed home with the children for nine months after my youngest 1
was born, and I hated the intellectual **stagnation** and social isolation
I felt. I kept very busy (all young mothers do) taking care of the children and the house, cooking, cleaning, gardening. But it was really
lonely work. An infant and a toddler, as sweet as they were, were not
great conversationalists. And when my husband came home tired
from work, he didn't want to talk about the world outside the house.
He wanted to spend time with the children. Besides, by 6:30 or 7:00
in the evening, I was too physically exhausted to be much of an intellectual companion anyway.

When I decided to return to work at the welfare department, I 2
felt somewhat guilty. Here I was going to a job that I didn't *have* to
have and leaving my children with a babysitter from 7:30 in the
morning until 5:30 or so at night. And, like my husband, I too came
home tired. But also like him, I really wanted to spend time with my
children when I got home.

There's been a lot written about "quality" versus "quantity" 3
time, and a lot of it is rationalizing the less-than-ideal situation of
busy parents who don't spend much time with their children. However, because I got the intellectual and social stimulation I require
from a job outside the home, I was a much happier person and, as a
result, I feel I was a far better parent than I had been when I was a
full-time homemaker.

CHILD CARE SACRED AS FRANCE CUTS BACK
THE WELFARE STATE
Marlise Simons

Martine Susini performs the thankless tasks of any day-care director: 1
picking up tricycles here, cleaning tiny hands there, stopping to

---

stagnation: inactivity, failure to progress

check on milk bottles or the state of the mini toilets. Yet here in France she is known as Madame la Directrice and her job holds considerable prestige.

Mrs. Susini heads a crèche, a municipal day nursery, in Paris that 2 occupies a spacious modern building on **Rue Edgar Faure.** As director, she gets an adjacent apartment to insure that she is available for emergencies. And to care for her 88 children she has the help of 25 trained employees, a ratio approaching that of a luxury hotel.

"We can manage, but more staff would be even better," said 3 Mrs. Susini, who keeps a neat office with files and charts worthy of an executive. She may not get additional employees on Rue Edgar Faure, but elsewhere the numbers of officially approved child-care workers and nurseries continue to expand.

That expansion, when France has reluctantly begun to trim its 4 swollen and costly **welfare state,** is a barometer of how strongly the French endorse government-provided child care and how much they have come to count on it. Strict budgetary rules required as Europe prepares to adopt a common currency have forced the government to make unpopular cuts in medical services and retirement benefits, but the generous subsidies for day care and health services for children up to the age of 3 continue to swell.

In Paris, for instance, a city of two million, there are already 520 5 subsidized nurseries, most of them run by the local government. In the last year, the municipality has opened eight new day-care centers and modernized six others. The city budget for day care rose by 60 percent between 1989 and 1994.

When the conservative government was elected in 1993, the 6 rate of spending on day care slowed, but each year spending levels continue to rise. In 1996, Paris spent $182 million on day care, 9 percent more than in 1994. The day-care network is expanding too in the rest of the country.

A number of other European countries, notably in Scandinavia, 7 continue to provide excellent child care for preschool children at relatively low prices, despite cuts in other aspects of the welfare state.

While American parents are deeply divided over day care for 8 small children and many feel that infants and toddlers are best off at

---

Rue Edgar Faure: Edgar Faure Street;   welfare state: a government that provides its citizens with services such as free medical care, inexpensive higher education, free old-age care, and free child care home tended by their parents, the French and many other North Europeans have few **qualms** about such care.

Demand, and even a sense of entitlement, has grown among 9
young parents in recent years as studies showed that children who attended day nurseries and pre-school centers performed better in the first years of elementary school. Parents seem widely convinced, surveys have shown, that group child care makes for more stable, less **rambunctious** teen-agers. On a Paris playground you can hear mothers of toddlers talk of "awakening" and "civilizing" their children.

Hélène Desegrais had to wait four months to get a place for her 10
daughter Diane, who is 2. Since then, a weight has fallen off her. It means she can look for a job and take some courses. As a single, unemployed mother, she pays the $33 minimum monthly fee, although the real cost per child is $800.

"I've been really lucky," Mrs. Desegrais said. "Diane is already 11
more open, she plays more and she is talking more."

One reason French parents feel so comfortable with govern- 12
ment child care is that it is generally of high quality. Another reason is that many Europeans, including the French, who are used to social-democratic traditions, have an attitude toward social spending that fundamentally differs from Americans; further, they are generally more comfortable with government involvement in society, particularly in education.

Outside experts have at times looked to France as a model be- 13
cause of the consistent quality of its system. Day care first grew notably here after World War II when the government sought to protect small children from malnutrition and disease. But expansion has been fastest in the last two decades as more and more women joined the work force. The Paris municipal government, for instance, has increased its budget for day care more than fivefold since 1977.

Paris takes particular pride in its network of public and private 14
nurseries. For its 70,000 children up to the age of 3, there are 24,200 city-sponsored places; some 6,000 infants are on waiting lists. It is not known exactly how many parents decline to send their children to day care because the mother is at home or the child is left with a **nanny** or baby sitter. The city also employs some 2,600 care givers licensed to receive up to three or four children in their home.

Finding a vacancy in Paris, though, can take up to a year. Some- 15
times it takes connections, at the town hall, for instance. Anxious

---

qualms: doubts;   rambunctious: disorderly;   nanny: live-in baby sitter mothers register for a vacancy during pregnancy, call on social workers, visit the local town councilor and pay regular visits to several nursery directors to plead their case.

Paris officials say the capital needs more nurseries than other   16
cities because proportionately more married women here work outside the home and fewer have the support system that relatives offer in the **provinces.**

Rosaria Methenni, 30, is one such Parisian. She picks up her 18-   17
month-old son, Kevin, from the Edgar Faure nursery after finishing her shift at the bakery where she works. Her husband, a car mechanic, has dropped Kevin off at 7:30 on his way to work. As is customary, they are charged 10 percent of their joint salary for Kevin's fees, which comes to $175 a month. Fees are also charged on a sliding scale, with poor parents paying as little as $33 and the richest a maximum of $640 a month. From ages 3 to 6, all children go to preschool, which is free.

"The nursery is marvelous but it's still a lot of money for us," said   18
Mrs. Methenni, who has another child, age 7. But without this day care, she concedes, she could not keep her bakery job and the family would have to live on the $882 her husband brings home. To pay the nursery fee, the couple does some janitorial work on weekends.

Last year, she sometimes paid a woman to look after Kevin at   19
home. "For all you know, the child gets smacked or ignored," she said. She added that the nursery had made Kevin livelier.

These are exactly the kind of comments Mrs. Susini, the nursery   20
director, loves to hear. "Our aim is to stimulate the children and to make them independent," said Mrs. Susini, who is licensed as a nurse and a teacher. Her nursery looks like a joyful place, with plenty of playrooms, toys, a paddling pool and tiny beds and cradles.

A psychologist calls regularly to discuss possible behavior problems and a pediatrician comes twice a week. "It's a disadvantage of   21
nursery life that when one child gets a cold or diarrhea or an eye infection many get it," Mrs. Susini said. Some parents have withdrawn their children altogether after a particularly unpleasant brush with a nursery-based epidemic.

This being France, even little children get tasty, wholesome   22
meals. Fresh produce is delivered every day and two cooks prepare lunch on the premises. On this day, it was poached fish with carrot mousse and a yogurt.

---

provinces: areas of a country outside its capital

To reduce noise and create a more intimate mood, the building 23
is divided into four sections, each with its own kitchen and playing
and bathing spaces. Age groups are mixed. "It's more natural and
calmer," said Françoise Goyard, who tracks when each child slept,
ate and had a diaper changed. "If you put only fierce 2-year-olds in
a room you get too much biting and scratching."

Besides nurseries, the city organizes other support systems. 24
There are day-care homes, where a supervised and trained baby sitter receives up to three children in her home. And there are licensed
play schools where a child may be dropped off just two half-days a
week. Two Paris nurseries keep extended hours from 5 a.m. to 10
p.m. to help parents who work unusual shifts in places like hospitals,
theaters or public transport.

One of them is The Magic House, in eastern Paris. "Both parents 25
must work difficult hours," a supervisor said. "Whatever the hours
they keep, the child should stay here only for eight hours. This cannot be the child's home."

Anne Husson said she had to wait more than six months to get 26
her 2-year-old into The Magic House. "But it was definitely worth
it," said Mrs. Husson, who organizes conferences and cultural events
and, like her husband, comes home late once or twice a week. "It
was always a panic and a scramble to have Alma looked after."

Some care givers see unwanted side effects to the system. Be- 27
cause sick children must stay at home, parents often give them drugs
to cure them, perhaps too quickly, a pediatric nurse said. "All of our
children already had a lot of medicines at their young age," the nurse
said disapprovingly.

As nurseries have increased in number, some care givers see a 28
shift in attitude toward raising children, an expectation that the state
will provide them with child care, that makes them uncomfortable.

"Young couples plan on a child and they automatically think 29
nursery," Mrs. Susini said. "Young people now approach us as if it is
our duty to take their child. Some become aggressive when there is
no room. There is a new definition of what it means to be a parent. I
wonder and worry about that."

Post-reading

Write brief summaries of each of the readings above, separating in each
case facts from emotions, feelings, desires, and opinions. Ask yourself the
following questions:

How sympathetic are you to women who don't necessarily have to work but who want to? What basis do you have for your feelings?

Is the child care "crisis" a real one? Explain in detail why you do or do not think so.

Do all women have the same problem with child care? If not, note carefully the differences for different women.

Just as women are mothers, men are fathers. Should fathers be playing more of a role in child care, and if so, what should it be?

Does the French system seem to you to represent a model for the US to follow? Why or why not?

Essay Assignment

Write an essay in which you discuss the issue of who should be primarily responsible for taking care of the children. You may want to take a position on this issue and make a recommendation, acknowledging, of course, that there's no "right" answer for everyone. On the other hand, your essay may simply illuminate this issue without offering a resolution or making a recommendation.

For more discussion of this issue and suggestions about organizing your essay, log on to http://devenglish.wadsworth.com.

Pre-writing

As you think about organizing your essay, keep these points in mind:

1. Give your readers enough background to understand the importance and complexity of the issue.
2. Acknowledge the strengths, as well as the weaknesses, of the arguments you cite—including your own.
3. Remember that a statement is not an argument; a statement needs to be supported with facts and/or well-founded opinions in order to become an argument.

Also refer to the section "Writing Discussion Essays" for ideas on structuring your essay. As you have in previous assignments, jot down a working thesis and outline.

Writing

Although you may feel strongly one way or the other on this issue, re-member that there's no right or wrong answer. There are, however, stronger and weaker arguments. In order to compose the strongest one you can, keep an open mind while you write and use the most compelling support you can muster. And be sure to review the Writer's Checklist on pages 426–428.

RATING THE MOVIES

The debate over what is and is not suitable for certain audiences has been going on at least since the fifth century B.C. when Greek dramatists and their critics considered the appropriateness of certain subjects for the stage. With the advent of motion pictures, the debate took on a new di-mension. Here was a medium that was widely and easily accessible to chil-dren and adolescents. On any given Saturday afternoon, young people could (and did) flock to the movie houses to watch whatever was being projected on the silver screen, and parents had no way of knowing whether those movies were appropriate—in subject matter or its treatment—for their children. As you can guess, sex and violence were (and remain) their primary concerns.

Different societies and cultures have taken widely different approaches to what is acceptable content in films and what isn't, and even within indi-vidual societies, what is or isn't acceptable has often changed with time. For instance, in the 1950s and early 60s in the United States, teenagers were not allowed to see a movie showing bare breasts, but they could watch movies featuring killings and other forms of violence. At the same time in France, violent movies were forbidden to those under sixteen years old while even small children could go to movies with nudity. Some societies have forbid-den showing kissing on the screen, while others have no restrictions of any kind on who can see what.

In the United States, feelings about what children and teenagers can and cannot see have gradually been changing. Attempting to inform poten-tial audiences, especially parents, of a film's suitability for children, the Mo-tion Picture Producers and Distributors of America established its first code in 1930. Since then the code has been revised twice—in 1968 and 1984—re-flecting views about what is or is not acceptable for young people to see. For instance, in 1969 the movie *Midnight Cowboy* was given an X rating; today it simply gets an R. Despite or because of the past revisions, some people continue to call for further changes.

Not surprisingly, these codes have raised serious concerns within the movie industry itself and among the public at large. The movie industry argues that the codes interfere with artistic freedom by limiting what a filmmaker can include in a film in order to get it a "general" rating—one that does not restrict an audience by age—and are therefore a form of censorship that forbids certain people to see a film because of its content. A number of people outside the film industry concur while a number disagree. The following reading assignments reflect much of the confusion and uncertainty over whether or not to rate movies and, if so, how best to do it.

Reading Assignment

Pre-reading

Before you begin reading this assignment, work out for yourself on paper what concerns *you* have about labeling or rating movies. Ask yourself questions like the following:

- Should movies carry ratings or labels of any kind? A basic question involved here is whether in a free society, where the First Amendment to the Constitution protects our freedoms to speak and write, movies should be any more censored than books are.

- Under what circumstances should movies be labeled or rated? Should labels describe a movie's content for the guidance of the audience or act as censors? Or should they do both? Why? What characteristics should be brought to the attention of a potential audience? Sex? Violence? Nudity? Why?

- If a rating system should act as a censor, who should be forbidden to see what?

This is a complex topic intellectually and emotionally. Intellectually, it involves our First Amendment rights as American citizens to freedom from censorship. Emotionally, it taps into people's most deeply held beliefs about issues like sex and violence.

Reading

Try to read the following material with as open a mind as possible, and remember to read actively.

THE MOTION PICTURE PRODUCTION CODE

This is the 1984 version of the code established by the Motion Picture Association of America that requires that movies be labeled G, PG, PG-13, R, or X.

This Code is designed to keep in close harmony with the mores, cul-   1
ture, the moral sense and change in our society.

The objectives of the Code are: 2

1. To encourage artistic expression by expanding creative
    freedom.
2. To assure that the freedom which encourages the artist re-
    mains responsible and sensitive to the standards of the
    larger society.

In our society, parents are the arbiters of family conduct. Parents 3
have the primary responsibility to guide their children in the kind of
lives they lead, the character they build, the books they read, and
the movies and other entertainment to which they are exposed.

The creators of motion pictures undertake a responsibility to 4
make available pertinent information about their pictures which will
assist parents to fulfill their responsibilities.

But this alone is not enough. In further recognition of our obli- 5
gation to the public, and most especially to parents, we have extended the Code operation to include a nationwide voluntary film
rating program which has as its prime objective a sensitive concern
for children. Motion pictures will be reviewed by a Code and Rating
Administration which, when it reviews a motion picture as to its conformity with the standards of the Code, will issue ratings. It is our intent that all motion pictures exhibited in the United States will carry
a rating.

These ratings are: 6

(G)	General audiences, all ages admitted.
(PG)	Parental guidance suggested. Some material may not be suitable for children.
(PG-13)	Parents are strongly cautioned to give special guidance to children under 13. Some material may be inappropriate for young children.
(R)	Restricted. Those under 17 must be accompanied by a parent or adult guardian.
(X)	No one under 17 admitted.

The ratings and their meanings will be conveyed by advertising; 7
by displays at the theaters; and in other ways. Thus, audiences, especially parents, will be alerted to the theme, content, and treatment
of movies. Therefore, parents can determine whether a particular

picture is one which children should see at the discretion of the parent; or only when accompanied by a parent; or should not see.

Standards for Protection

In furtherance of the objectives of the Code to accord with the 8
mores, the culture, and the moral sense of our society, the principles
stated above and the following standards shall govern the Administrator in his consideration of motion pictures submitted for Code approval:

- The basic dignity and value of human life shall be respected and upheld. Restraint shall be exercised in portraying the taking of life.
- Evil, sin, crime and wrong-doing will be justified.
- Special restraint shall be exercised in portraying criminal or antisocial activities in which minors participate or are involved.
- Detailed and **protracted** acts of brutality, cruelty, physical violence, torture and abuse shall not be presented.
- Indecent or undue exposure of the human body shall not be presented.
- **Illicit** sex relationships shall not be justified. Intimate sex scenes violating common standards of decency shall not be portrayed.
- Restraint and care shall be exercised in presentations dealing with sex aberrations.
- Obscene speech, gestures or movements shall not be presented. Undue profanity shall not be permitted.
- Religion shall not be **demeaned.**
- Words or symbols contemptuous of racial, religious or national groups, shall not be used so as to incite bigotry or hatred.
- Excessive cruelty to animals shall not be portrayed and animals shall not be treated inhumanely.

NC-17 Replaces X in Movie Ratings

In September 1990, the Motion Picture Association of America dropped its former X rating for movies considered unsuitable for minors and replaced it with a new rating, NC-17. Like the former X rating, the new NC-17 will be given to movies with scenes containing so-called "adult" content, chiefly sex but possibly also extreme violence.

---

protracted: drawn out, prolonged;   illicit: illegal;
demeaned: put down, lowered in value

The X rating had become a problem for the film industry since it was used by makers of pornographic films, but the new NC-17 rating will be trademarked so that others may not use it.

Once the X rating became associated almost exclusively with pornographic movies, filmmakers were extremely reluctant to make films that would get an X, and many newspapers refused advertisements for all X-rated movies. Also many movie theaters have rental contracts that forbid them from showing X-rated movies.

While some professionals in the filmmaking world have expressed cautious approval of the new rating, most feel that it will have little or no effect on the problem produced by X ratings. In fact, many newspapers are expected to refuse advertising for NC-17 movies, and the nation's largest chain of video rental stores, Blockbuster, has announced that it will not carry movies rated NC-17.

The 1995 movie *Kids* went into distribution without a rating because if it had been submitted for rating, it would have been given an NC-17. It is expected that many directors and producers will change movies in order to get R ratings rather than NC-17.

THE BIG CHILL
Lois P. Sheinfeld

In the following excerpts from an article published in Film Comment, *the author discusses the ratings of the Motion Picture Association of America in relation to the proposed ratings of the Parents Music Resource Center (PMRC), an organization founded by several politically prominent women who want to label rock music albums regarding their content. The PMRC argues that if labeling is good for movies, then it's good for music. However, Sheinfeld questions whether labeling is good for movies. She asks, "Are ratings good sense—or censorship?"*

Ratings went into effect in 1968, as the result of an agreement between   1
the MPAA, NATO (National Association of Theater Owners), and IFIDA
(International Film Importers and Distributors of America). . . .

The MPAA Rating Board, based in Los Angeles, has six full-time   2
members and a part-time chair, Richard Heffner. The members are
chosen by Heffner with the approval of Jack Valenti, MPAA president
and Heffner's boss. We know very little about them. Their names and
backgrounds are closely guarded secrets. . . . These few individuals
are paid to watch movies all day and, according to Valenti, to rate
them "as most parents" would "on each of several categories such
as theme, violence, language, nudity, sex." The MPAA's half-dozen
Supermoms-and-pops are supposed to guess what countless millions
of differing parents think. . . .

An examination of this system in the light of principles that the   3
Supreme Court has recognized as limiting governmental censorship
demonstrates how far the MPAA's rating scheme intrudes upon free
expression. Not only does this system compel the repression of
original work, it denies a willing audience access to that work.

First, state regulation of artistic expression has been strictly con-   4
fined to what fits the [Supreme] Court's definition of obscenity. Restricting speech merely because of its supposed offensiveness has
been unequivocally condemned. . . . "Above all," the Court held in
1972, "the First Amendment means that government has no power
to restrict expression because of its message, its ideas, its subject
matter, or its content." . . .

Second, even where obscenity is concerned, the Court has for-   5
bidden vague and open-ended standards for censorship. . . .

Third, . . . any system for banning movies or other forms of expres-   6
sion as obscene must provide rigorous procedural safeguards against
administrative error and unaccountability. The censor must bear the
burden of proof of obscenity, with prompt judicial review to follow.

Obviously, the MPAA Rating System is, on all of these accounts,   7
more repressive than any laws that a state could constitutionally enforce. Nevertheless, industry members suggest that it is the lesser
of two evils: that, but for the Rating System, the states might enact
censorship legislation that would be costly to upset in court. . . .

The notion that the Rating System is more benign than any po-   8
tential state censorship ignores its powerfully prescriptive effects. Its
supposedly "voluntary" character . . . is a gross misrepresentation.
Newspapers, television and radio stations refuse to carry ads for, reviews of, or stories about X-rated films. Theater owners refuse to play
them, and distributors refuse to handle them. No wonder *Variety*
likened an X rating to "a confession of guilt," carrying the punishment of being "shut out . . . from the market." . . . No wonder studios will order films cut, recut, and again recut until the Rating Board
is satisfied enough to remove the dreaded X. . . .

Thus is the "voluntary" nature of the Rating System—much em-   9
phasized by Heffner and Valenti—exposed for what it is. It amounts
to a "voluntary" choice between economic suicide and self-subjection
to a scheme of censorship more repressive than any government
could get away with. . . .

Finally, the Rating System not only provides precedent and sup-   10
port for those like the PMRC, who would model the censorship of other
media on it, but also invites ever-increasing pressure for more drastic

forms of artistic content regulation. A September 1985 report of the National Council of Churches (NCC) recommended improvement of the present [rating] system by adding "simple, short phrases" of explanation such as "Brief Frontal Nudity," "Mild Comic Violence," and "Strong Graphic Language," which would "accompany PG, PG-13, R and X ratings, be displayed at the box office and [be] included by theatres in telephone descriptions of the films." This would, according to the NCC, "considerably further the industry's own objective to provide advance information to enable parents to make judgments on movies they wanted their children to see." The NCC also advocates the application of the MPAA ratings to videocassettes and cable TV.

Some have suggested additional movie ratings: V for violence, L for language (profanity), S for sensuality. But the biggest battle took place over a proposed SA (substance abuse) or X rating for films depicting drug use. The Senate Permanent Subcommittee on Investigations held hearings on this subject in November 1985. Said Senator William Roth, subcommittee chair: "We're not holding the threat of censorship. . . . We're looking to encourage those in the movie industry to join us in the fight against drug abuse." Nancy Reagan and Dr. Carlton Turner, President Reagan's policy advisor on drug abuse, have also taken to proclaiming that the favorable portrayal of drug use in films has an adverse effect on children.   11

"If parental attitudes were strong enough and communicated to us," proposed Richard Heffner [chairman of the MPAA], "a movie that showed pot smoking could be rated X." *Parade Magazine* thereupon polled 55,000 people, finding that 96 percent favored an SA rating and 90 percent favored giving these films an X rating as well. Taking both Heffner and the poll at face value, the X rating would have had to be assigned to films like *Private Benjamin, Nine to Five, Poltergeist, Silkwood, Romancing the Stone, The Big Chill, Trading Places,* and *Desperately Seeking Susan.*   12

On April 8, 1986, MPAA and NATO (National Association of Theater Owners) disclosed the industry's new rule on drug use portrayal: Any films that depict or refer to the use of drugs will automatically receive a PG-13, R, or X rating. Barbara Dixon, spokesperson for the MPAA, cited John Hughes' and Universal's *Sixteen Candles* (PG) as a film which would have fallen within the new strictures because teenagers were shown "**gratuitously** smoking marijuana."   13

---

gratuitously: unnecessarily, for no purpose

AVOIDING THE CENSORS
Peter Stack

This article reports on a proposal to label videotapes and a suggested expanded rating system.

Next to television, home video is the most popular form of commer- 1
cial entertainment in the country. As it has grown, so has the interest
of many communities in codifying taped programs according to
moral values, sometimes called "community moral standards." At
least a dozen cities, and one state (New Hampshire), have proposed
rating systems for tapes that elude the familiar G, PG, PG-13 and R
system used for feature films. That system, devised by the Motion
Picture Association of America, was originally intended to apply to
movies released to theaters.

While feature films dominate the home video industry, the fact 2
is that movies on tape amount to only one sixth of all programs on
the home video market. There are dozens more documentary, how-
to, fitness, religious and arts programs available to the public than
there are films. So far, no organized efforts other than shelving-ac-
cording-to-genre at video stores have been undertaken to label video
materials. And some communities have grown alarmed that what
might seem like a harmless tape actually may contain values considered by some to be objectionable.

It came as no surprise that on Tuesday a group of video produc- 3
ers—joining under the name of Independent Video Programmers Association—came up with a system of rating tapes. The particular aim
was to devise a system for non-movie cassettes that have flooded the
video market in recent years. . . .

The system is simple, and consumers may soon start to see tapes 4
in video stores using the so-called FAB (Film Advisory Board) labels.
The first label deals with type of audience—C for children, F for family,
M for mature, MM for very mature, MMM for extremely mature. . . .

The second label would give the consumer a suggestion about 5
the program's content. L would indicate possibly objectionable language, EL would mean extremely offensive language, S would mean
sex, ES would indicate explicit sex, and N would mean nudity. V and
EV would note that a program contained violence or extreme violence.
The labeling system would also use X to indicate totally offensive.

"It's the content part of the rating system that really beats the 6
MPAA ratings," said Elayne Blythe (FAB's president). "We think our
plan is far more informative for parents."

Blythe gave as an example the first tapes to get one of the new 7
labels.

It's a tape scheduled for Valentine's Day release entitled "Cook- 8
ing with Beefcake Too." The $40, 69-minute cassette is designed for
"bored housewives or lonely but saucy gals" and features two men
who give cooking instructions while wearing nothing but aprons.
From time to time, they show their buns. The tape, said FAB's Blythe,
was rated MM-N, which meant it was for mature viewing and contained some nudity.

THE RATING GAME
Paul Attanasio

This essay, written by a movie critic for the Washington Post *and published
in the* New Republic, *discusses the whole issue of rating the movies along
the usual lines—including sex, violence, and profanity. Despite his humorous
tone, he does suggest an alternative to the present labeling system, which
he sees as artificial and arbitrary.*

The *Desperately Seeking Susan* you can see at your local **bijou** is not 1
the movie Susan Seidelman originally made. There's a scene, for example, in which Rosanna Arquette clambers out of Aidan Quinn's
bed. Look hard, but you still won't see her breasts—they've been
"optically darkened" to blend into the shadows. Then there's the
scene in which Robert Joy amorously mauls Madonna while she sits
atop a pinball machine; the joke is that the crescendo of bells and
buzzers comments on their passion. That scene's been edited, too,
even though Madonna never really gets undressed. Such is the work
of the Motion Picture Association of America's rating board, which
occasionally sees nudity even *through* clothes.

For almost 17 years, the MPAA has been rating the suitability of 2
movies for people under the age of 17. . . . The single, generally
phrased standard for ratings (taking into account the film's level of
violence, sexuality, nudity, and profanity) is: "Would the average
American parent consider this film suitable for children under 17?" A
movie is rated G if the average parent would consider it acceptable
for children of all ages; PG ("parental guidance") indicates that parents should use their discretion about whether it is suitable for their
kids to see on their own; PG-13 if the film contains disturbing material to a degree that it requires a closer look for preteens; R if the film

---
bijou: movie theater

is acceptable for children only with the attendance of the parent; and X for "clearly adult" films. In 1984 roughly 30 percent of the films rated got a PG; 60 percent got an R. . . .

A kind of common law of ratings has evolved, and inevitably, 3 the **parsing** of distinctions gets pretty silly. Nudity can get you a PG as long as it's in a pristine jungle setting with no men around (*Sheena*); if the nudity comes in a sexual setting, it's generally an R. Shots of the drawings of Aubrey Beardsley had to be cut from *Crimes of Passion* before the film could be rated R; the same drawings are available to children in any bookstore. . . . Generally the ratings board seems more tolerant of violence than sex—full frontal nudity is usually an automatic X, while lots of heads have to roll before a film will be rated X for violence. Then again, self-mutilation, like the scene in *The Evil Dead* where a creature bites off his own hand, is an X-rated no-no. *Dogs* got an R because it featured a pack of dogs—"children's favorite household pets"—gone berserk. And according to producer Don Simpson, Paramount's head of production at the time, *Prophecy* initially got an X because of a shot of a bear chewing an automobile tire. . . .

King David had the same decapitations, impalings, and assorted 4 slashings and hewings as *Friday the 13th: Part V*, but it was the Bible, the actors spoke with English accents, and most of all, had the good taste to keep their clothes while they lost their heads. It got a PG-13. And so forth. . . .

Partisans of the ratings system **couch** their defense in **pseudo-** 5 democratic rhetoric. Because ratings are "advisory," each parent is allowed to decide whether his children should see a movie. The problem is that in this democracy, the kids themselves count not at all; and once you start with this principle, it's hard to limit it. How would we feel if books received ratings, and a 15-year-old had to be accompanied by his parent before he could check *Huckleberry Finn*, or even *Ball Four*, out of the library? And why should movies be different?

The system's primary virtue—that it is a single, simple unified 6 system—is also its downfall. The psychology of children is complex; different kids get nightmares from different things. What's more, in a country as large and varied as ours, the idea of a central organ of taste is preposterous. A parent in the Bible Belt might find the chain

---

parsing: detailed analysis;   couch: to phrase, to word;
pseudo-: false, fake

saw murder of a woman perfectly appropriate Saturday night fun, while the utterance of a single "goddamn" would call for a gallon of earwash. A feminist in downtown Washington might feel exactly the opposite.

Part of the answer, then, is to return the judgment to the locali- 7 ties, just as the Supreme Court has done in its obscenity rulings. Most local papers, including my own, now include a parents' guide at the end of film reviews, describing the content of the picture in terms of nudity, violence, sex, and profanity. Besides the **salubrious** effect of forcing people to read their local movie critic, the substitution of the parents' guide for a ratings code, both more specific and more attuned to local mores, would allow parents to make better decisions for their children. And because such a system would be truly advisory, it would allow for one of the most time-honored traditions in American movies—a kid sneaking into a theater against his parents' order.

Post-reading

The reading selections discuss three approaches to labeling movies: (1) the MPAA's rating system, (2) the FAB's labeling system, and (3) Attanasio's parents' guide. In addition, Sheinfeld argues against any form of rating, claiming that ratings are simply censorship in another form. In order to analyze and evaluate the information, look at these approaches again, making notes on the following matters:

1. To what extent does each rating system involve censorship, forbidding some from seeing certain movies, and on what basis? Be sure to consider the economic effect to the moviemaker of having his or her audience reduced.

2. To what extent does each system merely describe movies?

3. What attitudes toward violence, profanity, nudity, sex, or other matters does each system reflect? In other words, if a war story with lots of "blood and guts" is rated PG-13 and a love story in which there is partial nudity is rated R, what does that say about the raters' sense of what teenagers should be able to see? That is, what values underlie each labeling system? Do you agree with these values?

Go back to the notes you took before you read these articles. Have your ideas on this topic changed in any way? If so, how and for what reasons? If not, what specific parts of the articles support your original ideas?

---

salubrious: healthful, wholesome

Essay Assignment
Write an essay in which you discuss one or more of the key issues involved in rating movies—the desirability of being able
to rate them, the danger of ratings acting as tools of censorship,
the key values that seem to underlie current or proposed rating
or labeling systems. If you can, come to your own conclusion
about what you think should be done in regard to rating
movies.

For more discussion of this issue and suggestions about organizing your essay, log on to http://devenglish.wadsworth.com.

Pre-writing

The first thing you need to do is to isolate the issues surrounding this
topic that you are most interested in discussing. Then, using your own experience and the ideas of the writers you have read, try to line up the positive and negative arguments for each issue. For instance, if you want to write
about the desirability of using a rating system but the dangers of censorship, you will want to consider both sides of each of those questions. If you
want to consider the different proposed systems, you will want to line up
the advantages and disadvantages of each.

It is extremely important to use concrete instances in your discussion. For
example, the person who argues that the First Amendment guarantees that
our artistic works will not be censored needs to consider whether children
should be allowed to see movies depicting extreme, graphic violence or explicit sexual activities. At the same time, the person who would forbid such
movies to children must be prepared to say what is wrong with having children see them. In discussions of these kinds, it is highly desirable to try to base
your examples on specific movies and, if possible, specific scenes from them.

In working out your ideas on a controversial issue like this one, a discussion with a person whose views are different from yours can be very helpful, as long as you don't start arguing with each other. Listening to the
points of an opponent and writing them down can be an excellent way of
developing your own thinking. In any case, you need not come to a firm
conclusion on this troublesome question. Your essay may simply discuss
what you feel are the main problems.

As you think about organizing your essay, remember these points:

1. Provide enough background so your readers understand the impor-
    tance and complexity of the issue.

2. Acknowledge both the strengths and the weaknesses of arguments you cite, including your own.

3. Remember that a statement is not an argument. A statement needs support from facts and/or well-founded opinions to become an argument.

For further ideas on structuring your essay, refer to the section "Writing Discussion Essays." As in previous assignments, jot down a working thesis and outline.

Writing

Your introduction should very briefly explain what the ratings problem is and the aspects of the problem you think are most important.

In the body of your essay, you will shape your discussion to cover the central issues involved for and against rating systems, or you may decide to discuss the relative merits and failings of different kinds of rating systems.

Your conclusion will either present your recommendations concerning using or not using ratings systems or, if you do not want to come to such a conclusion, restate the problem as you see it, much as you did in your introduction. Review the Writer's Checklist on pages 426–428 while you work on this assignment.

IS HATE SPEECH FREE SPEECH?

In recent years there have been occasional attacks on college campuses by students against other students—not physical attacks but verbal ones, taking the form of signs, pamphlets, handouts, and speech. The worst of these have constituted insults and name-calling based on the victims' being members of ethnic minorities or being homosexual. Some universities have chosen to try to prevent such language assaults by drafting rules forbidding them. At the University of Michigan, the following rule was passed:

> Physical acts or threats or verbal slurs, invectives or epithets, referring to an individual's race, ethnicity, religion, sex, sexual orientation, creed, national origin, ancestry, age, or handicap, made with the purpose of injuring the person to whom the words or actions are directed and that are not made as a part of a discussion or exchange of an idea, ideology, or philosophy, are prohibited.

The university also published guidelines giving the following examples, among others, of prohibited speech:

> Racist graffiti written on a door of an Asian student's study carrel.
>
> A male student makes remarks in class like "Women just aren't as good in this field as men," thus creating a hostile learning atmosphere for female students.
>
> Male students leave pornographic pictures and jokes on the desk of a female graduate student.
>
> You exclude someone from a study group because that person is of a different race, sex, or ethnic origin than you are.
>
> Your student organization sponsors entertainment that includes a comedian who slurs Hispanics.
>
> You laugh at a joke about someone in your class who stutters.

Eventually the guidelines were withdrawn and, under threat of legal action, the rules were rescinded.

Similar rules were drawn up at the University of Connecticut, and under these a student named Nina Wu was expelled for hanging a poster on the outside of her door listing "homos," among others, as unwelcome. She sued and was reinstated, and the university has changed its rules.

While most people will agree that none of us should use insulting speech based on race, sex, sexual orientation, and so on, it can become very difficult to decide what kinds of speech constitute insults. If a white student calls a black student a nigger, is that an insult? If the black student calls the white student a honkey, is that an insult? Should they both be kicked out of school? If a male student, because of his deficient background, genuinely thinks that females are inferior, are the females insulted? Should the male student be expelled from school for thinking that?

Following is the text of the First Amendment to the Constitution, our guarantee of freedom of speech, followed by three views on the issue of hate speech and free speech on university campuses.

Reading Assignment

Pre-reading

It is easy to think of kinds of speech, insults and so on, that one might want to prohibit if possible. Nobody wants to be called names or in any way belittled because of something one has no control over, such as one's ethnicity or sex or sexual orientation or some disability. But think now about other kinds of situations. Are students hurt or insulted if they are left out of social situations or professional groupings because of sex, sexual orientation, or ethnicity? Is there an objective way to tell whether speech or actions are insulting or offensive? Is there an objective way to tell whether speech or actions are *intended* to be offensive? Is it possible to offend someone without intending to do so? Have you ever told an ethnic joke or slurred someone in some way? Have you ever muttered, "That's a woman for you," or "That's just like a man"? Are these examples of insensitivity?

What kinds of actions, aside from expulsion, might universities consider in an attempt to reduce or eliminate offensive speech and actions from campuses?

Reading

THE FIRST AMENDMENT TO THE UNITED STATES CONSTITUTION

Congress shall make no law respecting an establishment of religion, or prohibiting the free exercise thereof; or abridging the freedom of speech, or of the press; or the right of the people peaceably to assemble, and to petition the Government for a redress of grievances.

Note: While the First Amendment specifically limits only Congress, later amendments and rulings extended the prohibitions of the First Amendment both to the federal government as a whole and to state governments. You should also note that the First Amendment extends to other forms of expression aside from speech. For instance, the Supreme Court has held that burning the American flag in protest of government policies is a form of protected "speech."

THE DEBATE OVER PLACING LIMITS ON RACIST SPEECH MUST NOT IGNORE THE DAMAGE IT DOES TO ITS VICTIMS
Charles R. Lawrence III

Charles R. Lawrence III is a professor of law at Georgetown University. His article, which appeared in the October 25, 1989, Chronicle of Higher Education, *is adapted from a speech to a conference of the American Civil Liberties Union.*

I have spent the better part of my life as a dissenter. As a high   1
school student, I was threatened with suspension for my refusal to participate in a civil-defense drill, and I have been a conspicuous consumer of my First Amendment liberties ever since. There are very strong reasons for protecting even racist speech. Perhaps the most important of these is that such protection reinforces our society's commitment to tolerance as a value, and that by protecting bad

speech from government regulation, we will be forced to combat it as a community.

But I also have a deeply felt apprehension about the resurgence 2 of racial violence and the corresponding rise in the incidence of verbal and symbolic assault and harassment to which blacks and other traditionally subjugated and excluded groups are subjected. I am troubled by the way the debate has been framed in response to the recent surge of racist incidents on college and university campuses and in response to some universities' attempts to regulate harassing speech. The problem has been framed as one in which the liberty of free speech is in conflict with the elimination of racism. I believe this has placed the bigot on the moral high ground and fanned the rising flames of racism.

Above all, I am troubled that we have not listened to the real 3 victims, that we have shown so little understanding of their injury, and that we have abandoned those whose race, gender, or sexual preference continues to make them second-class citizens. It seems to me a very sad irony that the first instinct of civil libertarians has been to challenge even the smallest, most narrowly framed efforts by universities to provide black and other minority students with the protection the Constitution guarantees them.

The landmark case of *Brown v. Board of Education* is not a case 4 that we normally think of as a case about speech. But *Brown* can be broadly read as articulating the principle of equal citizenship. *Brown* held that segregated schools were inherently unequal because of the *message* that segregation conveyed—that black children were an untouchable caste, unfit to go to school with white children. If we understand the necessity of eliminating the system of signs and symbols that signal the inferiority of blacks, then we should hesitate before proclaiming that all racist speech that stops short of physical violence must be defended.

University officials who have formulated policies to respond to 5 incidents of racial harassment have been characterized in the press as "thought police," but such policies generally do nothing more than impose **sanctions** against intentional face-to-face insults. When racist speech takes the form of face-to-face insults, catcalls, or other assaultive speech aimed at an individual or small group of persons, it falls directly within the "fighting words" exception to First Amend-

---

sanctions: penalties

ment protection. The Supreme Court has held that words which "by their very utterance inflict injury or tend to incite an immediate breach of the peace" are not protected by the First Amendment.

If the purpose of the First Amendment is to foster the greatest 6 amount of speech, racial insults disserve that purpose. Assaultive racist speech functions as a **preemptive** strike. The invective is experienced as a blow, not as a proffered idea, and once the blow is struck, it is unlikely that a dialogue will follow. Racial insults are particularly undeserving of First Amendment protection because the perpetuator's intention is not to discover truth or initiate dialogue but to injure the victim. In most situations, members of minority groups realize that they are likely to lose if they respond to epithets by fighting and are forced to remain silent and submissive.

Courts have held that offensive speech may not be regulated in 7 public forums such as streets where the listener may avoid the speech by moving on, but the regulation of otherwise protected speech has been permitted when the speech invades the privacy of the unwilling listener's home or when the unwilling listener cannot avoid the speech. Racist posters, fliers, and graffiti in dormitories, bathrooms, and other common living spaces would seem to clearly fall within the reasoning of these cases. Minority students should not be required to remain in their rooms in order to avoid racial assault. Minimally, they should find a safe haven in their dorms and in all other common rooms that are a part of their daily routine.

I would also argue that the university's responsibility for ensur- 8 ing that these students receive an equal educational opportunity provides a compelling justification for regulations that ensure them safe passage in all common areas. A minority student should not have to risk becoming the target of racially assaulting speech every time he or she chooses to walk across campus. Regulating vilifying speech that cannot be anticipated or avoided would not **preclude** announced speeches and rallies—situations that would give minority-group members and their allies the chance to organize counter-demonstrations or avoid the speech altogether.

The most commonly advanced argument against the regulation 9 of racist speech proceeds something like this: We recognize that minority groups suffer pain and injury as the result of racist speech, but we must allow this **hate mongering** for the benefit of society as a

---

preemptive strike: in warfare, an attack to prevent one from being attacked; preclude: prevent;   hate mongering: spreading hate whole. Freedom of speech is the lifeblood of our democratic system. It is especially important for minorities because often it is their only vehicle for rallying support for the **redress** of their grievances. It will be impossible to formulate a prohibition so precise that it will prevent the racist speech you want to suppress without catching in the same net all kinds of speech that it would be **unconscionable** for a democratic society to suppress.

Whenever we make such arguments, we are striking a balance   10
on the one hand between our concern for the continued free flow of ideas and the democratic process dependent on that flow, and, on the other, our desire to further the cause of equality. There can be no meaningful discussion of how we should reconcile our commitment to equality and our commitment to free speech until it is acknowledged that there is real harm inflicted by racist speech and that this harm is far from trivial.

To engage in a debate about the First Amendment and racist   11
speech without a full understanding of the nature and extent of that harm is to risk making the First Amendment an instrument of domination rather than a vehicle of liberation. We have not all known the experience of victimization by racist, **misogynist**, and **homophobic** speech, nor do we equally share the burden of the societal harm it inflicts. We are often quick to say that we have heard the cry of the victims when we have not.

The *Brown* case is again instructive because it speaks directly to   12
the psychic injury inflicted by racist speech by noting that the symbolic message of segregation affected "the hearts and minds" of negro children "in a way unlikely ever to be undone." Racial epithets and harassment often cause deep emotional scarring and feelings of anxiety and fear that pervade every aspect of a victim's life.

Brown also recognized that black children did not have an equal   13
opportunity to learn and participate in the school community if they bore the additional burden of being subjected to the humiliation and **psychic** assault contained in the message of segregation. University students bear an **analogous** burden when they are forced to live and work in an environment where at any moment they may be subjected to denigrating verbal harassment and assault. The same injury was addressed by the Supreme Court when it held that sexual ha-

---

redress: remedy;   unconscionable: excessive, not restrained by conscience; misogynist: women-hating;   homophobic: fear or hatred of homosexuality; psychic: mental;   analogous: similar rassment that creates a hostile or abusive work environment violates the ban on sex discrimination in employment of Title VII of the Civil Rights Act of 1964.

Carefully drafted university regulations would bar the use of   14 words as assault weapons and leave unregulated even the most **heinous** of ideas when those ideas are presented at times and places and in manners that provide an opportunity for reasoned rebuttal or escape from immediate injury. The history of the development of the right to free speech has been one of carefully evaluating the impor- tance of free expression and its effects on other important societal interests. We have drawn the line between protected and unpro- tected speech before without dire results. (Courts have, for example, exempted from the protection of the First Amendment obscene speech and speech that **disseminates** official secrets, that defames or libels another person, or that is used to form a conspiracy or monopoly.)

Blacks and other people of color are skeptical about the argu-   15 ment that even the most injurious speech must remain unregulated because, in an unregulated marketplace of ideas, the best ones will rise to the top and gain acceptance. Our experience tells us quite the opposite. We have seen too many **demagogues** elected by ap- pealing to America's racism. We have seen too many good liberal politicians shy away from the issues that might brand them as being too closely allied with us.

Whenever we decide that racist speech must be tolerated be-   16 cause of the importance of maintaining societal tolerance for all un- popular speech, we are asking blacks and other subordinated groups to bear the burden for the good of all. We must be careful that the ease with which we strike the balance against the regulation of racist speech is in no way influenced by the fact that the cost will be borne by others. We must be certain that those who will pay that price are fairly represented in our deliberations and that they are heard.

At the core of the argument that we should resist all government   17 regulation of speech is the ideal that the best cure for bad speech is good, that ideas that affirm equality and the worth of all individuals will ultimately prevail. This is an empty ideal unless those of us who would fight racism are vigilant and **unequivocal** in that fight. We

---

heinous: terrible, awful;   disseminates: spreads around;
demagogues: leaders who appeal to passions and emotions;
unequivocal: firm

must look for ways to offer assistance and support to students whose speech and political participation are chilled in a climate of racial harassment.

Civil-rights lawyers might consider suing on behalf of blacks 18 whose right to an equal education is denied by a university's failure to ensure a nondiscriminatory educational climate or conditions of employment. We must embark upon the development of a First Amendment **jurisprudence** grounded in the reality of our history and our contemporary experience. We must think hard about how best to launch legal attacks against the most indefensible forms of hate speech. Good lawyers can create exceptions and narrow interpretations that limit the harm of hate speech without opening the floodgates of censorship.

Everyone concerned with these issues must find ways to engage 19 actively in actions that resist and counter the racist ideas that we would have the First Amendment protect. If we fail in this, the victims of hate speech must rightly assume that we are on the oppressors' side.

FREE SPEECH ON THE CAMPUS
Nat Hentoff

Nat Hentoff is the author of The First Freedom *and is an editor for the* Village Voice.

A flier distributed at the University of Michigan some months ago 1 proclaimed that blacks "don't belong in classrooms, they belong hanging from trees."

At other campuses around the country, manifestations of racism 2 are becoming commonplace. At Yale, a swastika and the words WHITE POWER were painted on the building housing the University's Afro-American Cultural Center. At Temple University, a White Students Union has been formed with some 130 members.

Swastikas are not directed only at black students. The Nazi sym- 3 bol has been spray-painted on the Jewish Student Union at Memphis State University. And on a number of campuses, women have been singled out as targets of wounding and sometimes frightening speech. At the law school of the State University of New York at Buf-

---

jurisprudence: philosophy of law

falo, several women students have received anonymous letters characterized by one professor as **venomously** sexist.

These and many more such signs of the resurgence of bigotry   4
and know-nothingism throughout the society—as well as on campus—have to do solely with speech, including symbolic speech.
There have also been physical assaults on black students and on
black, white, and Asian women students, but the way to deal with
physical attacks is clear: Call the police and file a criminal complaint.
What is to be done, however, about speech alone—however disgusting, inflammatory, and rawly divisive that speech may be?

At more and more colleges, administrators—with the enthusias-   5
tic support of black students, women students, and liberal students—
have been answering that question by preventing or punishing
speech. In public universities, this is a clear violation of the First
Amendment. In private colleges and universities, suppression of
speech mocks the secular religion of academic freedom and free inquiry.

The Student Press Law Center in Washington, D.C.—a vital   6
source of legal support for student editors around the country—reports, for example, that at the University of Kansas, the student host
and producer of a radio news program was forbidden by school officials from interviewing a leader of the Ku Klux Klan. So much for free
inquiry on that campus.

In Madison, Wisconsin, *The Capital Times* ran a story in January   7
about Chancellor Sheila Kaplan of the University of Wisconsin branch
at Parkside, who ordered her campus to be scoured of "some anony-
mously placed white-supremacist hate literature." Sounding like the
legendary Mayor Frank ("I am the law") Hague of Jersey City, who
booted "bad speech" out of town, Chancellor Kaplan said, "This institution is not a lamppost standing on the street corner. It doesn't
belong to everyone."

Who decides what speech can be heard or read by everyone?   8
Why, the chancellor, of course. That's what **George III** used to
say, too.

University of Wisconsin political science professor Carol Tebben   9
thinks otherwise. She believes university administrators "are getting
confused when they are acting as censors and trying to protect students from bad ideas. I don't think students need to be protected

---

venomously: poisonously;   George III: king of England during the
American Revolution

from bad ideas. I think they can determine for themselves what ideas are bad."

After all, if students are to be "protected" from bad ideas, how 10 are they going to learn to identify and cope with them? Sending such ideas underground simply makes them stronger and more dangerous.

Professor Tebben's conviction that free speech means just that 11 has become a decidedly minority view on many campuses. At the University of Buffalo Law School, the faculty unanimously adopted a "Statement Regarding Intellectual Freedom, Tolerance, and Political Harassment." Its title implies support of intellectual freedom, but the statement warned students that once they enter "this legal community," their right to free speech must become tempered "by the responsibility to promote equality and justice."

Accordingly, swift condemnation will befall anyone who engages 12 in "remarks directed at another's race, sex, religion, national origin, age, or sex preference." Also forbidden are "other remarks based on prejudice and group stereotype."

This **ukase** is so broad that enforcement has to be alarmingly 13 subjective. Yet the University of Buffalo Law School provides no due-process procedures for a student booked for making any of these prohibited remarks. Conceivably, a student caught playing a Lenny Bruce, Richard Pryor, or Sam Kinison album in his room could be tried for aggravated insensitivity by association.

When I looked into this wholesale cleansing of bad speech at 14 Buffalo, I found it had encountered scant opposition. One protester was David Gerald Jay, a graduate of the law school and a cooperating attorney for the New York Civil Liberties Union. Said the appalled graduate: "Content-based prohibitions constitute prior restraint and should not be tolerated."

You would think that the law professors and administration at 15 this public university might have known that. But hardly any professors dissented, and among the students only members of the conservative Federalist Society spoke up for free speech. The fifty-strong chapter of the National Lawyers Guild was on the other side. After all, it was more important to go on record as vigorously opposing racism and sexism than to expose oneself to charges of insensitivity to these **malignancies.**

---

ukase: dictatorial order;   malignancies: evils

The pressures to have the "right" attitude—as proved by having 16
the "right" language in and out of class—can be stifling. A student
who opposes affirmative action, for instance, can be branded a racist.

At the University of California at Los Angeles, the student news- 17
paper ran an editorial cartoon satirizing affirmative action. (A student stops a rooster on campus and asks how the rooster got into
UCLA. "Affirmative action," is the answer.) After outraged complaints from various minority groups, the editor was suspended for
violating a publications policy against running "articles that perpetu-
ate derogatory or cultural stereotypes." The art director was also suspended.

When the opinion editor of the student newspaper at California 18
State University at Northridge wrote an article asserting that the
sanctions against the editor and art director at UCLA amounted to
censorship, he was suspended too.

At New York University Law School, a student was so disturbed 19
by the **pall of orthodoxy** at that prestigious institution that he wrote
to the school newspaper even though, as he said, he expected his
letter to make him a **pariah** among his fellow students.

Barry Endick described the atmosphere at NYU created by "a 20
host of watchdog committees and a generally hostile classroom reception regarding any student comment right of center." This "can
be arguably viewed as symptomatic of a prevailing spirit of academic and social intolerance of . . . any idea which is not 'politically
correct.'"

He went on to say something that might well be posted on cam- 21
pus bulletin boards around the country, though it would probably
be torn down at many of them:

> We ought to examine why students, so anxious to wield the Four-
> teenth Amendment, give short shrift to the First. Yes, Virginia, there
> are racist assholes. And you know what, the Constitution protects
> them, too.

Not when they engage in violence or vandalism. But when they 22
speak or write, racist assholes fall right into this Oliver Wendell
Holmes definition—highly unpopular among bigots, liberals, radi-
cals, feminists, sexists, and college administrators:

---

pall of orthodoxy: atmosphere of restriction;   pariah: outcast

If there is any principle of the Constitution that more impera-
tively calls for attachment than any other, it is the principle of free
thought—not free only for those who agree with us, but freedom
for the thought we hate.

The language sounds like a **pietistic** Sunday sermon, but if it   23
ever falls wholly into disuse, neither this publication nor any other
journal of opinion—Right or Left—will survive.

Sometimes, college presidents and administrators sound as if they   24
fully understand what Holmes was saying. Last year, for example,
when *The Daily Pennsylvanian*—speaking for many at the University of
Pennsylvania—urged that a speaking invitation to **Louis Farrakhan**
be withdrawn, University President Sheldon Hackney disagreed.

"Open expression," said Hackney, "is the fundamental principle   25
of a university." Yet consider what the same Sheldon Hackney did to
the free-speech rights of a teacher at his own university. If any story
distills the essence of the current decline of free speech on college
campuses, it is the Ballad of Murray Dolfman.

For twenty-two years, Dolfman, a practicing lawyer in Philadel-   26
phia, had been a part-time lecturer in the Legal Studies Department
of the University of Pennsylvania's Wharton School. For twenty-two
years, no complaint had ever been made against him; indeed, his
student course-evaluations had been outstanding. Each year students
competed to get into his class.

On a November afternoon in 1984, Dolfman was lecturing   27
about personal-service contracts. His style somewhat resembles
that of Professor Charles Kingsfield in *The Paper Chase.* Dolfman
insists that students he calls on be prepared—or suffer the consequences. He treats all students this way—regardless of race, creed,
or sex.

This day, Dolfman was pointing out that no one can be forced   28
to work against his or her will—even if a contract has been signed. A
court may prevent the resister from working for someone else so long
as the contract is in effect but, Dolfman said, there can "be nothing
that smacks of involuntary servitude."

Where does this concept come from? Dolfman looked around   29
the room. Finally, a cautious hand was raised: "The Constitution?"

---

pietistic: overly reverent;   Louis Farrakhan: African-American leader known
for anti-Jewish statements;   *The Paper Chase:* movie about law students

"Where in the Constitution?" No hands. "The Thirteenth 30
Amendment," said the teacher. So, what does *it* say? The students
were looking everywhere but at Dolfman.

"We will lose our liberties," Dolfman often told his classes, "if we 31
don't know what they are."

On this occasion, he told them that he and other Jews, as ex- 32
slaves, spoke at Passover of the time when they were slaves under
the Pharaohs so that they would remember every year what it was
like not to be free.

"We have ex-slaves here," Dolfman continued, "who should 33
know about the Thirteenth Amendment." He asked black students in
the class if they could tell him what was in that amendment.

"I wanted them to really think about it," Dolfman told me re- 34
cently, "and know its history. You're better equipped to fight racism
if you know all about those post–Civil War amendments and civil-
rights laws."

The Thirteenth Amendment provides that "neither slavery nor 35
involuntary servitude . . . shall exist within the United States."

The black students in his class did not know what was in that 36
amendment, and Dolfman had them read it aloud. Later, they complained to university officials that they had been hurt and humiliated
by having been referred to as ex-slaves. Moreover, they said, they
had no reason to be grateful for a constitutional amendment which
gave them rights which should never have been denied them—and
gave them precious little else. They had not made these points in
class, although Dolfman—unlike Professor Kingsfield—encourages
rebuttal.

Informed of the complaint, Dolfman told the black students 37
he had intended no offense, and he apologized if they had been
offended.

That would not do—either for the black students or for the ad- 38
ministration. Furthermore, there were mounting black-Jewish tensions on campus, and someone had to be sacrificed. Who better than
a part-time Jewish teacher with no contract and no union? He was
sentenced by—**George Orwell** would have loved this—the Committee on Academic Freedom and Responsibility.

George Orwell: author of the novel *1984*, depicting a future in which lies
are considered truth

On his way to the **stocks,** Dolfman told President Sheldon Hack- 39
ney that if a part-time instructor "can be punished on this kind of
charge, a tenured professor can eventually be booted out, then a
dean, and then a president."

Hackney was unmoved. Dolfman was banished from the cam- 40
pus for what came to be a year. But first he was forced to make a
public apology to the entire university and then he was compelled
to attend a "sensitivity and racial awareness" session. Sort of like a
Vietnamese reeducation camp.

A few conservative professors objected to the **stigmatization** of 41
Murray Dolfman. I know of no student dissent. Indeed, those students most concerned with making the campus more "sensitive" to
diversity exulted in Dolfman's humiliation. So did most liberals on
the faculty.

If my children were still of college age and wanted to attend the 42
University of Pennsylvania, I would tell them this story. But where
else could I encourage them to go?

HATE SPEECH ON CAMPUS
Joseph S. Tuman

*Joseph Tuman is the Director of Forensics and teaches argumentation,
debate, and constitutional law in the Speech and Communication Studies
Department at San Francisco State University.*

Recent efforts by large public universities and colleges aimed at stem- 1
ming the tide of hate speech on campus have caused all of us in the
academic community to carefully assess our position on this issue.
Hate speech refers to written or spoken words directed towards a
particular group (typically although not exclusively a minority group)
with the purpose or effect of verbally harassing and harming them.
In the educational setting, this can refer to language used both in
and outside the classroom, by teacher or student, while still within
the campus.

Schools such as the University of Michigan, the University of Wis- 2
consin, and the University of California have already written new regulations to restrict this form of speech, declaring that it disrupts the
educational process and retards progress made in bringing equal opportunity and access to education for all.

---

stocks: an ancient form of punishment;   stigmatization: being disgraced

Does hate speech harm the individual to whom it is addressed? I 3 can speak to this myself. My parents came to this country nearly four decades ago from the Middle East. I was born in Texas and later grew up in California's Central Valley. My early years were spent constantly trying to conform and avoid the appearance of being different. As a young person in public schools, I often heard comments, jokes and insults about my ethnicity and the place my parents had once called home. I can assure you that these comments hurt—and in a different way than they might if reversed against those in more populous numbers. If they caused me some pain as a white male, I can only imagine what they must feel like when they are directed to those already burdened with discrimination in our society.

As an adult and an educator, however, today I see this from a 4 different point of view, standing before the class instead of seated within the class. Consequently, I now find myself internally conflicted over this issue. I have always tried in my class to avoid promoting my own social and political agenda, believing instead that classroom discussions, within reasonable limits, should be open and accessible for all. This promotes participation from the broadest number of students, and enhances the learning process.

As a teacher, I thus look with unease at regulations which might 5 restrict what can be said in the classroom. My discomfort is grounded in the fact that I am not certain that clear regulations prohibiting hate speech can be designed without also entangling other forms of speech—speech that may otherwise be protected by the First Amendment.

A wise undergraduate student in my own Free Speech class debated me on this point last year, declaring that those rules aren't so 6 difficult. People know what kind of words and insults we're talking about, she said—and to illustrate her point, she promptly recited three different types of racist, sexist and homophobic slurs.

For me, however, her examples were the obvious ones. Yes, most 7 people do know about bigoted, hurtful insults and slurs—but should we draft a rule that prohibits only the obvious choices? Many forms of racist and sexist speech, for example, are oftentimes far more subtle, although their impact is no less devastating. How do we define rules prohibiting these? I assume we do this by making our restriction broader, but when we do so, how do we avoid prohibiting other speech which may not necessarily be hate speech?

This was the problem for Michigan, when a graduate student 8 teacher challenged the University of Michigan's rules, arguing they were so broad that they forced him to remove parts of his lecture material for fear of offending some unknown members of his class. He didn't in fact know if the material would offend anyone or not— but the rule was so broad that he feared the risk of penalty if he guessed wrong. The federal court hearing the case declared Michigan's rules unconstitutional.

In spite of the pain of my own past experience, I find I cannot 9 endorse rules such as these, either. Hate speech is the expression of bigotry and prejudice—and these in turn are the products of ignorance. I know no better place to address ignorance than in our schools, and no better way to do so than in exposing all of our ideas, good and bad, ugly and beautiful, to the light of scrutiny within our classes.

RETHINKING CAMPUS SPEECH CODES
Ben Wildavsky

Just a few years after rules banning offensive words began cropping 1 up at colleges and universities across America, the brief reign of these controversial campus speech codes appears to be drawing to a close.

A ruling earlier this week declaring Stanford University's hate- 2 speech ban unconstitutional is the latest in a string of legal setbacks for speech codes and anti-harassment rules.

The court decisions—and **derisive** attacks by critics of campus 3 "thought police"—are spurring colleges coast to coast to scrap or retool rules that may run afoul of the First Amendment.

The Stanford decision "is the final nail in the coffin of speech 4 codes," said Sheldon Steinbach, general counsel for the American Council on Education, which represents 1,700 colleges and universities.

"It sends a lasting **shot across the bow** of institutions that think 5 speech codes, as constructed in the late '80s and early '90s are the appropriate way of dealing with interpersonal conflict."

To be sure, campus wars over race and gender have hardly died 6 down. Indeed, such issues as affirmative action are more contentious than ever.

But speech codes have done little to ease campus tensions, leav- 7 ing other students fearful of making a race or gender **faux-pax.**

---

derisive: mocking; shot across the bow: warning—from the old naval custom of firing a cannon ball across the bow of a ship to warn it to stop; faux-pas: mistake—French for false step (pronounced foe-paw)

Speech and harassment rules may instead have fanned the flames of intolerance.

"If you're fearful that somehow you will misspeak," Steinbach 8 said, "you wind up avoiding the very people you need to get to know."

With its speech code now on hold, and no decision yet on 9 whether to mount a costly appeal, Stanford joins several major institutions whose campus rules have been held unconstitutional:

- In 1989, a federal judge overturned parts of the University of Michigan's speech code after a biopsychology graduate student said he feared the rules would prevent him from discussing controversial theories about biological differences among the sexes and races.
- In 1991, the University of Wisconsin's speech code was struck down as overly broad and "unduly vague." The university, one of the first to ban racial and sexual slurs, redrew its code more narrowly before scrapping it entirely in 1992.
- In 1993, a fraternity successfully sued Virginia's George Mason University after its members were disciplined for parodying an African American woman as part of an "ugly woman" contest. "Even as low-grade entertainment," the judge ruled, the skit "was inherently expressive and thus entitled to First Amendment protection."

Cross-Burning Decision

A major impetus behind the move away from speech codes was a 10 1992 Supreme Court ruling that struck down a hate-crime ordinance in St. Paul, Minn., and held that cross-burning could be considered protected speech under the First Amendment.

In some cases, colleges have abandoned anti-harassment and 11 speech codes after public outcry rather than legal action.

In one widely publicized incident, the University of Pennsylvania 12 disciplined a white male student for calling a group of five black sorority sisters "water buffalo" when they made noise outside his dorm room late one night.

The Hebrew-speaking student insisted the phrase was not racist 13 but simply a literal translation of an Israeli expression for noisy, disruptive people. The university dropped the charges and later withdrew its speech code.

The Stanford code, adopted in 1990, grew out of an incident 14 two years earlier in which two first-year students defaced a poster of Beethoven with racial caricatures.

"Fighting Words"

Unlike other broadly written rules, the Stanford code was carefully 15
crafted to avoid any "chilling effect" on debate of sensitive topics. It
forbade only "fighting words" linked to sex and race.

"It's about as narrow as you can get. All it prohibits is the face- 16
to-face use of racial **epithets**," said the code's architect, Stanford law
professor Thomas Grey.

Yet Santa Clara County Superior Court Judge Peter Stone still 17
found the rules a barrier to free expression.

"The Speech Code prohibits words which will not only cause 18
people to react violently, but also cause them to feel insulted or **stigmatized**," he wrote in his 43-page opinion. "(Stanford) cannot pro-
scribe speech that merely hurts the feelings of those who hear it."

Stone's ruling hinged on a 1992 state law extending free-speech 19
protections to private universities, which historically have not been
covered by the First Amendment.

Stanford Is Significant

Even though no other state has such a law, Stanford's prestige and 20
visibility mean this week's court decision is likely to send a national
message about speech codes.

"They're going out the door," said Robert Rosenzweig, former 21
president of the Association of American Universities. "I would be
surprised to see any significant number of institutions now adopting
codes, and where they exist they will be increasingly dead letters—
unenforced law."

Rosenzweig and others said the Stanford decision is particularly 22
significant because Stanford's rules were carefully drawn to pass constitutional muster.

"This ruling says that with the best of intentions and the best of 23
lawyers, it still is not possible to craft a speech code that doesn't violate the Constitution," said Paul McMasters, executive director of the
Freedom Forum First Amendment Center at Vanderbilt University.

"In a place where free-flowing dialogue and debate should be 24
revered," said McMasters, "speech codes put restrictions on that
very ideal."

A survey of 384 public colleges and universities conducted by 25
the center last year found that 36 percent had rules punishing "hate

---

epithets: insulting names;   stigmatized: labeled as inferior speech." Many of the rules, the center concluded, are probably un-constitutional.

The University of California, which adopted a system-wide 26 speech code in 1989 prohibiting "fighting words" that create a "hostile and intimidating environment," is studying the Stanford ruling, said UC deputy general counsel Gary Morrison.

"The issue, it seems to me, is whether at some point words lose 27 their essentially protected, expressive nature," he said, "and become simply tools for purposes of angering and intimidating someone, just like a slap in the face."

As speech codes fall by the wayside, some colleges are turning 28 instead to other rules of conduct to punish student behavior considered offensive.

"Now they have sexual harassment codes and racial harassment 29 codes so broadly drawn that they include a lot of speech," said attorney John Howard of the individual rights foundation in Los Angeles, one of several conservative groups that have helped students bring legal challenges to campus harassment rules.

"Instead of using them as a tool to fight harassment," he said, 30 "they use them as a political weapon to silence people with whom they disagree."

Post-reading

The article by Hentoff presents a pretty straightforward argument—speech should not be censored—and Hentoff tries to show us why it shouldn't by showing us what can happen when it is censored in one way or another. You will need to decide whether the examples he gives represent sufficiently serious offenses against our freedom of speech so that what is lost in freedom to speak outweighs what is gained by the censorship.

Lawrence's article requires very careful reading. In it, he notes that the courts have, in fact, put limitations on the First Amendment in the past, and you will need to note carefully what those limitations are. Specifically, while speech in public places is protected, speech on private property is not. If you don't like what someone is saying in your house, you can throw him or her out. If you run a private university, you can make up whatever rules you want concerning expression on campus. The Supreme Court has also established what is called the "clear and present danger" test. That is, advocacy of *immediate* violence or lawlessness is not protected.

Lawrence also cites as being applicable here the landmark Supreme Court case *Brown v. Board of Education*. Prior to this decision, many states had set up what they called "separate but equal" schools and colleges for black and white students. Of course, the schools weren't equal at all, though they were certainly separate. The *Brown* decision abolished racially segregated educational systems. Look back at the fourth, twelfth, and thirteenth paragraphs in Lawrence's essay to understand how he sees this decision as being relevant to the hate-speech issue. (Of course, although Lawrence speaks primarily about hate speech against African-Americans, his argument extends to other kinds of racism as well as to sexism, homophobic speech, and slurs based on age and on disabilities.)

Tuman's article is a carefully thought-out consideration of the issue from someone who has found himself on both sides of it, a person who suffered slurs because of his background and ethnicity and who is now responsible for being an effective teacher trying to promote a free exchange of ideas.

Essay Assignment

Write an essay in which you discuss the issue of free speech versus hate speech on college campuses. You may come to the conclusion that some form of censorship (you should specify the form it should take) or some form of punishment (you should specify the kinds of punishment and what the punishments would be given for) should be instituted to prevent the abuses of hate speech, or, conversely, you may wish to argue that we will have to accept abuses of free speech in order to protect free speech. In discussion essays, another option is simply to discuss, to try to shed light on the issue rather than trying to resolve it.

For more discussion of this issue and suggestions about organizing your essay, log on to http://devenglish.wadsworth.com.

Pre-writing

As you think about organizing your essay, remember these points:

1. Present adequate background to enable your readers to understand the importance and complexity of the issue.
2. Be sure to acknowledge the strengths, as well as the weaknesses, of the arguments you cite, including your own.
3. Remember that a statement is not an argument; a statement needs to be supported with facts and/or well-founded opinions in order to become an argument.

The section "Writing Discussion Essays" contains further ideas on structuring your essay. As you have in previous assignments, jot down a working thesis and outline.

Writing

Although you may feel strongly on this issue, remember that even the United States Supreme Court has had difficulty deciding the question of what speech is protected and what isn't. In fact, the Court has changed its mind on this issue several times over the years. The issue is complex and difficult. Accordingly, you may simply wish to discuss the issue, showing its complications, rather than coming down on one side or the other. If, however, you do want to argue for one position or the other, keep an open mind and acknowledge the arguments on the other side. Review the Writer's Checklist on pages 426–428 while you work on this assignment.

SHOULD COLLEGE ATHLETICS BE REFORMED?

As universities and colleges with major athletic programs continue to compete with one another for the best high school athletes and for the championships that bring to them literally millions of dollars, the argument continues to rage as to whether such schools should continue their current emphasis on big-time sports. Those who favor the current situation point to the huge amount of income such sports generate, at least at the most successful schools, and argue that many otherwise disadvantaged young men and women may get college educations because of their athletic talents, whereas otherwise they would not. Opponents claim that universities should be in the business of teaching academic subjects, not providing a training ground for professional basketball and football leagues.

Part of the problem is that although the organization governing college athletics, the National Collegiate Athletic Association (NCAA), has issued firm rules on recruiting and scholarships for athletes, cheating among major institutions has continued. Another difficulty is that at many schools with big-time programs, athletes are isolated from the rest of the student body, living in special dorms, being given make-work jobs created especially for them, and taking many (if not most) of their classes in programs designed by athletic departments. As a result, a large percentage of them never graduate, never earn a college degree, and are, ironically, incapable of competing professionally in the "real world" outside the college walls.

Reading Assignment

Pre-reading

As a way of beginning to think about this topic, ask yourself questions like the following: What are the problems surrounding college athletics? How are the athletes treated? Is the athletic program fair to them? Why or why not? Is it fair to the other students? Why or why not? What should be the role of athletics in a college?

Discuss this issue with your classmates, friends, and any college athletes you know. How do the athletes you know feel about this issue? You may wish to talk to coaches or others involved with your college's athletic program. Remember to take notes so you won't forget their arguments when it's time to write your essay.

Reading

The following passages address the role of athletics in colleges and thereby raise the fundamental question about what a university should be. They also illustrate that in this case, as with any complex issue involving individuals and institutions, what is best for the individual is not necessarily best for the institution and vice versa. Remember to read actively, taking notes, as you explore this issue.

REVIEW AT VIRGINIA TECH UNCOVERS SPORTS VIOLATIONS
Douglas Lederman

An internal committee has found at least 12 violations of National 1 Collegiate Athletic Association rules at Virginia Polytechnic Institute and State University, whose trustees were publicly **rebuked** for their sports policies only last month by the state's governor.

In a commencement speech last month, Governor Gerald L. 2 Baliles criticized the Virginia Tech Board of Visitors for permitting the university to risk scandal by turning to big-time sports. He warned the board that he would use his ability to appoint new members as a way of insuring the "re-direction of this university to its essential purpose."

The university committee, which is investigating allegations of 3 recruiting violations, said it had also found a pattern of what it called a "lack of regard for academic **integrity**" in the athletics department.

The most serious violation uncovered by the probe centered on 4 an unidentified basketball player who was given credit for a course

---

rebuked: criticized sharply;   integrity: strict adherence to a code of behavior in which he had done no work, in order to keep him eligible for athletic competition. The athlete, who in the fall of 1986 was failing a course in "house plants" that would have left him one credit short of eligibility, was assigned an independent-study project by a tenured education professor to provide that one credit. . . . The athlete was to write a paper on the history of the Metro Conference, of which Virginia Tech is a member, but he did not submit any work. The professor, however, gave him a grade of C plus.

Other rules violations discovered by the committee included: 5

A $7,200 automobile loan to a basketball player's wife;

A basketball coach's hiring of a tutor for a prospective player;

Free meals for recruited athletes at a restaurant owned by a booster;

Boosters acting as "foster parents" for two athletes, providing them Christmas gifts;

Two other boosters acting as "foster parents" for another athlete, providing him with meals and lending him their automobile.

Although the committee criticized the entire athletics program,   6
the basketball program received the most critical analysis. "In reviewing the academic records of basketball athletes, it is evident that most are not serious students," the report said. "Individuals have been advised to take courses in order to remain eligible, not to make progress toward a degree."

The graduate rate of basketball players was found especially wanting.   7
Of the players who came to the university between 1978 and 1981, 36 per cent graduated, 29 per cent flunked out, and 36 per cent withdrew. Of those who started at Virginia Tech between 1981 and 1986, none have yet graduated, 19 per cent flunked out, and 29 per cent withdrew. Of the 52 per cent who remain at the university, the report said, 80 per cent have grade-point averages of less than 2.0.

For athletes in the major sports—defined in the report as foot-   8
ball, men's basketball, and baseball—aptitude-test scores have tumbled badly. In 1979–80, the average Scholastic Aptitude Test score for scholarship athletes in those sports was 835, while for all students it was 1,050. By 1984–85, the **mean** for such athletes had dropped to 640, while the mean for all students had improved to

---

mean: the middle point between two extremes

1,080. "The total SAT spread between these athletes and other students now stands at 440, a difference in academic potential that places the student-athlete at a serious disadvantage in the classroom," the report said.

THE ROLE OF BLACK ATHLETES IN COLLEGE

One of the most sensitive aspects of the debate concerning the place   1
of athletics in colleges and universities is the concern over the fate of
black athletes. Well over half of the basketball players at major colleges are black, as is a very high percentage of football players. These
athletes, recruited from small towns and from large inner-city high
schools, often have minimal academic skills and show little interest
in studies. They dream of high-paying careers in the National Basketball Association or the National Football League. Until recently, they
could be admitted into an athletic program simply on the basis of
having a C average in their high school courses.

Then the NCAA decided that high school grades did not neces-   2
sarily indicate academic ability and imposed a minimal score on the
Scholastic Aptitude Test or the American College Test as a requirement for athletic eligibility. Proposition 48, passed in 1986, prevented athletes with low test scores from participating in sports at
major universities during their freshman year. It did not prevent them
from receiving scholarships or practicing with their teams. In 1989,
the NCAA passed a new regulation, Proposal 42, to prevent athletes
with low test scores from receiving scholarships during their freshman year. It did not prevent them from attending a community college in order to improve their academic skills.

In 1992, the NCAA again strengthened its academic require-   3
ments for athletes. Starting in 1995, college freshmen will have to
have a C plus high school grade average if they have a test score of
700 on the SAT or 17 on the ACT. Students who score 900 on the
SAT or 21 on the ACT will have to have only a C average. In addition, the number of "core" college preparatory courses required will
be raised from eleven to thirteen. Other rules have been added
requiring "satisfactory progress" in college degree programs. While
some black educators have charged that these new requirements are
discriminatory and will result in as many as 70 percent of black
athletes being denied admission to NCAA schools, Gerald Turner,
chairman of the NCAA Presidents Commission, said, "For the first time,

we have an accurate statement to kids about what it takes as a minimum foundation to have a chance to graduate from our universities."

FOES OF NEW ACADEMIC STANDARDS CRY "UNFAIR" AS TEST SCORES KEEP STAR STUDENT OFF THE FIELD
Douglas Lederman

Sidney Prince had an excellent football record last year as a line- 1
backer at Fox High School in the rural part of Oklahoma. That record, plus a formidable 6-foot-3-inch frame and a 3.4 academic average that qualified him as the high school's salutatorian, made him a top-notch college football recruit.

Coaches from Oklahoma State University and the University of 2
Oklahoma thought so, too. By the end of the academic year, Oklahoma's Coach Barry Switzer had persuaded Sidney to play for his Sooners, last year's national champions.

But Sidney Prince will not play a down of football this season. 3
He performed poorly on a standardized college-admission test and thus failed to qualify for eligibility under the NCAA's new academic standards for freshman athletes that went into effect in August.

Under the rules, known popularly as Proposition 48, freshman 4
athletes—to be eligible to play sports in their first year—must have earned a 2.0 grade-point average in a high-school core curriculum of 11 academic courses *and* have scored at least 700 on the Scholastic Aptitude Test or 15 on the American College Testing Program's standardized examination. "I'm all for eligibility standards, but I'm against this rule for reasons like Sidney," says Milton Cooper, principal and football coach at Fox High School. "It's unfair and it's discriminating."

In this first year for the rules, about 400 athletes—the vast ma- 5
jority of them black—have failed to meet the requirements and are ineligible to compete in athletics. Coach Switzer cites Sidney Prince as an example of a black athlete who has been victimized by the rules. "You're penalizing a kid severely, based on testing criteria that just don't determine whether you can be successful in a university environment," says Mr. Switzer.

Whether or not he has been treated unfairly, Sidney Prince's ex- 6
perience with the new standards points up the difficulty in designing academic rules that will treat all athletes equally.

Through his junior year in high school, Sidney attended tiny Per- 7
nell School, which has a total enrollment of about 100 students from
kindergarten through the 12th grade. Because it is so small, Pernell
plays eight-man football, a **truncated** version of the traditional game.
To improve his chances of getting a football scholarship, Sidney trans-
ferred to Fox for his senior year. Somewhat larger but still small by
city and suburban standards, Fox enrolls 425 students, including elementary grades. Sidney's graduating class numbered just 28 students.

Because of a limited teaching staff, geometry is offered only 8
every other year at Fox, says Mr. Cooper, its principal and coach.
"Some seniors don't get to take it because it's not offered that year."

Sidney took the ACT test in February, after studying a practice 9
book for a couple of weeks. He had studied basic algebra and only
"a little geometry" in the classroom. He says he was overwhelmed
by "a lot of stuff I hadn't even learned in school."

John R. Davis, president of the NCAA, says he is sympathetic with 10
the plight of those who have been declared ineligible. "Perhaps
[Proposition 48] was flawed in some ways, because some of those
who are ineligible are obviously well equipped to handle a college-
level curriculum." Mr. Davis believes it is likely that the NCAA will, in
time, develop a waiver system that will enable students to request a
review of their credentials, possibly overturning a decision declaring
them ineligible.

But he is not sure a waiver would, or should, help students who fail 11
to achieve the minimum test score. "I think we'll find that most of the
students who are ineligible will be so because they failed to meet requirements about core curriculum, not test scores. That test-score floor
is pretty low, and if a student isn't prepared to score 700 on the SAT,
he probably isn't prepared to handle the average college curriculum."

NCAA STIRS DEBATE—ARE SATS RACIST?

A new NCAA rule requiring freshmen receiving athletic scholarships 1
to achieve a minimum score on college entrance exams has revived
an old debate: Are such tests unfair to minority students?

The argument centers on the alleged bias of the Scholastic Apti- 2
tude Test and the ACT Assessment, each taken annually by about a
million college-bound high school seniors.

---

truncated: made shorter or smaller by cutting off an end

Georgetown University basketball coach John Thompson walked 3
off the court Saturday night at the start of a game against Boston
College to protest Proposal 42, an NCAA rule barring colleges from
granting athletic scholarships to freshmen who fail to achieve a minimum 2.0 grade-point average in high school and [who] score less
than 700 on the SAT or 15 on the ACT.

That's a tightening of the controversial NCAA Proposition 48 insti- 4
tuted three years ago which allowed such scholarships to athletes if
they met either standard, even though they may not be eligible to play.

Other coaches have joined in the outcry. Temple University bas- 5
ketball coach John Chaney said Proposal 42, which is to go into effect next year, will "punish these kids who come from a poor
background and have a poor educational opportunity."

An Associated Press survey in 1986 found that nearly one out of 6
10 college athletic recruits failed to meet the standards under Proposition 48. The results were not broken down by race.

Critics for years have charged that the SAT, sponsored by the 7
College Board in New York, and the ACT Assessment, sponsored by
the American College Testing Program in Iowa City, are culturally biased against women and minorities.

Such critics as FairTest, a Cambridge, Mass., group, have 8
charged that the only thing the tests reliably measure by requiring
knowledge of such words as **"regatta"** or **"aria"** is the family income
of the test-taker.

Bob Schaeffer, public education director of FairTest, said Mon- 9
day that his organization is sending a letter to the NCAA protesting
the new rule as a "blatantly improper use of test scores which must
be immediately abandoned."

The College Board has argued the test is fair; poor curricula and 10
home factors are to blame for the comparatively weak test results by
minority youngsters.

NCAA officials have justified their standards by citing the many 11
well-publicized instances of barely literate athletes who find few career opportunities after they have played their last college game.

Is the NCAA standard unreasonable? 12

The SAT is a two-part, multiple-choice examination of mathe- 13
matics and verbal aptitude, each consisting of roughly 80 questions.
The highest score on each part is 800. To meet the NCAA standard

---

regatta: sailboat race;   aria: song from an opera

of 700 [total on both parts], a student must average 350 each on the math and verbal sections, or answer roughly 13 out of 80 questions correctly on the math section and 24 correct on the verbal.

In other words, even with penalties for wrong answers, students 14 have a chance of meeting the NCAA standard through sheer guesswork.

Whites as a group have outperformed minority students. In 15 1988, white students averaged a combined 935 on the SAT, nearly 200 points higher than blacks.

But the NCAA standard is well within the grasp of the average 16 black student, according to College Board statistics. In 1988, black students averaged 384 on the math portion and 353 on the verbal—37 points above the NCAA guideline.

The NCAA standard, incidentally, is 204 points below the aver- 17 age SAT for all students in 1988: 904.

CHEERS TO JOHN THOMPSON'S EMPTY CHAIR
John Eisenberg

It happened before the opening tip. As soon as the officials whistled 1 for the players to come to center court to start the game, John Thompson, coach of the Georgetown Hoyas, grabbed the **ubiquitous** towel on his shoulder, tossed it to an assistant and walked across the court toward the locker room.

As soon as he took a step, the crowd in the Capital Centre stood 2 in unison and cheered, as though the Hoyas had won a big game. A sign in the student section was raised: "Give 'em Hell, Coach Thompson." Accompanied by an official, he walked through a battery of photographers off the end of the court. And then he was gone, not to return. The game was about to begin.

These bizarre circumstances came about as a result of a vote 3 taken at the National Collegiate Athletic Association convention last week all the way across the country, in San Francisco. There, members voted in favor of Proposal 42, an amendment to Proposition 48. Thompson walked out on the Hoyas' game with Boston College Saturday night to protest the passage of Proposal 42.

OK, bear with me here; try to keep these numbers and issues 4 straight, and we'll weed through this. Proposition 48 is a three-year-old rule preventing athletes with low grades and test scores from

---

ubiquitous: ever present

participating as freshmen at Division I colleges. Proposal 42, scheduled to take effect in August 1990, will prevent these athletes from
taking athletic scholarship money as freshmen.

Thompson believes this rule discriminates against athletes from   5
disadvantaged backgrounds. He walked out Saturday night to draw
attention to what he feels is a bad rule. And while such disobedience
sets a dangerous **precedent**, Thompson is on the right side of this
issue. Proposal 42 is a bad rule. Allow me to use a fictional example
to illustrate why.

Say you are a senior at a Baltimore high school. You are an ex-   6
cellent basketball player and a mediocre student and your family is
poor. Your grades and test scores fall below the Proposition 48 guidelines. Still, several schools in the Atlantic Coast Conference would
like you to come play for them. They are willing to give you an athletic scholarship.

Before Proposal 42 was passed, you could choose your school   7
and **matriculate** as a freshman—on an athletic scholarship. You simply sat out your freshman year, hopefully concentrating on your
classwork, then became eligible the next year. Not the worst idea.
But when, and if, Proposal 42 goes into effect, you will have to scare
up the tuition money for your freshman year.

Obviously, if you can't afford the tuition, you can't go to school.   8
That means that, because you are from a disadvantaged family, you
can't go to a major college that is willing to give you a scholarship.
Anyone with any sense of social justice can see that is discriminatory
and unfair.

Still, I have to admit, this remains a difficult issue for me. It is no   9
secret that academics have become a minor part of major college
athletics. Far too many of the athletes don't even belong in college.
The whole system is sleazy and cheap and in need of rewakened priorities. And the administrators who passed Proposal 42 were, among
other things, attempting to improve the quality of scholarship. That's
not wrong.

At many schools, the academic **disparity** between athletes and   10
the rest of the student body already is wide enough. Attempts to
limit this disparity are to be commended. It's just that this attempt is
all wrong.

---

precedent: example;   matriculate: enroll;   disparity: difference, inequality

(I must admit: **Altruism** from college coaches generally gives me 11
a slightly upset stomach. It would be different if these coaches
weren't getting rich off their game. If Thompson, Temple's John
Chaney and these other angry coaches feel so strongly, I would like
to see them offer up some money from their shoe contracts to help
these poor kids go to school.)

But I digress. The bottom line is that Thompson had reason to 12
walk out. It is just not right to deny a teenager an education at, say,
a major state university, just because he can't afford it. That creates a
caste system based on wealth, and we should be trying to tear down
such structures, not create more.

As well, it is a fact that a majority of the students affected by Pro- 13
posal 42 would be black. The NCAA is not a racist organization, as
some (not Thompson) have suggested. But it is racially insensitive.
Proposal 42 demonstrates an alarming lack of understanding of the
plight of the black, disadvantaged athlete. Thompson apparently
was just too offended to stand by. Bully for him.

Obviously, Thompson hopes that boycotting Saturday night's 14
game will sustain dialogue on the proposal.

A KINDER, GENTLER RACISM
Mona Charen

When 6-foot-9-inch basketball star Kevin Ross played for Creighton 1
University in Omaha, Nebraska, he didn't know the score. Literally.
According to his lawyer, "Kevin couldn't even figure out what the
score of a game was. He just knew if they were ahead or behind."

Ross may have been an **aberration** among college athletes, but 2
the howls of protest over the National Collegiate Athletic Association's Proposal 42 make you wonder. Proposal 42 requires that athletes achieve a total of 700 (out of a possible 1,600) on the SAT and
a grade point average of 2.0 (C) to qualify for athletic scholarships.

Is that too **onerous** for institutions of higher learning? Former 3
Wimbledon [tennis] champion Arthur Ashe, a supporter of Proposal
42, notes that "they give you 400 points for just showing up and
spelling your name right."

---

altruism: selflessness, concern for others;   caste system: rigid classification
by social rank;   aberration: untypical occurrence, not the norm;   onerous:
burdensome, oppressive

But since blacks account for 52 percent of college basketball 4
players and 36 percent of football players, and since an uncounted
number of those athletes would have been ineligible under the
new standard, the NCAA has touched the ever-exposed racial
nerve.

"Prop. 42 is an elitist, racist **travesty**," says Harry Edwards, the 5
University of California professor who orchestrated the "black
power" salute at the 1968 Olympics in Mexico City.

But it was not just hotheads who reacted angrily. John Thomp- 6
son, coach of the Georgetown University basketball team and one of
the nation's finest coaches, walked off the court before a game
against Boston College to dramatize his contempt for Proposal 42,
which, he argues, rests upon a culturally biased test (the SAT) that
puts minorities at a disadvantage.

Dr. Frederick P. Whiddon, president of the University of South 7
Alabama and a member of the executive committee of the NCAA,
doesn't see it that way. "I know how the media will play this," he acknowledged. "I'm a white from Alabama going up against a black
[John Thompson] from Washington, D.C. Lots of people will assume
I'm a racist. But someone has got to say that these kids are being ex-
ploited. Seventy-five to 90 percent never graduate. Only one in
2,000 goes on to professional sports. Do you know what happens to
the rest? Most wind up in menial jobs or in no jobs at all, because
while they have attended college, they haven't been given the necessary skills to grasp firmly the first rung of the ladder."

Whiddon doesn't sound like a racist. Fourteen percent of his un- 8
dergraduates are minorities—and all, athletes included, are expected
to maintain passing grades or be flunked out. Athletes get special
help—reduced course loads and special tutors—but even stars have
been asked to leave if they failed their academic courses.

Is it fair to ask students from disadvantaged backgrounds to 9
achieve an arbitrary score of 700? Well, nationally, the average black
score is 737, and it's reasonable to ask why college-bound students
shouldn't score well above average. Besides, as Arthur Ashe argues,
those who cannot manage a combined SAT of 700 can always attend a junior college until they're adequately prepared for the academic big leagues.

The seduction of young athletes begins very early. Recruiters are 10
forbidden to approach high school players before the 10th grade,

---

travesty: exaggerated imitation intended to ridicule;

but it's an open secret that coaches get around that obstacle. Alumni and others fawn over the kids, assuring them that they're NBA or NFL material. By age 14, Chris Washburn, a star at North Carolina State before going pro, had received thousands of letters from colleges. On the day of the SAT exam, he signed his name and fell asleep.

Opponents of Proposal 42 see **insidious** racism in the attempt 11
to reinstitute standards. But **patronizing** black youngsters, telling them we don't *expect* them to perform as well as whites, is kinder, gentler racism.

In the movie *Stand and Deliver*, based on a true story, Jaime Es- 12
calante, a high school teacher in poor, Hispanic East Los Angeles, alarms his colleagues by teaching his students calculus. They are dismayed. The kids don't have the proper background, they protest. To ask something beyond their capabilities will destroy their self-esteem.

No, says Escalante. To expect too little destroys their self-esteem. 13
And, in the end, all of his students passed the Advanced Placement calculus test.

So who is being racist? Those who say blacks can't score 700, or 14
those who say they can?

THE IVY LEAGUE AT 30: A MODEL FOR COLLEGE ATHLETICS OR AN OUTMODED ANTIQUE?
Douglas Lederman

The Ivy League was officially born 30 years ago this fall, the product 1
of a protest movement by eight college presidents who were dismayed by the growing professionalism of intercollegiate athletics. To ensure the amateurism of their athletic programs, the league's members agreed to forbid athletic scholarships and admissions breaks for athletes, oppose freshman eligibility, shorten athletic seasons, and ban off-season practice.

Many scoffed at the arrangement then, and many cynics still do 2
today. But even its critics admit that the Ivy League has, with minor adjustments, stayed its original course and, in most cases, held true to its ideas.

That course, however, has led the Ivy League away from the 3
mainstream of big-time intercollegiate athletics, where its members once competed. Four years ago, the Ivy institutions were forced out of the National Collegiate Athletic Association's top level of play by new standards governing stadium size and minimum attendance.

---

insidious: harmful spreading;   patronizing: treating like a child

Such a demotion may have been inevitable, since even Ivy offi- 4
cials admit that the league's ability to compete successfully at a national level in the major revenue sports is a thing of the past. Beyond
the issue of competitiveness, however, observers both inside and outside the conference raise questions about what may lie ahead as the
Ivy League . . . continues to march somewhat out of step with other
college sports programs. Has the league's adherence to its principles—ideals shared by few other colleges that compete seriously in
sports—isolated its members? Can the Ivy League be a model for the
way intercollegiate athletics should be run, or is it just an **antiquated**
reminder of the way things once were? Will other colleges eventually
follow the Ivy League's lead, or will the competitive gap that already
exists simply continue to widen?

In the late 1940's and early 1950's, gambling scandals rocked 5
college basketball, and a case of academic fraud **decimated** the football team at the U.S. Military Academy. Commentators, citing esca-
lating competition and rapidly expanding stadiums, bemoaned the
burgeoning professionalism of major college sports. In response, the
NCAA adopted sweeping rules governing recruiting and financial aid
that became known as the "sanity code." The name suggested measures of desperation; the rules were abandoned as unworkable in a
vote by NCAA members.

Eight prestigious Northeastern institutions—Brown, Columbia, 6
Cornell, Harvard, Princeton, and Yale Universities, Dartmouth College, and the University of Pennsylvania—formulated their own response: a new confederation designed to make sure that
intercollegiate sports remained in their proper place. Although the
colleges had been playing each other in football for decades, the
1954 Ivy Group accord brought them together formally in all sports.
In the agreement, the presidents of the eight institutions insisted that
"players shall be truly representative of the student body and not
composed of specially recruited athletes. . . . In the total life of the
campus, emphasis upon intercollegiate competition must be kept in
harmony with the essential educational purposes of the institution."

The league adopted two major **tenets**: athletes would be admit- 7
ted under the same criteria as the rest of its students, and the colleges would provide financial aid based only on need.

---

antiquated: too old to be useful;   decimated: destroyed;
tenets: principles, doctrines

There has been some tinkering over 30 years: the restoration of   8
freshman eligibility in most sports, the lengthening of the football
season from 9 to 10 games, and a stricter system for monitoring admissions standards, in response to what Brown's president Howard
Swearer calls "some slippage" in such standards within the league in
the 1970's.

Recruiting has also changed. The Ivy colleges have intensified   9
their recruiting in an effort to keep pace with their peers in the league
and with other top colleges that offer athletic scholarships. "I think
we've been caught up in recruiting more than the founders would
have hoped," says Al Paul, the athletic director at Columbia, "but we
do it within our predetermined rules and regulations."

Some observers have questioned the purity of Ivy motives on   10
other issues, such as playing major powers like Penn State and the
firing of coaches who don't win enough games. But despite some
adaptations to keep up with the times, the Ivy League has clung
tenaciously to its guiding ideals, its officials say.

"The league's underlying principles from 30 years ago are still   11
our underlying principles today," says Columbia's Al Paul, "and we've
stuck to them even though we've been alone much of the time."

Recent examples of national prominence by Ivy teams have been   12
rare. Penn made the final four in men's basketball in 1979, Columbia
was national runner-up in men's soccer in 1982, and Harvard was
runner-up in the men's hockey championships in 1983 and 1986.
But Ivy teams have lost substantial ground in football and basketball.
"Our ability to compete in the major sports has surely gone down,"
says Mr. Paul. "Recruiting outside the league has gotten too intense."
"In the so-called major sports we found ourselves playing opponents
who were simply outclassing us on a regular basis," adds Joan S. Gir-
gus, dean of the college at Princeton and an Ivy League policy committee member. The Ivy teams have thus altered their goals. "We're
very happy shooting for the Ivy title."

Officials at the institutions most frequently compared to the Ivy   13
colleges in terms of balance between sports and academics—Duke,
Northwestern, Rice, Stanford, and Vanderbilt Universities, for example—admire the league but suggest that its situation is unique. Roy
Kramer, athletic director at Vanderbilt, says the Ivies' lack of dependence on income from sports is the single biggest difference between Vanderbilt and the Ivy colleges. "Because of the Ivy set-up,

---

tenaciously: persistently, stubbornly

those schools are in the enviable position of not having to worry about gate receipts to pay for athletics," he says. "But because of the region we're in and the people we play, we couldn't do that unless the entire mold of intercollegiate athletics changed."

Post-reading

As a way of beginning to examine this issue, return to the reading selections and list the following:

- The benefits of college athletic programs for (1) students and (2) the institution
- The negative aspects of college athletic programs for (1) students and (2) the institution

Additionally, think about the role of higher education and answer the following questions and explain the reasons for your responses:

- Should colleges focus solely on academics?
- Are universities appropriate training grounds for professional athletes?
- Should college athletes be forced to compete academically with other students or should they be on a separate track?
- Do separate academic tracks—one for athletes and one for other students—diminish the value of a college's degree?

Essay Assignment

Write an essay in which you discuss the role of athletics in colleges. You may conclude that certain reforms should be made and wish to recommend some. Or you may prefer to discuss the issue in general in order not to recommend reform but to shed light on this heated debate.

For more discussion of this issue and suggestions about organizing your essay, log on to http://devenglish.wadsworth.com.

Pre-writing

As you think about organizing your essay, remember these points:

1. Present adequate background to enable your readers to understand the importance and complexity of the issue.

2. Be sure to acknowledge the strengths, as well as the weaknesses, of the arguments you cite, including your own.

3. Remember that a statement is not an argument; a statement needs to be supported with facts and/or well-founded opinions in order to become an argument.

The section "Writing Discussion Essays" contains further ideas on structuring your essay. As you have in previous assignments, jot down a working thesis and outline.

Writing

Although you may feel strongly one way or the other on this issue, remember that there's no right or wrong answer. There are, however, stronger and weaker arguments. To compose the strongest one you can, keep an open mind while you write and use the most compelling support you can generate.

THE WRITER'S CHECKLIST

The Idea Draft

1. Does your idea draft *respond fully* to the assignment?
2. Are your ideas *organized* in the way you want?
3. Does your *introduction* explain what the essay will be about and what its purpose is?
4. Do you have a *thesis* that states your point or indicates the issue the essay will address?
5. Do the *body paragraphs* each have a *topic sentence*? Do they develop the main points by giving *specifics and examples* to support those points?
6. Does your *conclusion* state your belief about the issue, make a recommendation for change, or summarize your main points?
7. Have you *collaborated* with at least one trusted friend or fellow student who has read your draft *critically*, looking for lapses in logic or other weaknesses in content?

Sentence Combining

In revising your idea draft, keep in mind the possibility of using verbal phrases in a few of your sentences. Use your

sentence-combining exercises and the sentences below as
models for how you can use these structures:

In "High School Papers Grow Up," notice how Jerry
Carroll uses an end-of-sentence verbal phrase to tie together
two points instead of making two sentences of them:

> Written by Kathryn Pallokoff, 17, the article is a careful and responsi-
> ble account of the problem, <u>giving figures on the spread of the disease</u>
> <u>and warning of the importance of "safe sex."</u>

In "Censorship: A Fact of Life Students Are Forced to
Face," Jonathan Yardley writes a similar sentence and then
one in which he puts a verbal between the subject and verb
of his sentence; in the latter case, many writers would have
started the sentence with the verbal phrase instead:

> The majority quite specifically reaffirmed that broad principle,
> <u>qualifying it only by the observation . . . that a school need not</u>
> <u>tolerate student speech that is inconsistent with its "basic educational</u>
> <u>mission.".</u> . .

> The principal of Hazelwood High School, <u>in restricting the contents of</u>
> <u>an issue of *Spectrum*</u>, was attempting among other things to teach his
> journalism students a lesson about what is and is not a responsible ex-
> ercise of journalistic freedom.

In "The Ivy League at 30," Douglas Lederman shows a
common use of *to* verbal phrases:

> <u>To ensure the amateurism of their athletic programs</u>, the league's mem-
> bers agreed to forbid athletic scholarships and admissions breaks for
> athletes, oppose freshman eligibility, shorten athletic seasons, and ban
> off-season practice.

Later Drafts

1. Taking into account the constructive criticism you have received,
    have you *revised* accordingly—that is, reorganized, if organization
    was a problem, or given additional support, if support was?
2. Have you read your essay *aloud*, listening closely to what it *actually
    says*, not just what you think it says? (This is another good place to
    work with a trusted fellow student or friend. Have him or her read
    your essay aloud; both of you should listen closely to what it says.)
3. Have you *revised your sentences* if they seemed unclear or awkward
    as you read them aloud?

4. Have you checked for those *mechanical difficulties* that you know you sometimes have? Have you used the dictionary to check words that you think may be *misspelled*?

Final Draft

If you have followed this assignment step by step, you have worked exceedingly hard on this essay. Therefore, make sure your final draft reflects your care and effort; make it as professional looking as possible.

1. Type it neatly, using the format your instructor has assigned.
2. Proofread slowly and carefully, word by word, line by line. (One last time, ask a trusted friend to proofread it *after* you have, or exchange your essay with another student and proof each other's.)

*S*entence Combining

SHAPING SENTENCES TO SHOW RELATIONSHIPS: VERBAL PHRASES

You have already used two verb forms—*ing* and *have*—as noun modifiers. These same kinds of words plus one other verb form, the *base* form, are frequently used to combine ideas.

From your dictionary work and previous sentence-combining practice, you remember, of course, that all verbs have *base, -ing,* and *have* forms such as these:

base	-ing	have
walk	walking	walked
laugh	laughing	laughed
think	thinking	thought
take	taking	taken

You may also recall that the base form is often preceded by the word *to* (to walk, to laugh, and so on), and so we will call these *to* forms from now on. We use these *to* forms in many ways, as in the following example:

The road to take was supposed to be the one on the left.

But we use the *to* form in these ways automatically, without thinking about it. However, all three verb forms—*have, -ing,* and *to*—have a function that students do not automatically use them for, at least not as much as experienced writers do, and that is to join into one efficient sentence ideas that would otherwise be in two sentences. Here are examples using each of the three verb forms; the phrases made from these three verb forms, by the way, are called *verbal phrases*.

> **Two sentences:** The police were watching a drug dealer from the window of a second-floor apartment. They photographed him making a sale.
> **One sentence:** <u>Watching</u> a drug dealer from the window of a second-floor apartment, the police photographed him making a sale.
>
> **Two sentences:** The children were enchanted by the Christmas play. They shrieked and laughed throughout.
> **One sentence:** <u>Enchanted</u> by the Christmas play, the children shrieked and laughed throughout.
>
> **Two sentences:** I wanted to help my roommate get an A on a crucial midterm. I stayed up half the night working with her on her math.
> **One sentence:** <u>To help</u> my roommate get an A on a crucial midterm, I stayed up half the night working with her on her math.

The *to* form of the verb used this way can also be preceded by the words *in order*. Whether or not you use *in order* makes no difference to the meaning of the *to* phrase or of the sentence; the use of *in order* is purely a stylistic option open to the writer. The following two sentences mean exactly the same thing:

> To get the car started, you have to turn the key and smack the dashboard simultaneously.
>
> In order to get the car started, you have to turn the key and smack the dashboard simultaneously.

One other option you need to be aware of is that you can also end sentences with these kinds of verbal phrases. There is no law that says they always have to come at the beginning. In fact, it has been shown statistically that published writers use them at the ends of sentences more than they do at the beginnings.

Finally, it is important to remember that although these verbal phrases don't actually have subjects, there must be in the sentence a word that tells the reader what you mean their subjects to be and that word is usually the subject of the sentence. Look at this example:

> Singing loudly, John walked into the side of a truck.

Who is singing loudly? John, of course, the subject of the sentence. Now look at this example:

> Singing loudly, a truck ran over John.

This doesn't work because we know that trucks can't sing. The same rule holds when the verbal phrase comes at the end of the sentence, as here:

> I walked through the forest, observing the birds and the bees. (This works because I, the subject, am doing the observing.)

> The forest was a pleasure to stroll through, observing the birds and the bees. (This doesn't work very well because there is no word in the sentence to tell who is doing the observing, and the subject, *forest*, cannot be the observer.)

EXERCISE

In the exercise below, make the second sentence in each pair into a verbal phrase attached to either the beginning or the end of the first sentence. In deciding where to place the phrase, test the sound of the sentence first; sometimes a phrase will work equally well at the beginning or the end, and sometimes it will not. In the first five exercises, the verbal phrases are underlined to help you. Example:

> Mary saved her money.
> She wanted to buy a new guitar.
> **Solution:** To buy a new guitar, Mary saved her money.
> > Or:
> > Mary saved her money to buy a new guitar.

A note on punctuation: We normally set off all three of the verbal phrases with a comma when they come at the beginning of the sentence, and we normally set off the *-ing* and *have* forms with a comma when they come at the end of the sentence. But, for no particular reason, writers usually do not set off sentence-ending *to* phrases. As always, the rule is, when in doubt about whether to use a comma, don't.

A Day in the Country

1. John and Mary planned to leave at 8:30 in the morning.
   They were hoping to get a good spot at the picnic grounds.
2. They made trip after trip from the house to the car.
   They were loaded down with things they simply couldn't leave behind.
3. They finally had to leave behind their bicycles and Schnoz, their pet anteater.
   They wanted to get the car doors closed.
4. The car developed a flat tire.

The car was <u>packed</u> to the ceiling with every manner of picnic and camping gear.

5. Mary unloaded some of the supplies.

   She was <u>muttering</u> some phrases she should not have muttered.

6. John finally got the tire replaced.

   He was burdened with a great ignorance about spare tires.

7. They decided to take a shortcut down a back road.

   They wanted to save some time.

8. They saw no identifiable landmarks.

   They were pausing finally to get their bearings.

9. The ants at the picnic grounds were getting edgy and irritable.

   They were waiting for John and Mary to show up.

10. Schnoz had given them some crumbs of information about the picnic.

    He wanted to get even for having been left at home.

EXERCISE

In the following exercise, you will practice two new aspects of verbal phrase use. One is placement. Verbal phrases may introduce sentences or they may end sentences. Normally, we use them to introduce sentences when they provide background to the main idea of the sentence:

> Mary had decided to throw a big party. (background)
> She began to make a list of possible guests. (main idea)

> Having decided to throw a big party, Mary began to make a list of possible guests.

On the other hand, when the verbal phrase *develops* the idea of the main sentence, we usually put it at the end. This is where you will find most verbal phrases in the work of professional writers.

> Mary began to make a list of possible guests. (main idea)
> She first wrote down the names of her closest friends. (development)

> Mary began to make a list of possible guests, first writing down the names of her closest friends.

The second aspect of verbal phrase use you will practice here is using more than one verbal at the ends of sentences in order to develop the idea as completely as possible:

> Mary began to make a list of possible guests. (main idea)
> She first wrote down the names of her closest friends.

She next noted people she couldn't stand.
She finally considered the borderline group.

Mary began to make a list of possible guests, first writing down the names of her closest friends, next noting people she couldn't stand, and finally considering the borderline group.

In these exercises, the main-idea sentence is always the first one. In the first five, the sentences to be turned into verbal phrases have been identified as background or development.

The Movie Critic

1. John decided to become a movie critic.

   He was watching two movie critics on a television show one night. (background)

2. He began to go to the movies four or five times a week.

   He wanted to polish up his critical skills. (background)

3. He invited Mary to come with him.

   He thought she would be a good audience for his criticism. (development)

4. She was happy to go to the movies with him.

   She thought John was really getting interested in her. (background)

5. She began to grow tired of these dates.

   She was seeing movies she hated. (development)

   She was listening to John's stupid comments about them. (development)

   She was losing a lot of study time. (development)

6. She began to turn down John's movie invitations.

   She pretended she had a headache.

   Or she said she had too much work to do.

7. She wondered why he didn't want to do anything but see movies.

   She was thinking about John's peculiar new dating pattern.

8. She began quizzing him about all these movie dates.

   She wanted to find out what he was up to.

9. When she found out that he just wanted an audience for his dopey practice criticism, she hit the ceiling.

   She realized that he was just taking advantage of their friendship.

10. Then she gave him a good lesson in constructive criticism.

    She told him what an insensitive clod he was.

    She made him understand how she felt.

EXERCISE

One last point having to do with verbal phrases. Frequently, we will put prepositions in front of *-ing* verbals in order to make our intended meaning clearer. For instance, instead of writing this:

Having considered all the pros and cons, John decided to buy a new car rather than a used one.

we could write this:

<u>After</u> having considered all the pros and cons, John decided to buy a new car rather than a used one.

Similarly, this:

Working out every day, I feel a lot better.

could become this:

<u>By</u> working out every day, I feel a lot better.

Or this:

John grew sleepy doing his homework.

could become one of these:

John grew sleepy <u>while</u> doing his homework.
John grew sleepy <u>when</u> doing his homework.

Try adding prepositions in as many of the following sentences as you can, but don't feel that you have to add a preposition in every case. Some phrases will sound better without one. Remember that you can add a preposition only if you are working with an *-ing* verb form.

Be sure to consider carefully whether the verbal phrases are background or development so you know whether to put them at the beginning or the end of the sentences. In each of these sentences, *the main idea is in the first sentence.*

The Concept of Tribute

1. Glenisha discovered some interesting new ways to make money.
   Glenisha took a course in ancient history.

2. She discovered the concept of tribute.

   She pored over her history texts.

3. She considered how to produce sufficient gratitude.

   She realized that her boyfriend, Raymont, wasn't sufficiently grateful to her to pay tribute.

4. She decided not to see him for three weeks.

   She wanted to produce some gratitude.

5. Raymont tried everything to get in touch with her.

   He called.

   He rang her doorbell.

   He sent messages via her roommate.

   He slid notes under the door.

   He sent a telegram.

6. Glenisha called him up.

   She began to note a certain desperation in his messages.

   She felt he was achieving the proper state of gratitude.

7. She told him that she now required one movie and one dinner each week in exchange for the pleasure of her company.

   She explained the concept of tribute.

8. Raymont began to study ancient history.

   He wanted to learn how to handle the tribute problem.

9. He called up Glenisha right away.

   He discovered that ancient peoples avoided tribute by developing new allies.

10. He told her that he had developed a new ally, Joanne.

    He explained that the concept of shortness of funds was more powerful than the concept of tribute.

REVIEW

In the following exercises, you will practice using everything you have studied so far by combining each group of sentences into a single sentence.

The Original Olympics

1. The citizens of Elis decided to add contests to their celebrations.

   They wanted to honor Zeus.

   Zeus was the foremost of the gods of ancient Greece.

   Elis was a small Greek city-state.

The contests were athletic.

The celebrations were religious.

2. These celebrations were held in a place and were run by the citizens of that city.

The place was called Olympia.

Olympia was a holy site near Elis.

It was dedicated to Zeus.

The citizens served as judges of the contests.

3. The Olympic games lasted for more than a thousand years.

They began in 776 B.C.

They were held every four years.

They ended when a Christian ruler stamped them out.

4. The games began as part of a celebration.

The celebration was small.

The celebration was local.

[join]

They soon grew into the most important sports event of ancient times.

They attracted athletes.

They attracted spectators.

The athletes were the greatest.

The athletes were from the whole Mediterranean area.

The spectators were numerous.

5. Spectators had to endure poor living conditions.

Spectators wished to attend the games.

The living conditions were no housing.

They were little water.

They were no sanitation facilities.

The water was for drinking or bathing.

[join]

The men were willing to make almost any sacrifice to attend.

The men were the wealthiest.

The men were of that time.

6. The games were open only to men, and the ranks of spectators were closed to women.

The men competed naked.

The women were married.

The women could be executed if caught there.

7. Chariot races usually opened the games.

   The races were violent affairs.

   They were filled with accidents and injuries.

   They attracted the attention of the spectators.

8. Besides chariot and horse racing, the contests included wrestling and boxing, the pancratium, and the pentathlon.

   The pentathlon was a mixture of five sports.

   The five sports were the long jump.

   They were the discus throw.

   They were the javelin throw.

   They were a foot race.

   They were wrestling.

9. Today we think of the Greeks as a people.

   They loved philosophy.

   They loved poetry.

   They loved science.

   [join]

   The pancratium was a fight.

   The pancratium was the favorite event of the spectators.

   The pancratium was the bloodiest of the Olympic contests.

   The fight was to the finish.

   The fight was between two contestants.

   The two contestants were punching.

   They were kicking.

   They were wrestling.

   They were strangling.

   They were biting.

   They were gouging each other.

   They did these things until one gave up, was knocked out, or died.

10. Contestants sometimes resorted to bribery, for all honors went to the winners, and nothing went to the losers.

    The contestants wanted to win in the Olympics.

    The contestants were desperate.

    The winners were glorious.

    The winners were often given great sums of money and even lifetime pensions by the citizens of their cities.

    The losers were miserable.

    The losers were jeered and treated with scorn, even by their own families.

Hobbyists

1. We tend to associate people mostly with their jobs.
    [join]
    An aspect of human behavior is the ways.
    The aspect is fascinating.
    People choose to entertain themselves in these ways.
    They entertain themselves in their spare time.
2. Of course, most people do things.
    The things are obvious.
    The things are watching television.
    The things are going to the movies.
    The things are reading.
    [join]
    Some choose other forms of entertainment.
    These forms are more active.
    This entertainment is some hobby to get involved in.
3. Interestingly, women tend to find ways of amusing themselves.
    These ways can be seen as useful.
    They are tending a garden.
    They are knitting.
    They are working for organizations.
    The organizations help needy people.
4. Men most often get involved in hobbies.
    They want to entertain themselves in their odd hours.
    The hobbies are much more like play.
    They are collecting stamps.
    They are building model ships or trains.
    They are playing golf.
    They are making pointless improvements on their cars.
5. Most men get a large part of their self-esteem from their work.
    [join]
    Many men can't wait to get home.
    They are bored with jobs.
    The jobs are dreary.
    The jobs keep them locked in offices all day.
    There they can escape into worlds of their own creation.
6. The model railroader might spend an entire evening.

The model railroader is dedicated.

He is trying to get effects on a boxcar.

The boxcar is miniature.

The effects are just the right ones.

The effects are of rust, dust, and mud.

7. The model shipbuilder will happily put in hours.

He is fascinated by the beauty of rigging and sails.

He will be studying ships-of-the-line of the mid-eighteenth century.

The ships are British.

8. A group of people are the ones.

The group is particularly interesting.

They play war games.

The games are usually recreations of famous battles of the past.

9. The wargamers will spend hours or even weeks.

They are slurping their beer or their soft drinks.

They are refighting a battle.

The battle is between the French and the Austrians in 1797. Or the battle is between the North and the South in 1864.

10. The hobbyist might seem to be wasting time.

The hobbyist is busy.

The hobbyist is living in his fantasy world.

The time is valuable.

[join]

The hobbyist is a man or a woman.

The man or woman is happy.

The man or woman is bothering no one.

SHAPING SENTENCES TO SHOW RELATIONSHIPS: PARALLELISM

Three of the FANBOYS words, the coordinators, can join parts of sentences: *and, or,* and *but.* The one we use most frequently is *and.* When we use one of these words to join sentence parts, we have to make sure that the parts they join are alike, that they are grammatically similar. Here are some common examples; the sentence parts being joined have been underlined:

John and Mary didn't know what to do on their day off.

They liked to walk but didn't feel like hiking.

They considered going to a movie or driving out of town.

Because the sentence parts being joined are like one another, they are said to be in parallel with each other, and the joining of such structures with *and, or,* or *but* is called parallelism.

In the exercises below, you will be given pairs of sentences. In each case, you should find the parallel structures within each pair of sentences and join them using *and, or,* or *but.* You can tell what the parallel structures are by eliminating repetition of words in the sentence pairs, as in these examples:

> She bought a dog.
> ~~She bought~~ a cat.
> **Solution:** She bought a dog and a cat.

> He rowed his boat up the creek.
> ~~He~~ tied it to a tree.
> **Solution:** He rowed his boat up the creek and tied it to a tree.

> John hates television.
> Mary ~~hates television~~.
> **Solution:** John and Mary hate television.

> She bought her house with her savings.
> ~~She bought her house with~~ money she made on her book.
> **Solution:** She bought her house with her savings and money she made on her book.

Notice that in these examples, no comma has been used before the coordinators. Normally, we use the comma only when the coordinator joins two complete sentences, rather than parts of sentences.

EXERCISE

In the following pairs of sentences, the word *and, or,* or *but* in parentheses follows the first sentence to tell you which word to use in creating the parallel structures.

Maria Makes a Decision

1. Maria was looking for part-time work as a secretary. (or)
   She was looking for part-time work as a receptionist.
2. She hoped for a good job. (but)
   She found a bad one.
3. She worked for a fast-food outlet serving gristly hamburgers. (and)
   She worked for a fast-food outlet serving greasy fries.

4. The hamburgers were tasteless. (but)
   The hamburgers were cheap.
5. The employees were overworked. (and)
   They were underpaid.
6. All of them were fed up with the low pay. (and)
   They were fed up with the poor working conditions.
7. Maria disliked the work. (but)
   She made several friends on that job.
8. One of her friends, Martha, was saving to go to college. (and)
   She was saving to buy a used car.
9. Martha hoped to get a scholarship. (or)
   She hoped to get a student loan.
10. Discouraged by her job, Maria decided to return to school. (and)
    She decided to pursue a major in engineering.

Parallelism in Series

As you know, we often join three or more elements in sentences with coordinators, particularly with *and*. In these cases, the basic rule of parallelism still holds: All of the elements being joined should usually be *similar* grammatically, as in these examples:

I took French, history, math, and psychology.
Mary, John, and I went to see a play.
She got a loan, a scholarship, and a cash award from a large company.

You will notice that in the first example, the elements in the series are all the same, all nouns naming a school subject. In the second example, the elements are not quite the same; they all indicate people, which is the main thing, but one is a pronoun rather than a noun. In the third example, the first two elements are simple nouns without modifiers, but the third noun has a lot of modifiers.

There is no problem with that. The only important thing is that all of the elements are nouns; the nouns may or may not have modifiers, as you wish. The same is true for verbs in parallel; it makes no difference what the forms of the different verbs are or what kinds of words follow them so long as all the verbs will work with the same subject. Here is a sentence with a string of nouns that are parallel despite the differences in how the nouns are modified:

Under the Christmas tree, the children found
  three books for each of them,

a <u>tricycle</u>,

an incredible new <u>doll</u> with a vocabulary of 200 words,

and a <u>train</u> that made sounds like the real thing.

Here is a sentence with a string of verbs that are parallel despite the different forms of the verbs and the different kinds of structures following them:

By the end of the day, John

<u>had seen</u> his car destroyed,

<u>had been taken</u> to the hospital for X-rays, which turned out negative,

<u>was</u> two hundred dollars poorer,

and <u>wished</u> he had stayed in bed.

You should notice also that when we join three or more elements in a parallel series, we put commas between all of them, including one before the coordinator.

EXERCISE

Combine the following groups of sentences to make parallel series of two, three, or four elements. In some cases, you will also have to join complete sentences with coordinators or subordinators.

A Day at the Mall

1. John went to a shopping mall.
   Mary went to a shopping mall. (and)
   Uncle Fred went to a shopping mall.
2. They hoped to buy a few clothes.
   They hoped to have a good lunch. (and)
   They hoped to see what was what.
3. John was looking for a light sweater. (or)
   He was looking for a new shirt in the latest style.
4. Mary wanted a silk blouse. (and)
   She wanted some earrings.
5. Uncle Fred hoped to find a rich widow.
   He hoped to find a wealthy divorcee. (or)
   He hoped to find a cute teenager looking for a good time.
6. John did not like the sweaters he saw. (and)
   He did not like the shirts he saw.

He was tempted to spend a lot of money on some shoes he didn't need.

7. Mary looked at a lot of blouses. (but)

She didn't like any of them.

None were cut in the style she wanted.

8. Uncle Fred approached widows.

He stopped divorcees. (and)

He accosted cute teenagers who seemed to be looking for a good time.

None would have anything to do with him.

Several threatened to call the police.

9. By the end of the day, John had not found a sweater he liked. (or)

He had not found a shirt he liked.

Someone had stolen his shoes.

He was trying on the ones he didn't need.

10. Mary had had enough of the mall.

She had had enough of John. (and)

She had had enough of looking at silk blouses.

She had absolutely had enough of Uncle Fred.

11. Uncle Fred was marching off to the car unhappy. (and)

He was marching off to the car displeased with the day.

12. Instead of a pretty widow, he had a sheriff's deputy on one arm. (and)

Instead of an attractive divorcee, he had a city police officer on the other.

Instead of a cute teenager, a state police officer was following him with a stern look on his face.

REVIEW

In the following exercises, you will practice using all the sentence-combining skills you have studied so far.

The Story of Pepper

1. Pepper originally came from Malabar.

It also came from Sumatra.

Pepper is the fruit of a vine.

The fruit is dried.

The vine is called *Piper nigrum*.

Malabar is a coastal region of India.

Sumatra is the second largest island of Indonesia.

2. Now it comes from five nations.

It comes from India.

It comes from Indonesia.

It comes from Malaysia.

It comes from Sri Lanka.

It comes from Brazil.

These nations have joined to form the International Pepper Community.

3. Pepper is made by picking peppercorns.

   The pepper is black.

   The peppercorns are green.

   It is made by leaving them in the sun to dry.

   Pepper is made by letting the peppercorns dry even longer.

   The pepper is white.

   It is made by washing the husks from the peppercorns.

   The husks are dried.

   The peppercorns are black.

4. We take pepper for granted now.

   It used to be a commodity.

   It was one of the rarest commodities.

   It was one of the most expensive commodities.

   It was one of the most prized commodities.

   The commodities were in the Western world.

5. The ancient Greeks loved pepper.

   The Romans loved pepper.

   The Romans learned where it came from.

   They established trade routes.

   The routes were between the Red Sea and the Malabar Coast.

6. They were interested in pepper.

   They were also interested in other goods.

   The goods were rare.

   The goods were from the East.

   The goods were cloves.

   The goods were nutmeg.

   The goods were cinnamon.

   The goods were pearls.

   The goods were ivory.

7. Alaric captured Rome in 408 A.D.

   Alaric was king of the Visigoths.

He demanded a ransom.

The ransom consisted partly of gold.

The ransom consisted partly of silver.

The ransom consisted partly of three thousand pounds of pepper.

8. In 1101 the army of Genoa won a great victory.

Genoa is an Italian city.

Each soldier was rewarded with two pounds of pepper.

Around this time, peppercorns were even used as currency.

The currency was between individuals and cities.

9. The explorers were seeking pepper.

The explorers were seeking the other spices.

The explorers undertook voyages into uncharted seas.

The explorers undertook voyages to unknown lands.

The explorers were great Europeans.

They were men like Columbus, Magellan, da Gama, and Cabot.

10. Explorers discovered plants.

The discovery was in the New World.

The plants produce effects.

The effects are pepperish.

The plants are paprika.

The plants are cayenne.

The plants are jalapeño peppers.

These are unrelated to true pepper.

They were considered inferior by the Europeans.

11. Pepper is so common now.

We scarcely think of it.

It was once almost as valuable as gold.

Language of the Eyes

1. Humans communicate through speech.

They also communicate through writing.

They also communicate in other ways.

The other ways are nonverbal.

The nonverbal ways are through posture.

They are through gestures.

They are through facial expressions.

They are through clothing.

2. One of our most important means of communication is governed by a set of rules.

   The means is the language of the eyes.

   The rules are fairly complex.

   We learn the rules without realizing it.

3. "Eye language" varies according to a number of criteria.

   One criterion is sex.

   Another is social class.

   Another is ethnic or national background.

   Another is even regions within countries.

4. Most Americans are looking at other people.

   They are governed by one basic rule.

   That rule is we stare at objects.

   We do not stare at people.

5. Americans want to be polite when meeting a new person.

   They practice the "look-and-look-away" stare.

   This stare says that we recognize the existence of the person.

   We do not consider him or her an object.

6. An American male stares at another American male.

   The one will usually interpret the look.

   The one is being stared at.

   The look is the starer's.

   He will interpret it as being hostile or sexual.

   He sees himself as being turned into an object.

7. A male stares at an American female.

   She may also resent the stare.

   She will do so for the same reason.

8. But it is not considered rude for a man to look closely at the parts of a woman's body.

   This is in France.

   It is in Italy.

   It is in Mexico.

   It is in many other countries also.

   The parts of her body are her shoulders.

   They are her arms.

   They are her breasts.

   They are her hips.

   They are her legs.

9. American women are usually embarrassed by this kind of examination.

   They are new to such countries.

   The examination is close.

   The examination is of their bodies.

   French, Italian, and Mexican women are accustomed to it.

   They expect it.

10. Americans like to be looked at.

   It shows that we are interesting or attractive.

   Most of us don't like to be looked at too much.

CHAPTER 7

Writing the In-Class Essay

Rarely, if ever, in "real" life will you be asked to write an extended piece of prose on the spur of the moment, especially on a topic you haven't had time to think about at some length. True, your boss may want you to whip out a last-minute report, so you may have to write feverishly for a few hours to meet her deadline. But, because it is the "stuff" of your job, you will have thought about the material you are dealing with and therefore have plenty to say in a report. Consequently, organization will be your first concern, then revision, and finally proofreading.

In college, however, you are occasionally presented with in-class writing assignments. This chapter will focus on the two most common ones—the essay exam and the writing test.

THE ESSAY EXAM

Frequently, an instructor will assign an in-class essay exam in order to test your knowledge and understanding of the subject matter of the course. The following assignments might sound familiar: "Write an essay in which you discuss the major causes of the Revolutionary War," or "Based on what we have discussed about the major theories of gender role development, write an essay in which you make predictions about the personality traits of children raised by a single father."

447

As in "real" life, these assignments ought not to hit you cold, since you will have spent class and study time discussing, thinking, and reading about the topics. Therefore, as long as you have studied the material, your job should be fairly straightforward although made somewhat stressful given the time constraints.

Don't, however, let those constraints panic you. Approach in-class essay assignments as you do any other writing task.

1. Read the question *carefully*, noting what *exactly* the instructor is asking for. If the question asks for the main causes of the Revolutionary War, then what are they? (Do not get sidetracked by the minor causes, although you may want to mention them in passing—in your introduction, for example.) If your instructor wants you to exhibit your knowledge of the major theories of gender role development and how they relate to the development of certain characteristics in a particular situation, focus on those two aspects of the course work. *Whatever the assignment, make sure you understand what the instructor is asking you to write about.*

2. Jot down on scrap paper or in your examination book the main points your essay will address: the several main causes of the war or the major theories and the personality characteristics of children raised by a single father, to continue with our examples.

3. Decide in what order you are going to discuss the points and number them. You may, for example, want to give the most important cause of the war first or start with the most important theory.

4. Look at what you've written down and compose a thesis that states your points and indicates the problem (the assignment) your essay will address.

What you've got now is a rough idea draft, and that's probably all you'll have time to do with the in-class idea draft. However, ask yourself the same kinds of questions you do when you're writing an essay outside of class; use the same kind of Writer's Checklist.

- Does this idea draft *respond fully* to the assignment?
- Are the ideas *organized* in a way that makes sense?
- Does the *thesis* point clearly to the direction the essay will take?

When you have adequately addressed these questions, it's time to write a working draft.

1. Using your rough idea draft as a guide, write your essay, making sure you cite examples and specifics from your textbook, lectures, and discussion notes to support your points. When you have written all that you want to say, STOP. Don't fret about a rhetorically brilliant conclusion at this

point. (One small piece of advice that you will appreciate when you begin to revise: Write on every other line, unless the instructions say you should not.)

2.   After you've finished your essay, go back and read over it slowly and carefully, thinking about the ideas it presents and noting any places where the writing makes you stop or is confusing. (Because you have to write exam essays without benefit of other readers, you have to become "another reader," as best you can, and read your essay with as much distance as possible, as though it were someone else's essay.)

3.   When you've finished reading the whole thing, go back and revise, fixing up confusing sentences, adding words that got left out, crossing out a part that may not belong, and so on.

4.   Now is the time to double-check your conclusion. You've got a "working" draft just about ready to submit, so does it need a more complete conclusion? Would a brief restatement of the main causes of the war wrap it up more effectively? If so, go ahead and write a short, concluding paragraph. However, if you think the essay has done its job in responding to the assignment and ends appropriately, write no more.

5.   One last task, if you have time: Read the essay once more, looking for spelling and mechanical errors that you know you sometimes make. This is the proofreading part of the process. When you've done this, turn the essay in.

THE WRITING TEST

Sometimes in-class essay assignments are designed not to test your knowledge of course material but to test your ability to write, period. Sometimes these serve as "exit exams" from particular writing courses (Freshman English, for example) or, more alarmingly, as a graduation requirement; both have to be dealt with successfully.

The only way they differ from the essay exam discussed above is that frequently the question asks you to write about a topic you've given no thought to. You have to think about the topic, then, on the spur of the moment.

Again, do not panic. Just take a piece of notepaper and start thinking— *in words, on paper*—about the assignment. Here's an example of the kind of question used often in such an exam.

Write an essay in response to the following question:
Who is an historical figure you admire and why?

Okay, think historical figures and jot down a few names such as Marie Curie, Martin Luther King, Jr., Eleanor Roosevelt, Babe Ruth, Julius Caesar, and so on. The very fact that these names enter your mind suggests that the people have meaning for you, and, consequently, you probably have something to say about why they do. Then quickly ask yourself which one you admire most (which one you have the most ideas about) and jot those ideas down. Now that you've got a topic and few ideas about it, go back to the section in this chapter on the idea draft and follow the steps outlined.

One last word about the writing test: These questions are usually designed so that many students with different backgrounds and experiences can respond to the topic. They tend to be, therefore, quite broad. Your job is to find a specific topic you know something about as quickly as possible and write an essay. Do not worry about a "right" answer. Just respond as thoughtfully as possible—and be relieved that this exercise is unlikely to be repeated in your professional life. But, in case it is, you know how to approach the writing test.

PLANNING YOUR TIME

In both writing tests and essay exams, part of what is being tested is your ability to plan your time. Here's a possible formula, but one to be modified as appropriate.

- One-quarter of your time for planning your idea draft and writing a thesis.
- Half of your allotted time for writing the essay.
- A quarter of the time for revising and proofreading.

Remember what you have learned about beginning to write any essay. *Do not just leap in and start writing.* Calmly think about the topic; jot down ideas, examples, and thoughts. Ask yourself questions about the topic. Thoughtfully organize your idea draft as you would if it were an assignment to write outside of class, and then start writing the draft. If you schedule your time wisely, you will have plenty of time to reread your essay and make whatever revision or editing is necessary.

Despite its added pressure, the in-class essay exam is still just an essay assignment, so the effective writing habits you have learned from this text will work for you in this situation, too.

PART III

Proofreading Skills Workbook

*There are three rules for writing well.
Unfortunately, no one knows what
they are.*

W. Somerset Maugham

INTRODUCTION

Grammar versus Usage

This part of your book contains rules, explanations, and exercises in many common matters of English usage. Usage is not the same as grammar. While every native speaker of English has a full command of its grammar, many of us are a little shakier when it comes to usage. Usage covers, for the most part, rules that apply only to *written* English—not to the spoken language: spelling words correctly, for instance, or using apostrophes. Fortunately, we don't have to worry about spelling or apostrophes when we speak.

What, Me Worry?

Many students size up usage issues in the following ways:

1. They are a pain in the neck—no more, no less.
2. They are the picky stuff that only English teachers care about.
3. They will drive you crazy if you worry about them (so it's better not to worry about them).
4. Finally, they have nothing to do with expressing your ideas.

Point 4 is correct, and point 1 is mostly correct, but the other two points are mistakes, and they can cost you.

Suppose you are the manager of a large business and you are planning to hire someone to an executive position. One of the application letters you get is full of spelling errors and other kinds of obvious mistakes in English. Are you going to hire that person?

Most English teachers know that usage issues have nothing to do with how well you express yourself, but they also know that to everyone else, usage errors are the most important part of writing. A letter or a memo full of errors in usage says to most of the world that the writer is sloppy, incapable, or, even worse—stupid. The moral is that usage may drive you crazy, but you'd better worry about it anyway.

Since people differ quite a bit from one another in which rules of written usage they know and which ones they don't, the first thing you will find in this section is a little quiz designed to help you and your teacher find out whether you have any weaknesses in common matters of usage and, if so, what they are. Then you can work on just your problems without having to plod through exercises on matters you already know.

In most cases, the following materials are designed so that you can work on them outside of class on your own. When you have worked through a particular usage lesson, you will then know the rules governing it, and when you have done the exercises correctly, you will have shown that you know how to apply the rules. But—and this is a big "but"—reading rules and doing exercises do not automatically translate into handling these usage issues correctly forever more.

Learning versus Doing

When you find out that you have a particular usage problem—say, your subjects and verbs don't agree often enough or you tend to leave *-ed* endings off verbs—you can be sure of one thing: You've been practicing doing it the wrong way for years. Every time you've made the mistake, whether you've had the mistake pointed out to you or not, you've gotten more practice in doing it wrong. That probably adds up to a lot of practice. Doing a couple of sets of exercises in which you do it the right way can't compare with all that previous practice in doing it wrong. So even when you learn the right way, you'll still do it the wrong way unless you make a big effort to overcome all that negative practice.

When to Worry—and When Not to Worry

But make the effort when you're proofreading, not when you're writing. If you get all hung up on questions of usage when you try to write, it really will drive you crazy, and you won't write well. Remember what you learned about writing in drafts, and proofread for your own usage problems in your final draft. Keep handy a list of just those usage errors you are likely to make, and proofread for each one of them separately (or two at a time, at the most). Gradually, you will get to the point where your positive practice will start to outweigh your negative practice, and then you'll start handling most of your usage issues well almost automatically.

PROOFREADING QUIZ

Part I

Correct any punctuation errors you find in the following sentences. If any of your punctuation changes require that you change a capital letter to a small one or vice versa, make those changes also. Some of the sentences may be correct.

1. Joanne bought an expensive car. Although she had recently quit her job.

2. When her husband found out about it, he was furious.

3. She reminded him of the extravagant stereo he had bought recently, it was much more powerful than they needed or could use.

4. He replied that they could both enjoy the stereo. While only she could enjoy her car.

5. He didn't know that she hated the stereo. A fact he was soon to find out.

6. When the dust finally settled, he had returned the stereo, Joanne still had the car.

7. Their marriage was saved, even though they still had a car they couldn't afford.

8. There are only a few problems I can't handle. The worst being my finances.

9. Money comes into my life in small quantities, however it leaves in large ones.

10. There seems to be nothing I can do about this, it just seems to be a characteristic of mine.

11. I took a course entitled "Love Your Money." Thinking that if I loved it more, I'd hang on to it longer.

12. That helped for a little while, then I just returned to my old habits.

13. I'd like to get this problem under control. Because it is getting me into serious financial difficulties.

14. I might be in trouble right now, I just got a bank statement today and it looks pretty bad. My savings having fallen to an all-time low.

15. The situation looks pretty serious, therefore I think I'd better do something about it.

Part II

Each of the sentences below contains one verb, together with its subject. If the verb is correct, write C in the blank at the end of the sentence. If the verb is incorrect, write the correct verb form in the blank.

Example:

a. John bit the cow.   _____**C**_____

b. There are a tavern in the town.   _____**is**_____

1. My friends and I loves to travel.   _____

2. There is only a few places in the country still unvisited by us.   _____

3. Some of my best friends like to travel too.   _____

4. One of them prefer to stay home, however. _____

5. Each of them have individual preferences. _____

6. A study of several thousand very experienced travelers show some interesting results. _____

7. There's a great many wealthy people among them. _____

8. But the wealthiest ones in the study has not always traveled more than the others. _____

9. The results of the study were of value to the travel industry. _____

10. The basis of many of our problems, especially the big ones, are our ways of approaching them. _____

11. Sheila and Mary hates to be late to parties. _____

12. Working short hours and earning a good salary are my main requirement in life. _____

Part III

Carefully proofread the following sentences, correcting the mistakes. Some sentences may contain more than one error.

1. Its a bad idea to go grocery shopping when your hungry.

2. The cat stuck its claws into my leg, and it was to painful for words.

3. There are many things people can do to make there lives worse than they have to be, and to often these are exactly the things that they do.

4. When you know who's seat you have taken, you will know who's going to be on you're case.

5. The dog took it's time getting into there truck; it was to lazy to hurry.

6. I can't stand the mess in my two sisters rooms.

7. The new father hated to change his babies diaper, so he was glad his wife didn't have twins.

8. In north america we mostly speak english, but central americas dominant language is spanish.

9. I had planned to take history 301, but since I had already signed up for another history class, I decided to take calculus instead.

10. The president of the united states is also the commander-in-chief of the armed forces, though, of course, he isn't actually a general.

11. I am use to getting good grades, but I know that college is a lot harder than valley view high school.

12. When I was in high school, I knew I was suppose to study, but I often didn't.

13. When they were juniors, several friends of mine drop out because they hate to do the assign work.

14. They had never realize the importance of school to one's future.

15. Of all those in my group, only me and John Williams graduated.

16. They tell you that anyone who doesn't at least get a high school diploma will never get a good job; they might as well forget it.

17. A person who drops out won't be able to compete in the job market; they will have to turn to crime or just stay poor.

18. High school didn't mean much to John and I, but we stuck with it.

Part IV

In the blanks in the following sentences, write the correct form of the verb indicated. (In some cases, you will have to add *has, have,* or *had.*)

1. By the time Maria got there, her friends_____(leave).

2. Last week, I_____(forget) my assignment when I_____ (leave) home for school.

3. For the past three years, I_____(jog) three miles every morning.

4. The plane crashed simply because the pilots_____(forget) to adjust the wing flaps properly.

5. We_____(do) it that way for as long as I can remember.

6. Since Maureen was a child, she_____(act) that way.

7. When you_____(buy) your car last month, you_____ (should + know) that you were paying too much.

8. When we complained, they said they_____(make) a mistake and_____(give) us our money back.

9. I went to the airport to meet my friend, but later I found out he_____(take) the train.

10. It_____(rain) for the last forty days and forty nights.

1. IDENTIFYING SUBJECTS AND VERBS

Fundamental to doing almost any kind of work with sentences is being able to identify subjects and verbs. Every sentence, as you know, has to have a subject and a verb; otherwise, it isn't a sentence. Although the subject usually comes before the verb in English sentences, it is easier to start by finding the verb.

You may have learned that verbs are words that express actions. That is true, but it isn't helpful, for while most verbs do express actions, many verbs don't and lots of words that are not verbs do. Look at this sentence:

Swimming is my favorite sport.

What is the action word? Obviously, it is *swimming*, but *swimming* isn't the verb. One could even say that *sport* is an action word, in a sense, since sports are, by definition, active. But *sport* isn't the verb either. As you probably have realized, *is* is the verb. Look at the same sentence rewritten slightly:

Swimming was my favorite sport.

Which word has been changed? How has the meaning of the sentence changed?

The verb *is* has been changed to its past-tense form *was* and so the meaning of the sentence has changed slightly. It now describes how I used to feel about it. We could also write the sentence this way:

Swimming will be my favorite sport.

Now the sentence tells how I think I will feel about swimming in the future. The question now is, So what? And the answer is that since all English sentences have to be in some tense or time—present, past, or future—and since the verbs in our sentences tell what that tense or time is, we can easily find the verbs in our sentences by changing the time of them and seeing what word changes. Look at the following examples.

What is the verb in this sentence?

The student in the back row sleeps through the lectures.

If we change the sentence to put the action in the past—last week, say—what changes?

The student in the back row slept through the lectures.

What is the verb?

sleeps / slept

Let's change the following sentence so that its action takes place in the future:

The people downtown threw paper out their windows.
The people downtown will throw paper out their windows.

What is the verb?

threw / will throw

Some verb forms, as you probably know, consist of more than one word. The future form is one example. Here are some others:

She is throwing a party.
She has thrown a party.
She used to throw parties.

EXERCISE 1.A

The sentences below are all in the present tense; locate the verbs in them by rewriting them twice, first in the past and second in the future (using *will*). It might help you to imagine the sentence beginning with the word *Yesterday* when you want to change it to past tense and *Tomorrow* when you want to change it to the future. Underline the verbs in your rewritten sentences.

Example:
John buys too many records.
(Yesterday) John bought too many records. (past)
(Tomorrow) John will buy too many records. (future)

Sentences followed by (2) have two verbs; be sure to change the tense of both of them and underline both in your rewrites.

1. Mary takes business courses.

   _____

2. She plans to own her own corporation.

   _____

3. A huge corporation is a desirable thing to own.

   _____

4. Mary also studies English and mathematics.

   _____

   5. Corporations run on letters and numbers.

_____

   6. Executives need solid writing skills.

_____

   7. They require a good command of math.

_____

   8. The Brand-X Corporation is failing because its president uses his fingers to count. (2)

_____

_____

   9. Executives of the Brand-Y Corporation study writing, and so they write superior letters. (2)

_____

_____

10. Brand-Y Corporation, which makes ballpoint pens, earns an excellent profit. (2)

_____

_____

EXERCISE 1.B

The following short paragraph is written in the present tense. Change the verbs in it to the future tense by drawing a line through each verb and writing the future form above it.

The party is a huge success. Almost all of the invited guests accept the invitations. They all arrive on time. No one who is not invited tries to come. Everyone is happy. The guests enjoy the food and drink. They like the music and dance enthusiastically. No one argues, breaks anything, or drinks too much. The hosts and the guests are all delighted.

EXERCISE 1.C

Through an amazing oversight, a friend wrote the following paragraph the other day in the present tense, only realizing afterward that the events described there had actually taken place the week before. In short, she should have written it in past tense. Revise it by drawing a line through each present-tense verb and writing the past-tense form above it.

I go to a bookstore that also sells picture frames, for I wish to price their frames.

The reason I do that is that earlier in the week I visit a print shop and see many

attractive prints that I want to buy. But in frames they are very expensive. I de-

cide to buy the prints inexpensively and to frame them myself. At the book-

store I discover where to find such frames, and so I buy two prints from the

print shop and two frames from the bookstore, and then my living room looks

more attractive.

Locating Subjects: The First-Noun Rule

Once you can locate the verbs in a sentence, it is easy to find their subjects. The subject is the word in front of the verb that answers the question *who* or *what* in relation to the verb.

> Storms rage in California.
> (What rages? Storms.)
> George is beating on the door.
> (Who is beating on the door? George.)
> The car in the garage is mine.
> (What is mine? The car.)
> The cat and the dog belong to Julia.
> (What belongs to Julia? The cat and the dog.)

You will notice that in these sentences, the subject is the first noun in the sentence (or, in the case of the last one, the first noun and the noun joined to it with *and*). This rule—the first-noun rule—will hold true in perhaps 90 percent of the sentences you or anyone else ever writes. You can't count on it every time, but when in doubt, look to the very first noun.

To practice identifying subjects, return to Exercise 1.A and draw two lines under the subjects in each sentence.

Subjects Separated from Verbs

The only tricky part about identifying subjects and verbs comes when there is more than one noun in front of the verb.

> The sweater in the drawer is made of wool.

Usually the *who* or *what* question will solve the problem. Who or what is made of wool, the sweater or the drawer? In this case, it's obvious. But sometimes the *who* or *what* question won't solve the problem or will even be misleading:

The hole in the sweater will have to be fixed.

Who or what will have to be fixed—the hole or the sweater? In this situation, remember the first-noun rule; the first of the nouns will be the subject—in this case *hole*. *Sweater* is not the subject of the sentence even though it makes sense to say that the sweater will have to be fixed.

Most exceptions to the first-noun rule occur when the sentence begins with a word or group of words followed by a comma, as in these cases:

Tomorrow, she will buy the parachute.
In the afternoon, she will use it.

In these circumstances, the subject is the first noun following the comma.

The only other exception to be careful of is nouns in the possessive form, that is, ending in an apostrophe (my *sisters'* boyfriends) or an apostrophe and *s* (my *sister's* boyfriend). Possessive nouns cannot normally be the subjects of sentences.

EXERCISE 1.D

Locate the verbs in the following sentences and underline them once. Then look for the subjects and underline them twice.

1. The peaches on the trees are ripe now.

2. The blue of the sky is extremely beautiful.

3. The people in that neighborhood litter their streets with trash.

4. Flowers and weeds grow in Juanita's garden.

5. Up in the sky, the birds from the north are flying south.

6. The argument of the president makes no sense.

7. The basis of this plan is a good one.

8. My sister's friend hangs out with some dangerous people.

9. My best friend's father takes English classes in the evening.

10. At the end of the street, two houses and an old warehouse are falling down.

There Sentences

There is a special kind of sentence in English that does not begin with a noun, and you have just read one of them. It is the *there* sentence:

There is a tavern in the town.
There are two taverns in the town.

In this type of sentence, the subject is the noun that *follows* the verb. Notice that in the first example above, the verb is *is*—that is, it is singular—while in the second example, the verb is *are*, the plural. Notice also that the noun following the first verb is singular and the noun following the second is plural. They are the subjects of the sentences and the reason for the difference in the verbs.

EXERCISE 1.E

Identify the subjects in the following *there* sentences and underline them.

1. There are many people in the woods.

2. There are animals around here also.

3. There will be a problem soon.

4. There were troubles in that part of town yesterday.

5. There was a loud clap of thunder last night.

6. There was a bunch of strange people in here yesterday.

7. There is too much water in that lake.

8. There are three newspapers published in this town.

9. There are frequently loud noises in that deserted house.

10. There used to be a barrel of rainwater at the corner of the house.

2. AGREEMENT BETWEEN SUBJECTS AND VERBS

Imagine that you are an alien who has just landed on a spaceship from the planet Blog, and you are studying a strange Earthling language called English. The person you are studying with shows you how English verbs work in the present tense by writing them down this way, using the verb *walk*:

Singular		**Plural**	
I	walk	we	walk
you	walk	you	walk
he/she/it	walks	they	walk

You examine this for a moment and then say, in your native Blogese, "Wait a minute. You made a mistake here. One of these verbs is wrong." Look at them yourself. Which verb would seem illogical to a creature from another planet? Which one doesn't fit with the rest?

Of course, the *he/she/it* form of the singular doesn't fit with the rest because it is the only one with an *s* ending. Every other one is *walk* and it is *walks*. It's totally illogical, and it's even useless, but there it is.

It is true that in some forms of spoken English people say "he walk" or "she walk" or (in the case of an alien from Blog) "it walk." That makes sense logically, but it still isn't the correct form in writing.

By the way, agreement between subject and verb almost exclusively involves this present-tense form. The only time it's a concern in the past tense is when we use the verb *be*, and then we get these changes:

I was	we were
you were	you were
he/she/it was	they were

In the present tense, the verb *be* has these endings:

I am	we are
you are	you are
he/she/it is	they are

If you can keep *was* and *were* straight, which most people do, you only have to watch for verbs following *he/she/it* nouns when you're writing in the present tense.

What's a *he/she/it* noun? Here are a few examples. Note that they all refer to one person or thing.

he = George, Juan, my father, the man in the car, the outfielder who won the batting title, a zoologist (Any of these nouns or phrases could be replaced by *he*.)

she = Michelle, your sister, the woman over there, the little girl playing in the sand, your attorney (Any of these nouns or phrases could be replaced by *she*.)

it = your pen, my paper, our class, discovering gold, excitement, a gigantic mess on the floor (Any of these nouns or phrases could be replaced by *it*.)

All of these words or phrases appearing as the subject of a sentence in the present tense would need a verb ending in *s*:

George <u>likes</u> Michelle.
The outfielder who won the batting title <u>comes</u> from Puerto Rico.
Michelle <u>thinks</u> George is a dope.
The little girl playing in the sand <u>looks</u> very happy.
Your pen <u>is</u> writing on my paper.
The gigantic mess on the floor <u>needs</u> to be swept under the sofa.

Basic Subject-Verb Agreement

The basic subject-verb agreement problem is simply to remember that in the *he/she/it* form of the present tense, the verb has to end in *s*. All the other present-tense verb forms end with their normal letter.

Here is a small complication to the basic rule. If your verb has two or more subjects joined by an *and*, the subjects become *they*, plural instead of singular, and the verb doesn't get an *s*:

Carlos and Lois feel like taking a walk.

But if two subjects are joined by *or*, the subjects become singular and the verb does get an *s*:

Carlos or Lois thinks I'm wrong.

(Note that only *one* of them thinks it.)

EXERCISE 2.A

In the following sentences, do the following things:

* Identify the subject of the verb, which is in parentheses.
* Decide whether the subject can be replaced by *he, she, it,* or *they*.
* Write *he, she, it,* or *they*, whichever is correct, and the correct form of the verb in the blank below the verb.

Example:
Maylene (write) her aunt the latest news.
    she writes

Thirty people (think) I'm wrong.
   they think

John and Willie (know) about the problem.
   they know

1. Lois (think) Carlos (look) down on the alien from Blog.

   _____   _____

2. The alien (hate) being called an alien.

   _____

3. The alien (prefer) being called a Blogite.

   _____

4. Carlos (feel) that if people from China (be) called Chinese, the alien

   _____   _____

   should be a Blogese.

5 Actually the alien (have) a name, Dork.

   _____

6. Most people (dislike) aliens from outer space, but Lois and Carlos (find)

   _____   _____

   Dork a pleasant companion, once one (get) over his complexion.

   _____

7. His skin (have) a texture similar to library paste coated with egg white.

   _____

8. Most of his legs (be) covered with green bristles, but the left front one (be)

   _____   _____

   smooth and brown, while the right front one (look) bumpy and orange.

   _____

9. The planet Blog (circle) a sun twenty light-years from us.

   _____

10. Its atmosphere (be) a mixture of hydrogen, oxygen, and bug spray.

   _____

11. Lois or Carlos (want) to visit there someday.

   _____

12. Lois (feel) sorry for Dork because the poor alien (long) to return to his

   _____   _____

   native planet.

13. Here, he (have) to squirt himself with bug spray every hour or die.

   _____

14. His breathing organs (require) the atmosphere of his home.

   _____

15. The bug spray (make) him smell bad, and his popularity (suffer) as a result.

   _____   _____

EXERCISE 2.B

   We often use nouns that don't indicate people or physical things as the subjects of our sentences. Words such as *agreement, conflict, entertainment, gardening, history,* and *maturity* are examples. These, of course, are *it* subjects, and it is important to remember that when two of them are joined by *and* in the subject spot, they take a plural verb:

   Analysis [it] of these documents reveals that illegal activities [they] are still
      occurring.

   The discovery and publication [they] of these documents have embarrassed
      the government.

Write the correct verb form on the line beneath the verbs in the following sentences:

1. The history of the United States (affect) us today.

   _____

2. Conflict between opposing points of view often (make) our government

   _____

   inefficient, but the framers of the Constitution designed it that way.

3. Fear of a tyrant and distrust of the masses (be) why they set up a system

   _____

   based on conflict.

4. Other European and Asian democracies (employ) a parliamentary system in

   _____

which the ruling party (have) all the power.

_____

5. Conflicts of the past, such as the Civil War, still (affect) us today.

_____

6. Distrust of government and fear of big business, the results of nineteenth-
century labor strife, still (influence) labor relations today.

_____

7. Past African slavery and discrimination against Chinese immigrants
still (play) negative roles in our society.

_____

8. Getting rid of some of these old influences (be) necessary for us to grow

_____

productively in the future.

9. At the same time, retaining the best of the past (help) us keep our unique

_____

national identity.

10. A positive American characteristic (have) always been a willingness to

_____

recognize and try to correct our own failures.

EXERCISE 2.C

Write the correct verb form on the line beneath the verbs in the following sentences:

1. The issue of whether women should pursue careers in the world of work
(involve) many genuine issues as well as many old prejudices.

_____

2. Probably almost nobody now (believe) in the old saying "Women's place is

_____

in the home."

3. Most people (accept) that most women who can will at least find jobs, if

   _____

   not careers.

4. But many of those who seem to accept this fact really (act) as though they

                                                _____

   (be) opposed to women working.

   _____

5. The person who (say) he or she (be) for women in the workforce but at the

                    _____

   same time (oppose) maternity leave (be) not in favor of women working.

       _____   _____

6. For regardless of whether a woman (work) or not, she (be) still the only one

                              _____   _____

   who can have children.

7. And to have children, one (need) to be able to have time off to give birth

              _____

   and to care for the infant during its early years.

8. Other countries, particularly in Europe, (have) made practical provisions

              _____

   for women to be able to work.

9. France, for instance, (have) established "écoles maternelles" or preschools

          _____

   that (provide) care for the children of working parents.

   _____

10. Since most women now (want) satisfying careers of their own, and since

           _____

   in most families the wife (have) to work for the family to make ends meet,

           _____

   it (seem) only right that government (set) up licensed, properly staffed

   _____   _____

   pre-schools to meet this need.

Subject-Verb Agreement in *There* Sentences

One kind of sentence begins with the word *there*, and this *there* does not refer to the location of anything. Here are some examples:

There is a tavern in the town.
There was some ice cream in the house yesterday.
There's going to be a big party tonight.
There are three buttons missing from my shirt.

Although *there* is the first word of these sentences and comes right in front of the verb, it isn't the subject. Read the following short passage, in which the verbs in the *there* sentences are underlined, and see whether you can figure out why some of the verbs are singular (*is*) and some plural (*are*):

There <u>is</u> an old saying. It goes, "There <u>are</u> more ways than one to skin a cat." There <u>is</u> a great truth in this saying. It means that usually there <u>are</u> several possible solutions to any problem.

Why is the verb singular in the first sentence below? Why is it plural in the second sentence?

There is a problem here.
There are two problems here.

What are the subjects of these sentences? Where do we find the subject of *there* sentences? Write here the rule for subject-verb agreement in *there* sentences:

_____

_____

_____

_____

EXERCISE 2.D

Write the correct form of the verb *be* in the blank in the following sentences and underline the verb's subject. When the word *past* appears after the verb slot, use *was* or *were*; when the word *present* appears, use *is* or *are*.

Example:

There_____(present) a coat in the closet.

There ___**is**___ a <u>coat</u> in the closet.

There_____(past) two coats in the closet.

There ____**were**____ two coats in the closet.

1. There_____(present) 50,000 books in our library.

2. Of them, there_____(present) one that I am anxious to read.

3. There_____(present) an excellent chance that it won't be there when I try to find it.

4. There_____(past) three days last week when I felt unwell.

5. There_____(past) one in particular when I was quite sick.

6. There_____(present) no feeling worse than some physical illness unless it's being unprepared for an exam.

7. We learned that though there_____(past) a lot of rules on one

 in high school, there_____(present) a lot of responsibilities on one in college.

8. There_____(present) a major project waiting for me at home, but

 there_____(present) little I can do about it now.

9. There_____(present) several reasons why I need to get at least a B in this course, but there_____(present) one major obstacle in my way.

10. There_____(past) quite a few people at the party, but there

 _____(past) only one I was hoping to meet.

3. PAST TENSE AND PAST PARTICIPLES

Past Tense

Every sentence you write will indicate the time of the sentence—that is, whether it expresses present time, future time, or past time. Like most other Western European languages but unlike most Eastern languages, English shows its sentence-time through its verbs. Present tense generally uses the base form of the verb, future tense uses *will* plus the base form, and past tense adds *-ed* (most of the time) to the base form, as in these cases:

Today, I walk to the store.

Tomorrow I will walk to the store.

Yesterday I walked to the store.

There are two little complications to this otherwise fairly simple system. One of them, covered in Chapter 1, is that not all past-tense verbs end in *-ed*, as in these cases:

Present	**Past**
I think	I thought
I sink	I sank
I eat	I ate

For a review of these verbs, see Chapter 1 ("Recognizing Verb Forms," page 46 in the Sentence Combining section).

The other complication applies only to the *-ed* verb endings; when we speak, we don't pronounce all *-ed* endings. Read the following sentence aloud—not silently—in your normal voice, as though you were speaking it; listen to see whether you hear the *-ed* endings on the verbs *walk* and *talk*:

Yesterday I walked to the record store and talked to my friend there.

Most people either will not pronounce the verb endings at all or will pronounce them only as a very slight, almost inaudible *t* sound. Other *-ed* endings most of us do pronounce quite noticeably:

I conducted an experiment to see whether anyone would return a borrowed book.

But the fact that we don't pronounce many *-ed* endings distinctly means that when we write, we may not hear them in our minds and so leave them off. But whether pronounced or not, they must always be there in writing. So if you're having trouble getting the *-ed* endings on your verbs, you'll need to work on it, but at least you know that there's a logical explanation for your problem.

Correcting an *-ed* problem is a pretty easy proofreading task. All you have to do is remember three things:

1. When you proofread, check each of your paragraphs to see what time you are expressing. If you are talking about the past, check each verb in each sentence to make sure it has a needed *-ed* ending. (But remember that even a passage in the past tense may legitimately have some present-tense sentences or parts of sentences in it.)

2. There are two common words that *always* have *-ed* endings: *supposed* and *used*. It's best to get used to (see that?) writing these words the way they're supposed to (and that?) be written in the first place.

3.   Any verb form that has the word *to* in front of it *never* takes an *-ed* ending: She wanted <u>to talk</u> to her friend on the phone, but her mother needed <u>to use</u> it for business.

EXERCISE 3.A

Rewrite the following sentences, changing the verbs in each from present tense to past tense:

1. In the high school cafeteria, Suzanne looks at Ramon and her heart stops beating.

    _____

2. She walks up to him and tries to start a conversation.

    _____

3. But she learns that only baseball interests him.

    _____

4. Getting no response in person, she finally mails him a letter inviting him to a party.

    _____

5. She believes this might do the trick.

    _____

6. In a few days, she walks to her mailbox and notices a letter for her from Ramon.

    _____

7. She hurries to open it.

    _____

8. Ramon invites her to a baseball game he is playing in.

    _____

9. In the high school cafeteria, Suzanne gazes at Glenn and her heart stops beating.

    _____

10. She strolls up to him and asks, "Do you play baseball?"

    _____

EXERCISE 3.B

The following passage is in the past tense. Proofread it for past-tense verbs that are missing their *-ed* endings, and look for any misspelled instances of *used to* or *supposed to*.

In the 1920s and 30s, some European military theorists believe that in the future, wars could be won simply by airplanes bombing civilian populations. They argue that the people being bombed would be driven mad, and they convince most airmen of the time that their planes would be able to destroy totally a nation's industry. In 1941, Germany attempt to put this theory into practice by bombing England night and day. But the English, who were suppose to be driven mad, hardly let themselves be affected by it. They quickly got use to hiding in shelters when the bombers drop their bombs, and at the same time, the Royal Air Force destroy huge numbers of the German bombers. American and British bombers devastate much of Germany, but they were unable to destroy German industry. Aerial bombardment during World War II never accomplish what its proponents believe it would—until the atomic bomb was invented near the end of the war.

Past Participles

Frequently when we write, we use verbs that have more than one part, for instance:

She <u>might have walked</u> to school yesterday, but she <u>will take</u> the bus tomorrow.

Or:

He wants <u>to be considered</u> a serious person, but no one <u>wants to think</u> of him that way.

There is something a little curious about some of the verb words in these two sentences. In the first sentence, there are two verbs, *walk* and *take*. But one ends in *-ed* and the other one doesn't. Why is that? Similarly, in the second sentence, there are also two verbs, *consider* and *think*; again, one of them ends with an *-ed* and the other one doesn't.

The reason for these differences is that English has a distinctive pattern involving verbs using more than one word:

If the main verb is preceded by some form of the verb *be, have, become,* or *get,* the verb itself has to end in *-ed* (unless it takes an irregular form like *thrown* or *bought* or *taken*).

This pattern would not present problems for most of us if it weren't that we generally don't pronounce these *-ed* endings when we say them, and so it can be hard to remember to put them on when we write. This is another one of the many cases in which English pronunciation and spelling are different.

EXERCISE 3.C

In the following sentences, forms of the verbs *be, have, become,* and *get* are underlined; rewrite each sentence, correcting the verb following *be, have, become,* and *get* by writing it in its *-ed* ending version.

Example:

Pak was not prepare for class.

Change to:

Pak was not prepared for class.

1. Mai had always expect Pak to buy her something romantic for Valentine's Day.

2. But Pak preferred to be instruct in the kind of present Mai might like to have purchase for her.

3. He was also too embarrass to buy her lingerie; he became totally fluster when he saw bras and panties.

4. As a result, Mai usually got irritate as February 14th neared, and Pak was apt to get depress.

5. Pak felt he had been badly use in the past when he had purchase Mai some nice present, like the chain saw.

6. Mai was use to these kinds of presents, but she became determine to make Pak see the light.

7. Pak might have never pick up on the sort of thing Mai was interest in except that she had gotten an idea.

8. She had order for Pak a nice assortment of catalogues.

9. He <u>was</u> suppose to look at them and <u>be</u> inspire to buy her some perfume or sexy underwear.

10. Unfortunately, he <u>got</u> turn on by the Victoria's Secret catalogue, <u>was</u> particularly fascinate by page 10, <u>became</u> totally infatuate with a bra model there, and ran off to New York to find her.

EXERCISE 3.D

Rewrite the following sentences, underlining the verbs *be, have, become,* and *get* and changing the verbs following them to their *-ed* form. (Note that not every appearance of these four verbs is necessarily followed by another verb that has to be changed.)

1. In the history of first dates in the world, for the most part disaster has follow disaster.

2. To be sure, there have been times when couples have encounter their lifelong soul mates, but more often, one or both of the persons have been seriously disillusion.

3. Abelard became enamor of Eloise at first sight, and Romeo got snare by Juliet's beauty when he first saw her, but on many first dates, the couples are overwhelm with disinterest for each other.

4. Oftentimes, one person is fascinate by the other, but the other is bore by the first.

5. In my dating lifetime, I have encounter both situations.

6. Once I was totally enchant by a lovely young woman, but she got bore with me on sight.

7. She became so tire of my witty conversation, she fell asleep.

8. A friend of mine tried to be prepare for a first date by reading two newspapers and three news magazines, but his date was totally uninterest in anything but rock stars.

9. When the person who is thrill by politics meets the person who is turn on only by basketball, disaster results.

10. Many people have return from first dates swearing that they will never get involve with the opposite sex for the rest of their lives.

EXERCISE 3.E

The following passage is in the past tense. Proofread it for *both* past-tense verbs that are missing their *-ed* endings *and* verbs after *be, have, become,* and *get* that need *-ed* endings.

People became interest in building a transcontinental railroad across the United States only after the California Gold Rush, which happen in 1849. The population of California had suddenly expand, and the state contain great wealth. California had been admit to the Union, but it was cut off from the rest of the United States. Only Indians live between Omaha, Nebraska, and California, over a thousand miles away. Most people going to California travel by ship, but that require a trip all the way around the tip of South America. Some wagon trains attempt to cross the continent, and many manage to succeed, but the way was difficult and dangerous. Many such travelers were kill by the difficulties of the trip itself. Some trains were wipe out by Indian raiders. And the terrible ordeal of the Donner Party, most of whom were kill by the terrible Sierra winter, show what could happen when a group happen to make a few mistakes. As a result, many efforts got start to begin building a railroad. In Washington, the government became involve when Congress pass the Pacific Railroad Act of 1862, and out west, a man named T. D. Judah went into the mountains and survey a route across the Sierra Nevada. A group of entrepreneurs in Sacramento who became call the Big Four got interest, and while the Civil War was still raging, the effort to build a railroad had start.

4. THE PAST-TO-PRESENT TENSE (PRESENT PERFECT)

In addition to the regular past tense, which English uses to express actions completed in the past, we have another tense—the past-to-present, or present perfect, tense.

The past tense, of course, is simply the standard *-ed* form or one of its irregular cousins (like *bought, ate,* or *sank*). The past-to-present tense includes the words *has/have* or *has/have been* in front of the verb:

I have enjoyed baseball for many years.
She has found her new life satisfying.
We have been poor now for much too long.
He has been a sailor for twelve years.

While we use the past tense mostly for events that took place entirely in the past, we use the past-to-present tense for two other purposes. Look at the following two sentences; what is the difference in meaning between them?

1.   George attended college for two years.
2.   George has attended college for two years.

In the first instance, which involves the regular past tense, George attended college at some time in the past but is no longer doing so. The action of attending college started and ended in the past. In the second instance, which involves the past-to-present tense, George is still attending college. The action of attending college started in the past and is continuing into the present.

There is a second difference between the past tense and the past-to-present tense. Look at the following two sentences; what is the difference between them?

1.   Teresa bought her textbooks yesterday.
2.   Teresa has bought her textbooks.

In the first case, in which the regular past is involved, we know when the action took place. But in the second case, we don't know exactly when it took place.

And so we can see that there are two main differences between the regular past tense and the past-to-present tense.

Regular past:

Expresses an action completed in the past.

Expresses an action that took place at a specific time in the past.

Past-to-present:

Expresses an action begun in the past but continuing to the present.

Expresses an action that took place at some unspecific time in the past.

Finally, it is important to note that situations in which either the regular past or the past-to-present may be used are quite common in English.

In trying to remember whether to use the past tense or the past-to-present tense, it can be helpful to note that there are words and phrases in English other than verbs that also indicate the time of the sentence and typically go with either the past tense or the past-to-present tense.

Words and phrases that indicate the past tense are ones that point to specific times in the past such as these:

yesterday	last year
in the morning	on Wednesday
the other day	two weeks ago
at three o'clock	after dinner
then	next
soon	later

Words and phrases that indicate past-to-present actions or situations are ones like these:

since	since yesterday
recently	up to now
so far	for the time being
	for (plus any time word or phrase)

EXERCISE 4.A

Rewrite the following sentences to use either the regular past or the past-to-present tense. If there is a word or phrase in any sentence that helps you know which tense to use, underline it.

1. Last week I (buy) a new pair of shoes.

   _____

2. Up to now I (enjoy) them greatly.

   _____

3. Early in the fall, Joanne (decide) to study harder.

   _____

4. Since making that decision, she (get) much better grades.

   _____

5. I (cook) for only three years now.

   _____

6. It (take) me that long to learn the rudiments of that art.

   _____

7. I (start) to learn when I first (live) on my own.

   _____

8. It (be) a struggle at first, but it (be) a pleasure since then.

   _____

9. The world (experience) a lessening of tensions in recent years.

   _____

10. The Cold War between the United States and the Soviet Union (last) about forty years, but since then, animosities between the two countries (diminish).

    _____

    _____

EXERCISE 4.B

Rewrite the following sentences to use either the regular past or the past-to-present tense. If there is a word or phrase in any sentence that helps you know which tense to use, underline it.

1. Not long ago, Josefa (decide) that she (want) a pet to keep her company.
2. She (consider) getting a dog but (decide) that although dogs are good company, they are too fawning and undignified.
3. She (consider) getting a cat but (decide) that although cats are independent and dignified, they are not good company.
4. So she (decide) to buy an elephant.
5. Since she (purchase) last Thursday a medium-sized Indian elephant at the local pet store, Josefa (discover) some advantages and disadvantages to owning a pet elephant.
6. Max, the elephant, (prove) to be loyal, faithful, and affectionate.
7. Ever since Josefa got him, he (accompany) her on her morning jog, (sleep) at the foot of her bed at night, and (do) all the heavy lifting around the house.
8. Unfortunately, there (be) some problems too.
9. When Max (try) to jump into the car to go shopping with Josefa, he (flatten) the car.
10. When he (try) to curl up on her lap in the evening, he (squash) her.

11. Also, the bills for hay (be) awfully high since Max (be) around.

12. So fond of Max though she is, Josefa recently (consider) getting a somewhat smaller pet.

13. The other day in a pet store window, she (see) a particularly attractive black widow spider.

EXERCISE 4.C

Write the correct verb form, either past tense or past-to-present tense, in the blanks in the following paragraph.

Providing adequate medical care to all our citizens is a problem the United

States _____ (be) more avoiding than dealing with over the past

forty or fifty years. Shortly after World War II, every European country

_____ (adopt) some form of "socialized medicine" to take care of

their citizens. When I _____ (live) in France in the 1950s, the gov-

ernment _____ (pay) for most doctors' and dentists' fees and medi-

cines for every citizen. Since then, these coverages _____ (be)

expanded, and citizens of European countries _____ (be) secure

about being able to afford health care. Canada also _____ (adopt) a

system of government control over the costs of medical care. Over the same

period of time, the United States _____ (have) not been able to bring

itself to adopt a system like either the European or Canadian ones. "Socialized

medicine" _____ (become) almost a four-letter word here. As a result,

since World War II millions of Americans _____ (suffer) the effects of

ill health, including premature death. We _____ (show) that we value

our principles more than we value human life.

5. THE PAST-BEFORE-PAST TENSE (PAST PERFECT)

English uses a third form of past tense besides the other two—the regular past and the past-to-present. The third form is underlined in the following sentence:

We <u>had given up</u> on seeing them when they suddenly arrived.

As this sentence indicates, the past-before-past tense indicates a time further in the past than the regular past, a past *before* the normal past. This past-tense form, also called the past perfect, uses the word *had* before the base form of the verb. In the example above, the action "they suddenly arrived" takes place in the regular past while the action "we had given up on seeing them" takes place in the time before the regular past. Here are three other examples of the past tense and the past-before-past tense:

> The War of 1812 had already ended when the Battle of New Orleans was fought. (The battle was fought after the war was over.)
> Marcus got a C on the final exam, but he had previously gotten A's on all the quizzes.
> They had eaten dinner and cleaned up the dishes by the time their guests finally arrived.

Note that we do not use the *had* form of the past for any reason other than comparing two past times; we do *not* use it to sound more formal.

When we use the words *before* and *after* to show time relationships, we can use either the regular past tense or the past-before-past tense.

> She had tried four different models before she decided to buy the least expensive one.
> She tried four different models before she decided to buy the least expensive one.
> After she had tried four different models, she decided to buy the least expensive one.
> After she tried four different models, she decided to buy the least expensive one.

EXERCISE 5.A

Rewrite the following sentences, using either the regular past tense or the past-before-past tense. When you have a choice between the two in sentences using *before* or *after*, use the regular past.

1. Alisha (work) as a waitress and a dancer before she (go) to law school.

   _____

2. She (become) sick of being poor by the time she (graduate).

   _____

3. When I (see) her for the first time in years, she (change) her style completely.

   _____

4. She (begin) to wear expensive, stylish clothes.

   _____

5. She (look) much better and (seem) happier than she (have) in the days
   when she (work) for low wages.

   _____

   _____

6. When Eric (buy) a used car, the man who (own) it previously (tell) him he
   (take) good care of it.

   _____

   _____

7. By the time the new pitcher (come) to our team, he (play) for three other
   teams in his career.

   _____

   _____

8. When I (go) to the bookstore to get my texts, the clerk (say) they (not come
   in) yet, but they (be) on order for at least a month.

   _____

   _____

9. After Juanita (eat) at that restaurant, she (feel) ill.

   _____

10. I (make) the mistake of betting on a team that (lose) its past thirteen games.

   _____

EXERCISE 5.B

   Rewrite the following sentences, using either the regular past tense or
the past-before-past tense. When you have a choice between the two in sentences using *before* or *after*, use the regular past.

1. When she (graduate) from high school, Eva Martinez was not interested in
   going to college.

2. She (feel) she (study) enough in high school.

3. By the time she (graduate) she (read) about history, (learn) about science,
   (study) math, and (write) papers, and that was enough.

4. The time (arrive) to get a good job.

5. She (want) to start a career and make a lot of money.

6. When she (be) 14, she (decide) to be a TV newscaster.

7. She (be) attractive and (speak) well, and she (look) somewhat older than her age.

8. Before she (go) job hunting, she (prepare) by reading the newspaper to her reflection in the mirror.

9. When she (do) that several times, she (feel) she was ready.

10. The TV executive she (speak) to (ask) if she (have) any experience.

11. He (ask) if she (have) any training.

12. He (ask) if she (graduate) from college.

13. He (look) at her as though she (drop) in on him from Mars.

14. He (say) they didn't need anyone like her just at this time.

15. After three more experiences like that one, Eva (decide) she would go to college after all.

EXERCISE 5.C

Fill in the correct verb form—past or past-before-past—in the following paragraph.

In 1863, Abraham Lincoln _____ (be) faced with a serious problem. The American Civil War _____ (be) going on for two years, but the North still _____ (not make) significant progress against the South in Virginia. In the preceding two years, President Lincoln _____ (appoint) general after general to lead the Union's Army of the Potomac, but Robert E. Lee, the Confederate general in Virginia, _____ (defeat) every one of them. In the western theater, however, the Union _____ (be) successful. In particular, an unknown Union general named Ulysses S. Grant _____ (defeat) the Confederates every time he _____ (fight) them. Noticing Grant's success, Lincoln finally _____ (decide) to make him commander of all the Union's armies.

He_____(put) him in charge of the whole war. Grant immediately

_____ (formulate) a plan for defeating the Confederacy and

_____ (put) it into effect. The result _____ (be) a Union

victory. Until Grant's appointment, the Union _____ (struggle) to

defeat an opponent with only half its strength, but when he _____

(take) charge, victory _____ (become) inevitable.

EXERCISE 5.D

In the following exercise, fill in the correct verb form—present tense, past tense, past-to-present tense, or past-before-past tense.

Before doing this exercise, briefly review the instructions for using past-to-present and past-before-past tenses. Then carefully work out in the case of each verb whether its action is in the present, the regular past, the past-to-present, or the past-before-past.

Don't guess.

Roughly between 1953 and 1957, an automotive revolution _____

(hit) the United States. It _____ (be) during that period that the fa-

mous Volkswagen Beetle, or "Bug," _____ (arrive) on the American

automobile market, the first imported car to reach a mass market in the United

States. The history of this car before the 1950s _____ (be) rather

strange.

By the mid-1930s, Germany _____ (be) in the grip of a severe

economic depression for over a decade. Up to that time, people

_____ (have) a hard time getting work, and German industry

_____ (stagnate). Before he took power, the new German leader,

Adolf Hitler, _____ (develop) many new schemes to get the country

back on its feet, and one of them _____ (be) to develop a new, low-

priced automobile that everyone could afford. So when he became Chancellor,

he _____ (commission) the great automotive designer, Ferdinand

Porsche, to design a new "people's car." (*Volks* in German _____

(mean) *people's* and *wagen* _____ (mean) *vehicle.*) Porsche

_____ (be) also famous for designing sports cars and military tanks.

The Second World War _____ (put) an end to the Volkswagen, but after the war manufacture of them _____ (begin), and starting in 1949, a few of them _____ (begin) to trickle into the United States. The original design _____ (be) hardly changed at all, and the early VWs _____ (show) it. For instance, they _____ (have) no fuel gauges, totally inadequate rear windows and windshield wipers, and only six-volt batteries.

German production of the Beetle _____ (be) discontinued in 1979, but the love affair of Americans now in their 40s and 50s with the car _____ (have not) died. A friend of mine _____ (own) one since the mid-80s. Eric Hansen, author of *Motoring with Mohammed,* _____ (travel) all over looking for Beetles, and in 1972, he _____ (find) one in the mountains of Pakistan. Recently, a restored Beetle _____ (be) on sale at a rare car dealer in San Francisco for $12,900. The Beetle _____ (have) not died and gone to automobile heaven yet.

Now the Volkswagen company _____ (build) a new, modern version of the old Beetle. It remains to be seen whether it will ever achieve the original Beetle's popularity.

6. COMMA-SPLICE ERRORS

Comma splices occur when the writer joins two complete sentences with a comma only:

My elephant was a lot of fun, I liked her enormously.

Note that if you put a period after *fun*, where the comma is, you would have two correctly punctuated sentences. Remember that commas do not, by themselves, connect sentences.

While comma splices are errors, they are in some ways a good sign. One of the marks of immaturity in writing is long strings of short sentences, with no indications by the writer of the relationships among them. Comma splices at least tell the reader that the writer saw a close connection between the ideas in the two sentences joined by the comma. It is better, of course, to tell the reader the same thing in a more precise way or in a way that the reader is used to seeing.

Finding Comma-Splice Errors

The best way of finding comma-splice errors is to start by asking your teacher not to mark them but only to indicate in some way that you have made the mistake in a particular line or lines in your paper. Then you should read the sentence in that line, starting in a preceding line if that's where your sentence starts. Read the sentence aloud in your normal voice, as though you were reading it to someone else. When we read aloud, we do two things when we come to the ends of sentences. Our voice drops slightly on the last word, and we pause. Read listening to your own voice and when you pause, check for a comma-splice. Your teacher may be able to help you do this the first time or two, making sure you don't skip past the pauses too quickly.

Correcting Comma-Splices

The best way to correct them is to try to see what logical relationship there is between the two sentences and find a word that expresses that relationship. In many cases words like *but, although, while, because,* or *and so* will work well.

Another way to show that sentences are closely related to one another is to use a semicolon. You might think of this punctuation mark as a semi-period, since it is half period and half comma, working like the period to show the reader that a sentence has ended but also working like the comma to show that more of the same idea is coming.

Therefore and *However*

Please notice that we did not suggest joining sentences with *however, thus,* or *therefore*. These words do *not* join sentences. They may introduce sentences, but they do not join them, and so the following sentences contain comma-splice errors despite the presence of *however* and *therefore*:

Shortly after World War II, the American dollar was one of the world's strongest currencies, however now it is one of the weakest.

Most people know nothing about economics, therefore they can be easily fooled in this area by politicians.

For those sentences to be correct, there would have to be a period or a semicolon after the first sentence in each pair. In any case, use *however* and *therefore* very sparingly. You will find them used rarely in good writing, and it is

not wise to rely upon them much, for they are heavy words that call attention to themselves. Good writers use conjunctions (*and, but, so,* and the rest
of the FANBOYS) much more frequently than these words.

These Words Join Sentences	These Words Don't Join Sentences
for, and, nor, but, or, yet, so	therefore, thus, consequently, however
because, since	for example, for instance
although, though, while	now, then
even though, whereas	

EXERCISE 6.A

Read the following exercises aloud in your normal voice, trying to notice when you pause. When you've identified a comma-splice, correct it by
using a conjunction such as *but, although, while, because,* or *so,* or *and so* if
you can; otherwise use a semicolon. Some of the sentences are correct.

1. Our football team finished in the bottom ten again last year, they are pretty untalented.

2. The offense averaged only 3.6 points a game, the defense was worse.

3. When they scored their first touchdown, the coach fainted. *OK*

4. The heaviest player on the team weighed 240 pounds, he was the quarter-back.

5. The team needs new blood, *because* most of their old blood is on the football field.

6. They had one momentous triumph, *for* they won their last game of the season.

7. Our opponents were favored by 39 points, *for* they were probably a little over-confident.

8. It was the greatest upset of the year, *for* nobody ever expected anything like it.

9. The team tried to carry the coach around the field on their shoulders, *but* they couldn't lift him.

10. It is true that he's a little heavy, he weighs about 300 pounds, more or less.

11. He once played guard for the Sacramento Poltroons, a minor-league foot-ball team.

12. The effort to lift him injured three players, who had to be hospitalized afterward.

50

13. The team we beat, our arch-rivals, went into shock after the game, they had to see therapists to cure their depression.
    ~~for~~

14. Many became suicidal, they had lost to the worst team in the state.
    ~~for~~

15. Thus we can see the value of athletics, they are good for the pocketbooks of psychologists.

EXERCISE 6.B

The following passage contains some comma-splice errors. Rewrite the passage, making no changes except to correct those errors.

My history as a cook is very spotty, ~~for~~ it contains a lot more failures than successes. When I was in college, my earliest cooking efforts consisted largely of putting cheese spread on crackers, although making bologna sandwiches was also an early triumph. In the army, cooking consisted of getting *nothing* cans open, sometimes a problem with the can openers they gave you. Advanced cooking was heating the food in the cans, a task mostly beyond my abilities. Later in life, I began to specialize *in sandwiches,* the cheese sandwich became my first area of concentration. The cheese sandwich is a delicate dish, requiring great care in the preparation, ~~for~~ sloppiness can easily ruin it. First, it is important to choose the ^ *because* right cheese, not all cheeses make good sandwiches. Second, the bread must be ^ *for* chosen carefully, it must complement the cheese. Dark, strongly flavored breads *while* like pumpernickel are best with strong cheeses, light cheeses taste best on sourdough or other light white breads. For the gourmet cheese sandwich, butter on *and* the bread is a must, lettuce and mustard are also desirable. Having mastered the cheese sandwich, I am now thinking of getting into hot foods.

7. SENTENCE FRAGMENTS

Any group of words that isn't a complete sentence but is punctuated like one is a sentence fragment—or fragment for short. If you read magazines, you will find many sentence fragments used on purpose, usually for emphasis. Advertisements are often written in virtually nothing but fragments. Does that mean it's all right to have them in your essays or other school writing? Generally, no. You may find occasion to use a fragment once in a great while in a formal paper, but both academic and business writing do not favor them.

While an intentionally written fragment may be effective, fragments written accidentally almost never are. They just look wrong and may even confuse the reader momentarily. There are three causes of accidental fragments, and if you write them, you should be aware of these causes, for normally one of them—and only one—will be the reason for your fragments. After you read over this section, then, you should analyze your own fragments, with the help of your teacher if necessary, to see what kind they are and why you seem to be writing them. In that way, you can study this section selectively, concentrating on the part of it relevant to you.

Three Kinds of Fragments and Their Causes

The most common sentence fragment is actually not so much a fragment as a punctuation error. We will call it the *punctuation fragment*. The punctuation fragment looks like this:

> The legislature passed a mandatory seat-belt law. <u>An attempt to protect drivers from their own recklessness.</u>
> She became one of the most successful lawyers in the firm. <u>Simply because she was willing to work night and day.</u>

The underlined groups of words are not sentences, but they could easily be part of the sentences preceding them; all that is necessary is to change the periods after the sentences to commas and the capital letters of the fragments to lowercase letters.

Why do we sometimes write fragments like these? No one can be sure, but it is easy to make mistakes in areas where we know better when we are concentrating mainly on what we want to say.

A second kind of sentence fragment is the *knowledge fragment*. This fragment may look like the punctuation fragment and will often be correctable in the same way—that is, by simply attaching it to the sentence preceding it. But the knowledge fragment is the fragment that the writer really thinks is a complete sentence. Here is a common knowledge fragment:

> The North began the Civil War confident of a quick victory. <u>Whereas it took four years of hard fighting before the South was finally defeated.</u>

Many people don't realize that *whereas* is like *because* and that a group of words beginning with *whereas* can't stand alone any more than a group of words beginning with *because* can.

The least common kind of sentence fragment, fortunately, is the *process fragment*. This is what a process fragment looks like:

Women born in the first three or four decades of the twentieth century, who, despite intelligence and education, were rarely able to enter the professional worlds of business, medicine, and the law.

Here, the word *who* prevents this from being a complete sentence, just as in the following simpler example:

Women who were rarely able to become doctors.

The simplest correction is simply to delete the *who*, which would make both examples above correct, complete sentences. But why does anyone write a sentence like the first one? Because the writer lost track of the sentence as he or she was writing and simply didn't notice that the *who*, which is all right in itself, made the finished "sentence" into a fragment. In other words, the writer got lost in the writing process.

Correcting Fragments

Although most fragments are not knowledge fragments, it is best to start the study of fragments with a review of the kinds of nonsentence structures that are most likely to be written as fragments and with exercises to help distinguish them from complete sentences.

Punctuation Fragments

The following kinds of structures are the ones most often accidentally punctuated as sentences:

She just stared at her food. A soggy unappetizing mess.
This is just a noun phrase describing the food; it has no subject and verb.

She just stared at her food. Although she hadn't eaten for two days.
This group of words has a subject and verb, but the word although *makes it into a dependent clause that must be attached to a complete sentence.*

She just stared at her food. Thinking about all the problems she'd had.
There is a subject and verb buried in this phrase, but the phrase, beginning as it does with an -ing *verb, is just a verbal phrase and not a sentence.*

Knowledge Fragments

The following kinds of structures are the ones people most often think of as sentences, although they are not:

She just stared at her food. <u>Whereas John began eating right away.</u>

She just stared at her food. <u>While John dug into his.</u>

> Whereas *and* while *are subordinating conjunctions, making otherwise complete sentences into dependent clauses that cannot stand alone and must be attached to complete sentences.*

She just stared at her food. <u>Which was a silly thing to do.</u>

> Which *cannot introduce complete sentences unless they are questions ("Which hat is yours?"). To correct, either join the* which *structure to the preceding sentence with a comma or change* which *to* that *or* this.

She just stared at her food. <u>The reason being that she had eaten only an hour before.</u>

> *The phrase* the reason being, *which is a carryover from speech, is not a complete sentence because* being *is not a verb but a verbal. To make this phrase a complete sentence,* being *would have to be changed to* was *(or, in a present-tense sentence,* is). *You can also attach it to the sentence preceding it by changing the period after* food *into a comma. But the best thing to do is change* the reason being that *to* because *and change the period to a comma.*

The band went crazy on the stage. <u>The lead guitarist smashing his instrument.</u> <u>The drummer jumping onto the drums.</u> <u>Other band members tearing off their clothes.</u>

> *These structures are exactly like* the reason being. *Each is like a sentence except that following the subject is an* -ing *verb instead of a regular verb. As in the case of* the reason being, *the best correction is simply to make all of these structures into one sentence by replacing the periods with commas. The other alternative would be to change the* -ing *verb forms into regular verbs.*

EXERCISE 7.A

Recognizing Punctuation Fragments

In the following series of short passages, there are punctuation fragments. Correct all fragments by rewriting the whole passage as a complete sentence.

1. My Lien's high school was gearing up for its big event of the year, a turtle race.

   _____   _____

2. My Lien planned to enter. Although she did not own a turtle.

   _____

3. She went to the lake. Hoping to find one there.

_____

4. At the lake, she found sand, rocks, and water. But no turtles.

_____

5. At pet stores and the aquarium, she heard the same words. "No turtles."

_____

6. As the day of the race neared, My Lien grew despondent. Fearing she had no chance.

_____

7. Her parents remained cheerful. Because her father had a secret.

_____

8. He had a business acquaintance with an odd hobby. Breeding turtles.

_____

9. On the day before the race, her father came home with a big surprise. A brand-new, five-speed racing turtle.

_____

10. My Lien's turtle swept the field. Leaving the others in the dust.

_____

EXERCISE 7.B

Following is a series of short passages in which there are one or more punctuation fragments. Copy each passage carefully. Correct each punctuation fragment by attaching it to the sentence preceding it.

1. The people of Smeltsburg elected Ronald Muffin mayor for a second term. Thinking he would once again do a good job. They did not realize that he planned to sell City Hall, a building of great historical importance.

_____

_____

2. City Hall had been built in 1864 to house wounded Civil War veterans, but it was used for that purpose only one month. The time it took for the one wounded veteran to get better.

_____

_____

3. Historians have discovered that of the 105 Smeltsburg men who went into the army, few ever saw combat. Even though all were fit for duty.

_____

_____

4. Most of the Smeltsburg Company hid behind trees during the battles. A fact that came out after the war when it was found that they were the only company in both armies with no casualties.

_____

_____

5. The one wounded Smeltsburg man was hurt when a chicken attacked him. Giving him severe pecks on his hands and face, wounds that sent him home to Smeltsburg.

_____

_____

6. After he was healed, the Smeltsburg Veterans Hospital was made the City Hall. A place where the returning veterans could gather and lie about the war. Their favorite form of entertainment.

_____

_____

7. Since the town's population has dropped to thirty-four, Mayor Muffin believes a city hall is no longer necessary, thus making possible the sale of the building. While perhaps acquiring a new business or employer for the town.

_____

_____

EXERCISE 7.C

Recognizing Knowledge Fragments

Following are several short passages in which nonsentence constructions are punctuated as sentences. Copy the passages, correcting the errors either by making the nonsentence part of the sentence preceding it or by changing it into a sentence.

1. Most fast food is tasteless. Whereas most good food is expensive.

_____

2. Most people are happy with tasteless food. Which is why fast-food places make money.

_____

3. I prefer food with taste. While Glen doesn't care what he eats.

_____

4. I got a hamburger the other day. Its bun bursting with lettuce, tomato, pickles, and who knows what.

_____

5. I couldn't taste the meat. The reason being there wasn't any. [Revise using *because*.]

_____

6. The greasy meat in most fast-food places isn't nutritious. Whereas all the salad piled onto it is.

_____

7. Glen loves it all. Which mystifies me.

_____

8. He won't accept fake money or listen to manufactured music. While he will eat fake food.

_____

8. PRONOUNS

Pronouns as Subjects and Objects

As you know, pronouns (*I, you, he, she, we, they, it*) can be subjects of sentences or other structures with verbs in them:

I ordered the books that you and she ordered, but they didn't come and it was the mailman's fault.

As you also know, whether you know you know it or not, other pronouns (*me, you, him, her, us, them, it*) can be objects:

We sent them an order, but they lost it, and for me and him, that created difficulties.

Subject pronouns come in front of verbs, just as noun subjects do:

She found the problem.

He lost his wallet.

Mary found the problem.

John lost his wallet.

Object pronouns follow verbs or prepositions, just as noun objects do:

Mary found it.

Mary likes him.

John went with them.

Mary found the problem.

Mary likes George.

John went with George and Tom.

People run into a problem sometimes when they have two pronouns joined by an *and* in a subject spot. Have you ever heard anyone say a sentence like one of these?

Me went to a movie last night.
Me worked on the car all day.

Probably not. But how about one of these?

Me and her went to a movie last night.
Me and John worked on the car all day. (Or, John and me worked on the car.)

The "me and her went" or "me and John worked" are just as wrong as the "me went" and the "me worked" and for the same reason: The words *me, her,* and *him* are all object pronouns, but in these sentences they've been used as subjects.

Here is a list of the subject and object pronouns; just skim it:

Subject	**Object**
I	me
you	you
he	him
she	her
we	us
they	them
it	it

Normally, we don't put an object pronoun in a subject spot unless we pair it with another noun or pronoun. When we use pronouns as subjects all by themselves, we always use them correctly. So to check whether you've used a pair or one of a pair correctly, ask yourself which pronoun you would use if you were using it by itself. For instance, look at the following sentence with pronouns used as subjects:

Me and her left the party early.

To check the *me* pronoun, ask yourself whether you would say, "Me left the party early." To check the *her* pronoun, ask yourself whether you would say, "Her left the party early." You know you wouldn't say either of those things, so you also know how the sentence should be written:

She and I left the party early.

EXERCISE 8.A

For practice, check the subject pronouns in the following sentences; not every one is incorrect. Write in the correct pronoun where needed.

1. Mary and me took out John's garbage.

2. He and the cat brought it back in, bits at a time.

3. Me and the cat had a fight over some fish bones.

4. Him and John had similar tastes in food.

5. It occurred to Mary and me that we were quite different.

6. Mary felt that she and I should leave them to themselves.

7. She said that her and the cat could never get along.

8. I secretly hoped that me and her could sneak off together.

9. We agreed that John and her could never share the same kitchen.

10. The cat and John thought that Mary and me were lacking in taste.

Pronoun Order

There may be some activities in which "me first" is a good motto, but not in writing. In writing, *me* always comes second. So the following sentence is incorrect:

They gave the tickets to me and Susan.

It should, of course, be

> They gave the tickets to Susan and me.

Uses and Misuses of *They*

The word *they*, of course, is a plural pronoun. It refers to both people and things:

> The people on the corner were angry. They were waving their arms and shouting.
>
> I spilled the whole box of nails on the floor. They were scattered everywhere.

Informally, in speech, we often use *they* when it doesn't actually refer to anything at all, as in these examples:

> They say that lightning never strikes twice in the same place. (Who says it?)
>
> I'd hate working in a department store. They have to put up with too many irritating people. (Who does?)
>
> The Dropsocket Corporation is making news again. They have come out with an internal combustion pencil sharpener. (Note that while the company gets the singular verb *is* in the first sentence, it's referred to by the plural pronoun *they* instead of the singular *it*.)

Unfortunately, in writing, all our pronouns (except indefinite ones, which we don't need to worry about) are supposed to refer to some specific noun. We would do better to write the sentences above like this:

> People say that lightning never strikes twice in the same place.
>
> I'd hate working in a department store. Clerks have to put up with too many irritating people.
>
> The Dropsocket Corporation is making news again. It has come out with an internal combustion pencil sharpener.

EXERCISE 8.B

In the following practice sentences, locate the instances in which *they* is misused and correct the sentences in whatever way seems to you best. *Be sure not to change any* they *that is correctly used.*

1. They say that there is nothing new under the sun, but the Snidely Wingnut Company has proven this saying wrong.

2. They have developed a whole new line of self-cleaning dog food dishes.

3. People are always complaining about their dog food dishes. After the dog uses them three or four times, they get disgusting.

4. The advantage of this new dish is that they will never get dirty again.

5. When the dog has eaten, the dish dissolves all the leftover particles of food in acid so that they won't stick to the dish.

6. Down at the Snidely Wingnut Company they do admit that there is one little bug they have to work out yet.

7. That's the acid solution left in the dish, which kills the dog the next time they try to eat out of the dish.

Pronoun Reference

Other pronouns besides *they* must, of course, be used correctly too. As we write, concentrating on what we're trying to say, it's very easy to forget precisely *how* we've said what we've previously said. This sort of forgetting, which is natural in writing, can lead to many technical problems in the finished product, and that's why revising and proofreading are so important. One of the easiest problems to spot and fix is mixed-up pronoun references—that is, having a pronoun that refers to no noun at all or having a pronoun that is in the wrong number for the noun it refers to, for example, a singular pronoun referring to a plural noun.

You can use this table as a reminder, if you want one, of how pronouns work:

he, she:	refers to one male or one female
his, her:	possessive form of *he, she*
they:	refers to more than one male, more than one female, or more than one thing
their:	possessive form of *they*
we:	refers to more than one person, including the writer; also refers to today's society or world
our:	possessive form of *we*

EXERCISE 8.C

In the following passage, fill in the correct pronouns from the list above. In addition, underline the noun each pronoun refers to.

The relationship between New England parents in the seventeenth century and

(   ) children was very different from what we see now. Then as now,

parents often had to deal with sons and daughters who became somewhat rebellious when (   ) reached their teen years. One of (   ) solutions to this problem, particularly in the case of a boy, was to send (   ) away to be an apprentice to a skilled artisan or a businessman. (   ) would have to live apart from (   ) parents for most of the year, learning from a master how to be a blacksmith or a shoemaker. Girls could also be sent to live with another family where (   ) would have to learn the arts of cooking and making cloth from someone other than (   ) mother. A woman who was raising a girl other than (   ) own daughter would tend to be more strict with (   ) charge than with (   ) own child. In our time, parents no longer send (   ) children off to be apprentices to others, but many parents, faced with difficult teenagers in the house, often wish (   ) could.

Pronouns with Indefinite Nouns

Sometimes when we write, we don't want to refer to particular people but to people in general. At these times, we may find ourselves using words or phrases like the following:

people	people in seventeenth-century New England
a person	a person looking for a job
students	Japanese students
a student	a student who is falling behind in class
one	

English does not make life easy for us when we are using these *indefinite* nouns and phrases. In particular, there is one little awkward situation that bothers many people. It is this: When you want to refer to men or women, or people in general, or even things, there is one handy all-purpose pronoun for you to use: *they* or *them*. But when you want to refer to a single person or thing, you have to make up your mind whether you want to use the masculine pronoun, *he*, or the feminine pronoun, *she*, or the neuter pronoun, *it*. There's nothing so bad about this except that sometimes your pronoun follows an *indefinite* noun—that is, a noun that although singular refers to people in general. Here is an example:

A child should never be left unattended in a parked car.

The word *child* is clearly singular, but at the same time it clearly refers to any child or all children. Singular nouns that perform this kind of function are called indefinite nouns, or indefinites. Now, since this indefinite noun is singular, would you follow this sentence with the word *He* referring to *child* or the word *She*? How about the next sentence?

A person who attends school and works will have quite a few problems.

Would you want your next sentence to begin with *He* or *She*?

Traditionally, the rules of English usage always said that we use the masculine form to refer to indefinite nouns like *child, person, student, worker,* and so on. But in recent years, many people, women in particular, have argued that it is inappropriate always to use a masculine pronoun when referring to both men and women. In speech there has never been a problem because people have been in the habit for centuries of just using *they* to refer to indefinite nouns and pronouns. But in writing that is still considered incorrect because *they* is plural and most indefinite nouns are singular. What to do? Writers tackle this situation in different ways.

The His/Her Option

In this option, one uses "he or she" or "him or her" or "his or hers" when referring to indefinites:

A person who attends school and works will have quite a few problems. He or she will have to budget his or her time carefully so that the demands of neither school nor work will overwhelm him or her.

You can see how quickly this gets out of hand, and the trouble is, once you start doing it, you have to keep doing it. It's not usually a great option.

The Plural Option

In this option, the writer avoids singular indefinites whenever possible, using plurals instead:

People who attend school and work will have quite a few problems. They will have to budget their time carefully so that the demands of neither school nor work will overwhelm them.

The Alternating Option

In this one, the writer uses masculine pronouns sometimes and feminine pronouns other times. This is all right as long as it doesn't confuse the reader.

The Whatever-You-Want Option

In this one, women use feminine pronouns and men use masculine pronouns.

Pronouns with Indefinite Pronouns

Just as English has indefinite nouns, so it also has indefinite pronouns, and they too cause a lot of trouble. The most common indefinite pronouns are these:

anyone	anybody
someone	somebody
no one	nobody
everyone	everybody

each (whether followed by a noun or not)

Although all these words clearly refer to more than one person, they are still grammatically singular, at least most of the time. Notice that one group of them has the word *one* in it, a help in remembering that they are supposed to be singular, and notice that the other group has the singular word *body* in it. The following examples all illustrate correct pronoun usage with these indefinites (remember that the masculine/feminine problem exists with indefinite pronouns just as it does with indefinite nouns):

Anyone can get good grades if he (she) just studies hard enough.

I would like to find someone to do my work for me. She (he) could take as long as she (he) wanted.

Each of us will have to make up his (her) mind for himself (herself).

There are several exceptions to this rule, but the most common and important one is that when the indefinites *no one/nobody* or *everyone/everybody* refer to specific groups of people, they take plural pronouns, as in these cases:

No one at the party wanted to leave. They were all having too good a time.

Everybody was extremely happy with the concert. They all applauded and cheered at the end.

In summary, when one of the indefinite words, either noun or pronoun, is used to refer to people or a group of people in general, it is followed by a *singular* pronoun: *he/she, him/her*. When *no one/nobody* or *everyone/everybody* refers to a specific group rather than a general group, it is followed by a *plural* pronoun: *they/them*.

EXERCISE 8.D

In the following sentences, fill in the blanks with the correct pronouns. In the case of indefinite nouns, you may change the noun according to the "plural option" listed above.

1. A student who tries to work too many hours will pay the price.

   _____ social life will be a disaster.

2. Anyone who wants to live a happy life should find a balance between

   _____ need for rest and recreation and _____ need to work.

3. Everyone who wants _____ community to work effectively must

   contribute some of _____ own time to it. Each person must do

   _____ share. Each must contribute some of _____ own time and talent.

4. Society is greatly concerned about the abused child. The problem is that

   when _____ becomes a parent, _____ is likely to

   abuse _____ own children.

5. Everyone in the class was angry; _____ all complained to the department.

EXERCISE 8.E

For more practice in pronoun use, write sentences as directed here.

1. Write a sentence in which you use *anyone* followed by the correct pronoun.

   _____

2. Write a sentence in which you use *someone* followed by the correct pronoun.

   _____

3. Write a sentence in which you use the indefinite *everyone* followed by the correct pronoun.

   _____

4. Write a sentence in which you use *everyone* to refer to a specific group followed by the correct pronoun.

   _____

5. Write a sentence in which you use *each* followed by the correct pronoun.

   _____

6. Write a sentence in which you use *a person* as subject, followed by the correct pronoun.

   _____

7. Write a sentence in which you use *a student* as subject, followed by the correct pronoun.

   _____

One and You

Sometimes students get somewhat confused about whether to use *one* or *you* or the plural *they* in situations in which they are writing about people in general, as in the following passage from a student paper; note the underlined words:

> From this report a person will find out what is expected in certain positions and what kind of job one can expect. Most jobs fall into the following four main categories: jobs requiring the person to have experience; jobs requiring one to have some education; jobs requiring them to be a college graduate; and jobs aimed at particular age groups. One must keep all these questions in mind when looking for a job.
>
> Most employers' first question is whether you have had any experience relating to the type of job. With experience one can find better pay, more benefits, and you may even start your own business.

Since the idea is to be as consistent as possible in the pronouns we use, we should not switch back and forth between singular and plural without some logical reason for doing so. Otherwise we just confuse the reader. In the same way, we should not switch between *one* and *you*, unless we really want to refer to *anyone* with *one* and to the reader with *you*.

Since this writer switches constantly, he has a big problem. He has started with the indefinite noun *person* followed by the indefinite pronoun *one*, which is all right. Both of them are singular and both mean "anyone." But then he has gone on to use the plural *them* to refer to *person* and shifted from *one* to *you* and *your*.

If you want to start with a singular indefinite noun like *person*, stick to the pronouns *one* and the combination *he or she*. Don't switch to the plural *them*, and don't switch from *one* to *you*. If, as you go along, you find that the way you've started is awkward and uncomfortable—that you can't easily be consistent because of the way you started—*go back to the beginning and change that*; don't just change in midstream.

Remember:

one: means anyone in general
you: means *your reader* specifically

EXERCISE 8.F

For practice, rewrite the student passage above in two versions.

1. Rewrite it as the original writer did, starting with *a person* in the first line; after that, be sure to use singular pronouns; use *one* where the original writer did.

2. Rewrite it using *people* instead of *person* in the first line; after that, be sure to use plural pronouns throughout, including where the original writer used *one*.

9. USING *A* AND *AN*

While in speech it doesn't generally matter much whether we use the word *a* or the word *an* in front of a noun, using the wrong one in writing is, to most readers, a really glaring mistake.

The rule for using these two words is pretty simple. Most of the time, we use *an* in front of a word beginning with one of the five vowel letters:

a, e, i, o, u

And, of course, we use *a* in front of words beginning with all the rest of the letters. So normal usage works like this:

an *a*rmadillo	a toad
an *e*lephant	a giraffe
an *i*llness	a sickness
an *o*rphan	a child
an *u*mbrella	a raincoat

Naturally, there are exceptions, but at least they are sensible ones. Regardless of the actual spelling of a word, if its first letter *sounds* like a consonant, we will use *a* in front of it, as in this case. This happens fairly frequently with words beginning with *u*.

a united organization
a US army unit

Notice that the *u* in these two cases is pronounced like *y*.

Similarly, if a consonant *sounds* like a vowel, we will usually put *an* in front of it. This happens in San Francisco all the time when the city's name gets abbreviated to S.F., because the letter *s* all by itself is pronounced *ess*:

an S.F. restaurant guide

EXERCISE 9.A

In the following sentences, write in the correct word, *a* or *an*.

1. _____ major problem for our basketball team is that no player is more than 5 feet 10 inches tall.

2. Even _____ average referee tends to look down on this team.

3. It takes _____ awfully clever coach to devise plays that they can use.

4. And it takes _____ unusually bad team to lose to them.

5. They will have _____ occasional scoring spurt when someone gets hot, but _____ event like that is rare in their lives.

6. They have _____ talented guard but not _____ active front line.

7. But the guard is _____ undersized 5 feet 2 inches.

8. _____ slam dunk is out of the question for this team, and even _____ layup is pretty rare.

9. _____ equally talented team can always beat them, and it is terrible to watch what happens when _____ really good team comes to town.

10. They always present _____ interesting spectacle on the court, since they look _____ lot like children who have wandered into the wrong place.

10. NOUN PLURALS

Most nouns in English have both singular and plural forms, and in most cases, their plurals take an *s* ending—as in the words you have just been reading: *nouns, forms, cases, plurals,* and *words*. Everyone knows this.

But because we don't always pronounce those *s* endings when we speak, some of us find it difficult to remember to put them on plural nouns when we write.

An added complication for some of us is that our particular speech patterns have a rule that says we don't need to add *s* endings when it is obvious that the noun is plural—in other words, when the *s* would simply be redundant. For instance, if we use the word *two* in front of the noun *car*, then we know that we are talking about more than one car without adding an *s* on it. So what's the point of adding it? There is no particular point except that in written English it has to have an *s* or your reader will think that you've made a simple mistake and that you're a dope.

Notice too that English has an interesting pattern when the word *one* appears in front of a noun. Normally, of course, the word *one* means just that and so a noun following it would not be a plural:

one paper
one basketball

But if we write *one of*, then the noun following will be a plural:

one of the papers
one of the basketballs

The idea is that this means one out of several papers or many basketballs.

EXERCISE 10.A

In the following exercises, find the word indicating a plural noun (for example, a number, a word like *several* or *many*, or the words *one of*), then find the noun that should have a plural *s* ending and add that ending.

Sometimes making a plural noun near the beginning of a sentence will mean that other nouns further along will have to be changed to plurals too. *Underline all nouns you change into plurals.*

1. The high school prom was being looked forward to by almost all of the student.

2. Raquel was one of the person most anticipating the event.

3. She and three of her friend were on the planning committee.

4. Many of the prom in the past year had been failure, so they were determined to make this one of the rare success.

5. Several difficulty presented themselves, however.

6. One was a group of boy who had disrupted two dance earlier in the year.

7. Another was a bunch of girl who had bad attitude and caused trouble.

8. A third was they couldn't agree on which of several band to hire.

9. Raquel, many of whose family member were diplomat, came up with a solution to these problem.

10. She hired a band led by the older brother of one of the troublesome boy.

11. She told two of the other boy that some of the difficult girl really liked them and hoped they would take them to the prom.

12. The prom turned out to be the most successful dance in several year, but Raquel missed it because she was hired by the United Nation to solve some difficult problem in Asia and Africa.

EXERCISE 10.B

Do the following exercises in using noun plurals:

1. Write three sentences in which you use numbers before nouns (for instance, *three cats*).

2. Write three sentences in which you use the words *many of*.

3. Write three sentences in which you see the words *one of*.

4. Write a sentence in which you use the words *a family of*.

5. Write a sentence in which you use the word *several* in front of a noun.

6. Write a sentence in which you use the word *some* in front of a noun.

7. Write a sentence in which you use the words *a group of*.

11. NONCOUNTABLE NOUNS

Some nouns do not take plural forms. These are called *noncountable* nouns. English has the very curious practice of dividing up its nouns into two types—those representing things that can be counted and those representing things that can't be counted. The *countable* nouns are the ones that take *s* plurals. We can, for instance, count

grains of sand
drops of water
pieces of aluminum
kinds of beauty

But we can't count

> sand
>
> water
>
> aluminum
>
> beauty

So we don't put *s* endings on those nouns.

Noncountable nouns fall into two large categories: mass nouns and abstract nouns. Mass nouns, which indicate things in their generic or undivided forms, are such words as these:

> *foods*: meat, fish, chicken, coffee, tea, milk
>
> *elements, minerals, and gases*: aluminum, iron, neon, hydrogen, sand, water, air

Abstract nouns include words such as these, which do not have *s* plural forms:

information	clothing
research	weather
advertising	luggage
homework	money
housework	advice
experience	equipment
knowledge	

Sometimes it doesn't seem logical to think of some of these abstract nouns as representing things one can't count. For instance, we talk about counting our money all the time, and one could certainly count the number of homework items one had to do. But the language insists that we are actually counting not money but dollars and cents (note the *s* endings on these words) and the items of homework we have to do. When a noun refers to a concept rather than a thing itself, it is a noncountable noun and usually doesn't take a plural form.

To confuse things even more, some nouns can be used to indicate concepts or abstractions some of the time, in which case they don't have *s* endings, and at other times they can refer to specific things, in which case they do. For instance, we can say,

> The dorm serves chicken all the time.

But we can also say,

> George is raising chickens in his backyard.

The first use of *chicken* refers to the meat as an abstraction while the second use refers to the specific birds.

Similarly, we say,

I have been studying philosophy for years.

And in this case, we would mean that we have studied the specific *philosophies* of numerous philosophers.

In still other cases, some nouns will take an *s* ending whether they are being used to refer to generic forms or not. For instance, the following uses are correct:

The dorm serves carrots all the time.

The dorm serves beets all the time.

The dorm serves peas all the time.

On the other hand, the words *corn, broccoli,* and *spinach* never take an *s* form. It's a wonder that anyone ever learns English.

Often the best policy is simply to try to memorize common noncountable nouns. Start with the thirteen abstract nouns listed above, and if you make the mistake of adding an *s* ending to other noncountable nouns, memorize those words too.

12. DROPPED CONTRACTIONS OF *IS* AND *ARE*

Some spoken forms of English offer three alternative ways of using forms of the verb *be* in the present tense. In these forms, you can say any of the following:

She is going.	They are going.
She's going.	They're going.
She going.	They going.
We are going.	You are going.
We're going.	You're going.
We going.	You going.

While these are all equally correct in speech, unfortunately only two of the forms are correct in writing: the one using the full verb *is* or *are* and the one using the contracted form *'s* or *'re*. The third form, in which *is* and *are* are deleted, is not considered correct in written English.

EXERCISE 12.A

In the following sentences, write *both* correct forms of subject and verb in the blanks, as in this example:

This morning (John) _____John's_____ /_____John is_____ walking
to school.

1. (Lorene) _____ /_____ considering marriage.

2. She has had three dates with Ricky, and now (she) _____ /

   _____ thinking of marrying the man.

3. Her friends keep telling her (she) _____ /_____ making a big mistake.

4. (They) _____ /_____ taking these ideas of hers very
   seriously.

5. Several of (them) _____ /_____ thinking of talking to
   her parents about her plans.

6. Some of the (others) _____ /_____ actually considering kidnapping her to let her get over her passion.

7. Meanwhile, (Ricky) _____ /_____ going about his
   business.

8. (He) _____ /_____ not even sure he wants to date
   Lorene again.

9. Actually, (he) _____ /_____ sort of thinking of asking
   Valerie for a date.

10. (Lorene) _____ /_____ going to be somewhat
    surprised when she learns that her (wedding)

    _____ /_____ being postponed.

EXERCISE 12.B

In the following passage, locate the places where the verbs *is* and *are* are
missing, and write them in.

George trying to get together a group of friends to participate in historical reen-actments. He has gotten them interested in the 9th and 10th US Cavalry, the two black regiments of the old post–Civil War army, the famous "Buffalo Soldiers." They increasingly busy acquiring or having made uniforms and equipment of the period. They subscribing to magazines devoted to historical reenactments, and they planning to attend events with other men and women who interested in the same period. George spending amazing amounts of time in the library. He doing research on the US Cavalry of the last half of the nineteenth century. His wife being kept so busy making blue cavalry uniforms she starting to think of either going into the uniform business or divorcing George.

13. FORMING DIRECT QUESTIONS

Questions Beginning with Who, What, Why, Where, When, *and* How

In written English, unlike in some forms of spoken English, questions beginning with the *wh* words (plus *how*) have to flip-flop the normal sub-ject-verb word order:

normal:	He likes her.
	He likes it. (or He does like it.)
question:	Who does he like?
	What does he like?

With a verb other than the verb *be*, we don't simply switch the order of the subject and verb; rather, we put a form of the verb *do* in front of the subject and then use the regular base form of the main verb after the subject:

normal:	She misses her cat.
question:	Who *does* she miss?
normal:	They miss their mother.
question:	Who *do* they miss?
normal:	He found his money.
question:	What *did* he find?

Notice that in the present tense, the verb *do* has to agree in number with the subject following it.

When a form of the verb *be* is the main verb, it just moves in front of its subject in the question form:

normal:	She is there.
question:	Where is she?
normal:	They were unhappy.
question:	Why were they unhappy?
normal:	She is leaving.
question:	When is she leaving?
	How is she leaving?

In the case of questions in the future tense, it is the word *will* that moves in front of the subject:

normal:	She will leave.
question:	When will she leave?

REVIEW

In questions, when do we use a form of the verb *do* in front of the subject?
When do we use the original verb rather than *do*?
How do we handle the future tense in questions?

EXERCISE 13.A

In the exercises below, change the sentence into a question beginning with the word indicated:

1. Calbert lost his wallet.

   How _____

2. He is very absent-minded.

   Why _____

3. He lost it yesterday.

   When _____

4. He lost it in the gym.

   Where _____

5. He will eventually find it.

   How _____

6. He will then be happy.

   When _____

7. He will need it on Saturday.

   What _____

8. He is improving as a student.

   How _____

9. He is getting better in English.

   Why _____

10. His teachers like him.

    Why _____

EXERCISE 13.B

Write three questions beginning with *where, what,* and *when* in which you use a form of the verb *be*:

Example:
Where are my shoes?

Write three questions beginning with *where, what,* and *when* in which you use a verb other than the verb *be*:

Example:
Where have my shoes gone?

Write three questions beginning with *why, how,* and *what* in which you use a verb in the future tense:

Example:
Why will we have rain?
How will the game end?

Yes-No Questions

Questions that require only yes-no answers work in pretty much the same way as *wh* questions. If the verb has more than one part, the *first* part goes in front of the subject:

She *should* get a good grade.
Should she get a good grade?

He *will* be successful.
Will he be successful?

We *haven't* completed the work.
Haven't we completed the work?

He *could* have been the best.
Could he have been the best?

If the verb has only one part, then a form of the verb *do* has to be used in front of the subject:

She got a good grade.
Did she get a good grade?

He succeeded in business.
Did he succeed in business?

We completed the work.
Did we complete the work?

But if the verb is a form of the verb *be*, it just flip-flops with the subject:

He is successful.
Is he successful?

They were out of town.
Were they out of town?

REVIEW

What is the rule for yes-no questions in which the verb has more than one part?
What is the rule for yes-no questions in which the verb has only one part?
What is the rule for yes-no questions when the verb is a form of *be*?

EXERCISE 13.C

Change the following sentences into questions:

1. George could have gone to college.

   _____

2. George went to college.

   _____

3. Tanya should have studied hard.

   _____

4. Tanya studied hard.

_____

5. George was an outstanding student.

_____

6. The supplies will arrive tomorrow.

_____

7. The supplies arrived today.

_____

8. These supplies are totally inadequate.

_____

9. The game was lost through bad luck.

_____

10. We lost the game through lousy talent.

_____

EXERCISE 13.D

Write three questions using verbs that have more than one part (for instance, verbs beginning with *should, could, will,* or *have*).

Write three questions using one-part verbs. These sentences will have to start with a form of the verb *do*.

Write three questions based on one-part forms of the verb *be* (that is, *am, is, are, was, were*).

14. FORMING INDIRECT QUESTIONS

In addition to direct questions, all forms of English, both spoken and written, allow us to use what are called indirect questions. Here are two examples of direct questions and their indirect counterparts:

direct: What can I do?
indirect: I wonder what I can do.

direct: Can I do it?
indirect: I wonder whether (if) I can do it.

As you know, in direct questions we change the order, or flip-flop, the subject and verb, putting the verb in front of the subject. But in indirect questions, we don't; we continue to use the standard nonquestion word order of subject first and verb second. This is contrary to some forms of spoken English in which the subject and verb are flip-flopped in indirect questions.

An indirect question always appears in the second half of a sentence that starts out not being a question, like these:

> I asked her . . .
> I wonder . . .

In fact, the verbs *ask* and *wonder* are very common signs that an indirect question is coming up. The other signs are whether certain words follow them, specifically the question words beginning with *wh* (plus the word *how*) and the words *whether* and *if*. Here are some typical indirect question sentences:

> I asked her *what* she wanted.
> I asked her *why* she did it.
> I asked her *where* she was going.
> I wonder *whether* you'll like the concert.
> I wonder *if* the plane will be on time.
> I wonder *when* it will get here.

In these kinds of sentences, be sure to use the normal order of first subject, and then verb following the *wh* word or the words *if* and *whether*.

EXERCISE 14.A

Complete the following sentences:

1. I wonder whether _____

2. I wonder if _____

3. I wonder where _____

4. I wonder why _____

5. I wonder when _____

6. I asked him whether _____

7. I asked him if _____

8. I asked him what _____

9. I asked him why _____

10. I asked him when _____

15. APOSTROPHES TO SHOW POSSESSION

In English, we can show that someone possesses something in several ways. We can say, "The book belongs to Mary," or we can say, "Look out fo the tail of the cat," but, of course, we would normally refer to "Mary's book" and "the cat's tail." Here are three sentences with possessives in them:

I love John's limousine.
The boy's eyes got wider.
The dancer's dreams were shattered.

First rule: When a noun does not end in *s* (John, boy, dancer), we make it into a possessive by adding *'s*.

Here are three more sentences with possessives in them; they are slightly different from the first three:

I love Charles' limousine.
The two boys' eyes got wider.
The three dancers' dreams were shattered.

Second rule: When a noun does end in *s* (Charles, boys, dancers), we make it into a possessive by adding only *'* (although many writers prefer to add *'s*, as in *Charles's*, for singular nouns ending in *s*).

These two rules can be summed up in the following rule:

When you have a noun that should be a possessive, first write it the way you normally would *and then* add the apostrophe or the apostrophe + *s*.

There are a few more rules covering special cases, but this is the one you will use 90 percent of the time. Practice it in the following exercises.

EXERCISE 15.A

Rewrite each underlined group of words using apostrophes to show possession.

Example:
He washed the socks of his girlfriend.

    his girlfriend's socks

He remembered the addresses of all his girlfriends.

    all his girlfriends' addresses

1. She found the treasure of the pirate.

2. She found the treasure of the pirates.

   _____

3. We ate the apple of the farmer.

   _____

4. We ate the apples of the farmers.

   _____

5. George kept track of the home runs of his favorite player.

   _____

6. He did not keep track of the birthday of his girlfriend.

   _____

7. She wanted to know why he was more interested in the statistics of baseball players than he was in her.

   _____

8. He said it wasn't interest; it was that the home runs of ballplayers come more frequently than her birthdays.

   _____

9. Try as we might, the important days of people are hard for many of us to remember.

   _____

10. It would help if I could get the government to make national holidays of the birthdays of my best friends.

   _____

Two special situations come up occasionally in apostrophe use. One involves what are called *compound nouns*—that is, nouns made up of more than one word:

   mother-in-law   someone else

To these words, we simply add the 's at the end:

   mother-in-law's   someone else's

The other situation involves the possession of something jointly by two (or more) people:

Fred and John own a boat
Fred and John's boat

But if we want to show that Fred and John each own separate boats, we would write

Fred's and John's boats

EXERCISE 15.B

Rewrite each underlined group of words using apostrophes to show possession.

1. I loved the house of John and Marsha.

   _____

2. The house of my sister-in-law was right next door.

   _____

3. The house of the air force commander-in-chief was across the street.

   _____

4. At the stadium, the city refurbished the restrooms of the men and the women.

   _____

5. The foreign policies of Presidents Reagan and Carter were quite different.

   _____

6. But the basic tasks of their secretaries of state remained the same.

   _____

7. One of the famous events in American history is the journey west of Lewis and Clark.

   _____

8. The shoes of Mary and Charles are exactly the same color—yellow.

   _____

9. The interests of my stepfather are very broad.

   _____

10. The jointly owned Mercedes of Marie, Sue, and Ellen is starting to fall apart.

   _____

You now know practically everything there is to know about using apostrophes to show possession. People often get anxious about this simple matter and start using apostrophes all over the place, even when they aren't correct. Along a country road have you ever seen a sign like this?

FRESH EGG'S

Or a student will write

I thought it was hers.

and then say, "Wait a minute. *Hers* is possessive. I better use an apostrophe," and change it to

I thought it was her's.

The farmer is wrong and the student is wrong. All the farmer means is that he has more than one egg for sale; the eggs don't own anything. And we never use apostrophes with pronouns to show possession—never ever—on with nouns. So don't overdo it. Remember the following three guidelines.

1. When a noun that shows possession does not end in *s*, we add to it *'s*.
    The artist's skill was obvious.
    But when a noun that shows possession does end in *s*, we add to it only *'*.
    The clowns' antics were very funny.

2. In the case of compound nouns, we add the *'s* or the *'* to the last word.
    The Secretary of the Interior's plan was bad.
    The two mother-in-laws' disagreement was obvious.

3. When two or more nouns indicate joint possession of something, we add the *'s* or the *'* only to the last noun.
    Joan and Mary's airplane crashed.
    John and Charles' boat sank.
    But when two or more nouns possess the same kind of thing but possess it separately, we add the *'s* or the *'* to each of the nouns.
    Joan's and Mary's airplanes both won prizes.
    John's and Charles' boats both sank.

Don't worry about plurals and possessive pronouns.

1. We *never ever* use an apostrophe with an *s* when the *s* just indicates a plural.

   The eggs of the farmer are not as fresh as the farmer's sons.

2. We *never ever* use an apostrophe with a pronoun that shows possession.

   Now that they got theirs, I want mine.
   If she flaunts hers, he intends to flaunt his.
   If it flaunts its, you can flaunt yours.

EXERCISE 15.C

Rewrite each underlined group of words using apostrophes to show possession.

1. The marriage of Edgardo and Flora was a modern one in that they both worked.

   _____

2. The job of Flora was as a junior executive for a meatball company.

   _____

3. The job of Edgardo was inspecting feathers in a pillow company.

   _____

4. The jobs of Edgardo and Flora were both very tiring.

   _____

5. The demands of their bosses were heavy and frequent.

   _____

6. The tendency of the boss of Flora was to give her reports to work on over the weekend.

   Flora's boss' tendency

7. The boss of Edgardo often gave him extra bushels of feathers to inspect at the very end of the day.

   Edgardo's boss

8. They complained to each other that the jobs of their parents hadn't been as difficult as theirs were.

   their parents' jobs'

9. Edgardo noticed that <u>the supervisor of his brother-in-law</u> was considerate and kindly.

his brother in law's sup.

10. <u>The policy of this supervisor</u> was to treat his employees fairly.

The sup's policy

11. As a result, <u>the loyalty to the firm of the employees</u> was outstanding.

the emp. loyalty to the firm's

12. Theirs was a faithfulness that was comparable only to <u>the faithfulness to its master of a dog.</u>

the dog faith. to its master

13. <u>The grumblings of the workers at the company of Edgardo</u> indicated a lot of unhappiness there.

_____

14. Flora finally talked to her boss about <u>the morale of her and her co-workers.</u>

_____

15. Now the <u>morale of everyone</u> is very high, and the meatballs are coming out rounder than ever.

_____

16. HOMOPHONES

Homophones are words that sound alike but are spelled differently and mean different things. For example, in this sentence, "Only a few hours ago, that house was ours," the words *hours* and *ours* sound the same to most people and so are considered homophones. While very few students have trouble with words like those, some do get confused in other cases, particularly those in which one word is a contraction and the other is a possessive.

You're/Your

Read the following passage and underline *you're* and *your* every time you find them.

If your coat isn't ready at the cleaners, you're going to have nothing warm to

wear this evening, and your mother will probably have a fit. If you're really planning on going to the party, you'd better make plans to borrow a coat just in case, or your goose will be cooked.

Which shows possession?_____

Which is a contraction of *you are*?_____

EXERCISE 16.A

In the blanks below, write *your* or *you're*:

1. Now that _____ in college, _____ high school probably seems a million miles away.

2. When _____ ready to leave, it's irritating to be held up.

3. If _____ parents are understanding during _____ teen years, that time can be a good one.

4. If _____ always fighting with them, it isn't so pleasant.

5. When _____ all fired up during a basketball game, the

   adrenaline in _____ body is flowing.

Write three sentences using the word *your*:

6. _____

7. _____

8. _____

Write three sentences using the word *you're*:

9. _____

10. _____

11. _____

It's/Its

Read the following passage and underline *it's* and *its* every time you find them.

It's time to take the cat to the veterinarian again. It's gotten some scratches on its nose and ears, probably from a fight, and I'm pretty sure it's time for its shots as well. In some ways, it's kind of a nuisance to own a cat, but I find its company very pleasant.

Which shows possession?_____

Which is a contraction of *it is* or *it has*?_____

EXERCISE 16.B

In the blanks below, write *it's* or *its*:

1. When _____ time to be fed, the dog heads straight for
   _____ dish.
2. Now that _____ been decided who will wash the car,
   _____ time to get started on it.
3. When the cat got _____ tail caught in the refrigerator door, it
   yowled _____ head off.
4. Let's try to find out whether _____ too late to get the tickets.
5. I'm sure the table is expensive; _____ made of rosewood, and
   _____ surface is in beautiful condition.

Write three sentences using the word *its*:

6. _____
7. _____
8. _____

Write three sentences using the word *it's*:

9. _____
10. _____
11. _____

Who's/Whose

Read the following passage and draw a line under *who's* and *whose* every time you find them.

I don't know who's going to pay for the band at the party tonight, and I don't know whose problem it is, but it's not mine. The committee whose decision it was to hire the group should also decide who's to follow through on it, including who's going to have to come up with the money. The people whose actions have produced this mess should now clean it up.

Which shows possession?_____

Which is a contraction of *who is?*_____

EXERCISE 16.C

In the blanks below, write *whose* or *who's*:

1. When I found out _____ job you were taking, I wondered

   _____ I would get.

2. _____ responsible for this mess we're in?

3. I know _____ responsible, but I don't know _____
   going to get us out of it.

4. Try to find out _____ going on the picnic and _____
   car we'll be taking.

5. I think I know _____ woods these are.

Write three sentences using the word *whose*:

6. _____

7. _____

8. _____

Write three sentences using the word *who's*:

9. _____

10. _____

11. _____

The three pairs of homophones covered above—*you're/your, it's/its,* and *who's/whose*—have something in common. Notice that in each case, the word with the apostrophe is a contraction, a combination of two word

you're = you are
    it's = it is or it has
  who's = who is or who has

Notice also that in each case, the word without the apostrophe is a possessive pronoun:

    your = your hat (Pick up your hat.)
      its = its fur (The cat is licking its fur.)
  whose = whose coat (Whose coat is this?)

While nouns in their possessive forms always use apostrophes, pronouns in their possessive forms *never* use apostrophes.

There/Their

Read the following passage and underline *there* and *their* every time you find them.

There are three main kinds of pests at movie theaters. The worst are the ones who insist on talking to their friends throughout the whole film. About as bad are the mothers who bring their little children, who sit there not understanding anything and either ask questions all the time or cry. Then there are the ones crunching their way through a monster vat of popcorn. Unfortunately, there seems to be little one can do about most of these nuisances.

Which is a way of introducing a thought or indicates a location? _____

Which shows possession?_____

EXERCISE 16.D

In the blanks below, write *there* or *their*:

1. _____ are several ways of messing up a date.

2. One standard one is to plan to go to a concert but not get _____ on time.

3. Then _____ are the people who don't write down

   _____ dates and appointments and just plain fail to show up.

4. _____ dating histories tend to be short and sad ones.

5. People who are considerate of _____ dates and get

_____ acts together ahead of time generally have a happier
time.

Write three sentences using the word *there* to introduce an idea.

6. _____

7. _____

8. _____

Write three sentences using the word *their* to indicate possession.

9. _____

10. _____

11. _____

To/Too

Read the following paragraph and underline the words *to* and *too* every
time you find them.

A friend of mine has made a list of movies he wants to see, but it's much too
long. He must have four or five hundred titles on the list, and it would simply
take too many hours to try to watch them. He not only wrote down all those
titles, but he even added comments to each one, too, writing things such as
"not to be missed." I went to the video store to try to rent a few things on his
list but couldn't find any of them. They were too rare for my local store to handle. I thought I might make a similar list too, but mine would be a great deal
shorter.

Which form means either *also* or *very*?_____

EXERCISE 16.E

Write either *to* or *too* in the blanks in the following passage. If the word
also or *very* would fit, write *too*. Otherwise, write *to*.

Chung set out _____ buy a CD player, but he was thinking of

getting a new tape recorder too. The tape recorder he owned was

_____ old to function well anymore. The first CD player he

looked at had _____ many frills and was far _____

expensive. He was somewhat drawn to another machine, but that one was

rather expensive _____. He examined every machine carefully,

and an attractive saleswoman tried to help him out. Finally he found some

equipment that seemed _____ do about what he wanted, and

he decided _____ buy it. Unfortunately, he owed

_____ much on his credit card, and so the store told him

_____ hit the road. The saleswoman was not _____

interested in his proposal _____ go on a date either.

17. CAPITALIZATION

Rules for capitalizing nouns are particularly hard to remember because they are so arbitrary. They are even completely different from one language to another. Here are the most common ones in English:

1. The first word of every sentence must be capitalized.
    My cat ate the doughnuts.
2. People's names and initials and the names of animals are capitalized.
    George F. Handel
    P. D. Q. Bach
    Black Beauty (but not *horse*)
    Fido (but not *dog*)

3. Titles and abbreviated titles are all capitalized.
    Doctor Mary Jones
    Mary Jones, M.D.
    J. W. Birdwalk, Ph.D.
    President Lincoln
    Senator Wilson
    John Jones, Coordinator of Special Programs
    Mother (when used as a name)

4. When title words are not used as actual titles, they are not capitalized.

   She took her mother to the doctor, and they ran into one of their senators along the way.

5. Names of specific places with formal names are capitalized.

   Great Britain
   Thailand
   the Grand Canyon
   Arizona
   Cleveland
   the Algonquin Hotel
   Main Street

6. Words referring to places without naming them are not capitalized.

   We walked down the street, past several hotels. Being in a strange city, we weren't sure which one to choose.

The following passage illustrates rules 1 through 6:

My mother went to see Doctor Jones yesterday, but the doctor was not in. She stopped by City Hall on Franklin Street to visit with her old school friend, Mayor Jane Wilson, but the street was blocked off by the police. One of the police, Officer Johnson, told her that a big movie company was making a film in the building.

7. Names of languages and nationalities are always capitalized.

   English
   Chinese
   Mexican
   Canadian

8. But not when they don't refer to the language or the country.

   french fries
   canadian bacon
   russian roulette
   chinese checkers

9. In school, course titles are capitalized but not the names of subjects, except when the subject is a language (see rule 7 above).

Capitalize	**Do not capitalize**
Sociology 110	My best subject is sociology.
History of English	I am taking a course in the history of English.

Following is a passage that illustrates rules 7 through 9:

My friend Bo Ericksson, a Swedish exchange student, put another round of spanish onion on his hamburger and talked about his schedule. "I'm taking four courses, history, physics, math, and English. I'd like to take French too, but I don't have the time. My best course so far is History 230, Early American Colonies."

10. The names of religions are capitalized and so are the names of organizations.

Judaism (and Jewish)
Buddhism (and Buddhist)
Catholic Church
Democratic Party
Ford Motor Company
Business Students Association

11. The titles of stories, books, poems, movies, television shows, magazines, newspapers, and the like are capitalized, except for short words like *a, the, of, and,* and so on. These words are capitalized only if they are the first word of the title.

The New Yorker
The Atlanta Constitution
A Hazard of New Fortunes
The Lord of the Rings
Cat on a Hot Tin Roof

12. Periods or events in history are capitalized and so are organized current events that have names.

the Wars of the Roses
the Reformation
the Boxer Rebellion
the Senior Prom
the Boston Marathon

The following passage illustrates rules 10 through 12:

In an excellent book entitled *A Fall of Fortresses*, Elmer Bendiner describes the lives and experiences of the men who flew the bombers of the US Army Air Force over Europe during World War II. The book is particularly valuable in its treatment of the disastrous Battle of Schweinfurt.

13. Days, months, and holidays are capitalized but not seasons.

Monday
January
Martin Luther King's Birthday
fall
winter

14. Capitalize directions when they refer to specific geographical areas but not otherwise. The following passage illustrates this rule and also rule 13.

Joanne is going to drive south this summer because she comes from the South and wants to revisit her hometown. She plans to leave on a Monday early in May.

EXERCISE 17.A

The following exercises cover rules 1 through 6. In every instance in which there should be a capital letter, write the capital over the small printed letter.

1. on their trip to europe, my father and mother planned to visit ireland and scotland, where they had relatives, and then cross the english channel to spend some time in paris, where their best friend, a dentist, was planning to be.

2. as it turned out, the dentist, doctor sam jones, had to change his plans and was still in london, staying in a hotel on a street made famous in the 1960s, carnaby street.

3. i stayed home and took care of ping and pong, our two cats, and tried to flirt with professor fludge, the unmarried mathematics professor who lives next door.

The following exercises cover rules 7 through 14. Write in capital letters where they belong.

4. my roommate at the college of california is a spanish student named Rosa, who is in the united states for the first time.

5. her english is excellent, and she has done very well in english 100 and english 200 as well as all the classes in her major, political science.

6. although she is catholic and I am protestant, we get along extremely well, even when discussing religion.

7. for one thing, our tastes are quite similar; we both enjoy reading the new york times book review as well as the american edition of the french magazine elle, and we are both fans of the rock group slimy potato.

8. the biggest difference between Rosa and me is that she is very conservative by american standards; I am a republican from the midwest but I'm not nearly as conservative as she is.

9. one saturday last fall, we both went to the annual fall mixer, a big dance sponsored by the humanities students association, a dance where you didn't bring dates.

10. Rosa had a wonderful time, but her conservative spanish heritage really came to the fore when the boy she met tried to give her a french kiss, and she slapped him hard enough that you could hear it back in barcelona.

EXERCISE 17.B

The following exercises cover all fourteen of the capitalization rules.

1. Write a short sentence about the president of the United States in which you use the word *president* twice, once in its capitalized form and once in its ordinary form.

   _____

2. Write a short sentence in which you use the name of the town or city in which you live and tell about a place in another state or country you would like to visit.

   _____

3. Write a short sentence about a language you have studied or are studying or would like to study.

   _____

4. Write a short sentence in which you name all the subjects you are taking this term and the name of one course.

   _____

5. Write a short sentence in which you name your religion or an organization you have belonged to or have worked for.

   _____

6. Write a short sentence in which you name three out of the following four things: a television show, a book you have read, a newspaper, a movie.

   _____

7. Write a short sentence about a specific period of history that you know about or a well-known historical event.

_____

8. Write a short sentence in which you mention a favorite holiday and also the region of the country you live in.

_____

EXERCISE 17.C

The following exercises cover all fourteen capitalization rules. Write the capital letter in over the lowercase letter where a capital is appropriate.

1. When marvin drizzle decided to go to the west coast on a vacation beginning the july fourth weekend, he decided to visit an old friend of his in san francisco.

2. His friend, marlene snips, was now president of a small company manufacturing tourist items to be sold in shops in chinatown.

3. Her firm, it ain't what it seems, inc., also made fake plants, such as bushes, trees, weeds, and even spanish moss, for film studios.

4. Marvin had read in the newspaper and in newsweek that san francisco had a large hispanic, as well as asian, population, and since his mother was mexican-american, he was interested to see the mission district, the center of the city's hispanic population.

5. Marlene, who had taken a course in the history of san francisco at san francisco state university, told him that during world war ii, the city's population had been largely irish, italian, and chinese.

6. While many black workers and their families had come west during the second world war to work in the shipyards, the biggest influx of new groups had taken place in the sixties, seventies, and eighties.

7. Marvin said, "I came out to this city for a vacation, and I feel as though I've enrolled in a sociology class."

8. He admitted that he found it quite interesting to hear english, chinese, and spanish all being spoken on the same street.

9. Marlene took him to all the standard tourist sites, such as the golden gate bridge, and introduced him to her business friends, the president of the chamber of commerce, a few lawyers, and others.

10. When marvin returned to the east coast, he spent a week resting up from his vacation before going back to his job as a publisher.

CREDITS

Pages on which material appears in this book are indicated in **boldface** in parentheses at the end of each acknowledgment.

Chapter 1

Elizabeth Drew, "Letter from Washington," originally published in *The New Yorker, Election Journal: Political Events of 1987–1988*. Copyright © 1989 by Elizabeth Drew. Reprinted by permission of William Morrow & Co. **(7)**

John J. Macionis, "Aging and the Elderly," *Sociology* Fifth Edition. © 1995 Prentice-Hall, Englewood Cliffs, NJ. **(9–10)**

Jane E. Brody, "Fatigue: The Cause Is Usually Emotional," *The New York Times*, January 23, 1980. Copyright © 1980 by The New York Times Company. Reprinted by permission. **(16–19)**

Roger D. McGrath, *Gunfighters, Highwaymen, and Vigilantes: Violence on the Frontier*. Copyright © 1984 The Regents of the University of California. Reprinted by permission of The University of California Press. **(20–22)**

Robert L. Heilbroner, "Don't Let Stereotypes Warp Your Judgment," *Reader's Digest*, January 1962. Copyright © 1961 by International Business Machines Corp. Reprinted by permission of William Morris Agency, Inc. **(22–26)**

Joyce Maynard, "His Talk, Her Talk," *Viewpoints: Readings Worth Thinking and Writing About*, W. Royce Adams, ed., D.C. Heath & Co., 1988. Reprinted by permission of Robert Cornfield Literary Agency. **(30–31)**

Mark A. Sherman and Adelaide Haas, "Man to Man, Woman to Woman," *Psychology Today*, June 1984. Copyright © 1984 (PT Partners, L.P.). Reprinted with permission from *Psychology Today Magazine*. **(31–34)**

Chapter 3

John J. O'Connor, "What Are TV Ads Selling to Children?" *The New York Times*, June 6, 1989. Copyright © 1989 by The New York Times Company. Reprinted by permission. **(90–92)**

Chapter 6

Tammy Hansen, "Home Day Care Providers Face Increasing Demand," *Oakland Tribune*, January 11, 1998, pp. D1–D5. (**370–373**)

Marlise Simons, "Child Care Sacred as France Cuts Back the Welfare State," *The New York Times*, December 31, 1997, p. A1. Copyright 1997 by The New York Times Co. Reprinted by permission. (**373–377**)

Motion Picture Association of America, "The Motion Picture Production Code." (**380–382**)

Lois P. Sheinfeld, "Ratings: The Big Chill," *Film Comment*, June 1986. Reprinted by permission of the author. (**383–385**)

Peter Stack, "Avoiding the Censors," *San Francisco Chronicle*, January 7, 1988. © *San Francisco Chronicle*. Reprinted with permission. (**386–387**)

Paul Attanasio, "The Rating Game," *The New Republic*, June 17, 1985. Reprinted with permission of *The New Republic*. (**387–389**)

Charles R. Lawrence III, "The Debate over Placing Limits on Racist Speech Must Not Ignore the Damage It Does to Its Victims," October 25, 1989. Copyright 1989 *The Chronicle of Higher Education*. Reprinted by permission of the author. (**393–398**)

Nat Hentoff, "Free Speech on Campus," *Progressive*, May, 1989. Reprinted by permission of the publisher. (**398–404**)

Joseph S. Tuman, "Hate Speech on Campus," *Inside*, San Francisco State University. Reprinted by permission of the author. Joseph Tuman is an assistant professor in the Department of Speech and Communication Studies at San Francisco State University. (**404–406**)

Ben Wildavsky, "Rethinking Campus Speech Codes," *San Francisco Chronicle*, March 3, 1995, pp. 1, 15. Copyright *San Francisco Chronicle*, 1995. Used by permission. (**406–409**)

Douglas Lederman, "Review at Virginia Tech Uncovers Sports Violations," *The Chronicle of Higher Education*, July 15, 1987. Copyright 1987 *The Chronicle of Higher Education*. Reprinted by permission. (**412–414**)

Douglas Lederman, "Foes of New Academic Standards Cry 'Unfair' as Test Scores Keep Star Student off the Field," November 12, 1986. Copyright 1986 *The Chronicle of Higher Education*. Reprinted by permission. (**415–416**)

"NCAA Stirs Debate—Are SATs Racist?" *San Francisco Chronicle*, January 17, 1989. Reprinted with permission of the Associated Press. (**416–418**)

John Eisenberg, "Cheers to John Thompson's Empty Chair," *The Baltimore Sun*, January 17, 1989. © 1989 The Baltimore Sun Co. Reprinted by permission. (**418–420**)

Mona Charen, "A Kinder, Gentler Racism," *San Francisco Chronicle*, February 19, 1989. Reprinted by permission of Creators Syndicate. (**420–422**)

Douglas Lederman, "The Ivy League at Thirty: A Model for College Athletics or an Outmoded Antique?" *The Chronicle of Higher Education*, November 19, 1986. Copyright 1986 *The Chronicle of Higher Education*. Reprinted with permission. (**422–425**)

INDEX

INDEX OF AUTHORS AND TITLES